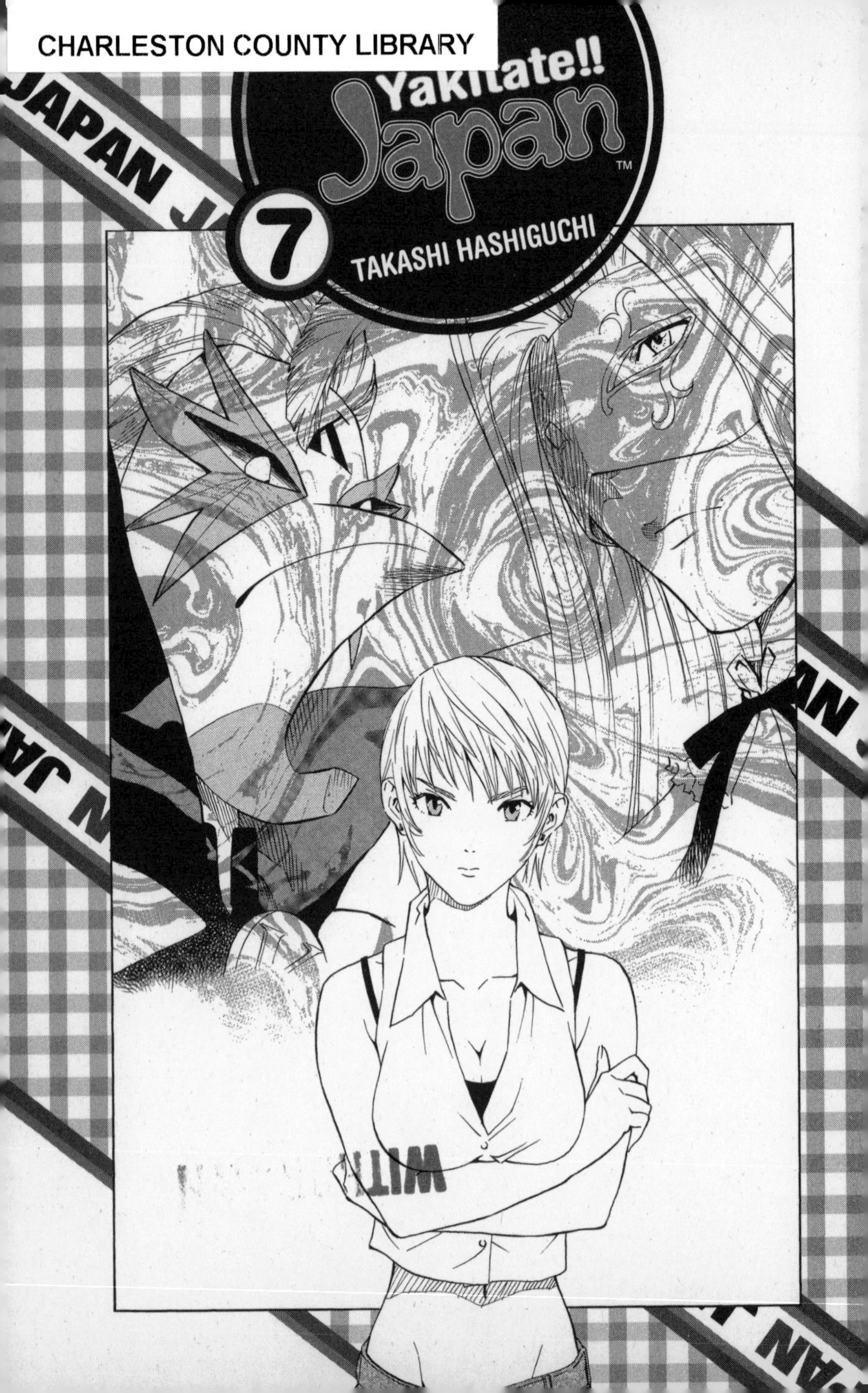
Yakitate!!
Japan™
7
TAKASHI HASHIGUCHI
JAPAN JA
JAPAN
JAPAN

YAKITATE!! JAPAN
7
VIZ Media Edition

★The Story Thus Far★

Genius bread craftsman Kazuma Azuma was scouted by Pantasia bakery empire scion Tsukino Azusagawa to work under the supervision of master baker Ken Matsushiro at the chain's South Tokyo branch. Azuma's ultimate goal is to create his country's signature bread—its "Ja-pan."

Enrolled in Pantasia Group's annual Pantasia Rookie Tournament, Kazuma advanced to the finals. His friend Kyosuke Kawachi—who works at the same branch—was defeated after Tsukino's half-sister Yukino sabotaged his materials. Dejected, Kawachi sought help at a very strange church.

In the finals match, Azuma faced Shigeru Kanmuri—who held the special Ocean Yeast as his trump card. Despite the overwhelming odds against him, Azuma won the Rookie Tournament with innovative baking that flew in the face of common sense.

The third-place match is now underway. Kawachi, who shows up with an Afro haircut for some reason, faces rival Kai Suwabara. Will his mysterious church training pay off...?!

CONTENTS

Research Assistance/Bakery Consultant:
Koichi Uchimura.

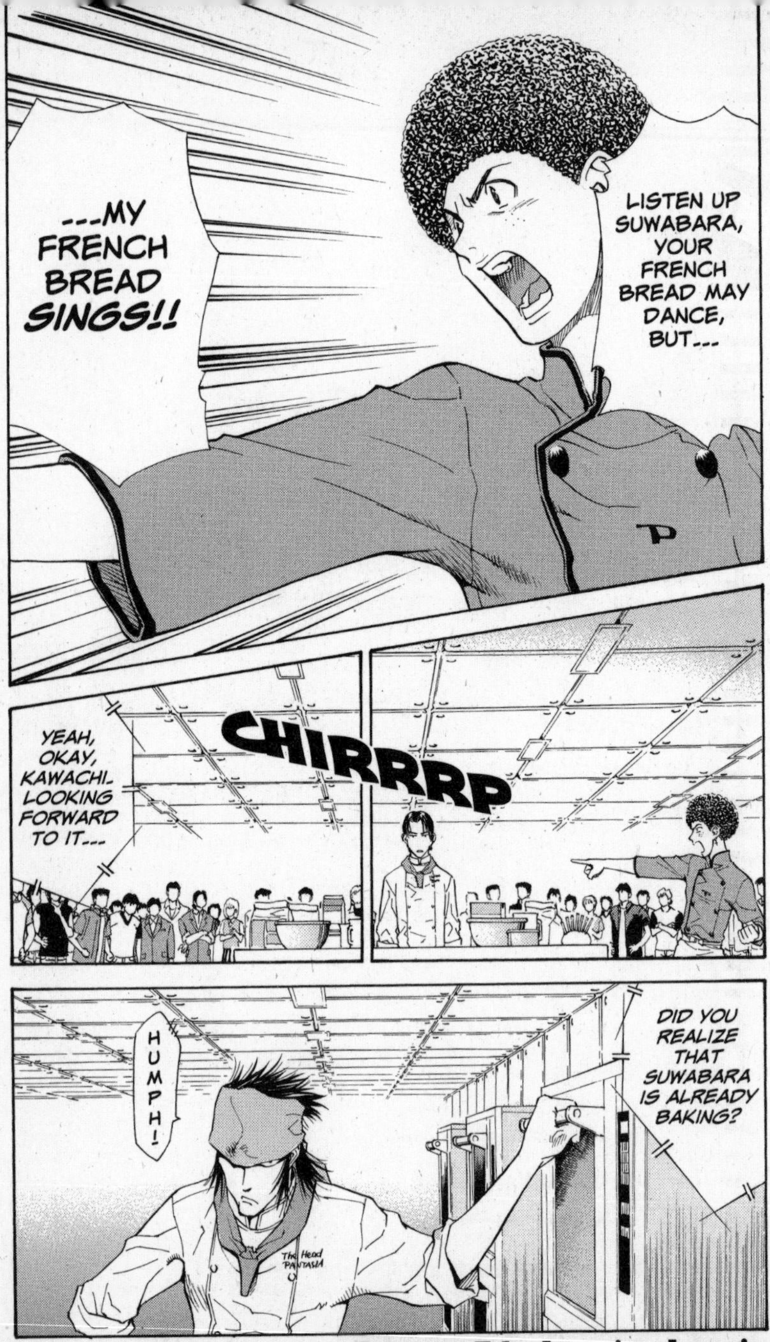
LISTEN UP SUWABARA, YOUR FRENCH BREAD MAY DANCE, BUT...
...MY FRENCH BREAD SINGS!!
CHIRRRP
YEAH, OKAY, KAWACHI. LOOKING FORWARD TO IT...
DID YOU REALIZE THAT SUWABARA IS ALREADY BAKING?
HUMPH!

Story 51: Louis, Louis

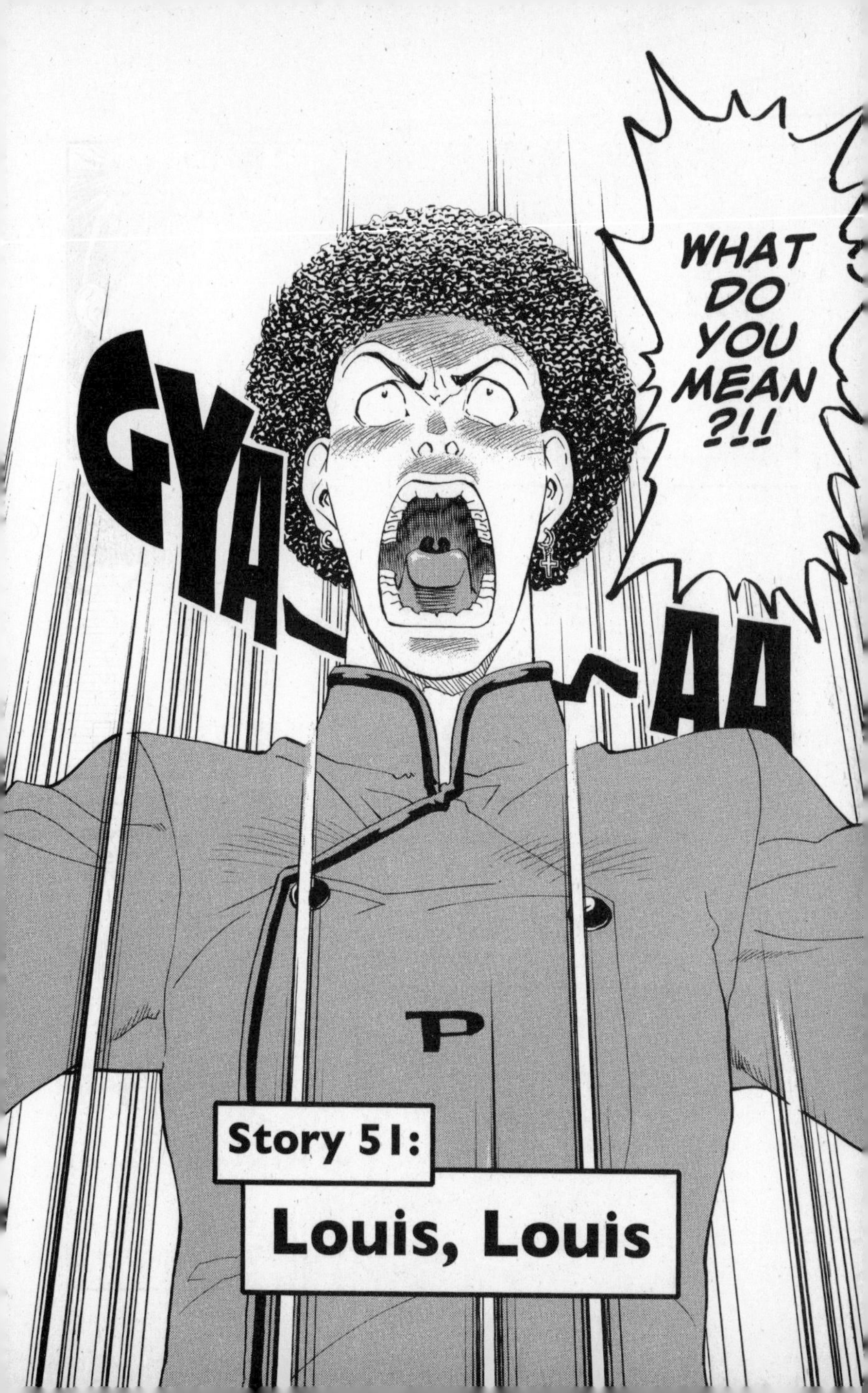
WHAT DO YOU MEAN ?!!
GYA—AA
P
Story 51:
Louis, Louis

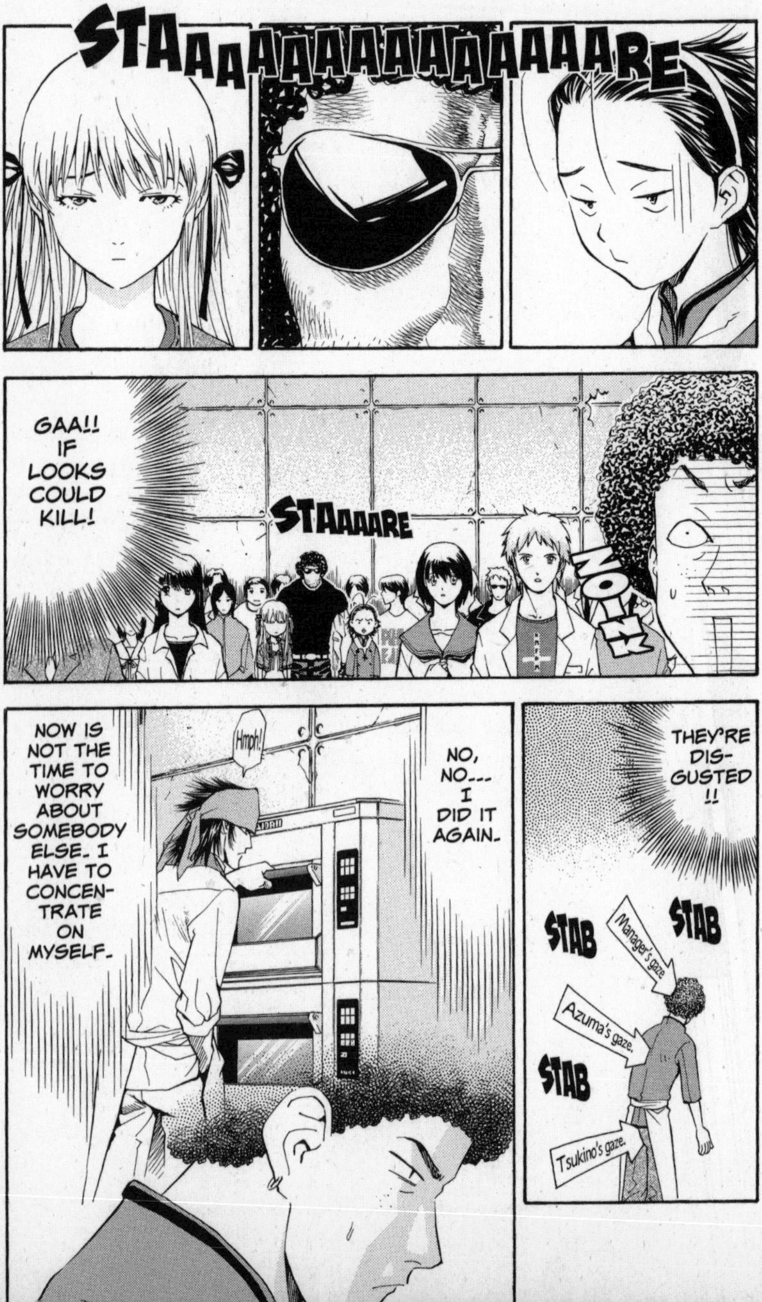
STAAAAAAAAAAAAAARE
NOINK
STAAAARE
GAA!! IF LOOKS COULD KILL!
THEY'RE DIS-GUSTED !!
STAB
Manager's gaze
STAB
Azuma's gaze.
STAB
Tsukino's gaze.
NO, NO... I DID IT AGAIN.
Hmph!
NOW IS NOT THE TIME TO WORRY ABOUT SOMEBODY ELSE. I HAVE TO CONCEN-TRATE ON MYSELF.

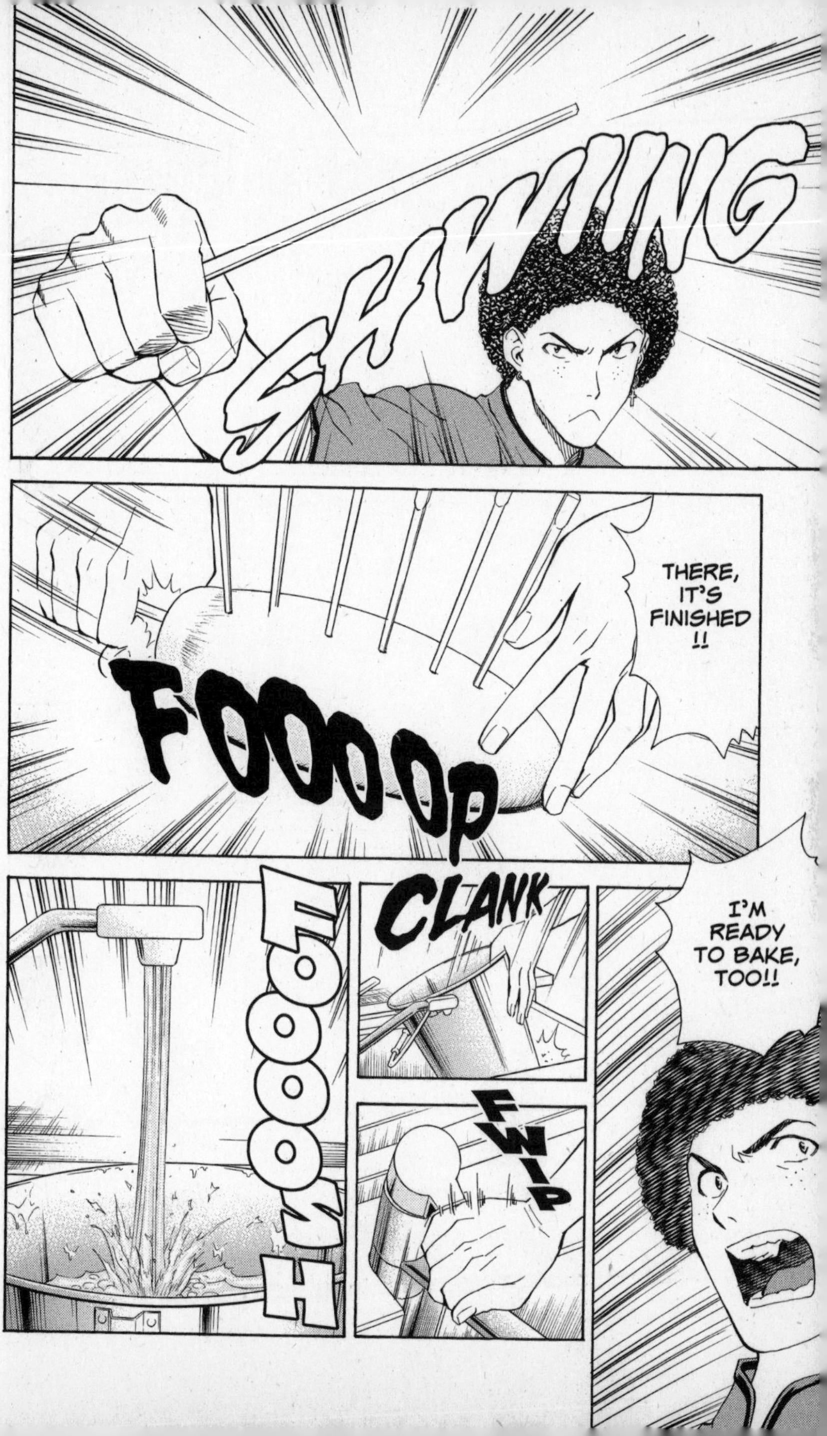
SHWING
THERE, IT'S FINISHED!!
FOOOOP
I'M READY TO BAKE, TOO!!
CLANK
FWIP
FOOOOOSH

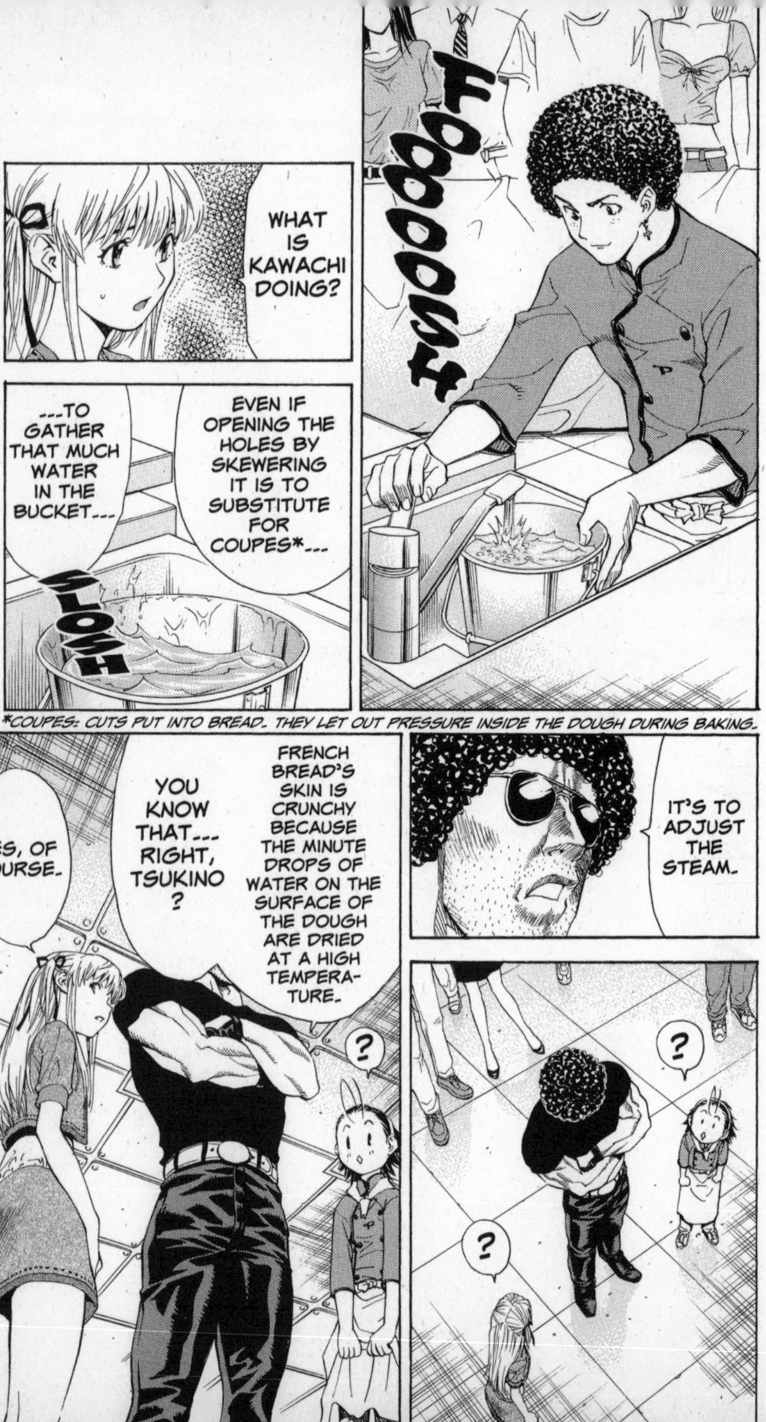
FOOOOOOSH
WHAT IS KAWACHI DOING?
EVEN IF OPENING THE HOLES BY SKEWERING IT IS TO SUBSTITUTE FOR COUPES*...
...TO GATHER THAT MUCH WATER IN THE BUCKET...
SLOSH
IT'S TO ADJUST THE STEAM.
?
?
FRENCH BREAD'S SKIN IS CRUNCHY BECAUSE THE MINUTE DROPS OF WATER ON THE SURFACE OF THE DOUGH ARE DRIED AT A HIGH TEMPERA-TURE.
YOU KNOW THAT... RIGHT, TSUKINO?
YES, OF COURSE.
?

*COUPES: CUTS PUT INTO BREAD. THEY LET OUT PRESSURE INSIDE THE DOUGH DURING BAKING.

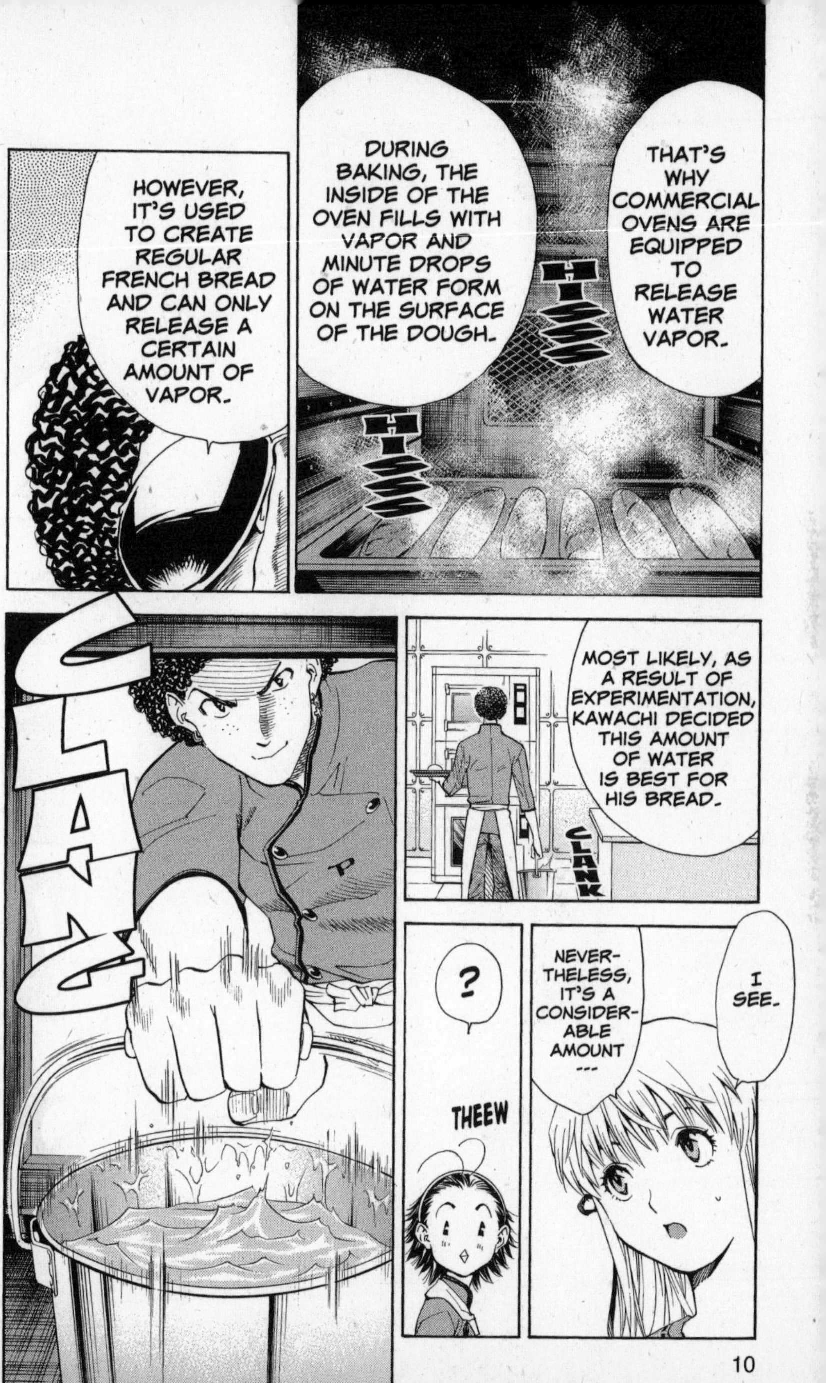
DURING BAKING, THE INSIDE OF THE OVEN FILLS WITH VAPOR AND MINUTE DROPS OF WATER FORM ON THE SURFACE OF THE DOUGH.
THAT'S WHY COMMERCIAL OVENS ARE EQUIPPED TO RELEASE WATER VAPOR.
HISSSS
HISSSS
HOWEVER, IT'S USED TO CREATE REGULAR FRENCH BREAD AND CAN ONLY RELEASE A CERTAIN AMOUNT OF VAPOR.
MOST LIKELY, AS A RESULT OF EXPERIMENTATION, KAWACHI DECIDED THIS AMOUNT OF WATER IS BEST FOR HIS BREAD.
CLANK
I SEE.
NEVER-THELESS, IT'S A CONSIDER-ABLE AMOUNT ---
?
THEEW
CLANG

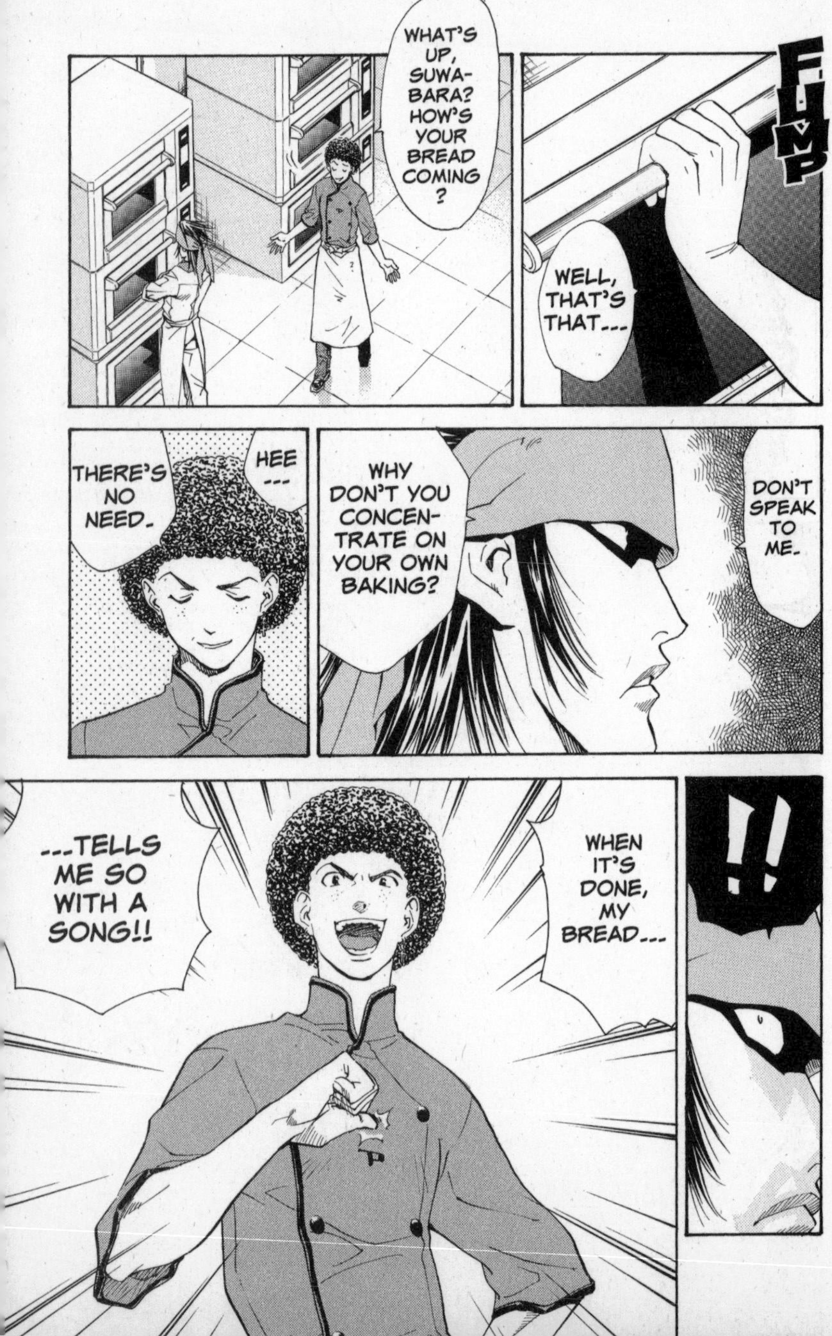
FUMP
WELL, THAT'S THAT...
WHAT'S UP, SUWABARA? HOW'S YOUR BREAD COMING?
DON'T SPEAK TO ME.
WHY DON'T YOU CONCENTRATE ON YOUR OWN BAKING?
HEE...
THERE'S NO NEED.
!!
WHEN IT'S DONE, MY BREAD...
...TELLS ME SO WITH A SONG!!

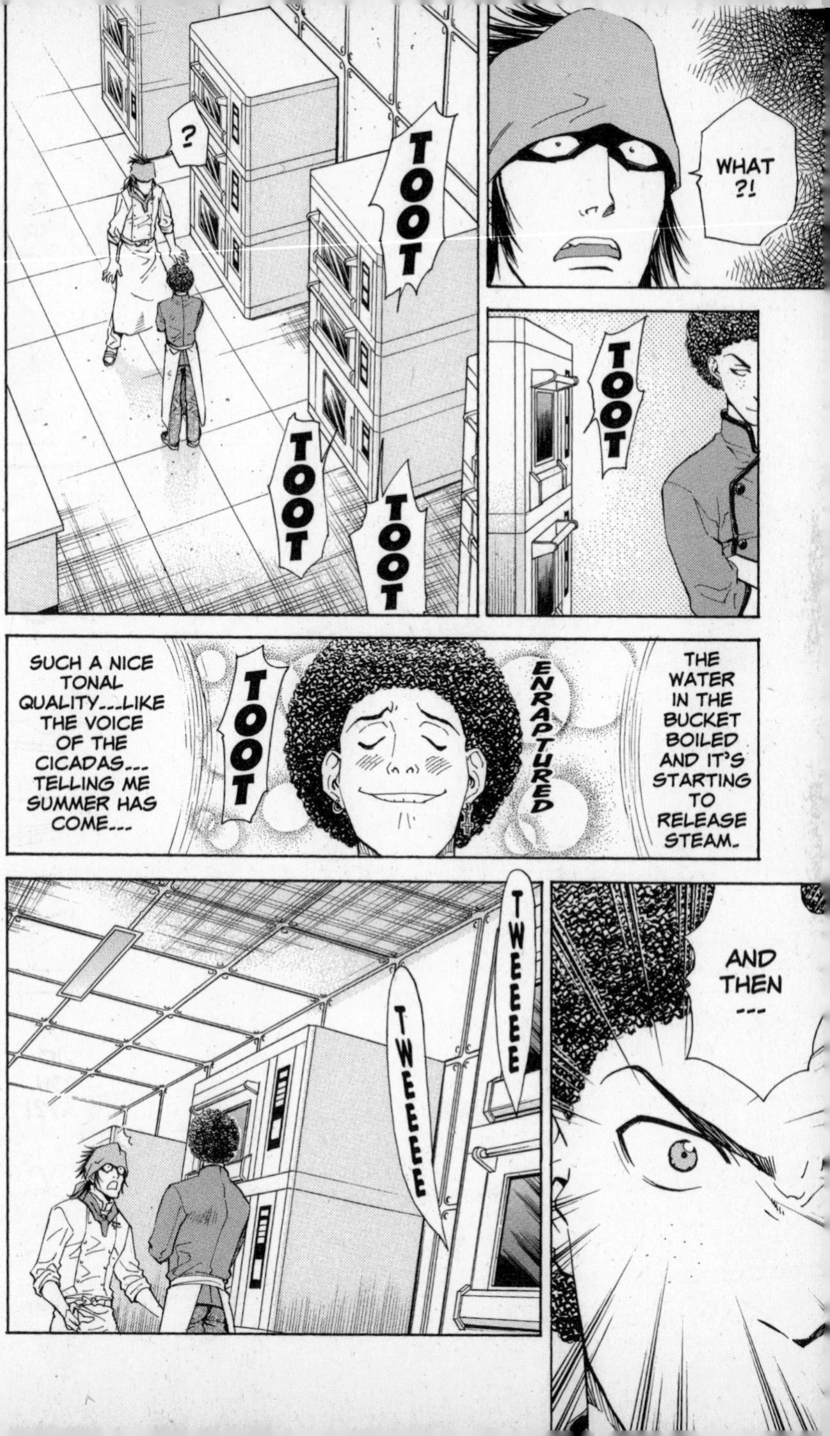
WHAT ?!
TOOT
TOOT
?
TOOT
TOOT
THE WATER IN THE BUCKET BOILED AND IT'S STARTING TO RELEASE STEAM.
ENRAPTURED
TOOT
SUCH A NICE TONAL QUALITY...LIKE THE VOICE OF THE CICADAS... TELLING ME SUMMER HAS COME...
AND THEN ---
TWEEEEE
TWEEEEE

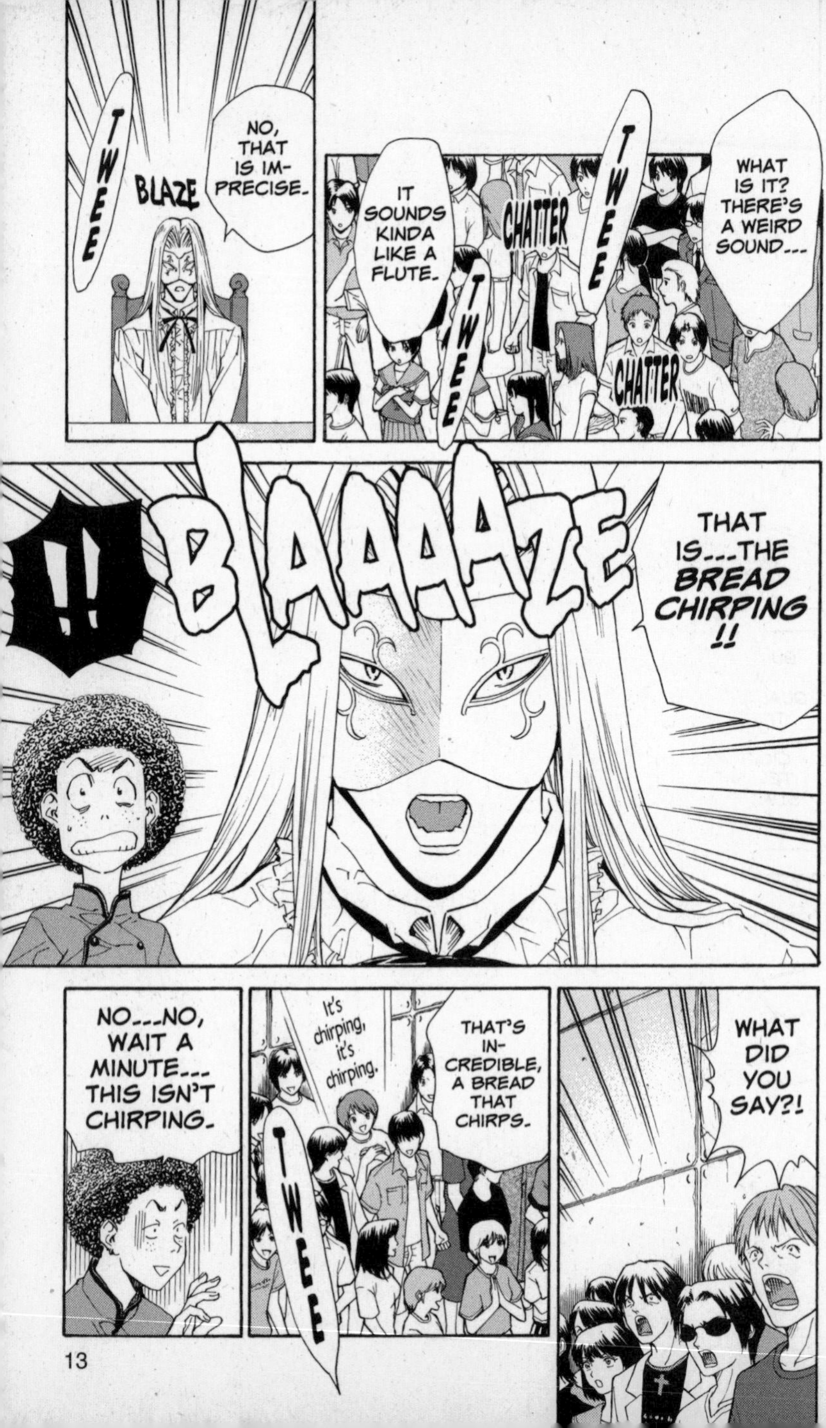
WHAT IS IT? THERE'S A WEIRD SOUND...
TWEE
CHATTER
IT SOUNDS KINDA LIKE A FLUTE.
TWEE
CHATTER
NO, THAT IS IM-PRECISE.
BLAZE
TWEE
THAT IS...THE *BREAD CHIRPING* !!
BLAAAAZE
!!
WHAT DID YOU SAY?!
THAT'S IN-CREDIBLE, A BREAD THAT CHIRPS.
It's chirping, it's chirping.
TWEE
NO...NO, WAIT A MINUTE... THIS ISN'T CHIRPING.

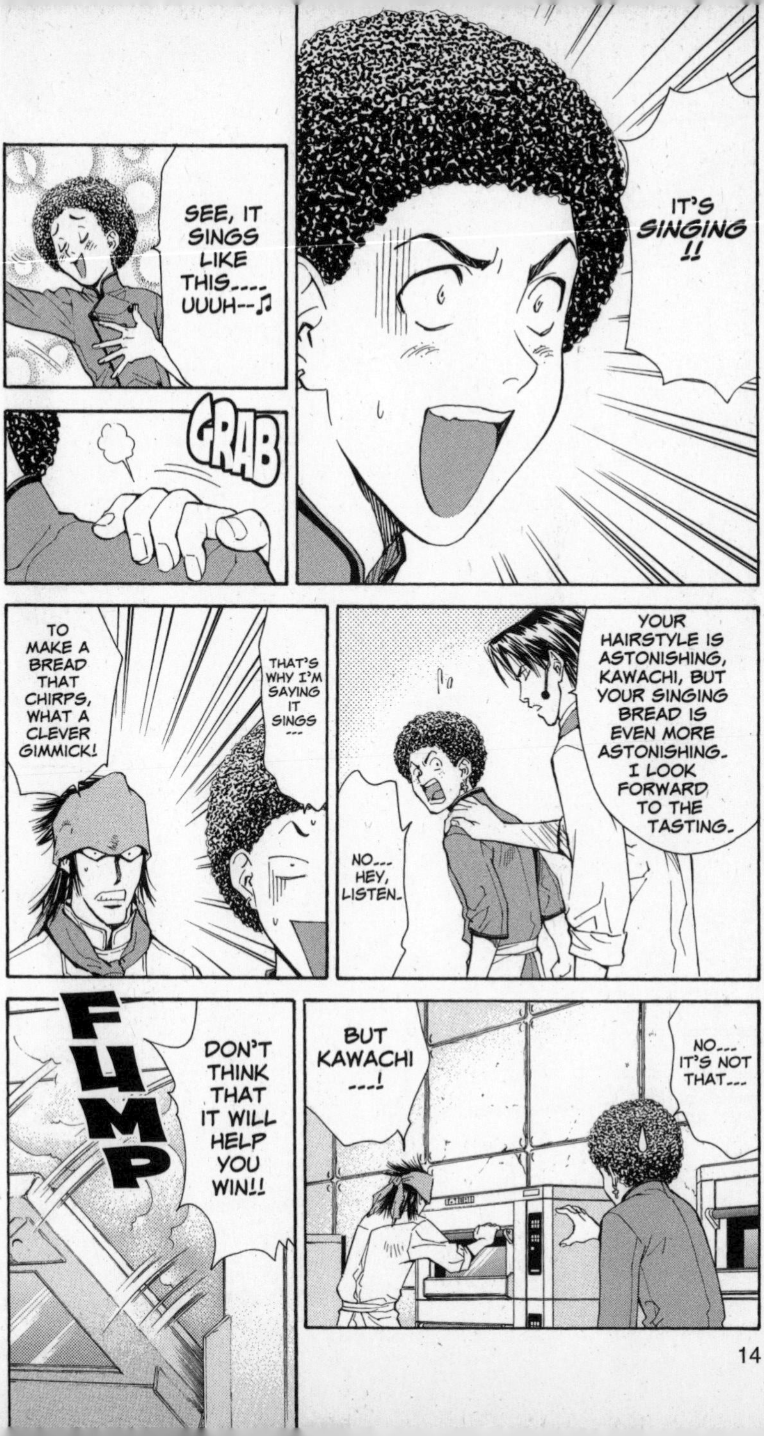
IT'S SINGING!!
SEE, IT SINGS LIKE THIS.... UUUH--♫
GRAB
YOUR HAIRSTYLE IS ASTONISHING, KAWACHI, BUT YOUR SINGING BREAD IS EVEN MORE ASTONISHING. I LOOK FORWARD TO THE TASTING.
NO... HEY, LISTEN.
TO MAKE A BREAD THAT CHIRPS, WHAT A CLEVER GIMMICK!
THAT'S WHY I'M SAYING IT SINGS...
NO... IT'S NOT THAT...
BUT KAWACHI...!
FUMP
DON'T THINK THAT IT WILL HELP YOU WIN!!

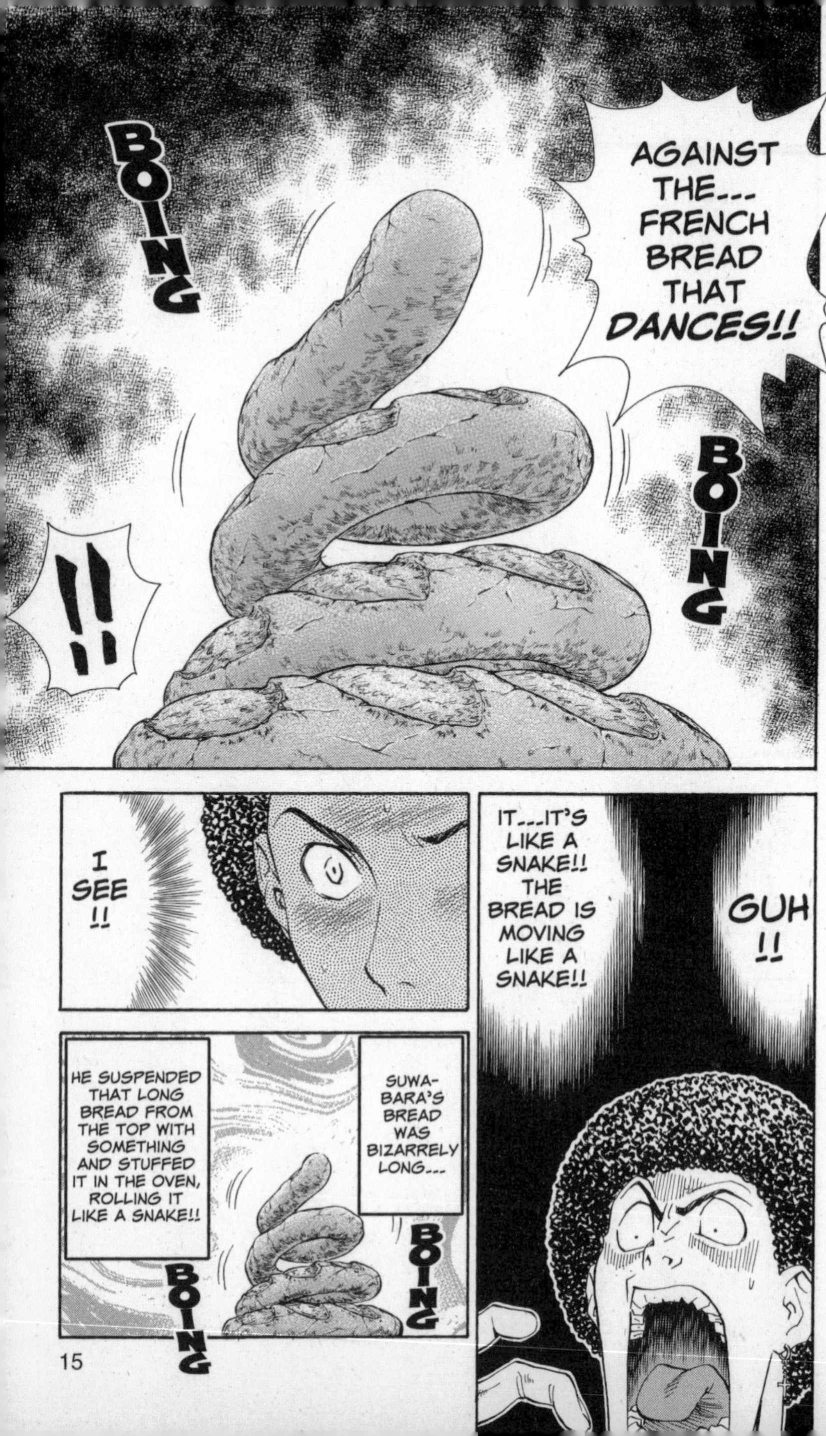
AGAINST THE... FRENCH BREAD THAT DANCES!!
BOING
BOING
!!
GUH!!
IT...IT'S LIKE A SNAKE!! THE BREAD IS MOVING LIKE A SNAKE!!
I SEE!!
SUWA-BARA'S BREAD WAS BIZARRELY LONG...
BOING
HE SUSPENDED THAT LONG BREAD FROM THE TOP WITH SOMETHING AND STUFFED IT IN THE OVEN, ROLLING IT LIKE A SNAKE!!
BOING

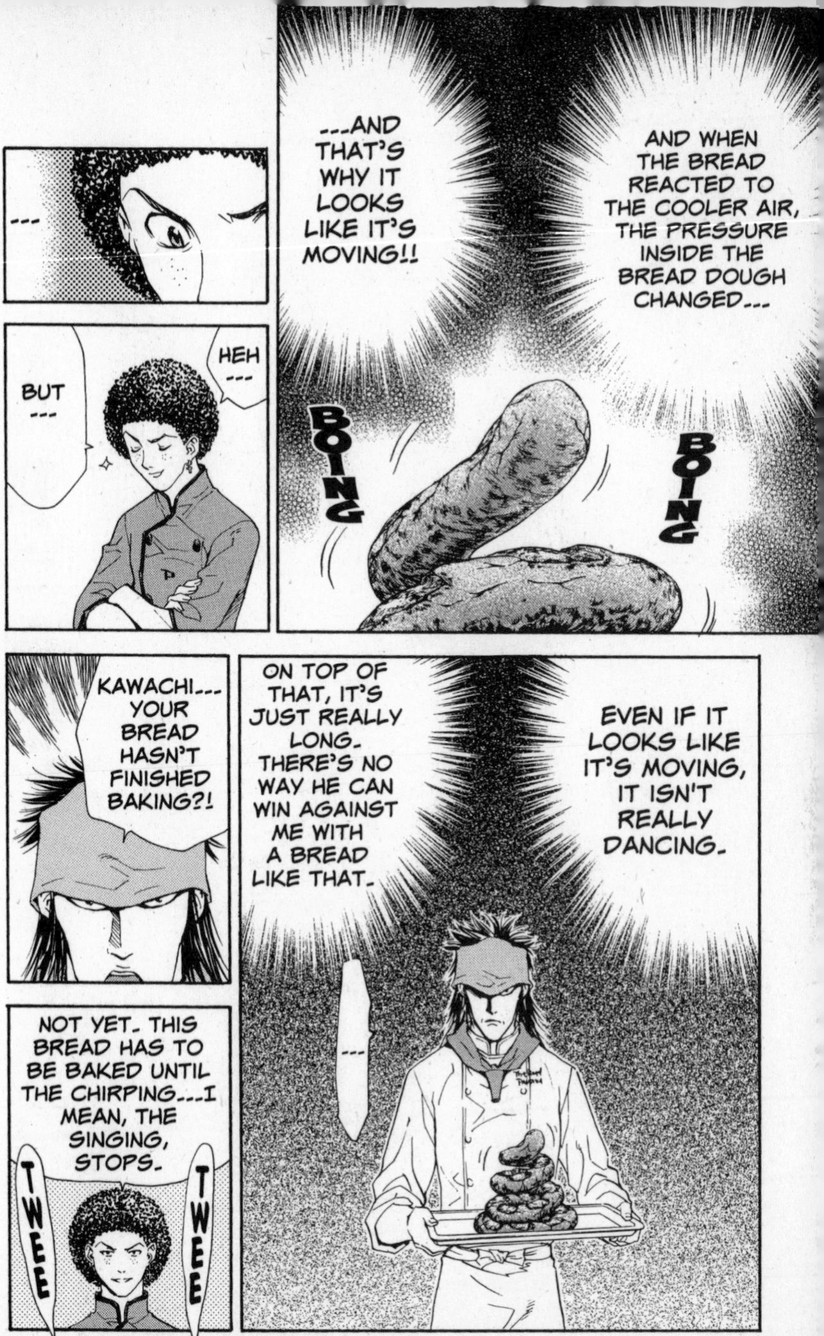
AND WHEN THE BREAD REACTED TO THE COOLER AIR, THE PRESSURE INSIDE THE BREAD DOUGH CHANGED...
...AND THAT'S WHY IT LOOKS LIKE IT'S MOVING!!
BOING
BOING
...
HEH...
BUT...
EVEN IF IT LOOKS LIKE IT'S MOVING, IT ISN'T REALLY DANCING.
ON TOP OF THAT, IT'S JUST REALLY LONG. THERE'S NO WAY HE CAN WIN AGAINST ME WITH A BREAD LIKE THAT.
...
KAWACHI... YOUR BREAD HASN'T FINISHED BAKING?!
NOT YET. THIS BREAD HAS TO BE BAKED UNTIL THE CHIRPING...I MEAN, THE SINGING, STOPS.
TWEE
TWEE

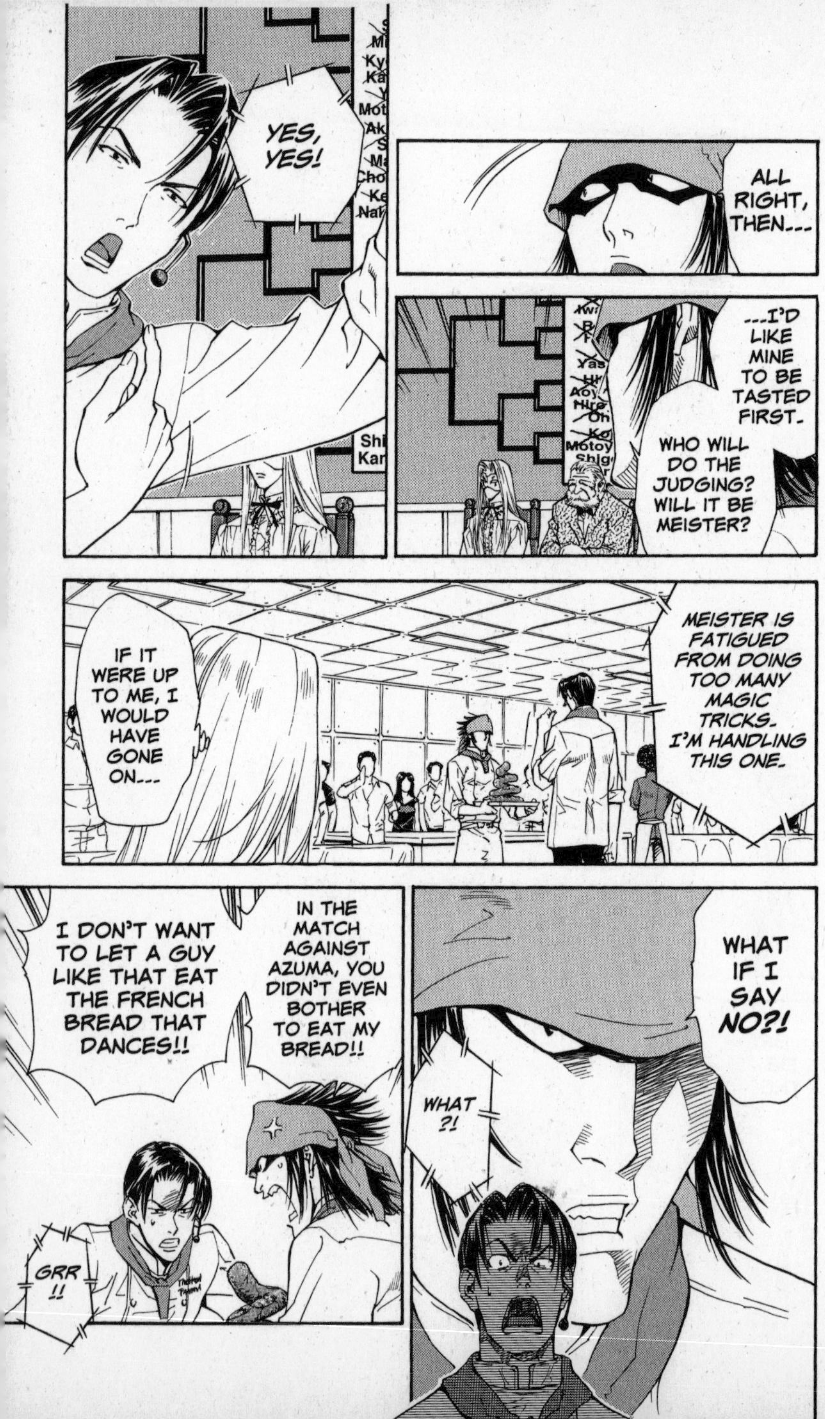
ALL RIGHT, THEN...
...I'D LIKE MINE TO BE TASTED FIRST.
WHO WILL DO THE JUDGING? WILL IT BE MEISTER?
YES, YES!
MEISTER IS FATIGUED FROM DOING TOO MANY MAGIC TRICKS. I'M HANDLING THIS ONE.
IF IT WERE UP TO ME, I WOULD HAVE GONE ON...
WHAT IF I SAY NO?!
WHAT?!
IN THE MATCH AGAINST AZUMA, YOU DIDN'T EVEN BOTHER TO EAT MY BREAD!!
I DON'T WANT TO LET A GUY LIKE THAT EAT THE FRENCH BREAD THAT DANCES!!
GRR!!

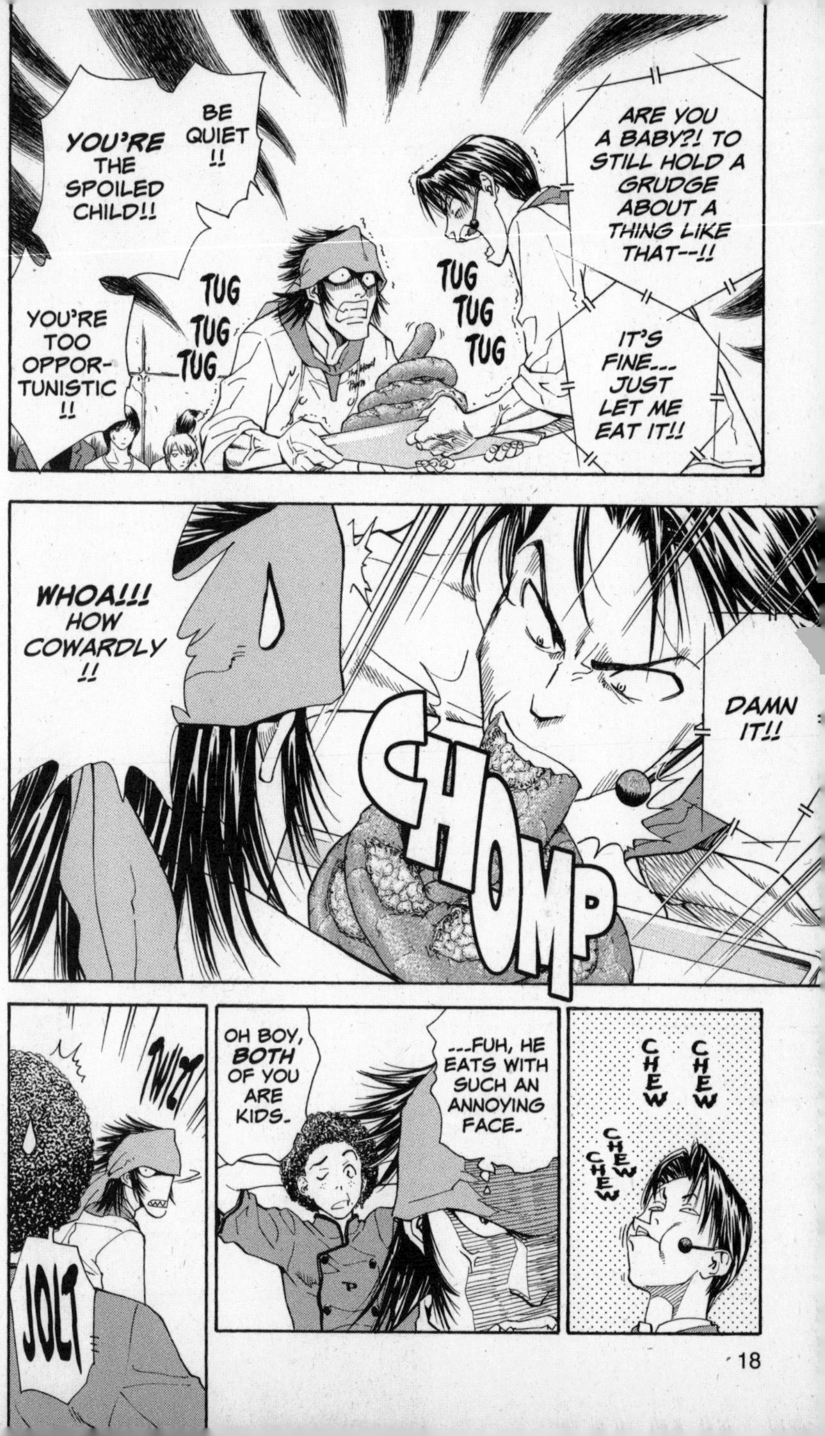
ARE YOU A BABY?! TO STILL HOLD A GRUDGE ABOUT A THING LIKE THAT--!!
BE QUIET !!
YOU'RE THE SPOILED CHILD!!
TUG TUG TUG
IT'S FINE... JUST LET ME EAT IT!!
TUG TUG TUG
YOU'RE TOO OPPOR-TUNISTIC !!
DAMN IT!!
CHOMP
WHOA!!! HOW COWARDLY !!
CHEW CHEW
CHEW CHEW
...FUH, HE EATS WITH SUCH AN ANNOYING FACE.
OH BOY, BOTH OF YOU ARE KIDS.
JOLT

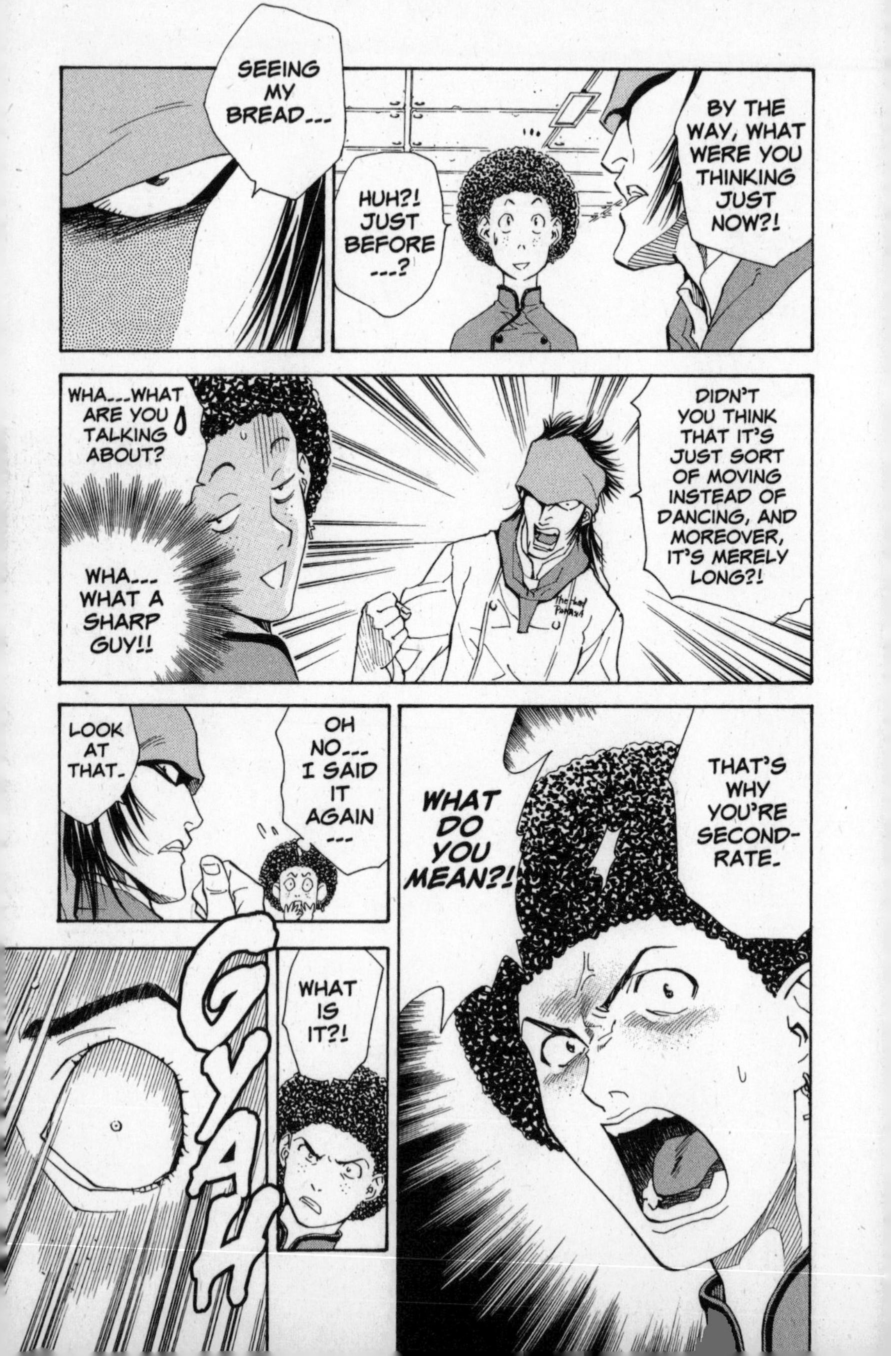
BY THE WAY, WHAT WERE YOU THINKING JUST NOW?!
HUH?! JUST BEFORE ---?
SEEING MY BREAD---
DIDN'T YOU THINK THAT IT'S JUST SORT OF MOVING INSTEAD OF DANCING, AND MOREOVER, IT'S MERELY LONG?!
WHA---WHAT ARE YOU TALKING ABOUT?
WHA--- WHAT A SHARP GUY!!
THAT'S WHY YOU'RE SECOND-RATE.
WHAT DO YOU MEAN?!
OH NO--- I SAID IT AGAIN ---
LOOK AT THAT.
WHAT IS IT?!
GYAH

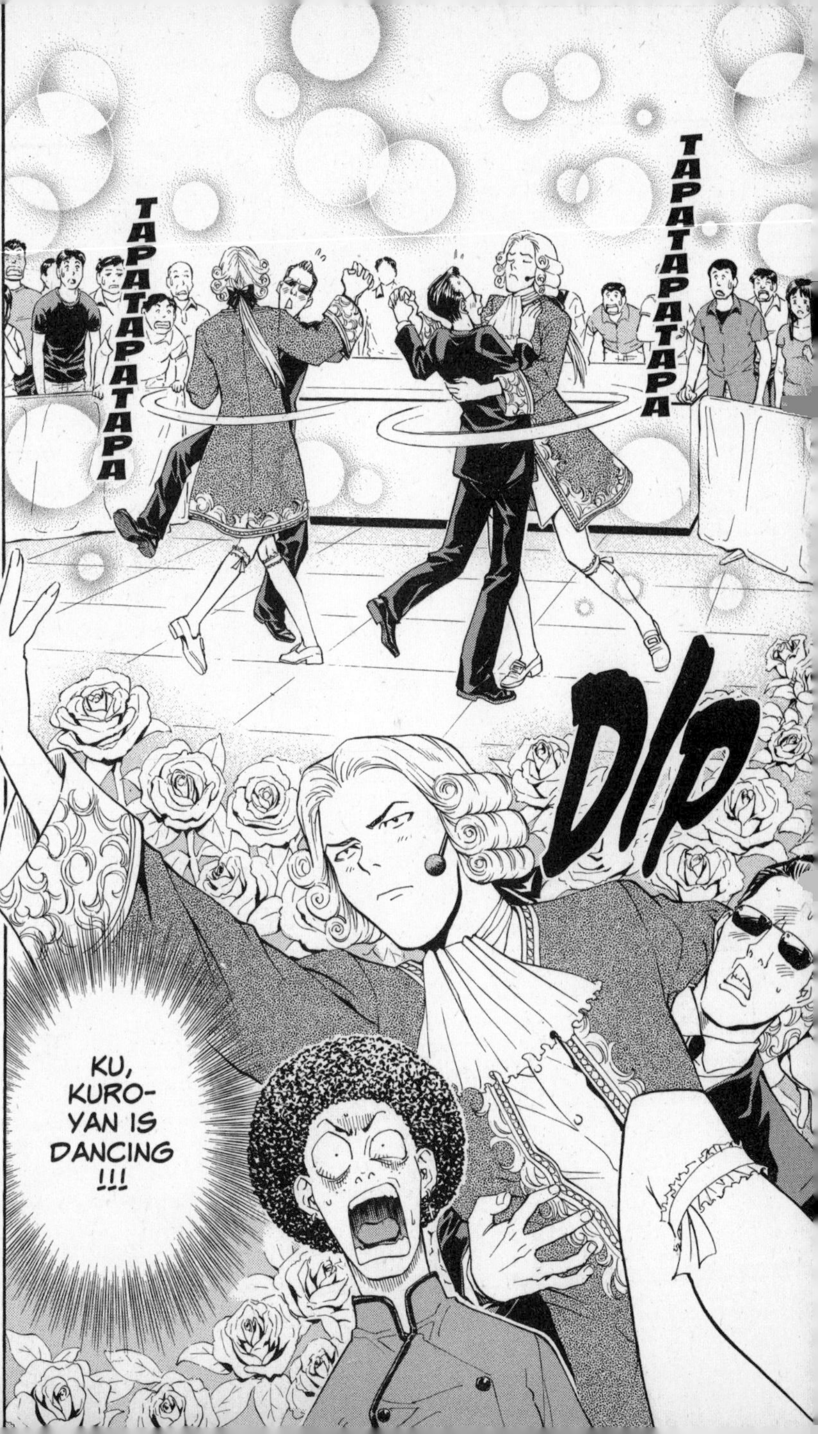
TAPATAPATAPA
TAPATAPATAPA
DIP
KU, KURO-YAN IS DANCING !!!

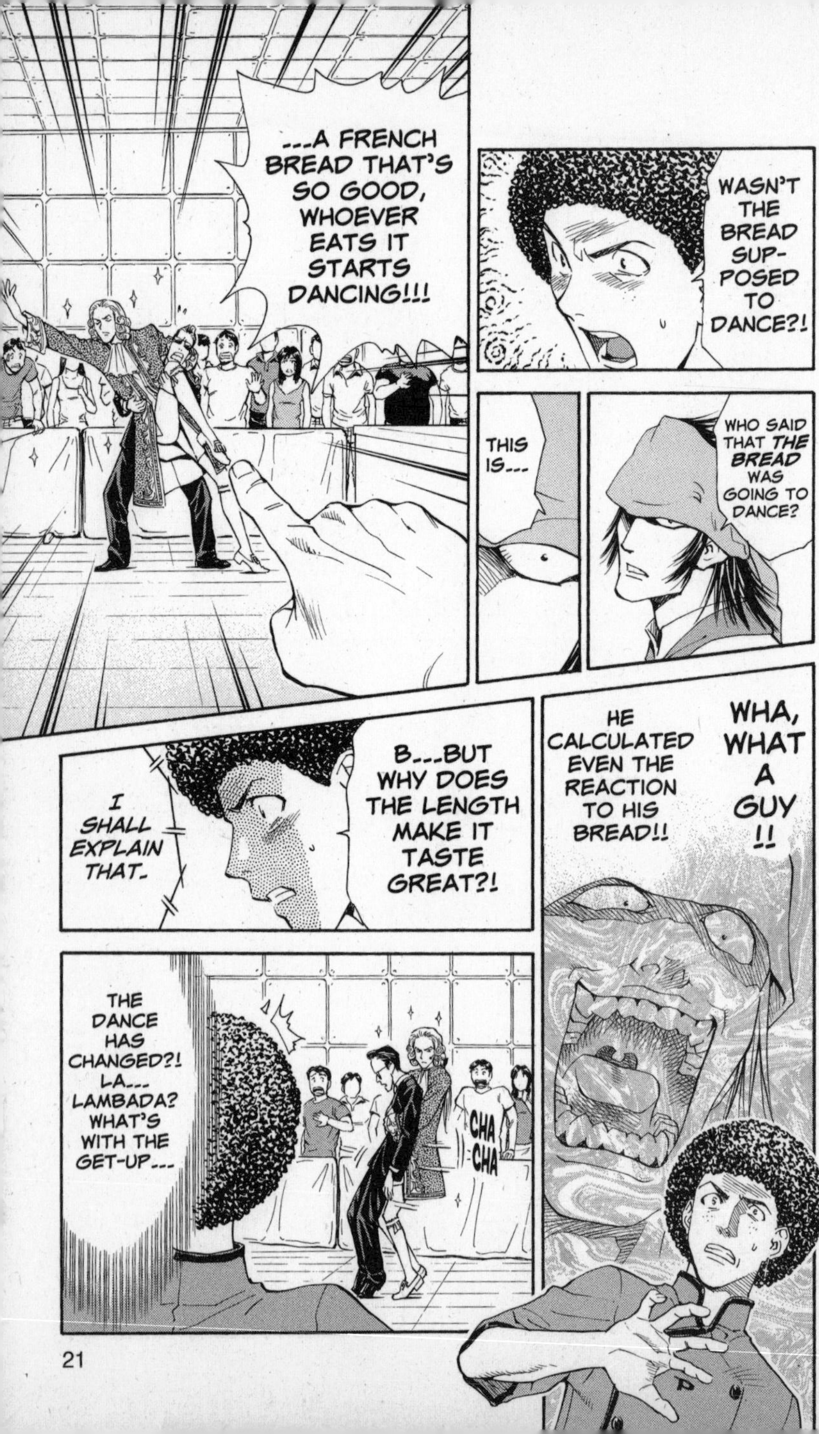
WASN'T THE BREAD SUP-POSED TO DANCE?!
WHO SAID THAT *THE BREAD* WAS GOING TO DANCE?
THIS IS...
...A FRENCH BREAD THAT'S SO GOOD, WHOEVER EATS IT STARTS DANCING!!!
WHA, WHAT A GUY !!
HE CALCULATED EVEN THE REACTION TO HIS BREAD!!
B...BUT WHY DOES THE LENGTH MAKE IT TASTE GREAT?!
I SHALL EXPLAIN THAT.
THE DANCE HAS CHANGED?! LA... LAMBADA? WHAT'S WITH THE GET-UP...
CHA CHA

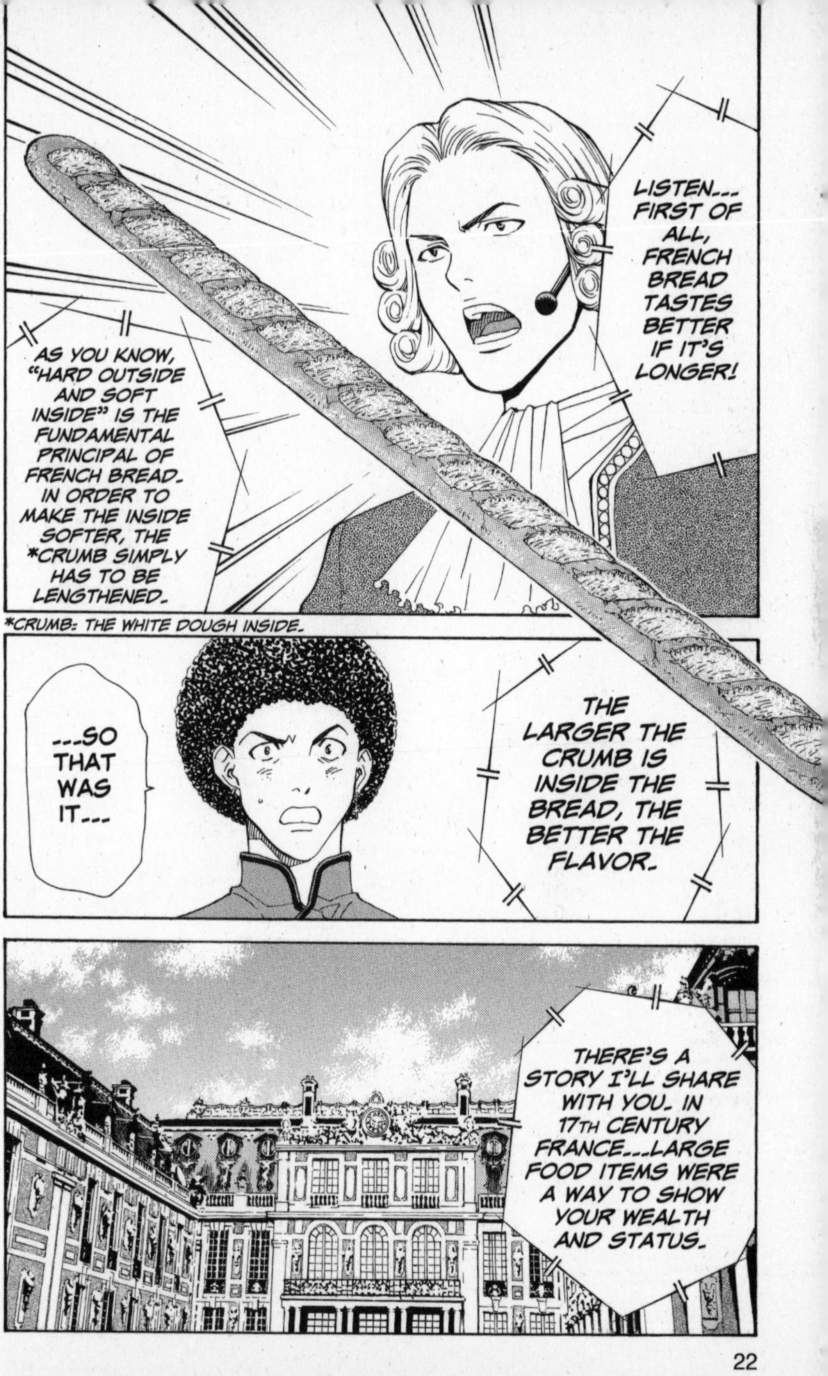
LISTEN... FIRST OF ALL, FRENCH BREAD TASTES BETTER IF IT'S LONGER!
AS YOU KNOW, "HARD OUTSIDE AND SOFT INSIDE" IS THE FUNDAMENTAL PRINCIPAL OF FRENCH BREAD. IN ORDER TO MAKE THE INSIDE SOFTER, THE *CRUMB SIMPLY HAS TO BE LENGTHENED.
THE LARGER THE CRUMB IS INSIDE THE BREAD, THE BETTER THE FLAVOR.
...SO THAT WAS IT...
THERE'S A STORY I'LL SHARE WITH YOU. IN 17TH CENTURY FRANCE...LARGE FOOD ITEMS WERE A WAY TO SHOW YOUR WEALTH AND STATUS.

*CRUMB: THE WHITE DOUGH INSIDE.

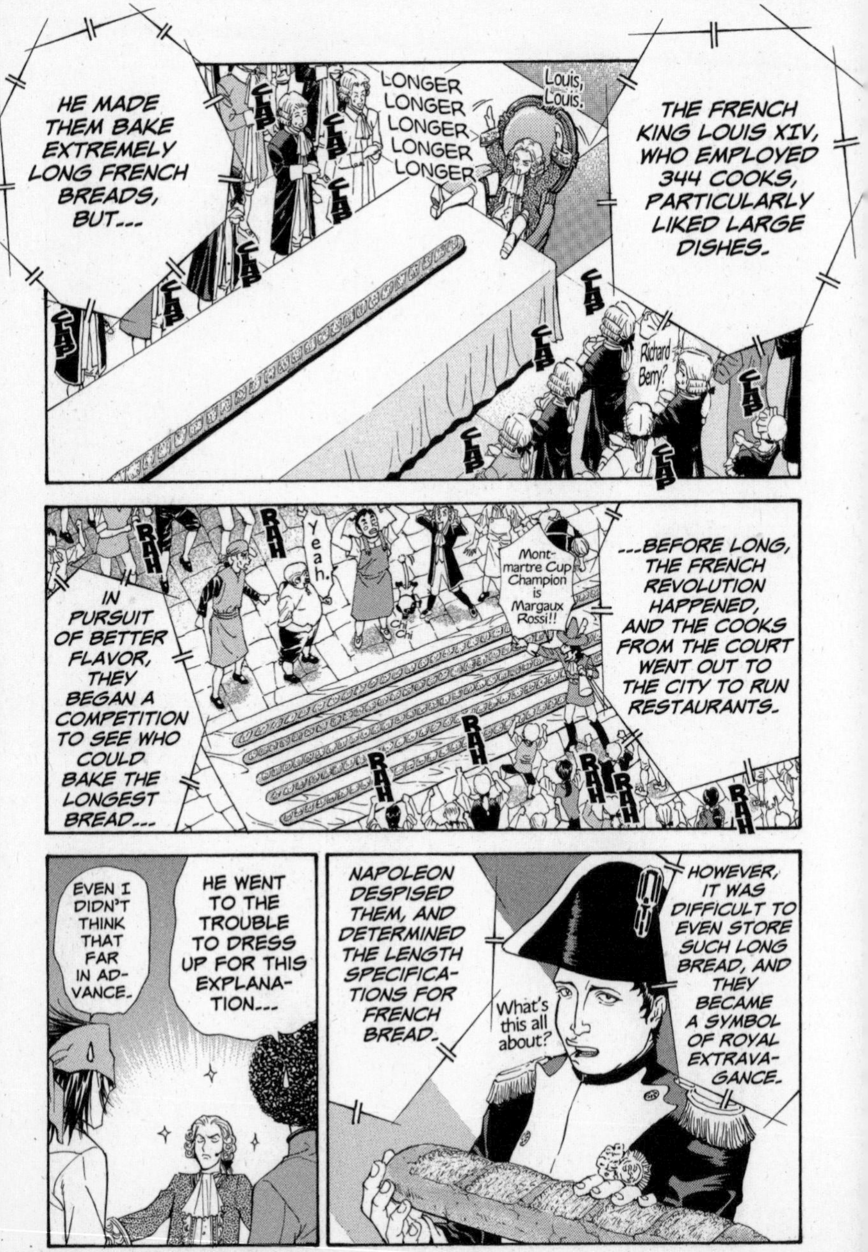
THE FRENCH KING LOUIS XIV, WHO EMPLOYED 344 COOKS, PARTICULARLY LIKED LARGE DISHES.
Louis, Louis.
LONGER
LONGER
LONGER
LONGER
LONGER
HE MADE THEM BAKE EXTREMELY LONG FRENCH BREADS, BUT...
CLAP CLAP CLAP CLAP CLAP CLAP
Richard Berry?
CLAP CLAP CLAP CLAP CLAP
...BEFORE LONG, THE FRENCH REVOLUTION HAPPENED, AND THE COOKS FROM THE COURT WENT OUT TO THE CITY TO RUN RESTAURANTS.
Mont-martre Cup Champion is Margaux Rossi!!
Yeah.
Chi Chi
RAH RAH
IN PURSUIT OF BETTER FLAVOR, THEY BEGAN A COMPETITION TO SEE WHO COULD BAKE THE LONGEST BREAD...
RAH RAH RAH RAH RAH
HOWEVER, IT WAS DIFFICULT TO EVEN STORE SUCH LONG BREAD, AND THEY BECAME A SYMBOL OF ROYAL EXTRAVA-GANCE.
NAPOLEON DESPISED THEM, AND DETERMINED THE LENGTH SPECIFICA-TIONS FOR FRENCH BREAD.
What's this all about?
HE WENT TO THE TROUBLE TO DRESS UP FOR THIS EXPLANA-TION...
EVEN I DIDN'T THINK THAT FAR IN AD-VANCE.

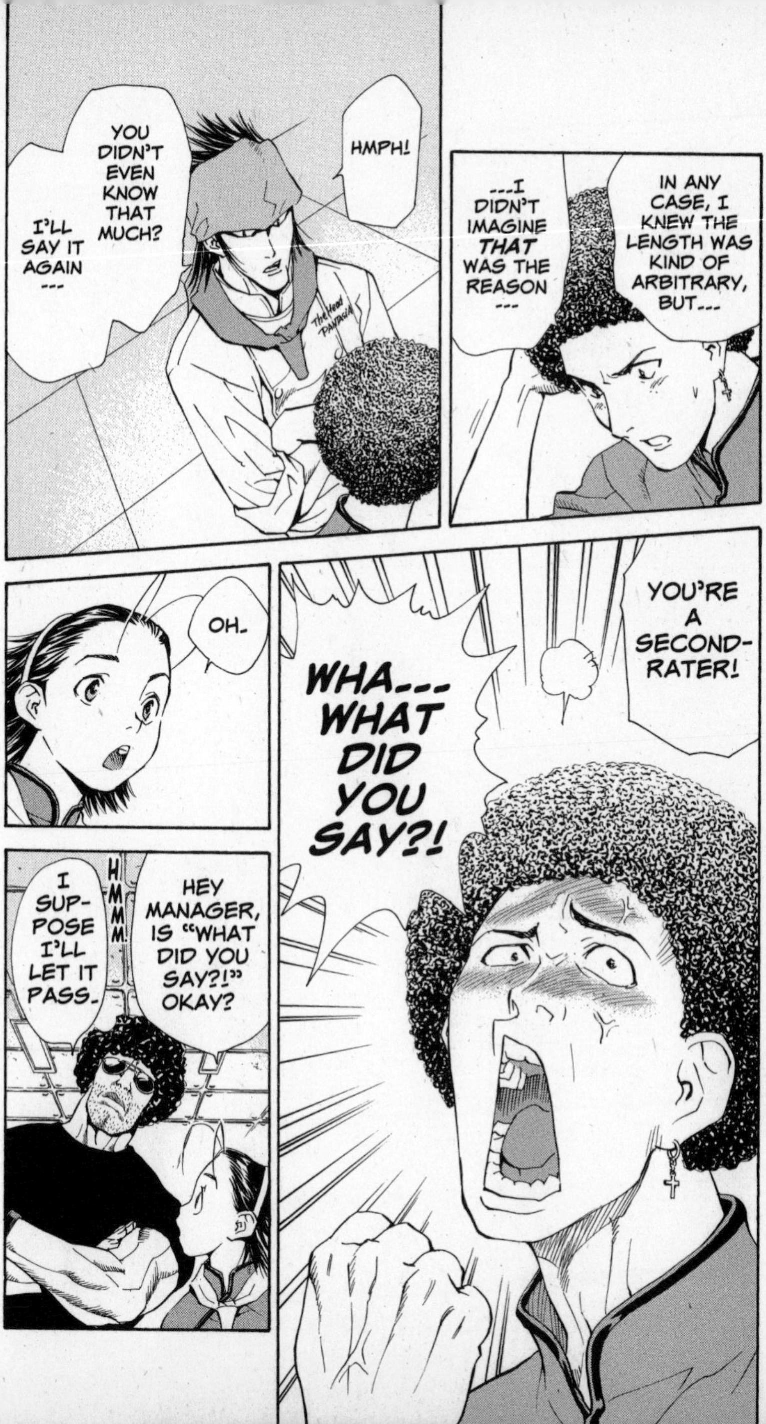
IN ANY CASE, I KNEW THE LENGTH WAS KIND OF ARBITRARY, BUT...
...I DIDN'T IMAGINE *THAT* WAS THE REASON...
HMPH!
YOU DIDN'T EVEN KNOW THAT MUCH?
I'LL SAY IT AGAIN...
YOU'RE A SECOND-RATER!
WHA... WHAT DID YOU SAY?!
OH.
HEY MANAGER, IS "WHAT DID YOU SAY?!" OKAY?
HMMM.
I SUPPOSE I'LL LET IT PASS.

Story 52:
Kidd!

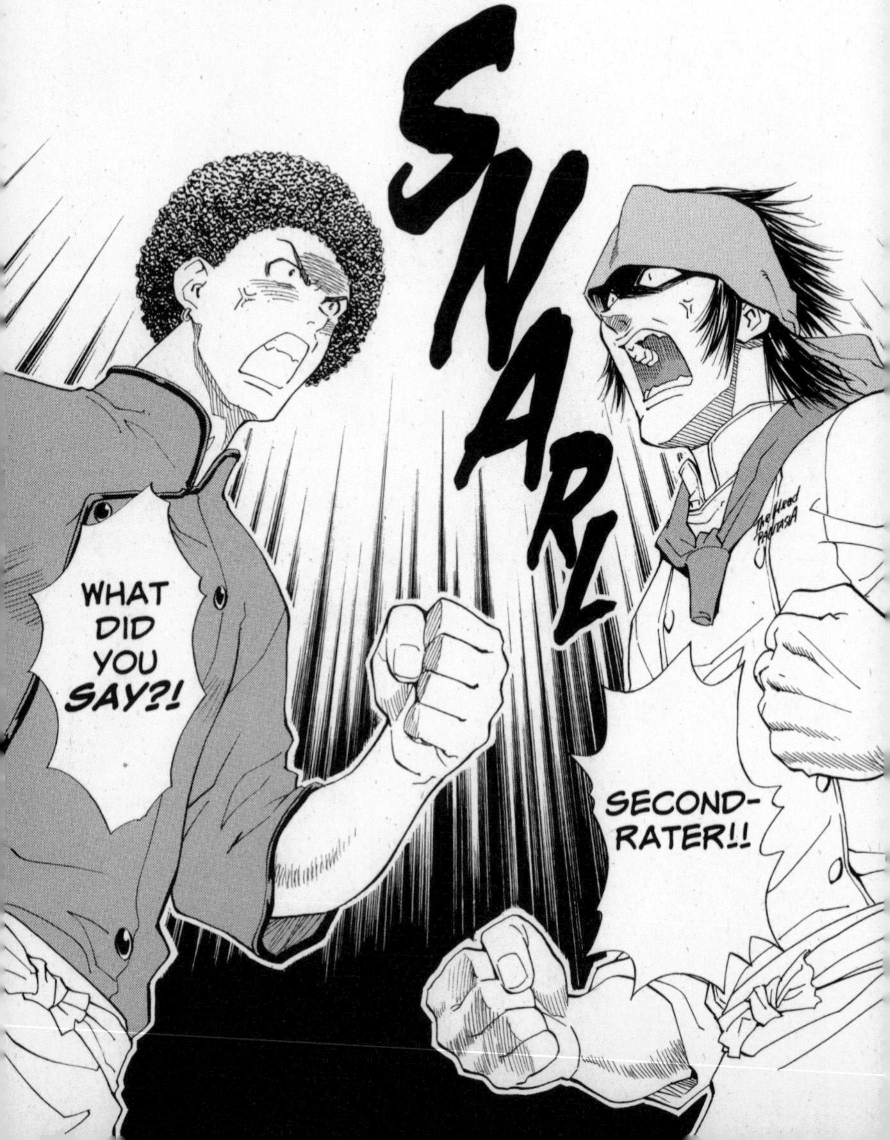
SNARL
SECOND-RATER!!
WHAT DID YOU SAY?!

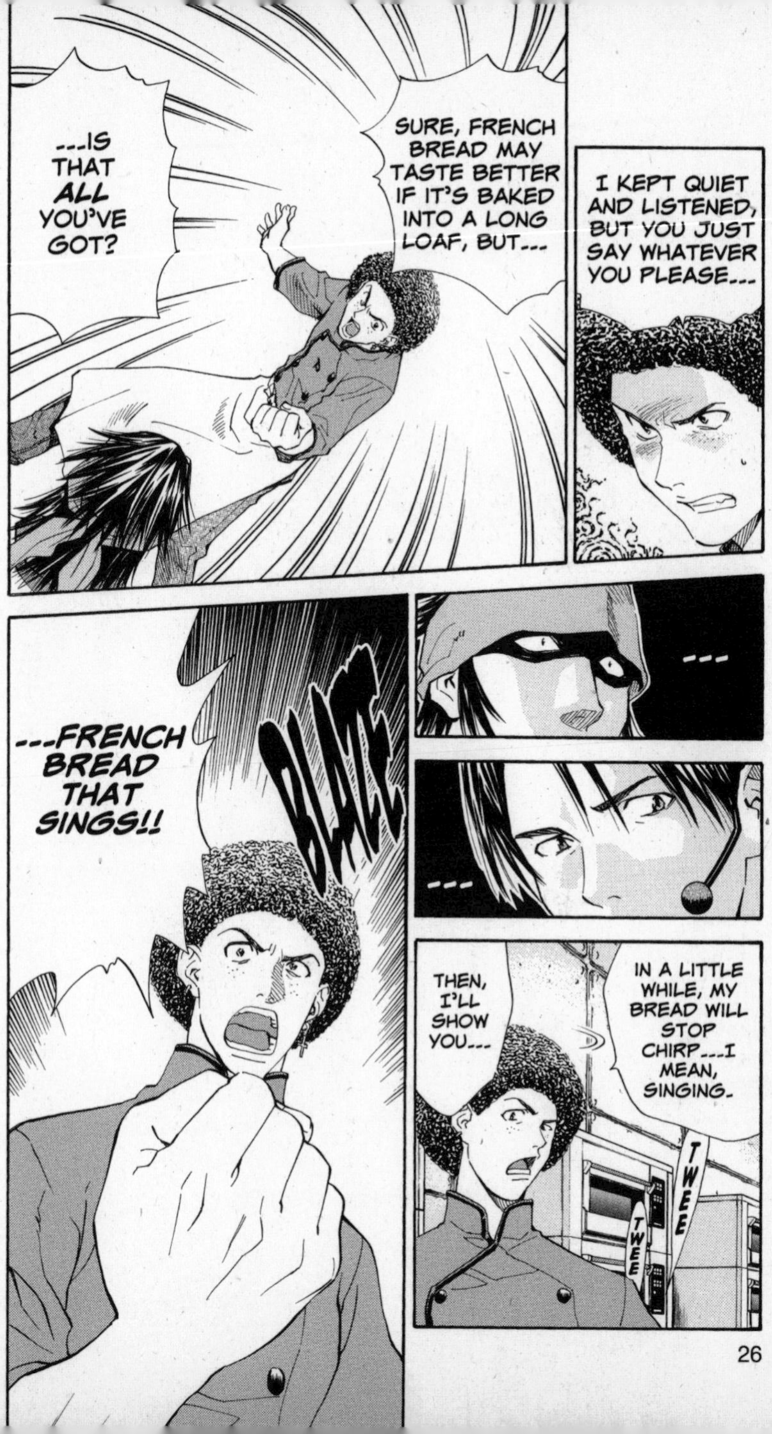
I KEPT QUIET AND LISTENED, BUT YOU JUST SAY WHATEVER YOU PLEASE...
SURE, FRENCH BREAD MAY TASTE BETTER IF IT'S BAKED INTO A LONG LOAF, BUT...
---IS THAT **ALL** YOU'VE GOT?

IN A LITTLE WHILE, MY BREAD WILL STOP CHIRP---I MEAN, SINGING.
THEN, I'LL SHOW YOU...
TWEE
TWEE
BLAZE
---FRENCH BREAD THAT SINGS!!

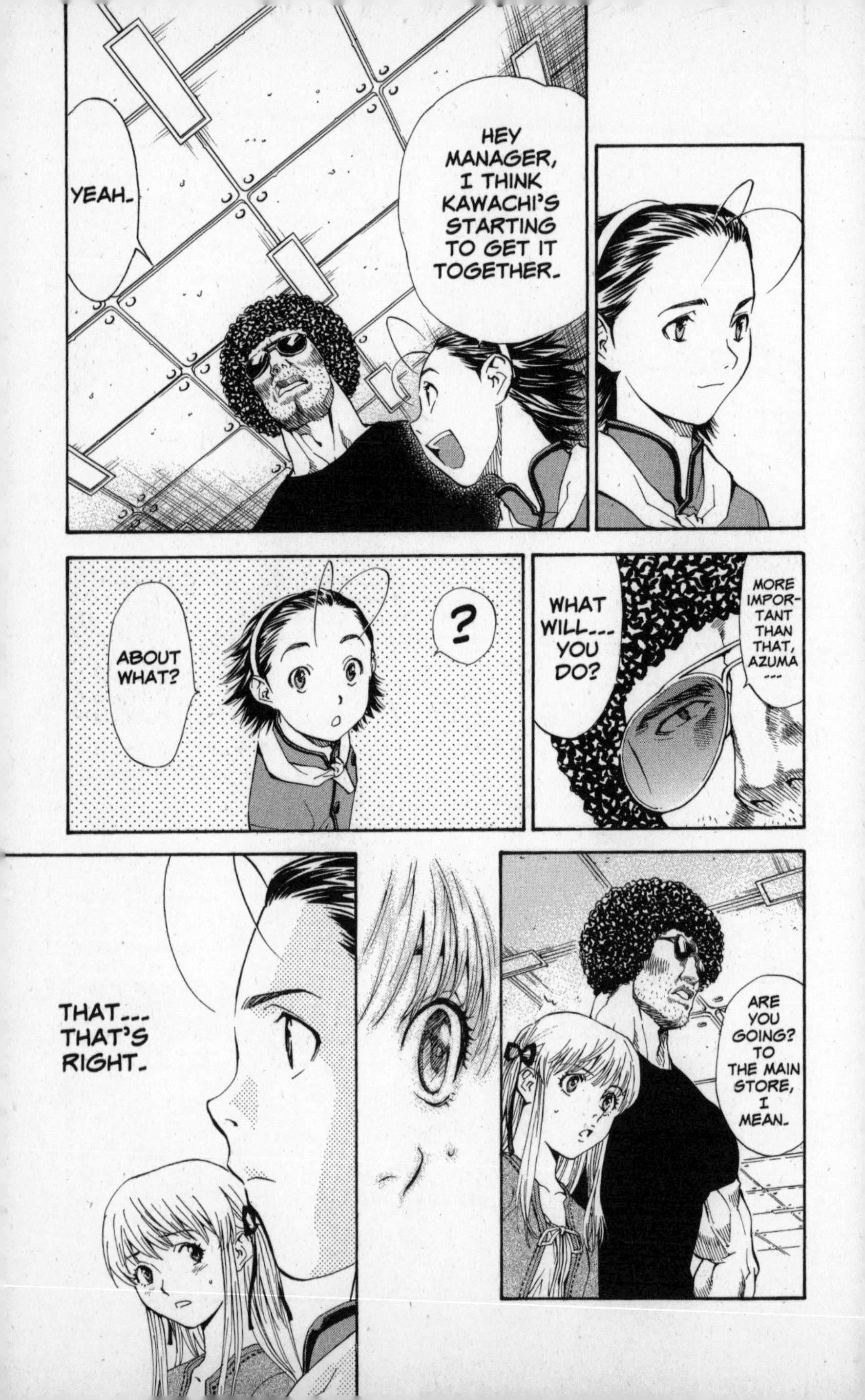
HEY MANAGER, I THINK KAWACHI'S STARTING TO GET IT TOGETHER.
YEAH.
MORE IMPORTANT THAN THAT, AZUMA...
WHAT WILL... YOU DO?
?
ABOUT WHAT?
ARE YOU GOING? TO THE MAIN STORE, I MEAN.
THAT... THAT'S RIGHT.

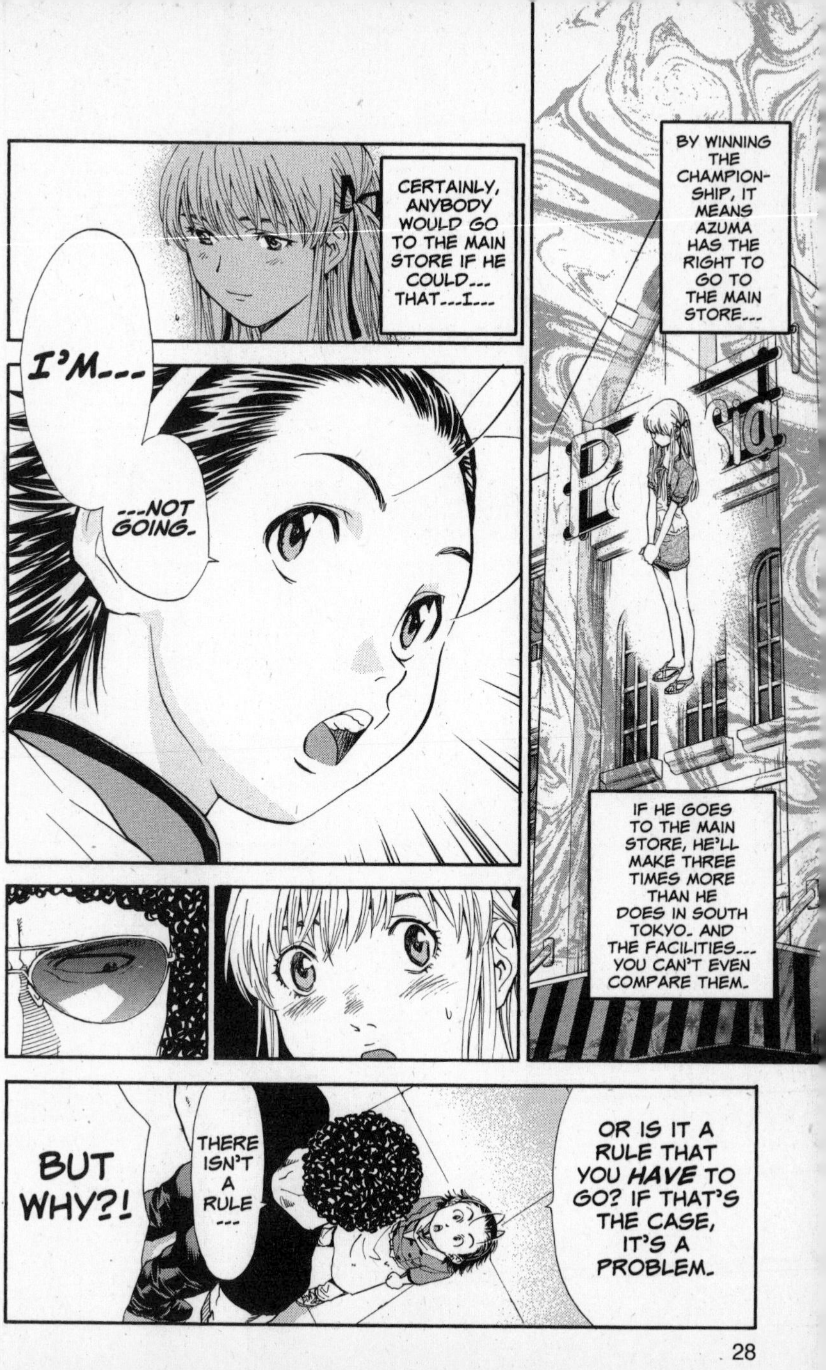
BY WINNING THE CHAMPIONSHIP, IT MEANS AZUMA HAS THE RIGHT TO GO TO THE MAIN STORE...
IF HE GOES TO THE MAIN STORE, HE'LL MAKE THREE TIMES MORE THAN HE DOES IN SOUTH TOKYO. AND THE FACILITIES... YOU CAN'T EVEN COMPARE THEM.
CERTAINLY, ANYBODY WOULD GO TO THE MAIN STORE IF HE COULD... THAT...I...
I'M...
...NOT GOING.
OR IS IT A RULE THAT YOU *HAVE* TO GO? IF THAT'S THE CASE, IT'S A PROBLEM.
THERE ISN'T A RULE ...
BUT WHY?!

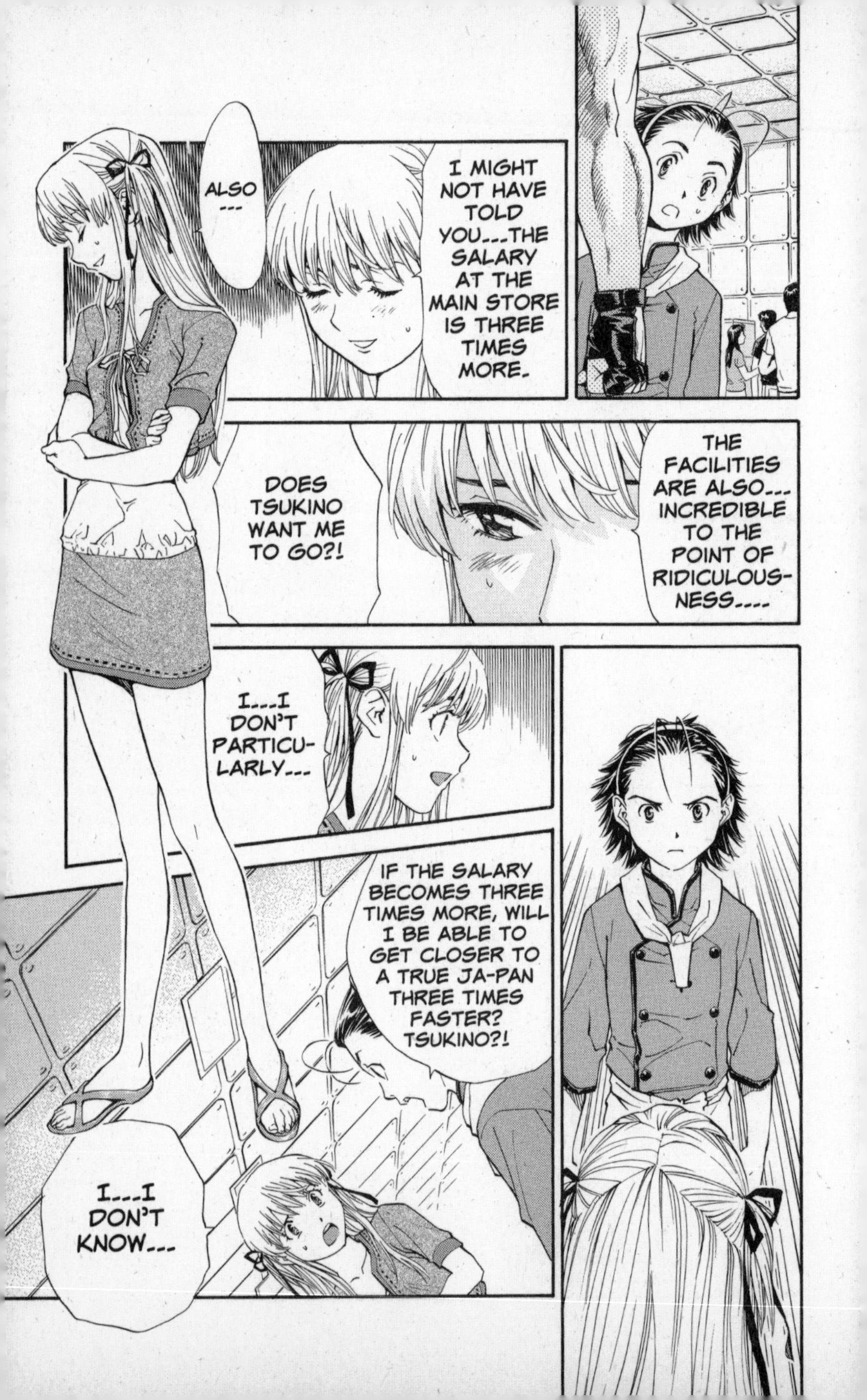
I MIGHT NOT HAVE TOLD YOU...THE SALARY AT THE MAIN STORE IS THREE TIMES MORE.
ALSO ---
THE FACILITIES ARE ALSO... INCREDIBLE TO THE POINT OF RIDICULOUSNESS....
DOES TSUKINO WANT ME TO GO?!
I...I DON'T PARTICULARLY...
IF THE SALARY BECOMES THREE TIMES MORE, WILL I BE ABLE TO GET CLOSER TO A TRUE JA-PAN THREE TIMES FASTER? TSUKINO?!
I...I DON'T KNOW...

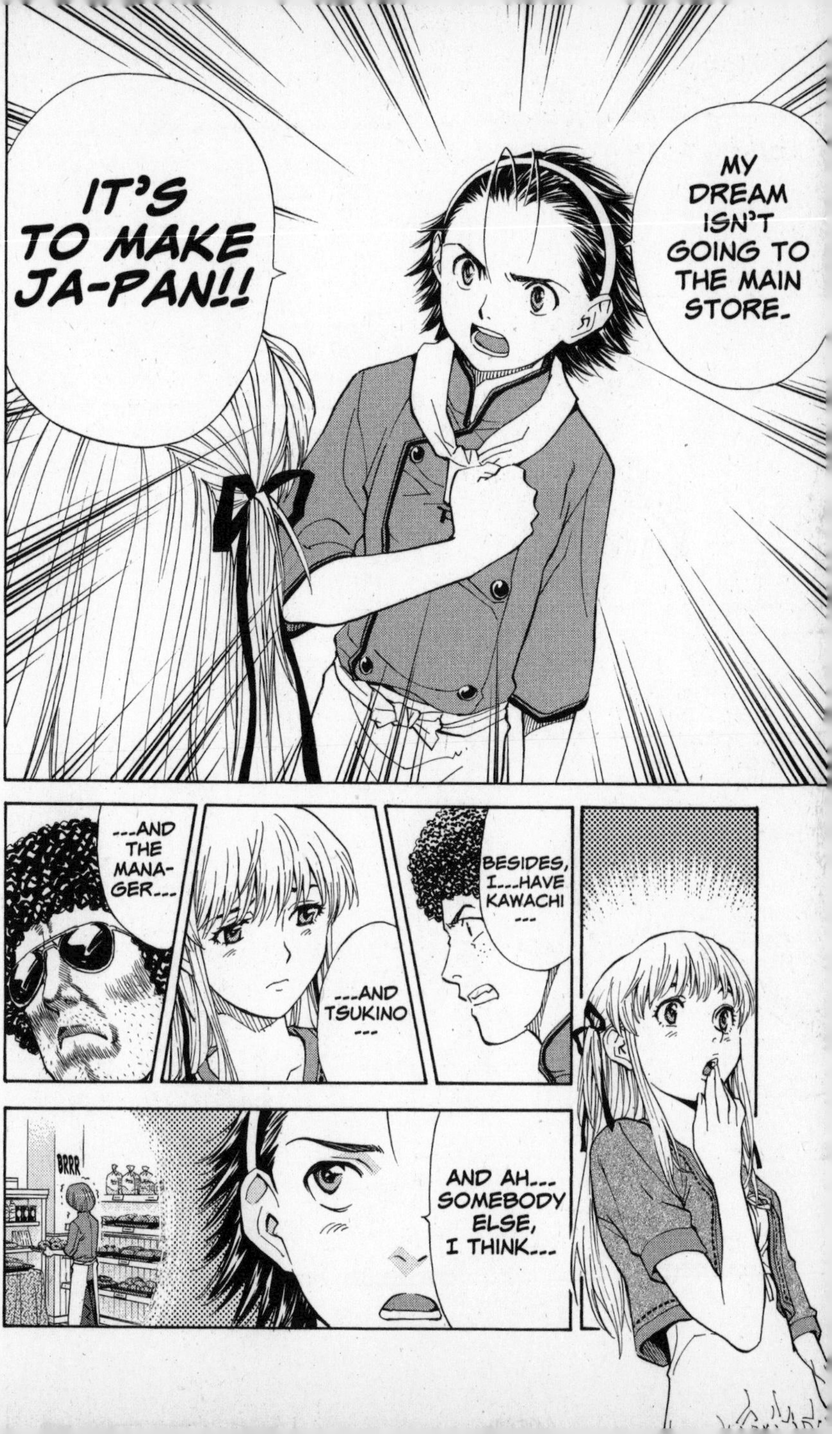
MY DREAM ISN'T GOING TO THE MAIN STORE.
IT'S TO MAKE JA-PAN!!
BESIDES, I...HAVE KAWACHI ...
...AND TSUKINO ...
...AND THE MANA-GER...
AND AH... SOMEBODY ELSE, I THINK...
BRRR

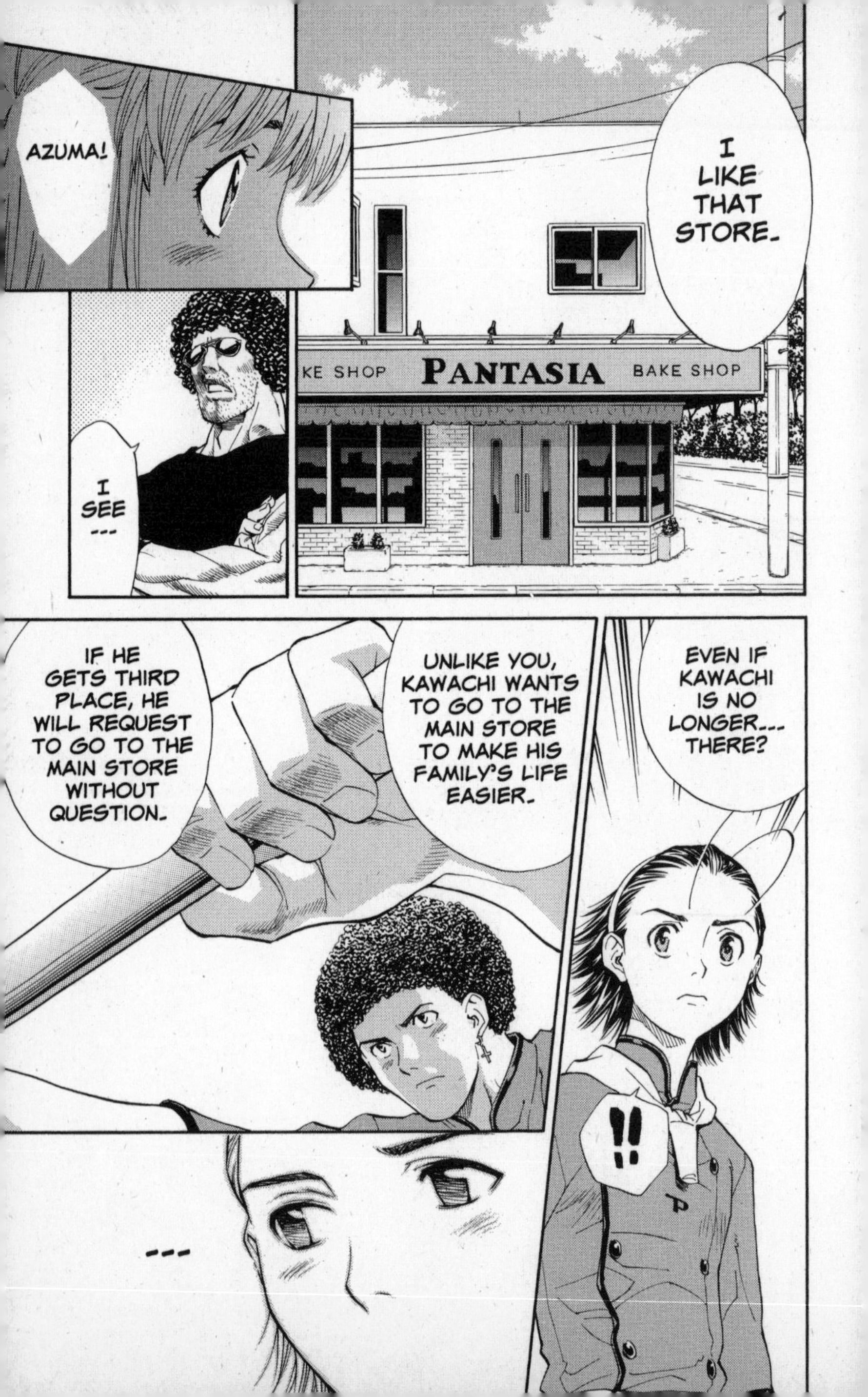
I LIKE THAT STORE.
PANTASIA
KE SHOP
BAKE SHOP
AZUMA!
I SEE...
EVEN IF KAWACHI IS NO LONGER... THERE?
!!
UNLIKE YOU, KAWACHI WANTS TO GO TO THE MAIN STORE TO MAKE HIS FAMILY'S LIFE EASIER.
IF HE GETS THIRD PLACE, HE WILL REQUEST TO GO TO THE MAIN STORE WITHOUT QUESTION.
...

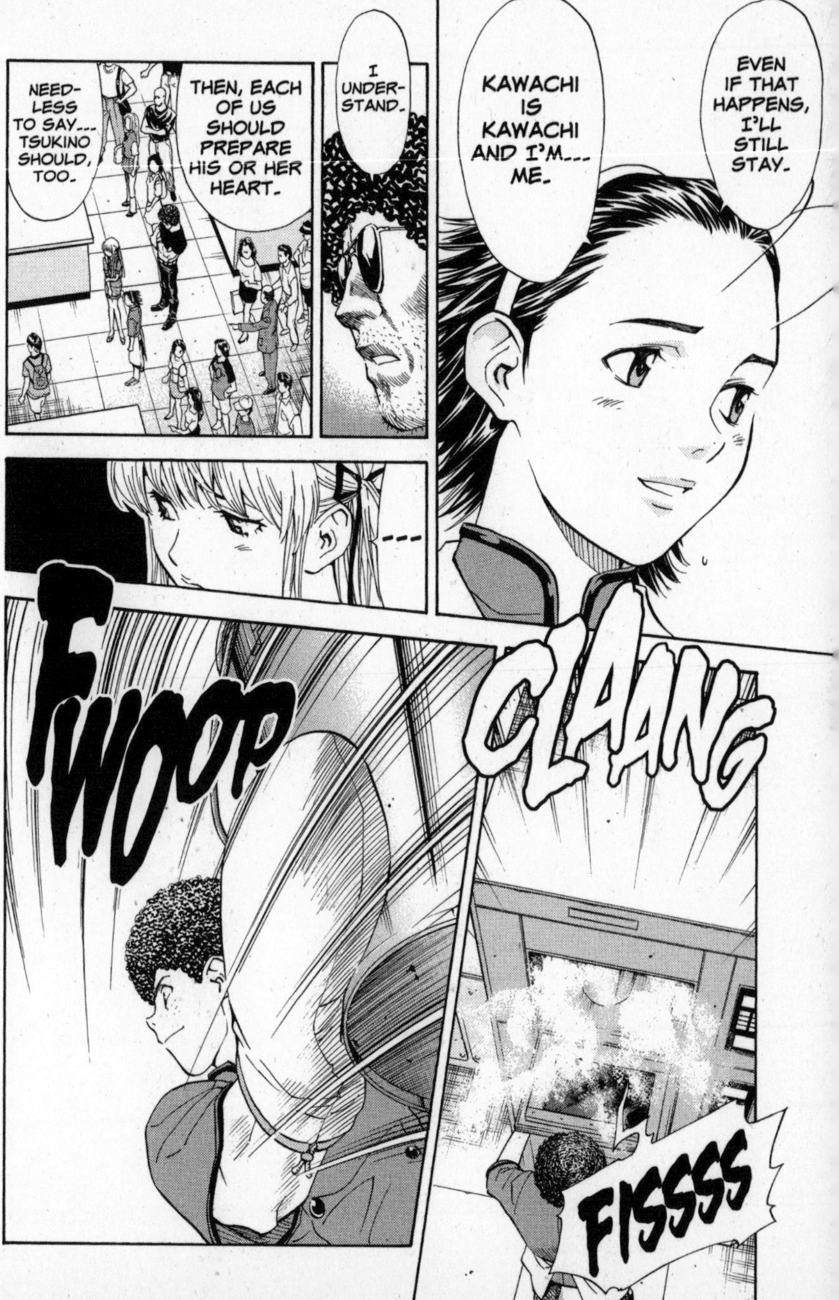
EVEN IF THAT HAPPENS, I'LL STILL STAY.
KAWACHI IS KAWACHI AND I'M... ME.
I UNDER-STAND.
THEN, EACH OF US SHOULD PREPARE HIS OR HER HEART.
NEED-LESS TO SAY... TSUKINO SHOULD, TOO.
...
CLAANG
FISSSS
FWOOP

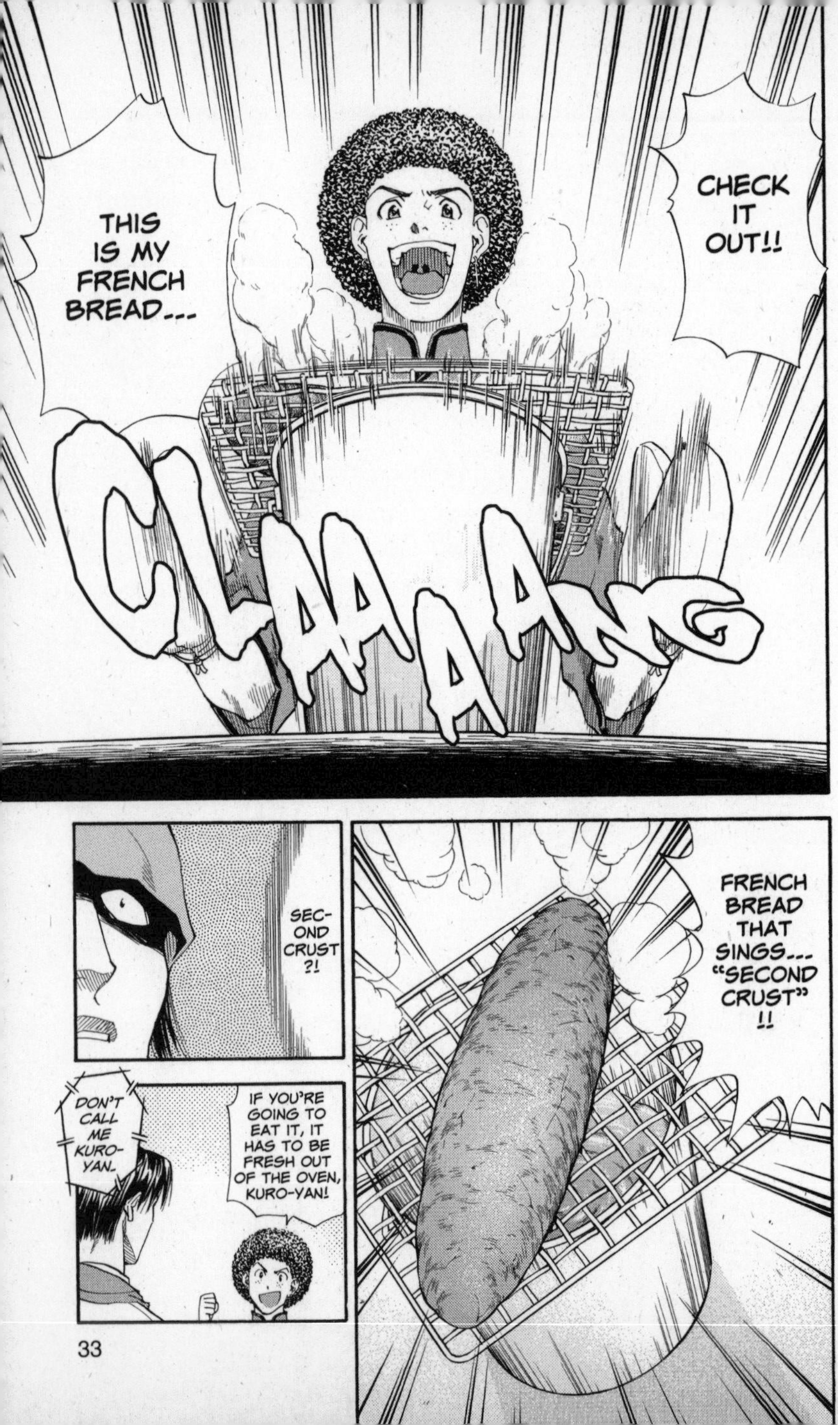
CHECK IT OUT!!
THIS IS MY FRENCH BREAD...
CLAAAAANG
FRENCH BREAD THAT SINGS... "SECOND CRUST" !!
SECOND CRUST?!
IF YOU'RE GOING TO EAT IT, IT HAS TO BE FRESH OUT OF THE OVEN, KURO-YAN!
DON'T CALL ME KURO-YAN.

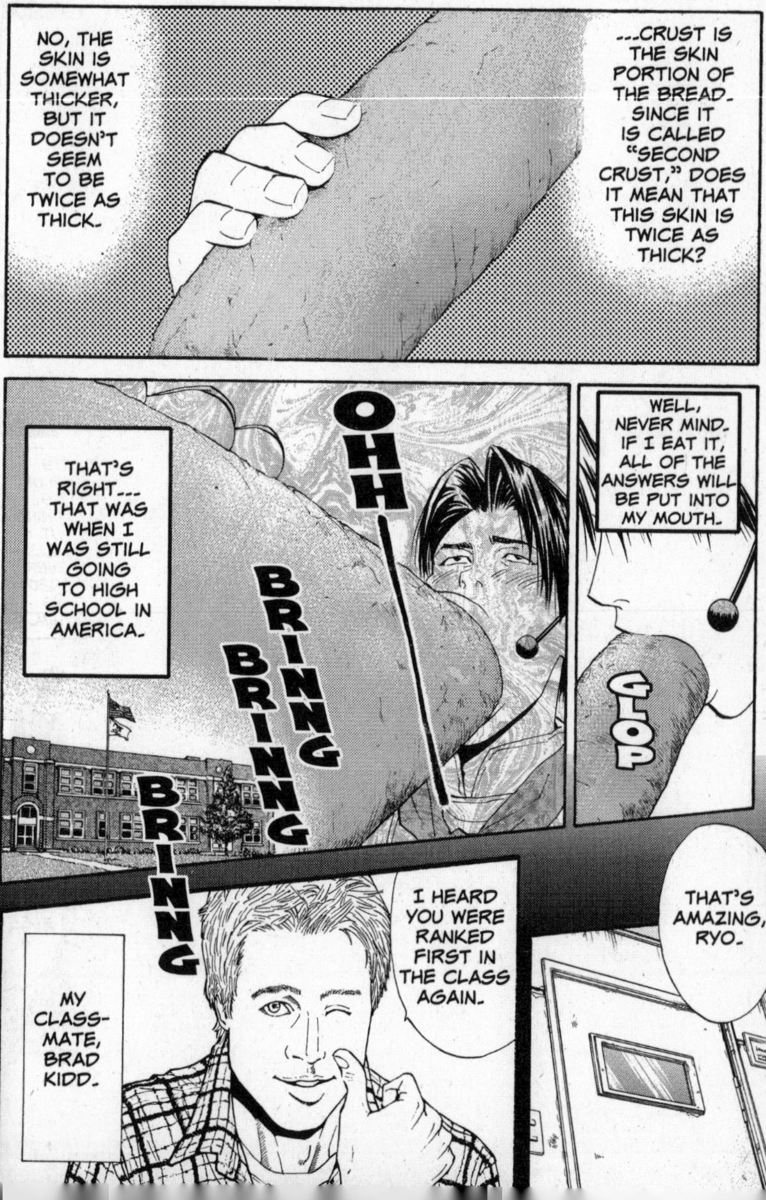
---CRUST IS THE SKIN PORTION OF THE BREAD. SINCE IT IS CALLED "SECOND CRUST," DOES IT MEAN THAT THIS SKIN IS TWICE AS THICK?
NO, THE SKIN IS SOMEWHAT THICKER, BUT IT DOESN'T SEEM TO BE TWICE AS THICK.
WELL, NEVER MIND. IF I EAT IT, ALL OF THE ANSWERS WILL BE PUT INTO MY MOUTH.
GLOP
OHH
BRINNG
BRINNG
BRINNG
THAT'S RIGHT--- THAT WAS WHEN I WAS STILL GOING TO HIGH SCHOOL IN AMERICA.
THAT'S AMAZING, RYO.
I HEARD YOU WERE RANKED FIRST IN THE CLASS AGAIN.
MY CLASSMATE, BRAD KIDD.

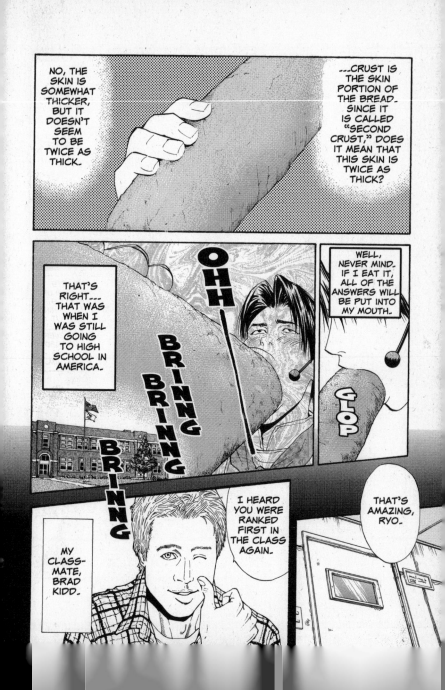

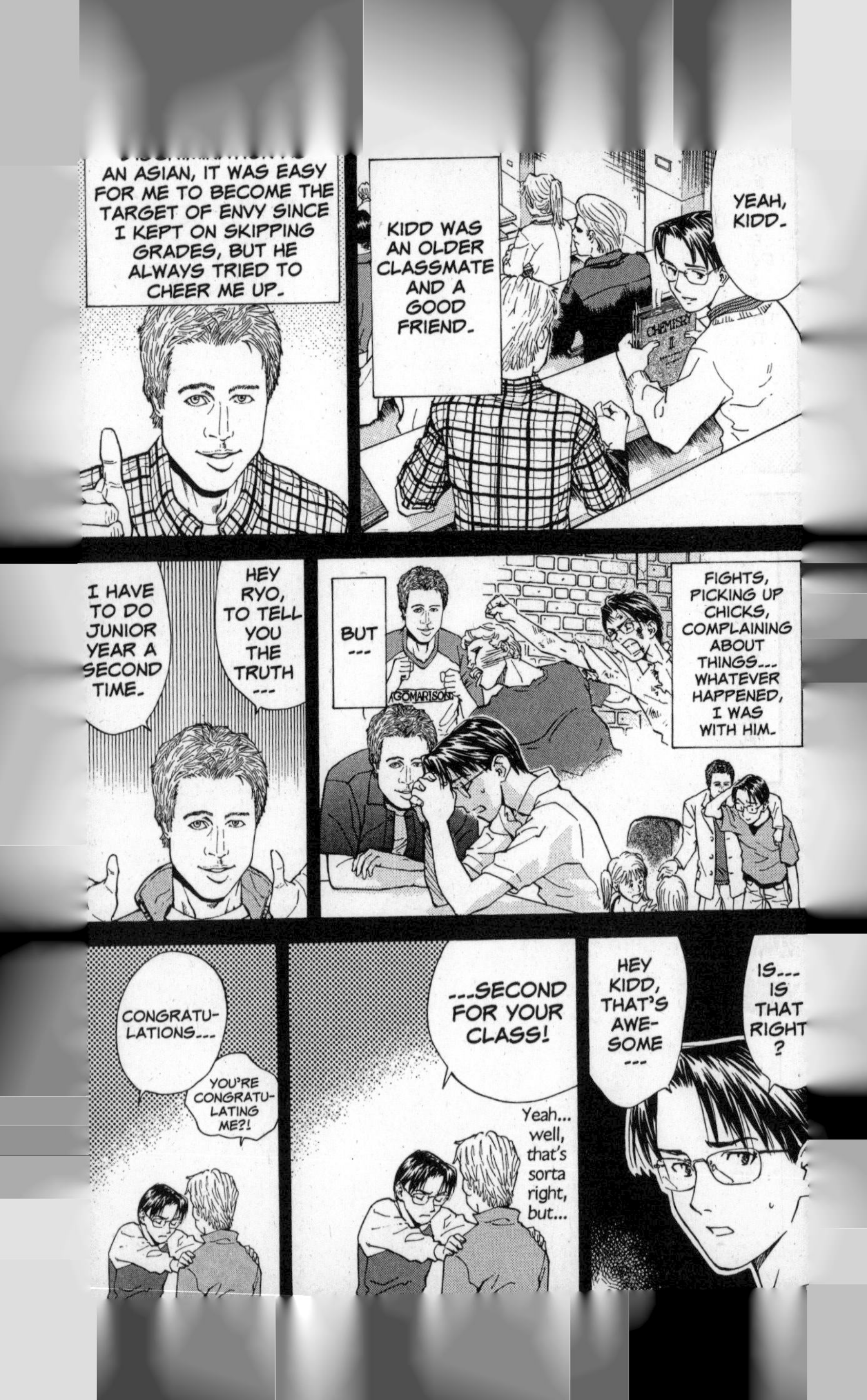
YEAH, KIDD.
KIDD WAS AN OLDER CLASSMATE AND A GOOD FRIEND.
AN ASIAN, IT WAS EASY FOR ME TO BECOME THE TARGET OF ENVY SINCE I KEPT ON SKIPPING GRADES, BUT HE ALWAYS TRIED TO CHEER ME UP.
FIGHTS, PICKING UP CHICKS, COMPLAINING ABOUT THINGS... WHATEVER HAPPENED, I WAS WITH HIM.
BUT...
HEY RYO, TO TELL YOU THE TRUTH...
I HAVE TO DO JUNIOR YEAR A SECOND TIME.
IS... IS THAT RIGHT?
HEY KIDD, THAT'S AWESOME...
...SECOND FOR YOUR CLASS!
Yeah... well, that's sorta right, but...
CONGRATULATIONS...
YOU'RE CONGRATULATING ME?!

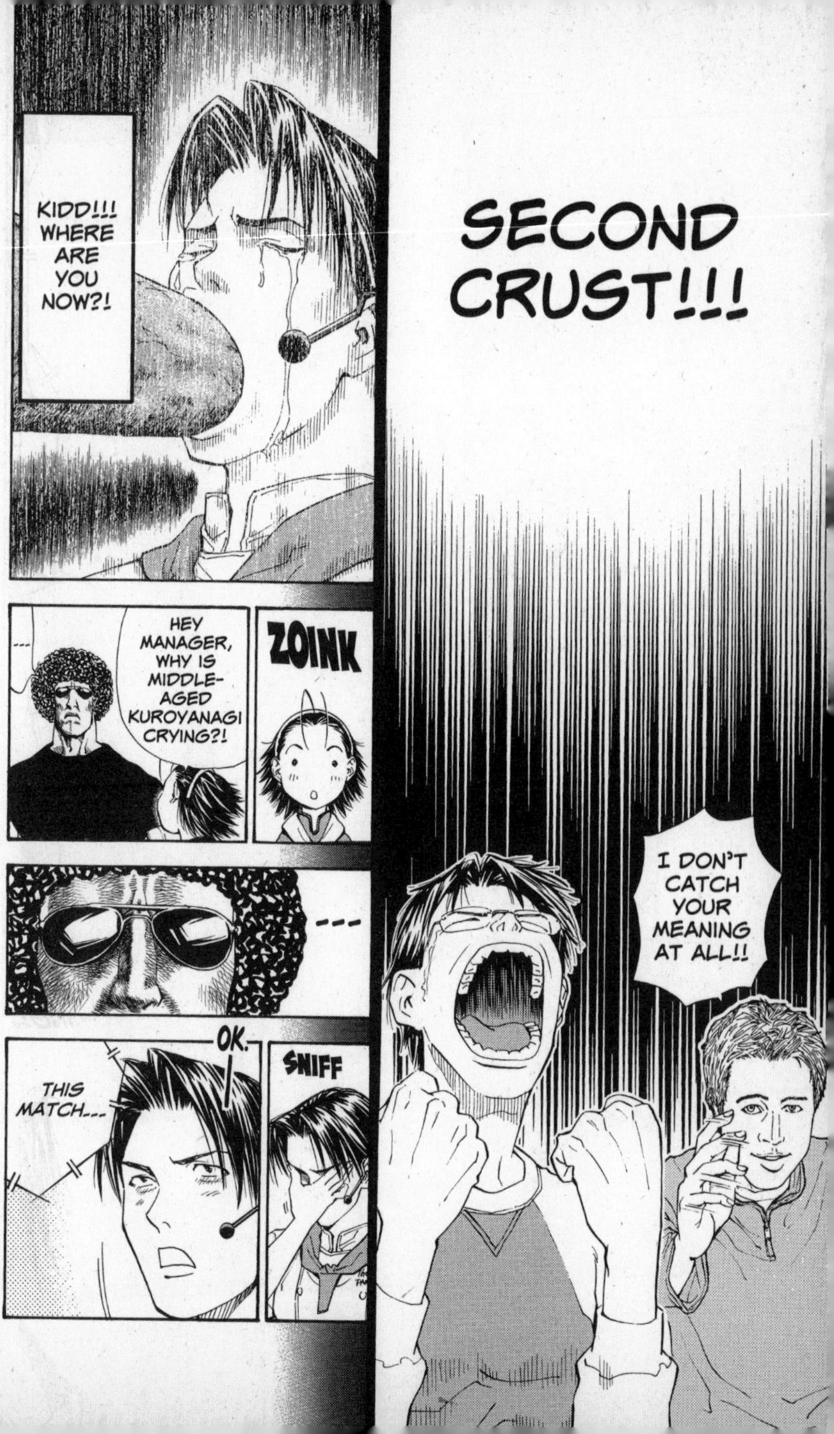
SECOND CRUST!!!
I DON'T CATCH YOUR MEANING AT ALL!!
KIDD!!! WHERE ARE YOU NOW?!
ZOINK
HEY MANAGER, WHY IS MIDDLE-AGED KUROYANAGI CRYING?!
...
...
SNIFF
OK.
THIS MATCH...

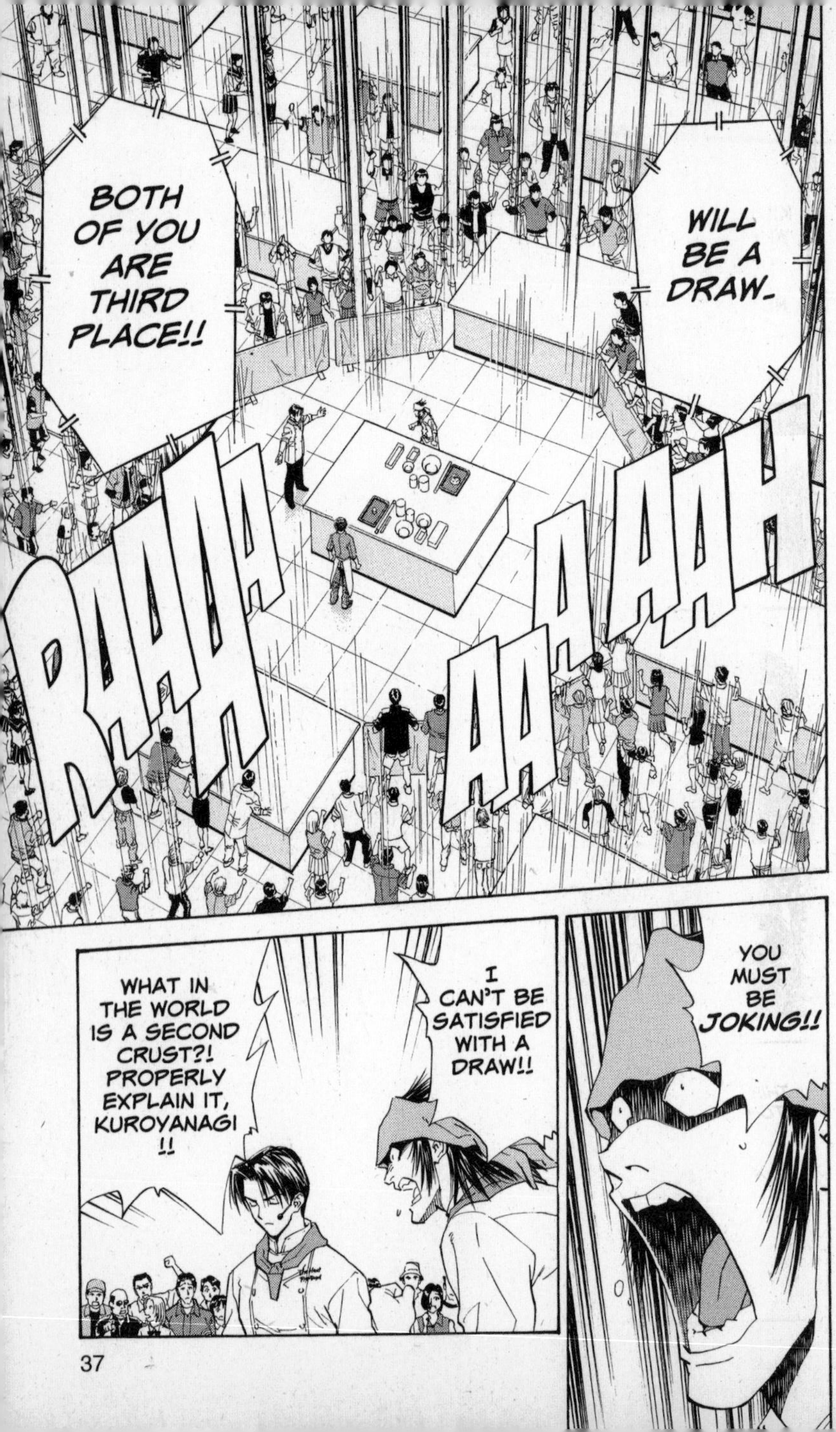

WILL BE A DRAW...
BOTH OF YOU ARE THIRD PLACE!!
RAAAAAAAAAH
YOU MUST BE JOKING!!
I CAN'T BE SATISFIED WITH A DRAW!!
WHAT IN THE WORLD IS A SECOND CRUST?! PROPERLY EXPLAIN IT, KUROYANAGI!!

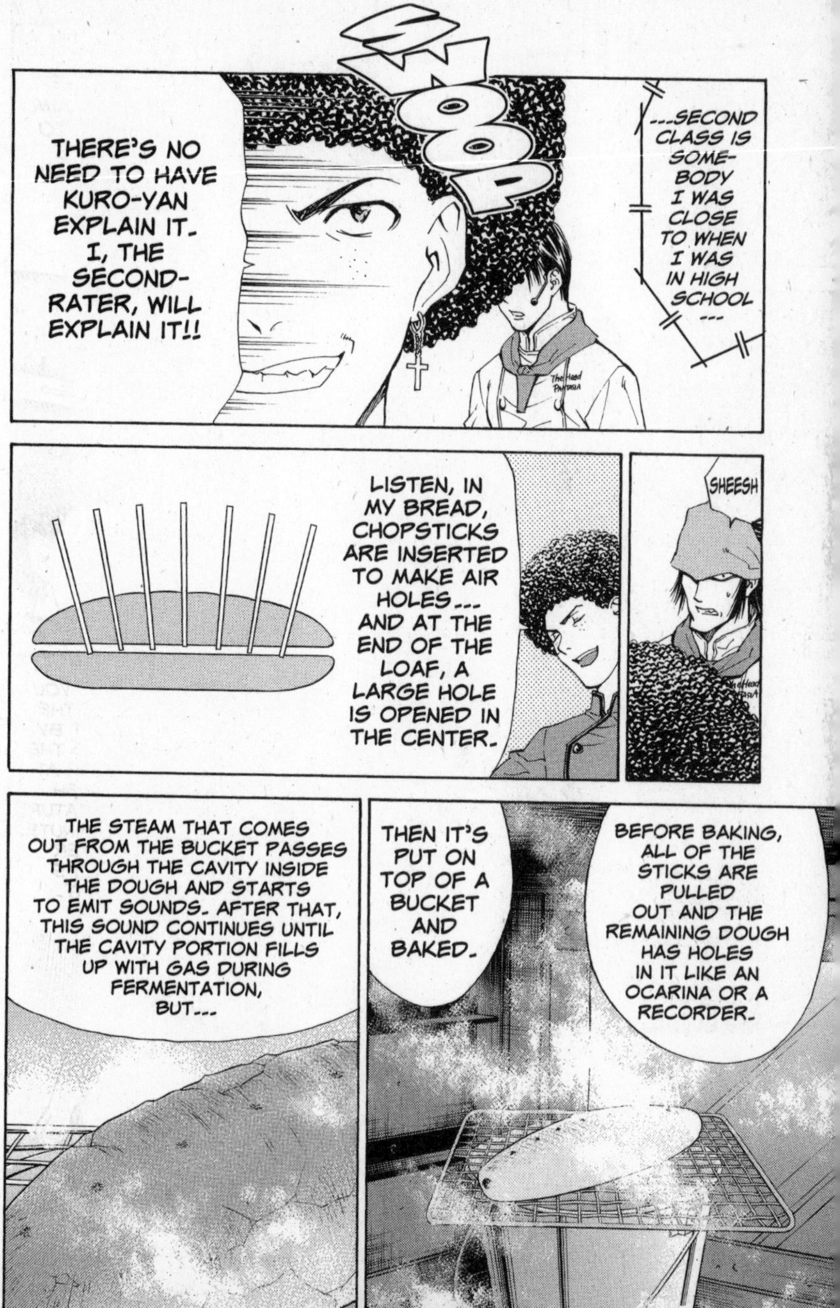
SWOOP
---SECOND CLASS IS SOMEBODY I WAS CLOSE TO WHEN I WAS IN HIGH SCHOOL---
THERE'S NO NEED TO HAVE KURO-YAN EXPLAIN IT. I, THE SECOND-RATER, WILL EXPLAIN IT!!
SHEESH
LISTEN, IN MY BREAD, CHOPSTICKS ARE INSERTED TO MAKE AIR HOLES... AND AT THE END OF THE LOAF, A LARGE HOLE IS OPENED IN THE CENTER.
BEFORE BAKING, ALL OF THE STICKS ARE PULLED OUT AND THE REMAINING DOUGH HAS HOLES IN IT LIKE AN OCARINA OR A RECORDER.
THEN IT'S PUT ON TOP OF A BUCKET AND BAKED.
THE STEAM THAT COMES OUT FROM THE BUCKET PASSES THROUGH THE CAVITY INSIDE THE DOUGH AND STARTS TO EMIT SOUNDS. AFTER THAT, THIS SOUND CONTINUES UNTIL THE CAVITY PORTION FILLS UP WITH GAS DURING FERMENTATION, BUT...

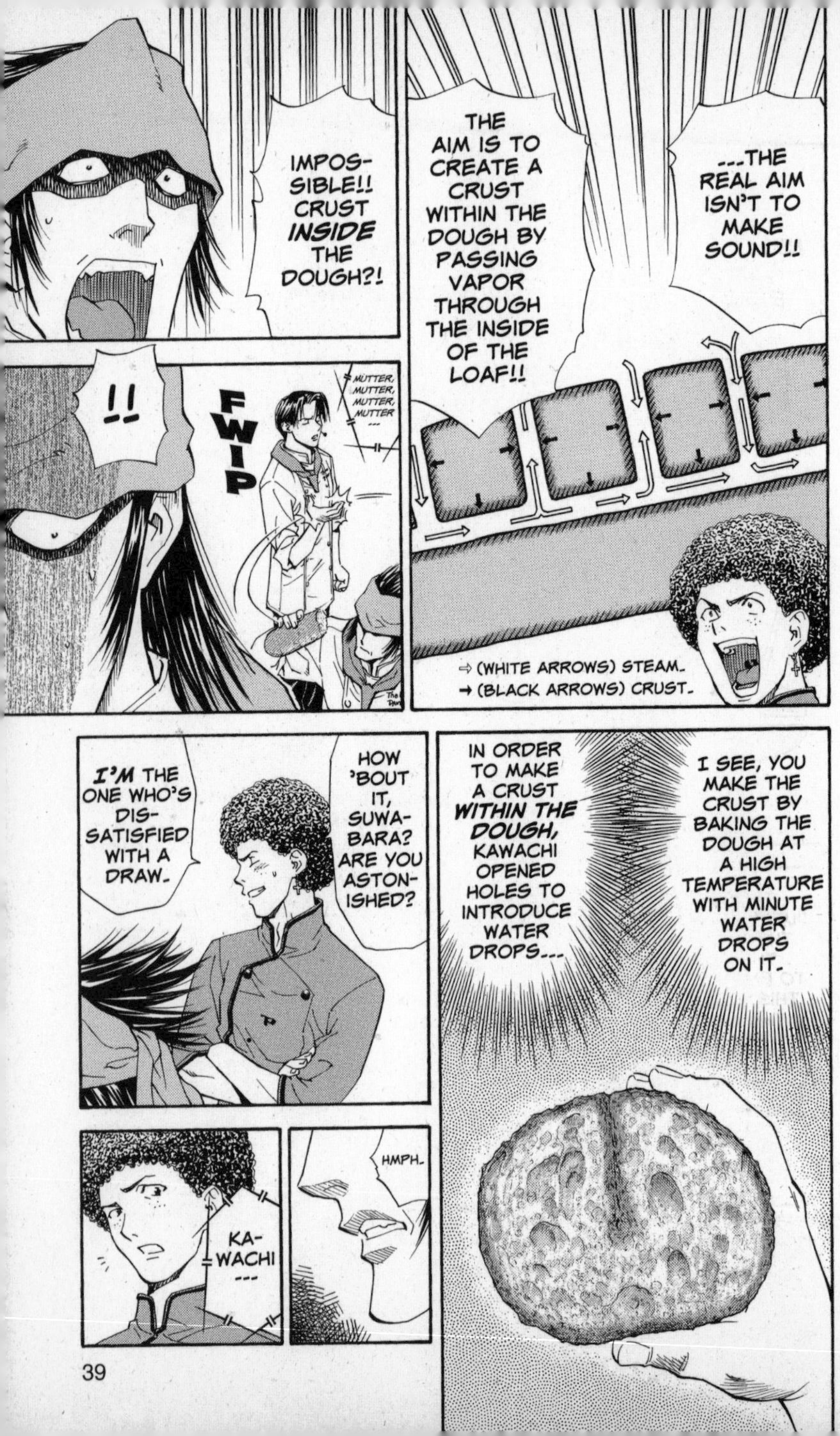
---THE REAL AIM ISN'T TO MAKE SOUND!!
THE AIM IS TO CREATE A CRUST WITHIN THE DOUGH BY PASSING VAPOR THROUGH THE INSIDE OF THE LOAF!!
⇨ (WHITE ARROWS) STEAM.
➜ (BLACK ARROWS) CRUST.
IMPOSSIBLE!! CRUST *INSIDE* THE DOUGH?!
!!
FWIP
MUTTER, MUTTER, MUTTER, MUTTER ---
I SEE, YOU MAKE THE CRUST BY BAKING THE DOUGH AT A HIGH TEMPERATURE WITH MINUTE WATER DROPS ON IT.
IN ORDER TO MAKE A CRUST *WITHIN THE DOUGH,* KAWACHI OPENED HOLES TO INTRODUCE WATER DROPS...
HOW 'BOUT IT, SUWABARA? ARE YOU ASTONISHED?
I'M THE ONE WHO'S DISSATISFIED WITH A DRAW.
HMPH.
KAWACHI ---

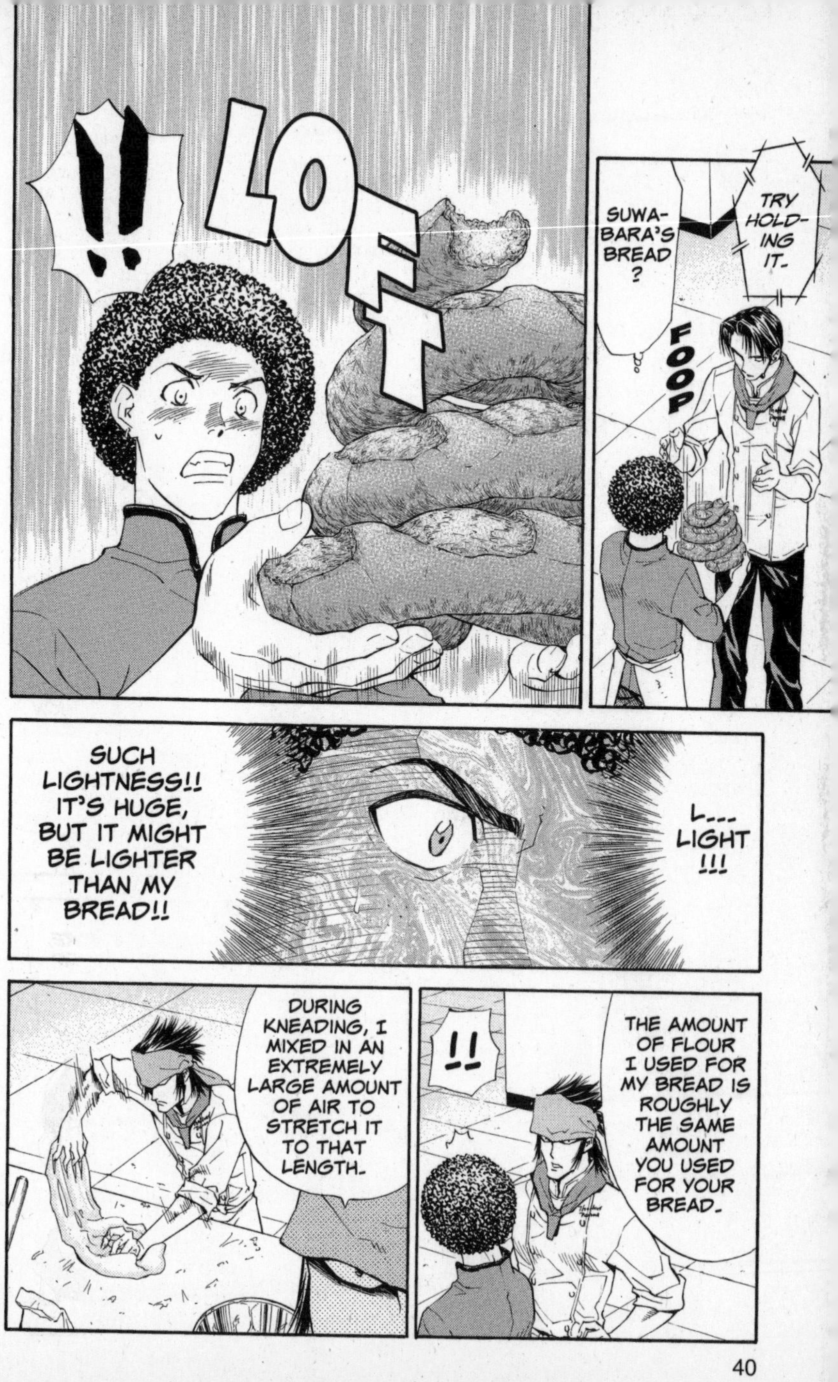
TRY HOLDING IT.
SUWA-BARA'S BREAD?
FOOP
LOFT
!!
L... LIGHT!!!
SUCH LIGHTNESS!! IT'S HUGE, BUT IT MIGHT BE LIGHTER THAN MY BREAD!!
THE AMOUNT OF FLOUR I USED FOR MY BREAD IS ROUGHLY THE SAME AMOUNT YOU USED FOR YOUR BREAD.
!!
DURING KNEADING, I MIXED IN AN EXTREMELY LARGE AMOUNT OF AIR TO STRETCH IT TO THAT LENGTH.

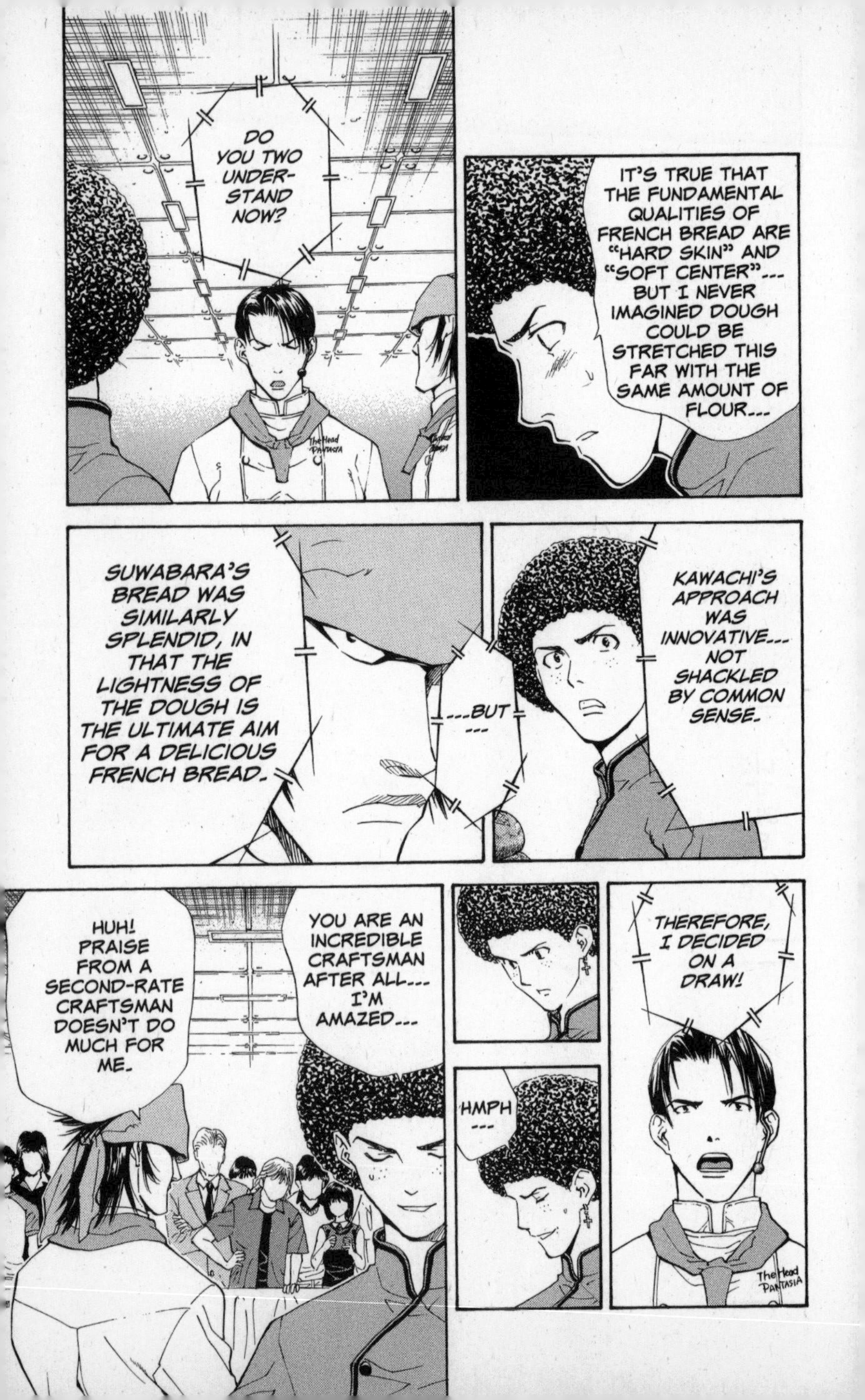
IT'S TRUE THAT THE FUNDAMENTAL QUALITIES OF FRENCH BREAD ARE "HARD SKIN" AND "SOFT CENTER"... BUT I NEVER IMAGINED DOUGH COULD BE STRETCHED THIS FAR WITH THE SAME AMOUNT OF FLOUR...
DO YOU TWO UNDER-STAND NOW?
KAWACHI'S APPROACH WAS INNOVATIVE... NOT SHACKLED BY COMMON SENSE.
...BUT ...
SUWABARA'S BREAD WAS SIMILARLY SPLENDID, IN THAT THE LIGHTNESS OF THE DOUGH IS THE ULTIMATE AIM FOR A DELICIOUS FRENCH BREAD.
THEREFORE, I DECIDED ON A DRAW!
The Head PANTASIA
HMPH ...
YOU ARE AN INCREDIBLE CRAFTSMAN AFTER ALL... I'M AMAZED...
HUH! PRAISE FROM A SECOND-RATE CRAFTSMAN DOESN'T DO MUCH FOR ME.

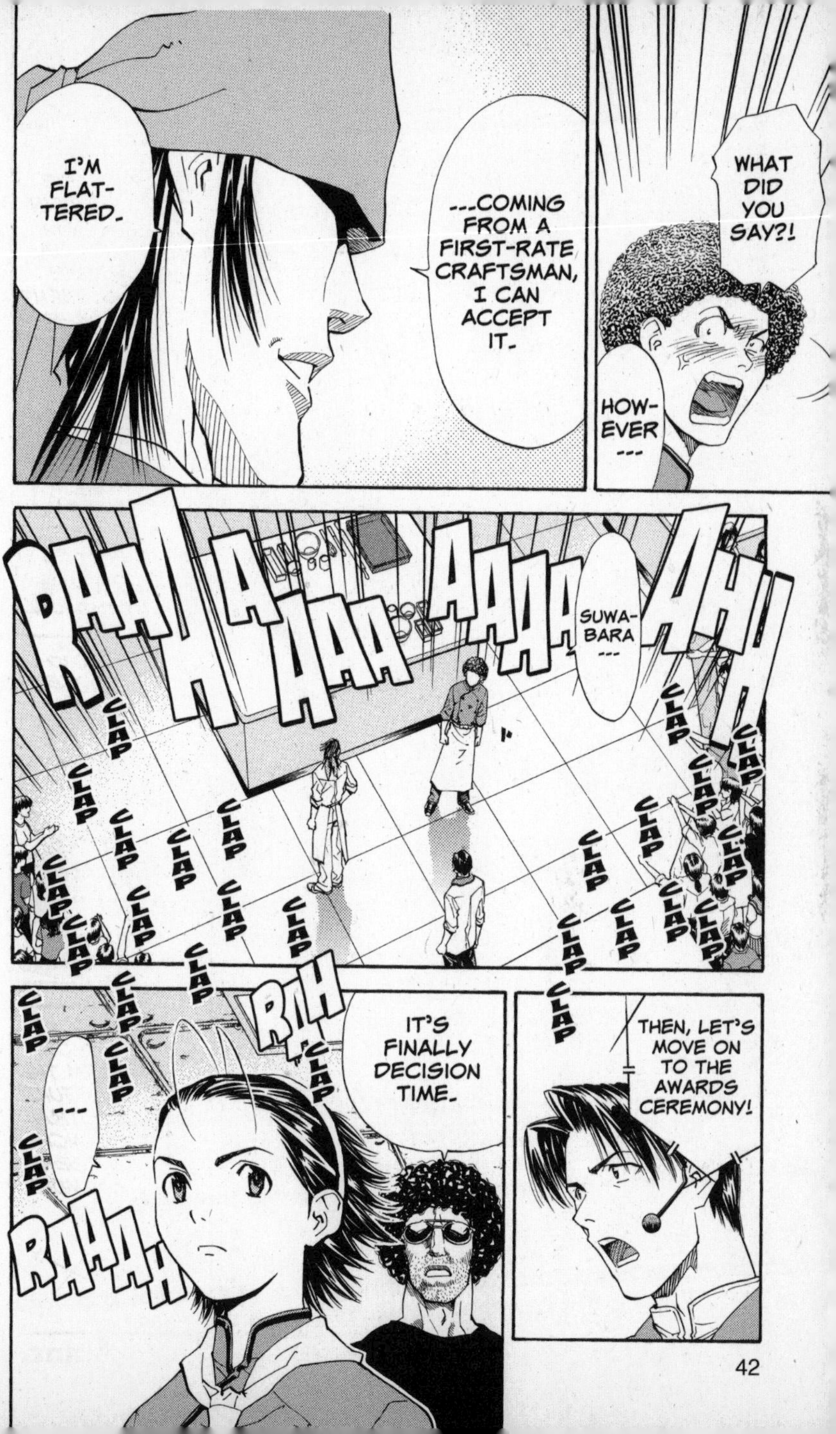
WHAT DID YOU SAY?!
HOW-EVER---
---COMING FROM A FIRST-RATE CRAFTSMAN, I CAN ACCEPT IT.
I'M FLAT-TERED.
RAAAAAAAAAAAAAAAAH
SUWA-BARA---
CLAP CLAP CLAP CLAP CLAP CLAP CLAP CLAP CLAP CLAP CLAP CLAP CLAP CLAP CLAP CLAP CLAP CLAP CLAP CLAP CLAP CLAP CLAP CLAP
THEN, LET'S MOVE ON TO THE AWARDS CEREMONY!
RAH
IT'S FINALLY DECISION TIME.

RAAAAH

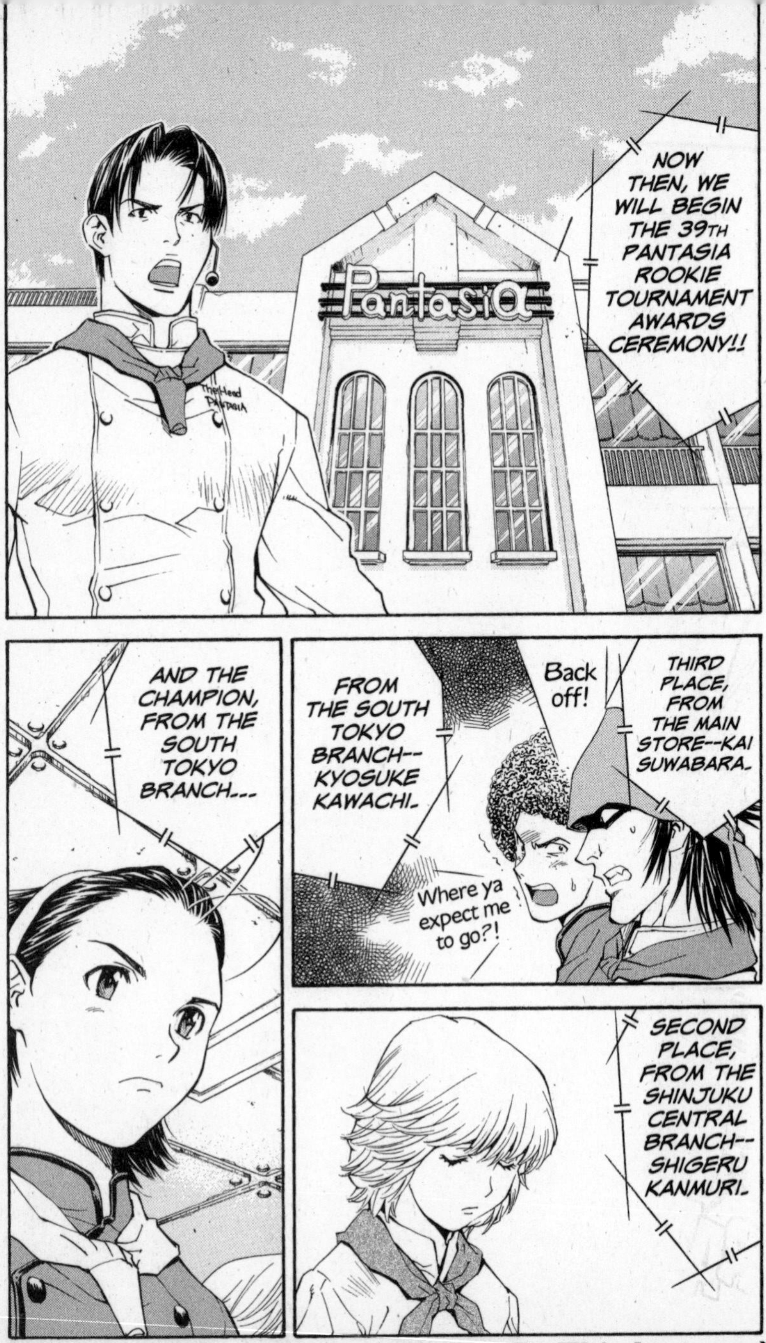
NOW THEN, WE WILL BEGIN THE 39TH PANTASIA ROOKIE TOURNAMENT AWARDS CEREMONY!!
Pantasia
THIRD PLACE, FROM THE MAIN STORE--KAI SUWABARA...
Back off!
FROM THE SOUTH TOKYO BRANCH--KYOSUKE KAWACHI...
Where ya expect me to go?!
SECOND PLACE, FROM THE SHINJUKU CENTRAL BRANCH--SHIGERU KANMURI...
AND THE CHAMPION, FROM THE SOUTH TOKYO BRANCH...

Story 53: "What do you mean?!" (In This Instance)

Story 53:
"What do you mean?!" (In This Instance)

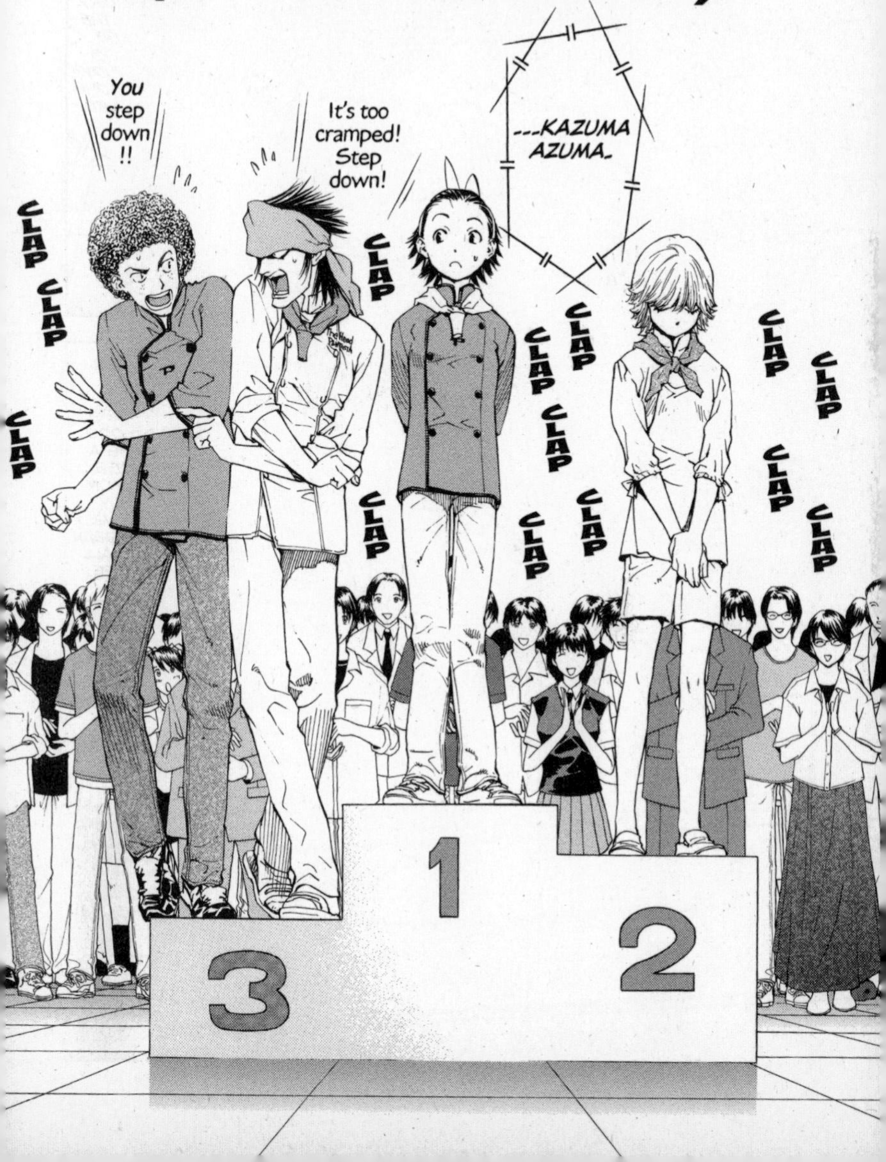
---KAZUMA AZUMA-
It's too cramped! Step down!
You step down!!
CLAP
CLAP
CLAP
CLAP
CLAP
CLAP
CLAP
CLAP
CLAP
CLAP
CLAP
CLAP
CLAP
CLAP
1
2
3

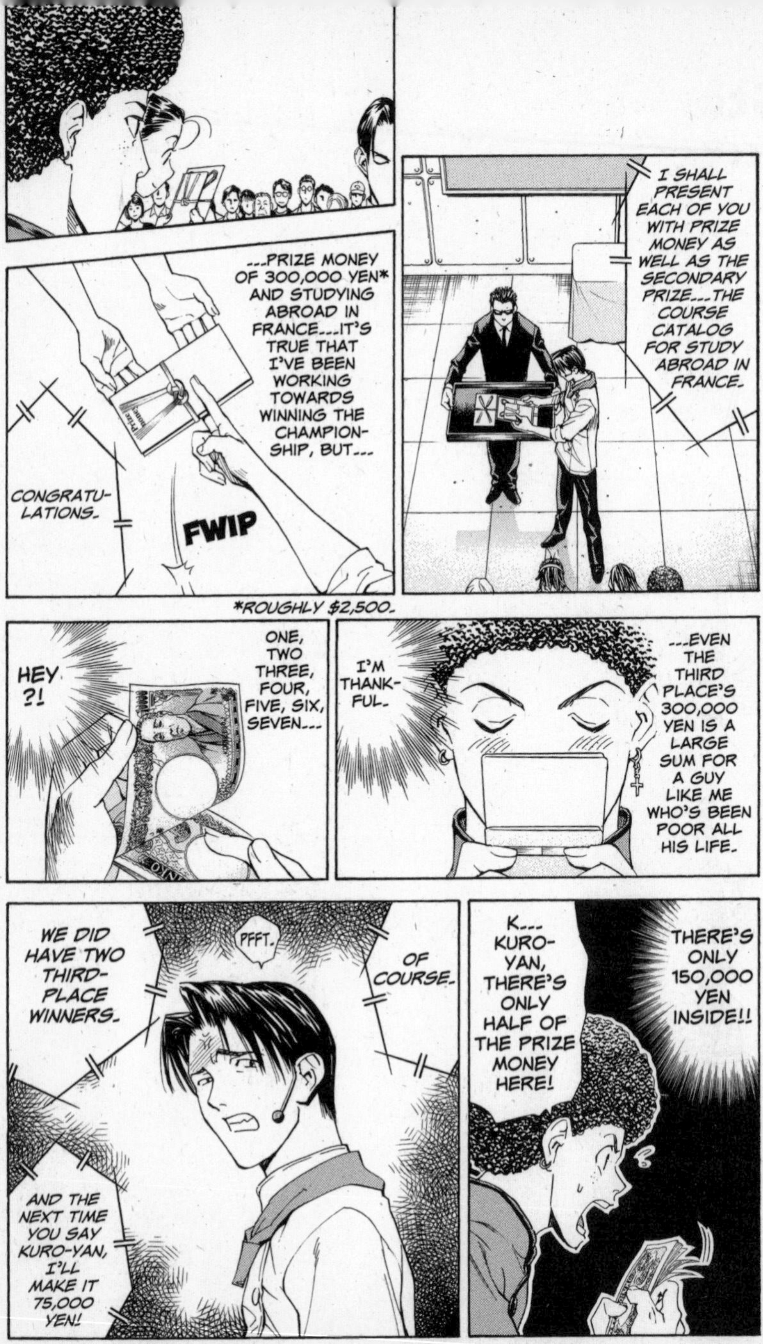
I SHALL PRESENT EACH OF YOU WITH PRIZE MONEY AS WELL AS THE SECONDARY PRIZE... THE COURSE CATALOG FOR STUDY ABROAD IN FRANCE.
...PRIZE MONEY OF 300,000 YEN* AND STUDYING ABROAD IN FRANCE... IT'S TRUE THAT I'VE BEEN WORKING TOWARDS WINNING THE CHAMPIONSHIP, BUT...
FWIP
CONGRATULATIONS.
*ROUGHLY $2,500.
...EVEN THE THIRD PLACE'S 300,000 YEN IS A LARGE SUM FOR A GUY LIKE ME WHO'S BEEN POOR ALL HIS LIFE.
I'M THANKFUL.
ONE, TWO THREE, FOUR, FIVE, SIX, SEVEN...
HEY ?!
THERE'S ONLY 150,000 YEN INSIDE!!
K... KURO-YAN, THERE'S ONLY HALF OF THE PRIZE MONEY HERE!
OF COURSE.
PFFT.
WE DID HAVE TWO THIRD-PLACE WINNERS.
AND THE NEXT TIME YOU SAY KURO-YAN, I'LL MAKE IT 75,000 YEN!

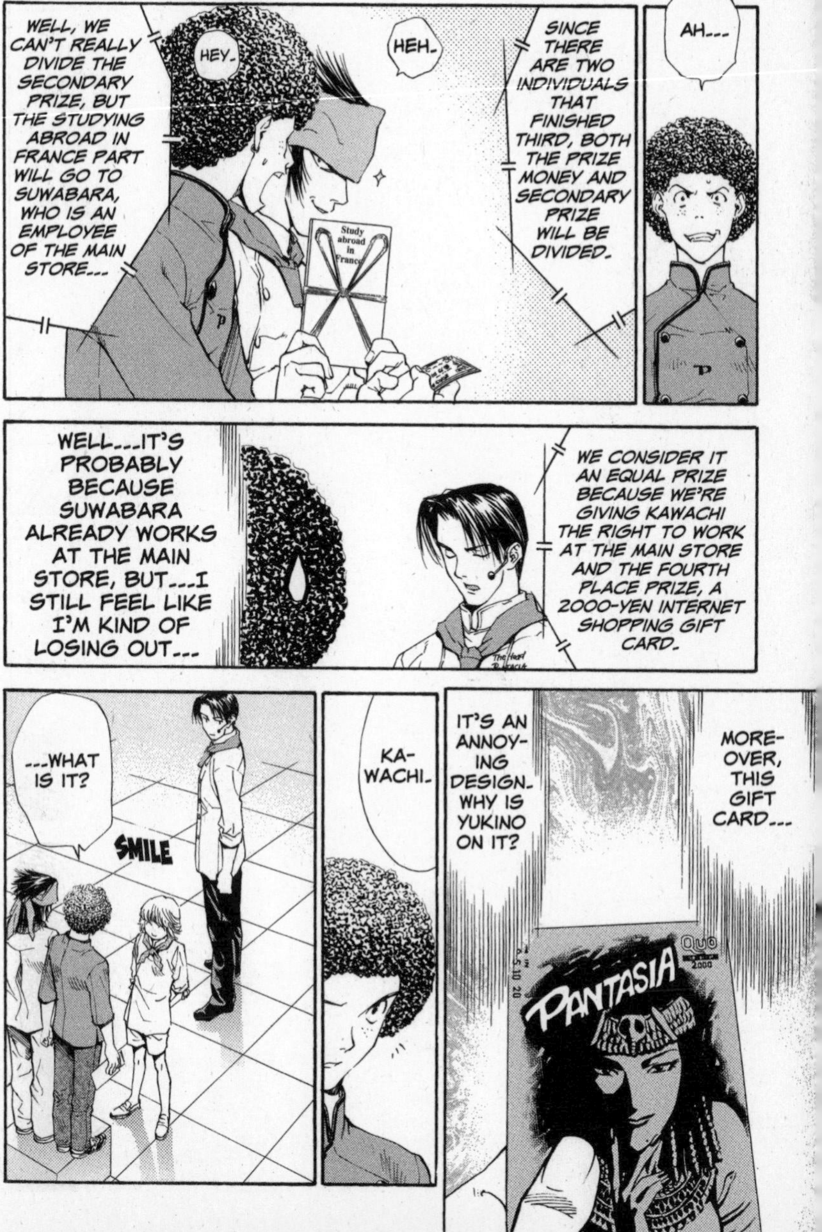
AH...
SINCE THERE ARE TWO INDIVIDUALS THAT FINISHED THIRD, BOTH THE PRIZE MONEY AND SECONDARY PRIZE WILL BE DIVIDED.
HEH.
HEY.
WELL, WE CAN'T REALLY DIVIDE THE SECONDARY PRIZE, BUT THE STUDYING ABROAD IN FRANCE PART WILL GO TO SUWABARA, WHO IS AN EMPLOYEE OF THE MAIN STORE...
Study abroad in France
WE CONSIDER IT AN EQUAL PRIZE BECAUSE WE'RE GIVING KAWACHI THE RIGHT TO WORK AT THE MAIN STORE AND THE FOURTH PLACE PRIZE, A 2000-YEN INTERNET SHOPPING GIFT CARD.
WELL...IT'S PROBABLY BECAUSE SUWABARA ALREADY WORKS AT THE MAIN STORE, BUT...I STILL FEEL LIKE I'M KIND OF LOSING OUT...
MORE-OVER, THIS GIFT CARD...
IT'S AN ANNOY-ING DESIGN. WHY IS YUKINO ON IT?
PANTASIA
KA-WACHI.
...WHAT IS IT?
SMILE

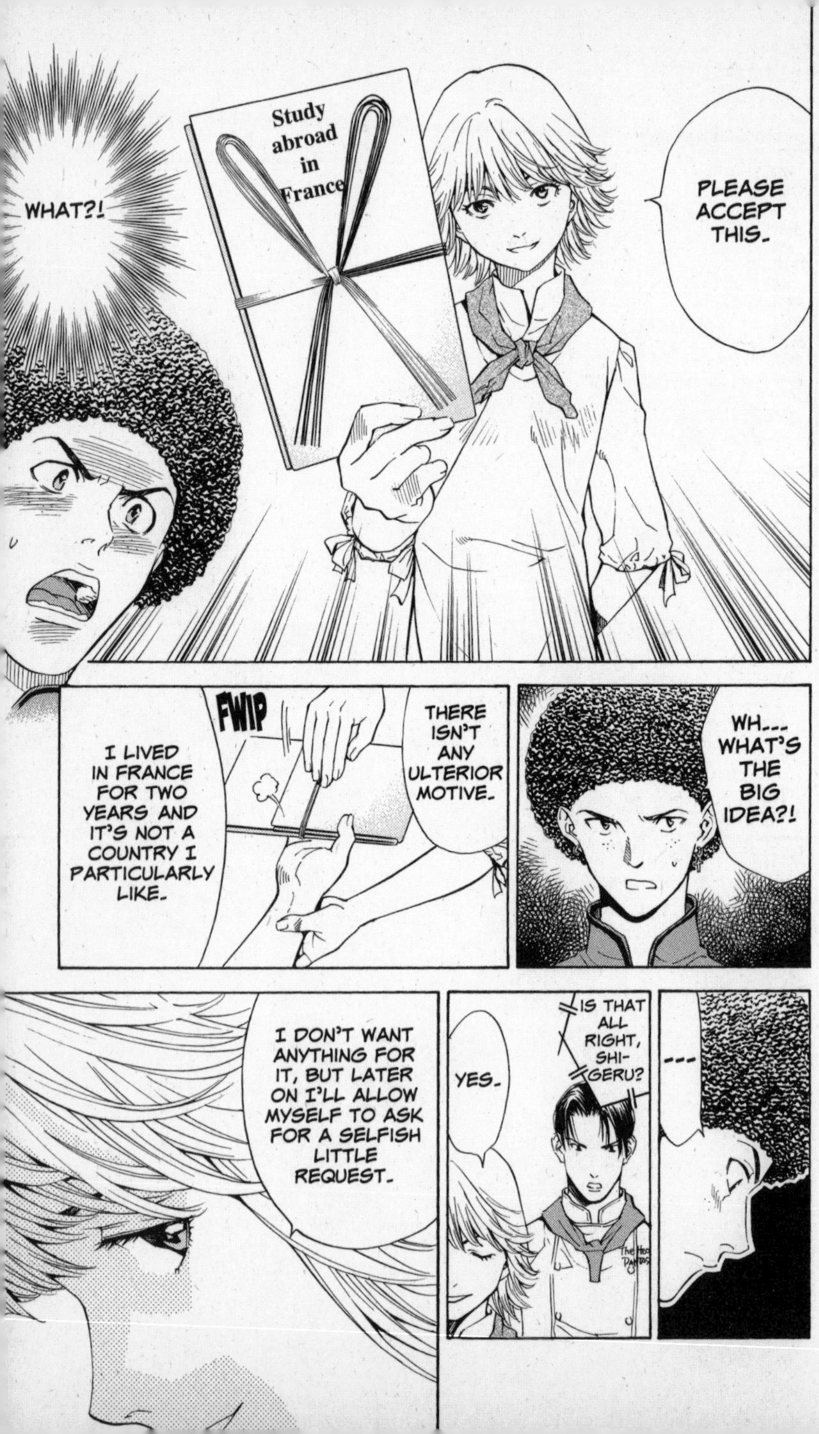
PLEASE ACCEPT THIS.
Study abroad in France
WHAT?!
WH... WHAT'S THE BIG IDEA?!
THERE ISN'T ANY ULTERIOR MOTIVE.
FWIP
I LIVED IN FRANCE FOR TWO YEARS AND IT'S NOT A COUNTRY I PARTICULARLY LIKE.
...
IS THAT ALL RIGHT, SHIGERU?
YES.
I DON'T WANT ANYTHING FOR IT, BUT LATER ON I'LL ALLOW MYSELF TO ASK FOR A SELFISH LITTLE REQUEST.

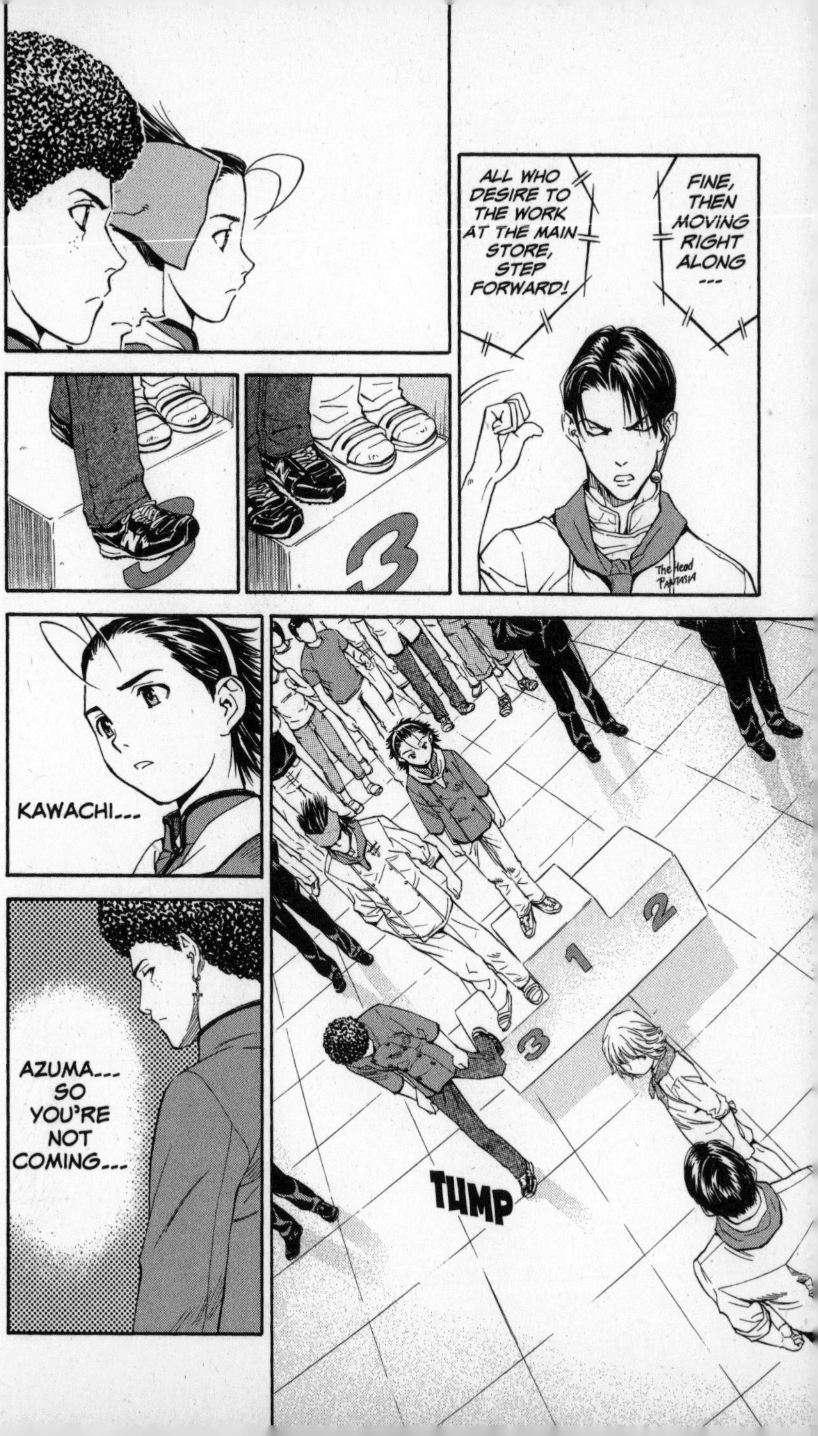
FINE, THEN MOVING RIGHT ALONG---
ALL WHO DESIRE TO THE WORK AT THE MAIN STORE, STEP FORWARD!
The Head PANTASIA
TUMP
KAWACHI---
AZUMA--- SO YOU'RE NOT COMING---

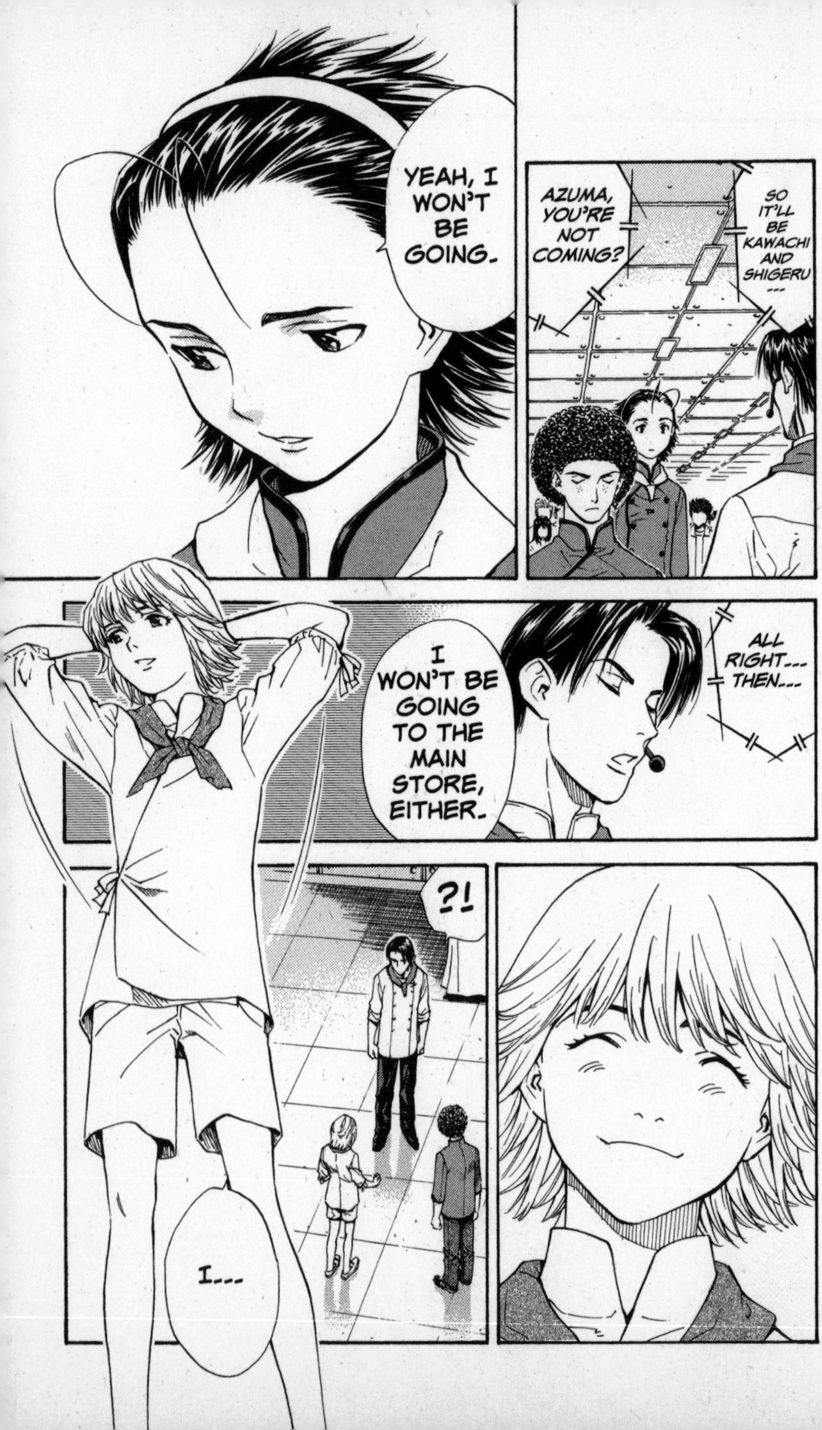
SO IT'LL BE KAWACHI AND SHIGERU...
AZUMA, YOU'RE NOT COMING?
YEAH, I WON'T BE GOING.
ALL RIGHT... THEN...
I WON'T BE GOING TO THE MAIN STORE, EITHER.
?!
I...

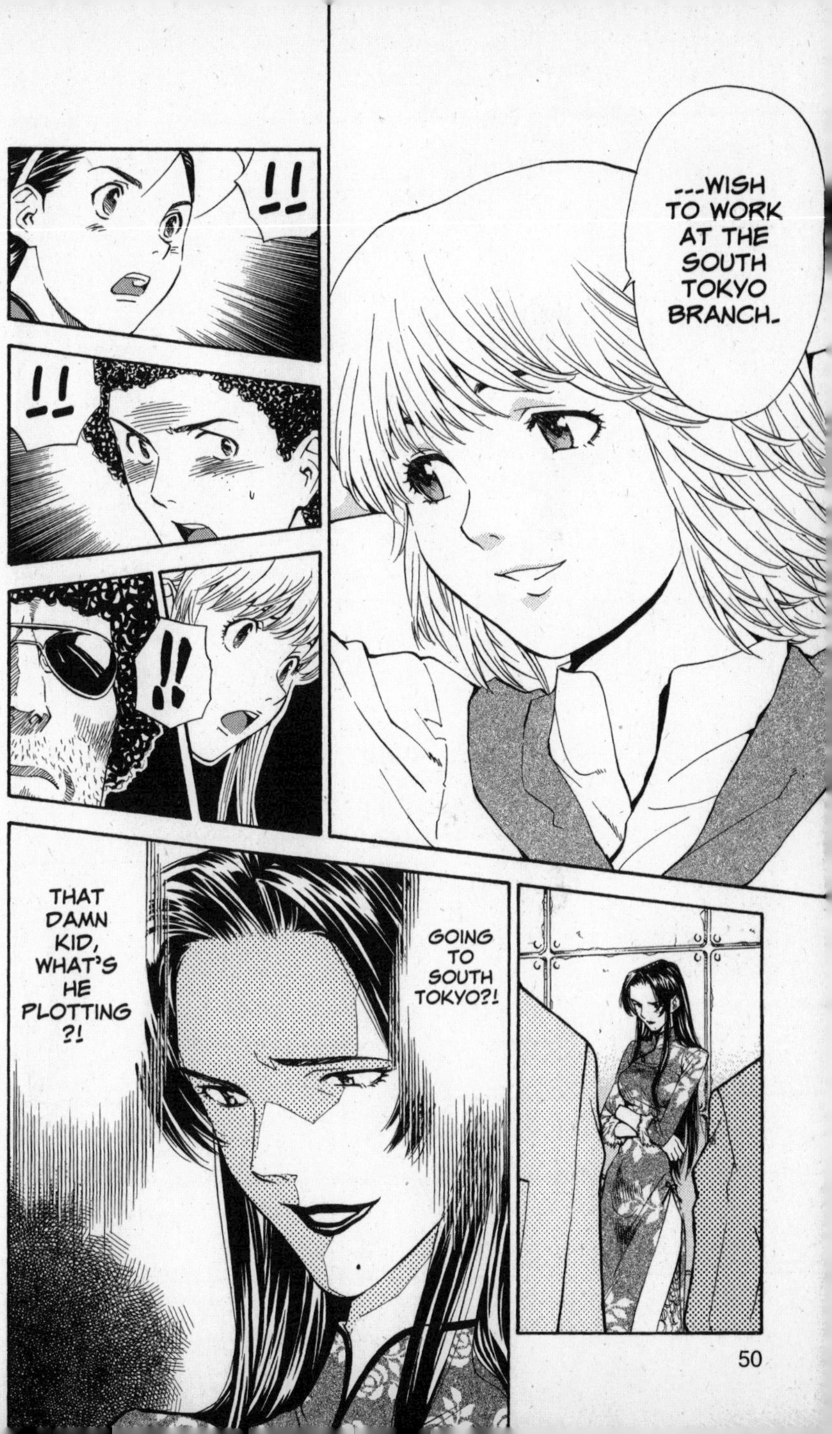
...WISH TO WORK AT THE SOUTH TOKYO BRANCH.
!!
!!
!!
GOING TO SOUTH TOKYO?!
THAT DAMN KID, WHAT'S HE PLOTTING ?!

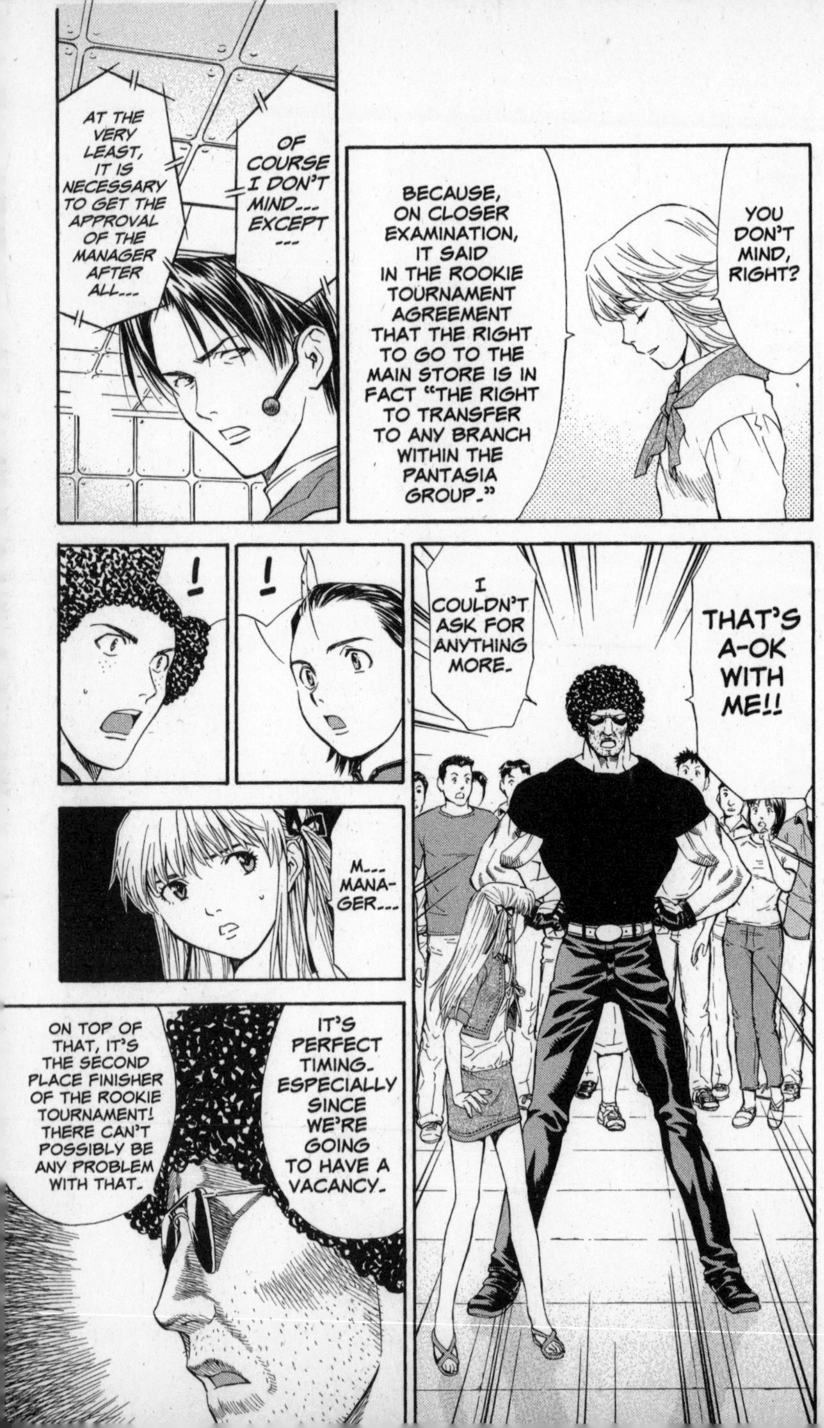
YOU DON'T MIND, RIGHT?
BECAUSE, ON CLOSER EXAMINATION, IT SAID IN THE ROOKIE TOURNAMENT AGREEMENT THAT THE RIGHT TO GO TO THE MAIN STORE IS IN FACT "THE RIGHT TO TRANSFER TO ANY BRANCH WITHIN THE PANTASIA GROUP."
OF COURSE I DON'T MIND... EXCEPT ...
AT THE VERY LEAST, IT IS NECESSARY TO GET THE APPROVAL OF THE MANAGER AFTER ALL...
THAT'S A-OK WITH ME!!
I COULDN'T ASK FOR ANYTHING MORE.
!
!
M... MANA-GER...
IT'S PERFECT TIMING. ESPECIALLY SINCE WE'RE GOING TO HAVE A VACANCY.
ON TOP OF THAT, IT'S THE SECOND PLACE FINISHER OF THE ROOKIE TOURNAMENT! THERE CAN'T POSSIBLY BE ANY PROBLEM WITH THAT.

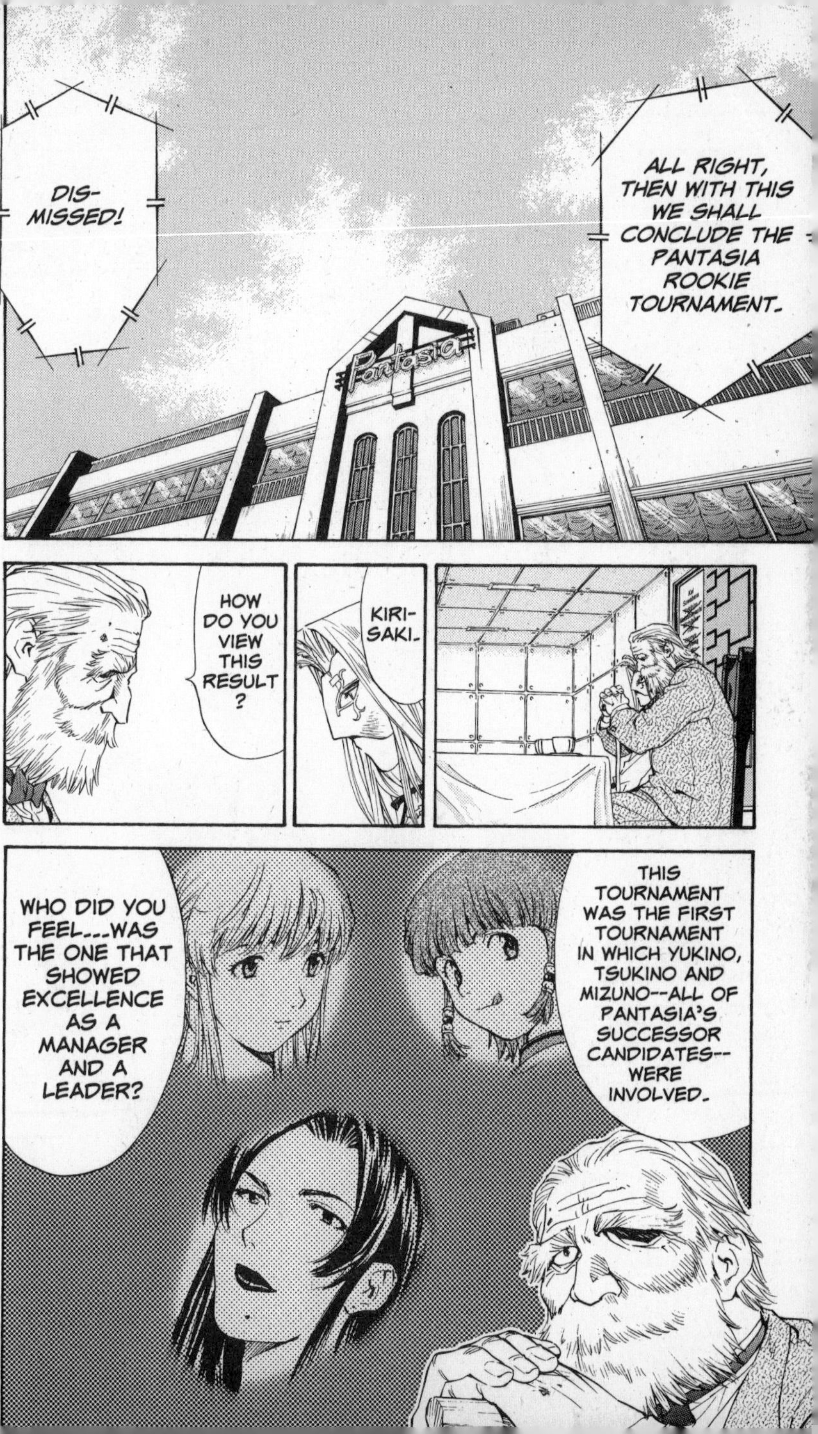
ALL RIGHT, THEN WITH THIS WE SHALL CONCLUDE THE PANTASIA ROOKIE TOURNAMENT.
DIS-MISSED!
Pantasia
KIRI-SAKI.
HOW DO YOU VIEW THIS RESULT?
THIS TOURNAMENT WAS THE FIRST TOURNAMENT IN WHICH YUKINO, TSUKINO AND MIZUNO--ALL OF PANTASIA'S SUCCESSOR CANDIDATES--WERE INVOLVED.
WHO DID YOU FEEL...WAS THE ONE THAT SHOWED EXCELLENCE AS A MANAGER AND A LEADER?

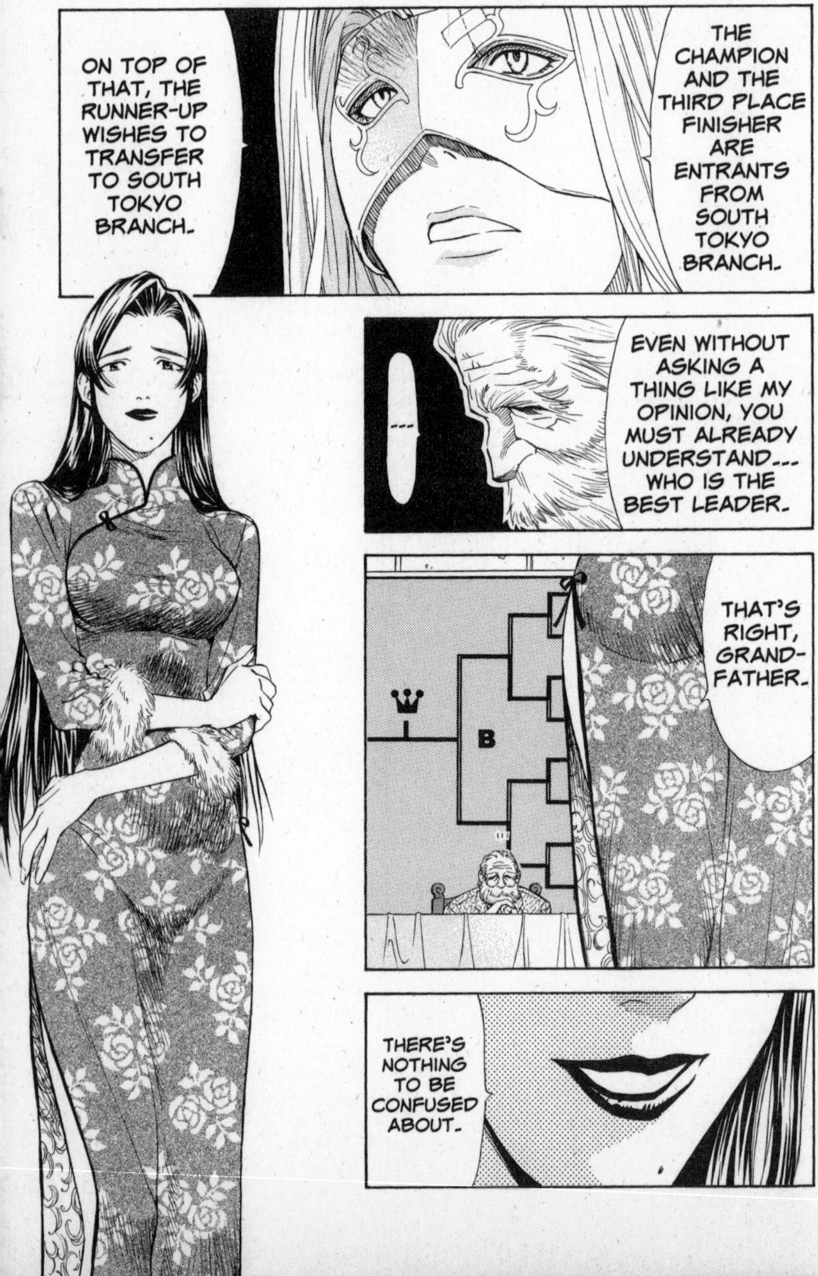
THE CHAMPION AND THE THIRD PLACE FINISHER ARE ENTRANTS FROM SOUTH TOKYO BRANCH.
ON TOP OF THAT, THE RUNNER-UP WISHES TO TRANSFER TO SOUTH TOKYO BRANCH.
EVEN WITHOUT ASKING A THING LIKE MY OPINION, YOU MUST ALREADY UNDERSTAND... WHO IS THE BEST LEADER.
...
B
THAT'S RIGHT, GRANDFATHER.
THERE'S NOTHING TO BE CONFUSED ABOUT.

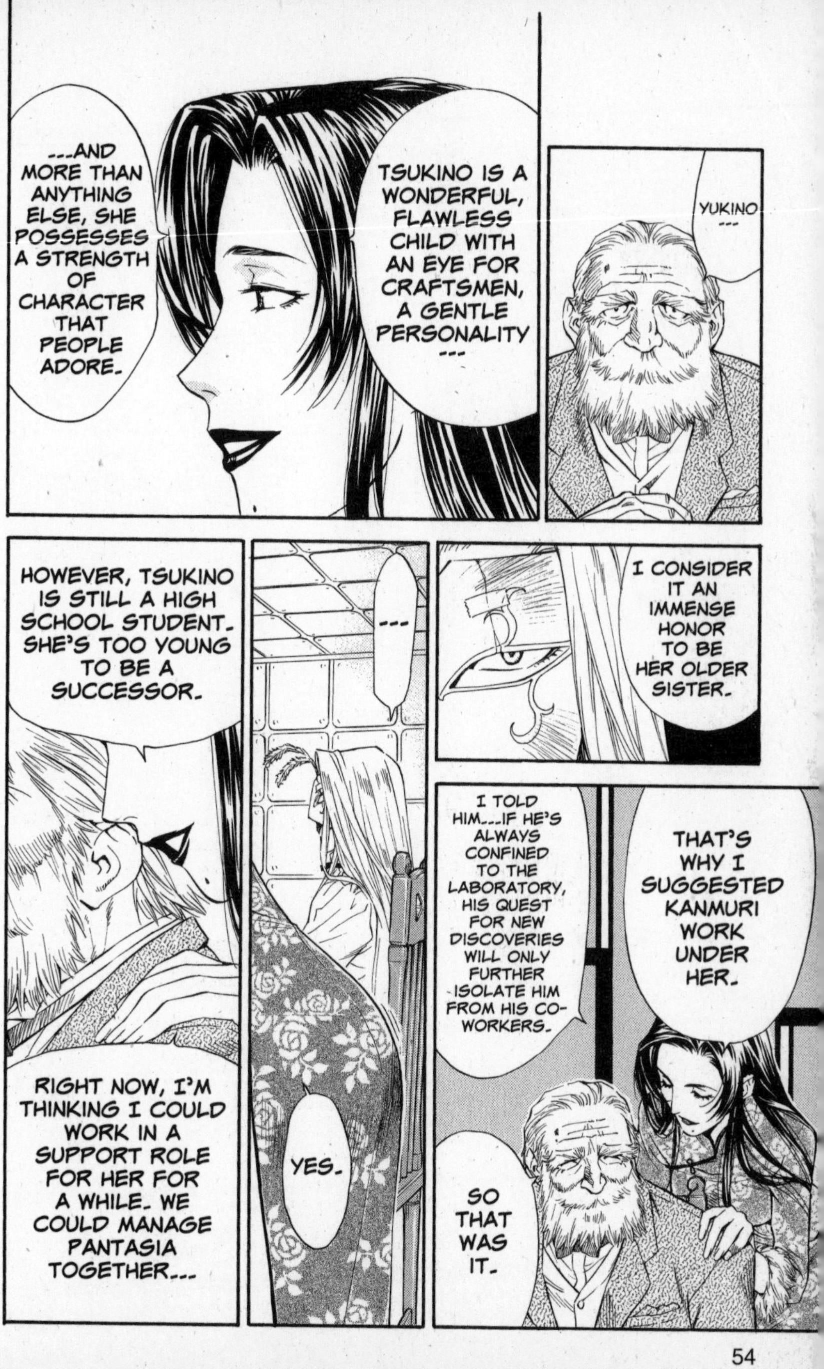

YUKINO ---
TSUKINO IS A WONDERFUL, FLAWLESS CHILD WITH AN EYE FOR CRAFTSMEN, A GENTLE PERSONALITY ---
---AND MORE THAN ANYTHING ELSE, SHE POSSESSES A STRENGTH OF CHARACTER THAT PEOPLE ADORE.
I CONSIDER IT AN IMMENSE HONOR TO BE HER OLDER SISTER.
THAT'S WHY I SUGGESTED KANMURI WORK UNDER HER.
I TOLD HIM...IF HE'S ALWAYS CONFINED TO THE LABORATORY, HIS QUEST FOR NEW DISCOVERIES WILL ONLY FURTHER ISOLATE HIM FROM HIS CO-WORKERS.
SO THAT WAS IT.

YES.
HOWEVER, TSUKINO IS STILL A HIGH SCHOOL STUDENT. SHE'S TOO YOUNG TO BE A SUCCESSOR.
RIGHT NOW, I'M THINKING I COULD WORK IN A SUPPORT ROLE FOR HER FOR A WHILE. WE COULD MANAGE PANTASIA TOGETHER...

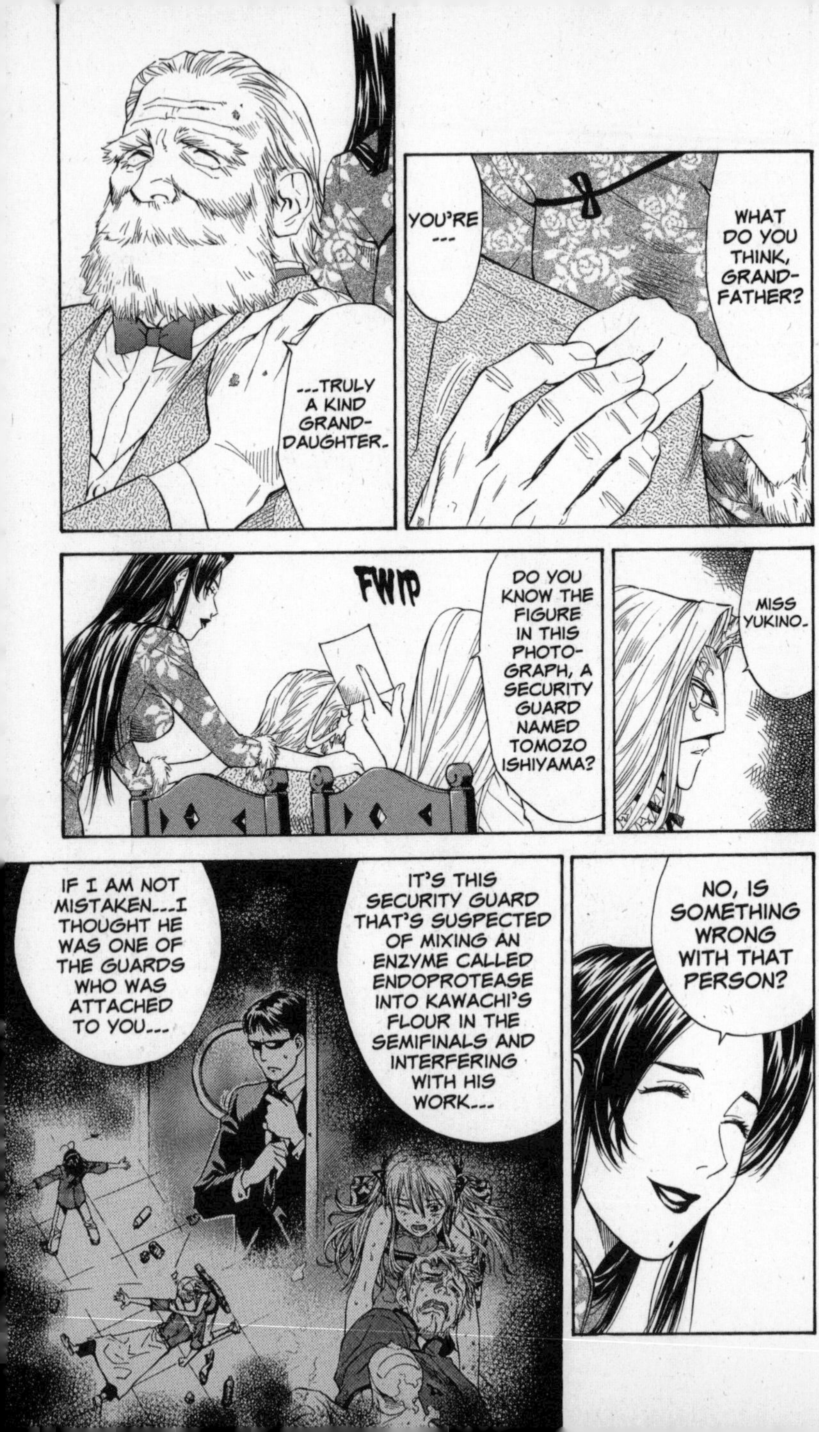
WHAT DO YOU THINK, GRANDFATHER?
YOU'RE ---
---TRULY A KIND GRANDDAUGHTER.
MISS YUKINO.
DO YOU KNOW THE FIGURE IN THIS PHOTOGRAPH, A SECURITY GUARD NAMED TOMOZO ISHIYAMA?
FWIP
NO, IS SOMETHING WRONG WITH THAT PERSON?
IT'S THIS SECURITY GUARD THAT'S SUSPECTED OF MIXING AN ENZYME CALLED ENDOPROTEASE INTO KAWACHI'S FLOUR IN THE SEMIFINALS AND INTERFERING WITH HIS WORK---
IF I AM NOT MISTAKEN---I THOUGHT HE WAS ONE OF THE GUARDS WHO WAS ATTACHED TO YOU---

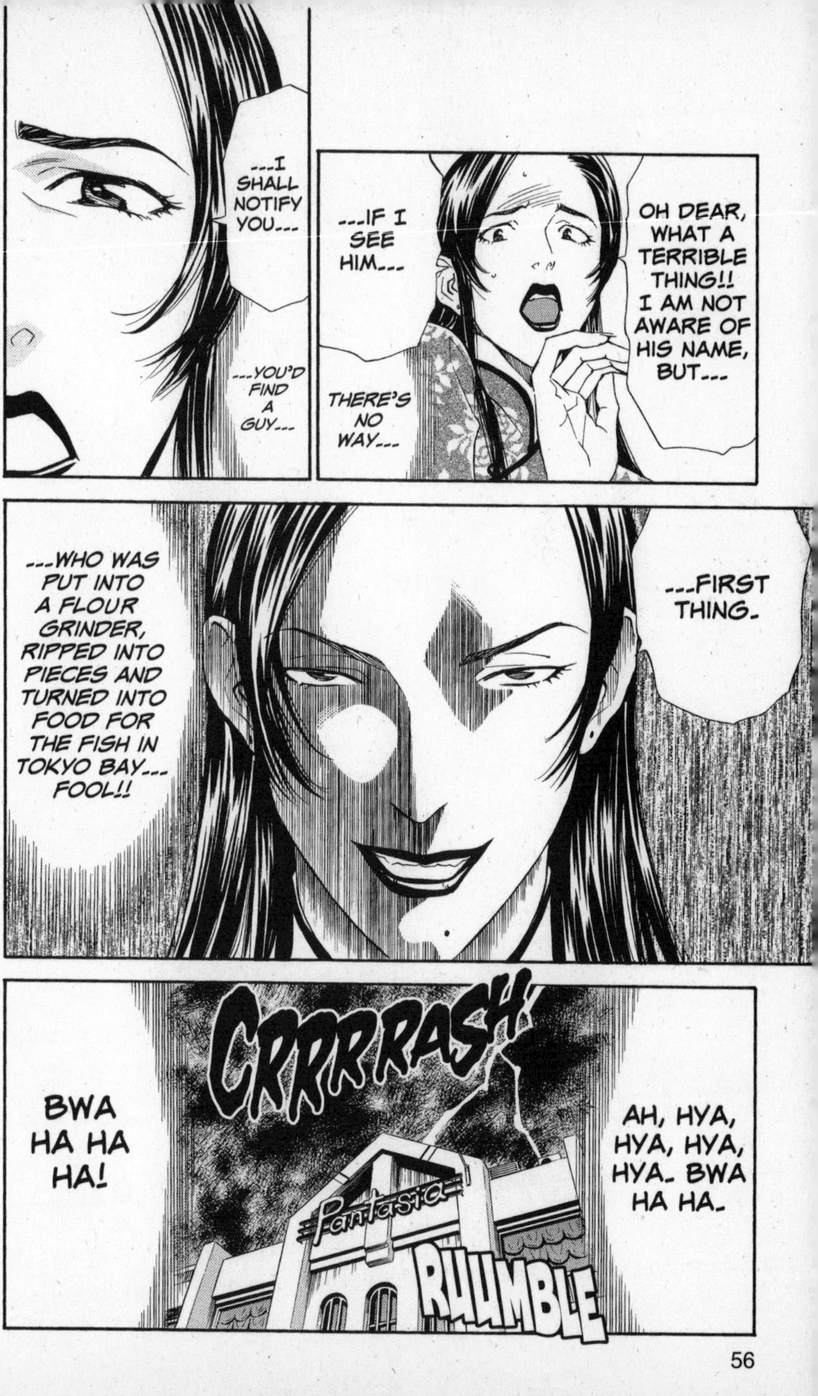
OH DEAR, WHAT A TERRIBLE THING!! I AM NOT AWARE OF HIS NAME, BUT...
...IF I SEE HIM...
THERE'S NO WAY...
...I SHALL NOTIFY YOU...
...YOU'D FIND A GUY...
...FIRST THING.
...WHO WAS PUT INTO A FLOUR GRINDER, RIPPED INTO PIECES AND TURNED INTO FOOD FOR THE FISH IN TOKYO BAY... FOOL!!
CRRRRASH
AH, HYA, HYA, HYA, HYA. BWA HA HA.
BWA HA HA HA!
Pantasia
RUUMBLE

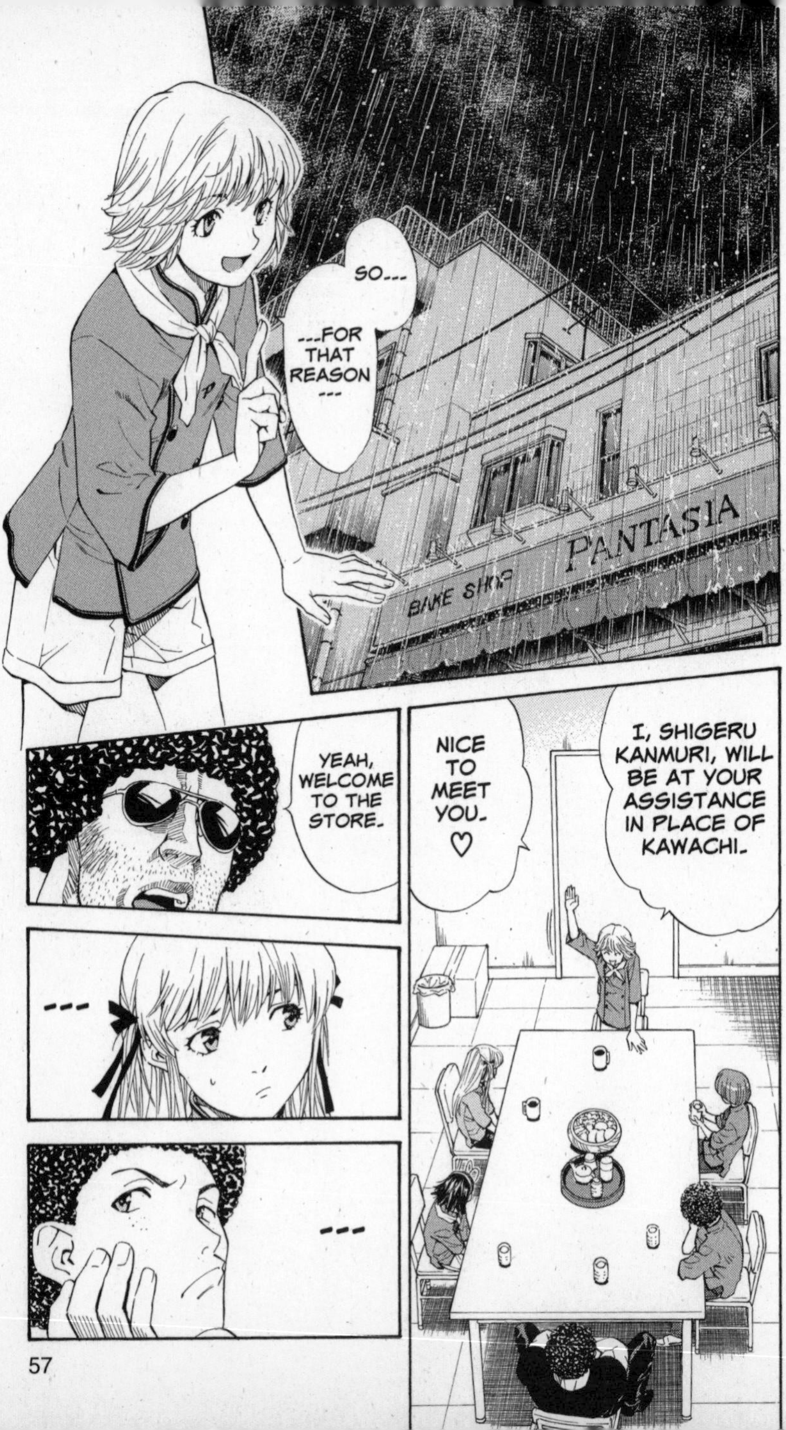
SO...
...FOR THAT REASON ...
BAKE SHOP
PANTASIA
I, SHIGERU KANMURI, WILL BE AT YOUR ASSISTANCE IN PLACE OF KAWACHI.
NICE TO MEET YOU. ♡
YEAH, WELCOME TO THE STORE.
...
...

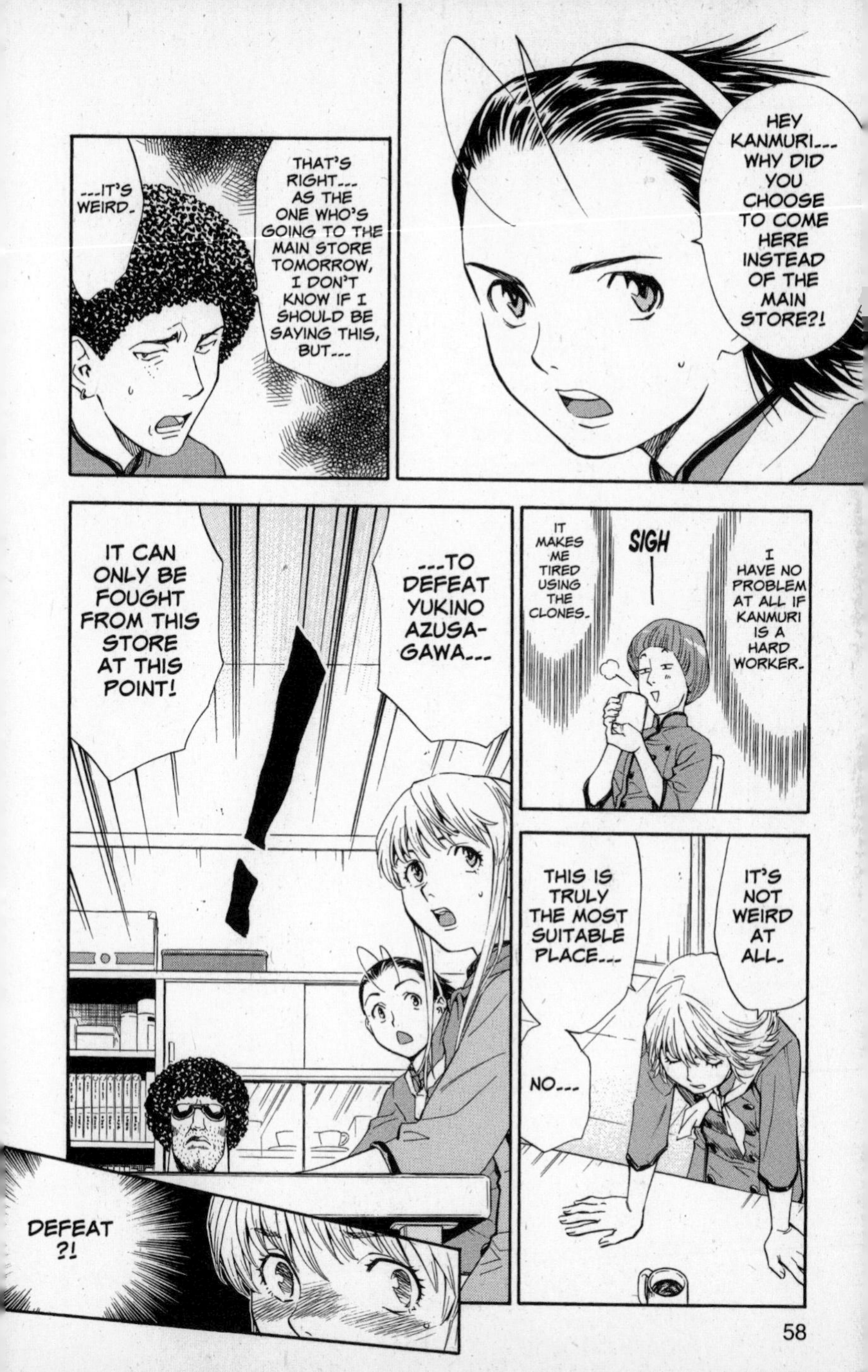
HEY KANMURI... WHY DID YOU CHOOSE TO COME HERE INSTEAD OF THE MAIN STORE?!
THAT'S RIGHT... AS THE ONE WHO'S GOING TO THE MAIN STORE TOMORROW, I DON'T KNOW IF I SHOULD BE SAYING THIS, BUT...
...IT'S WEIRD.
I HAVE NO PROBLEM AT ALL IF KANMURI IS A HARD WORKER.
SIGH
IT MAKES ME TIRED USING THE CLONES.
IT'S NOT WEIRD AT ALL.
THIS IS TRULY THE MOST SUITABLE PLACE...
NO...
...TO DEFEAT YUKINO AZUSA-GAWA...
IT CAN ONLY BE FOUGHT FROM THIS STORE AT THIS POINT!
DEFEAT ?!

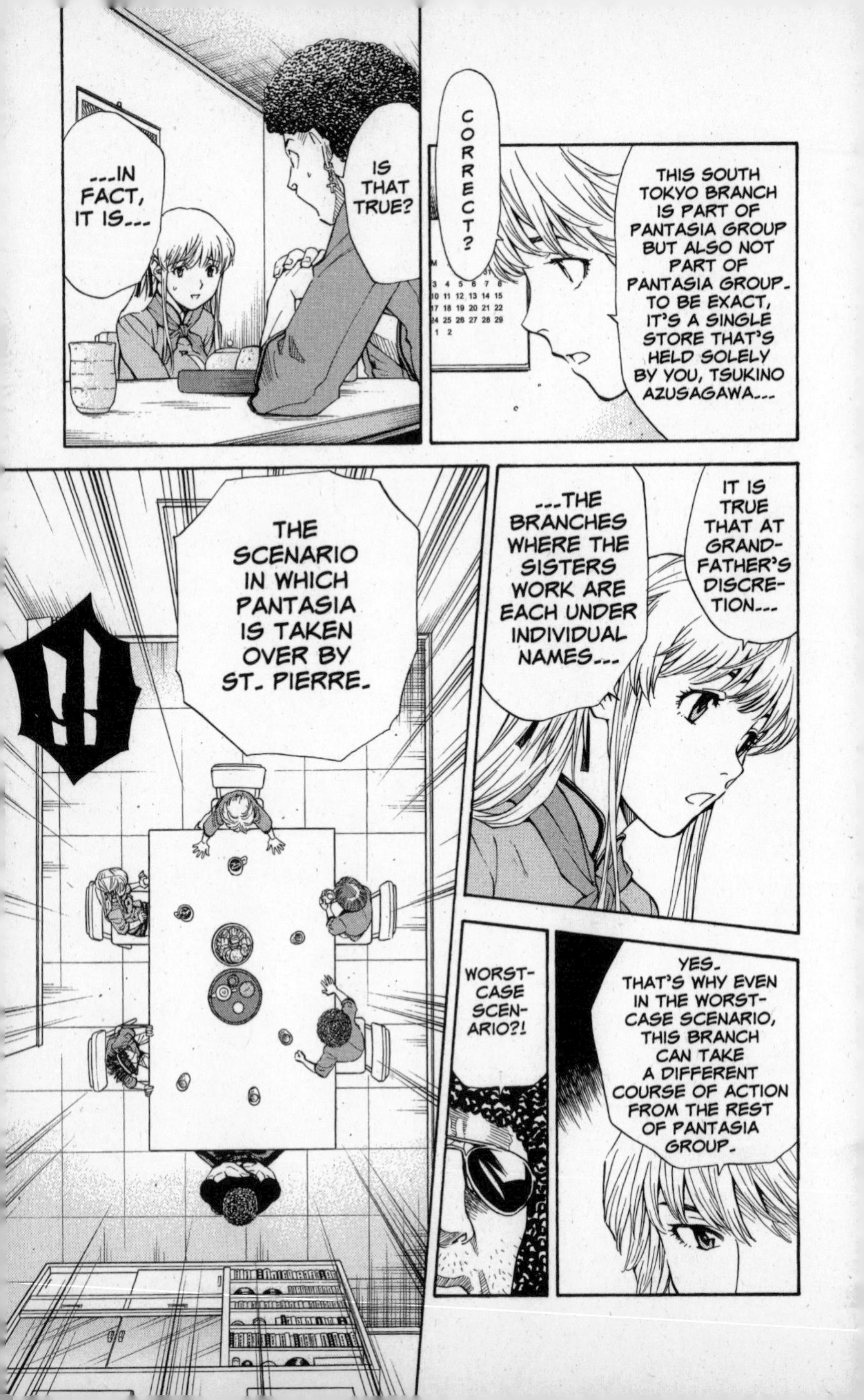

THIS SOUTH TOKYO BRANCH IS PART OF PANTASIA GROUP BUT ALSO NOT PART OF PANTASIA GROUP. TO BE EXACT, IT'S A SINGLE STORE THAT'S HELD SOLELY BY YOU, TSUKINO AZUSAGAWA...
CORRECT?
IS THAT TRUE?
...IN FACT, IT IS...
IT IS TRUE THAT AT GRAND-FATHER'S DISCRE-TION...
...THE BRANCHES WHERE THE SISTERS WORK ARE EACH UNDER INDIVIDUAL NAMES...
YES. THAT'S WHY EVEN IN THE WORST-CASE SCENARIO, THIS BRANCH CAN TAKE A DIFFERENT COURSE OF ACTION FROM THE REST OF PANTASIA GROUP.
WORST-CASE SCEN-ARIO?!
THE SCENARIO IN WHICH PANTASIA IS TAKEN OVER BY ST. PIERRE.
!!

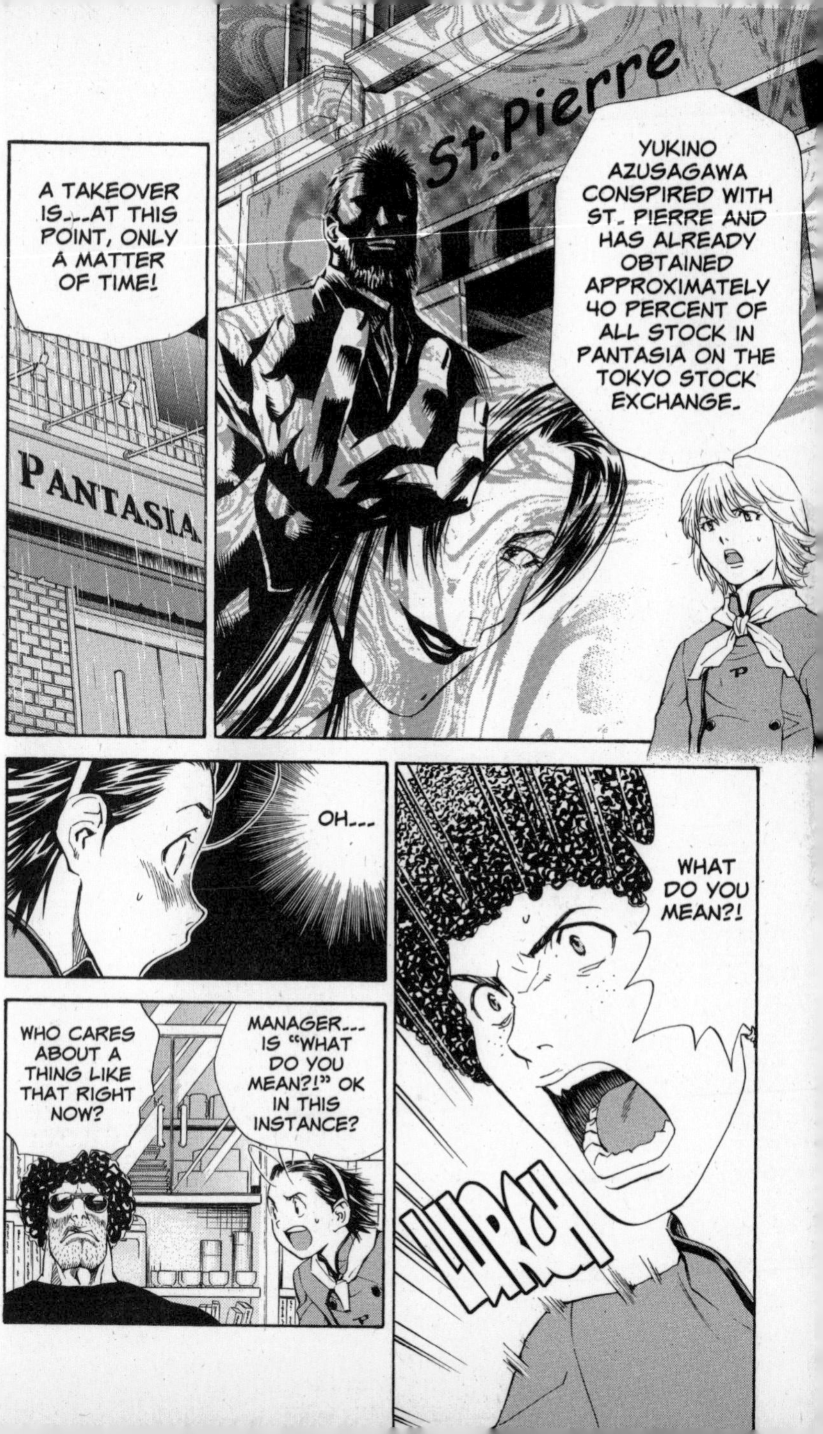
St.Pierre
YUKINO AZUSAGAWA CONSPIRED WITH ST. PIERRE AND HAS ALREADY OBTAINED APPROXIMATELY 40 PERCENT OF ALL STOCK IN PANTASIA ON THE TOKYO STOCK EXCHANGE.
A TAKEOVER IS...AT THIS POINT, ONLY A MATTER OF TIME!
PANTASIA
WHAT DO YOU MEAN?!
OH...
MANAGER... IS "WHAT DO YOU MEAN?!" OK IN THIS INSTANCE?
WHO CARES ABOUT A THING LIKE THAT RIGHT NOW?

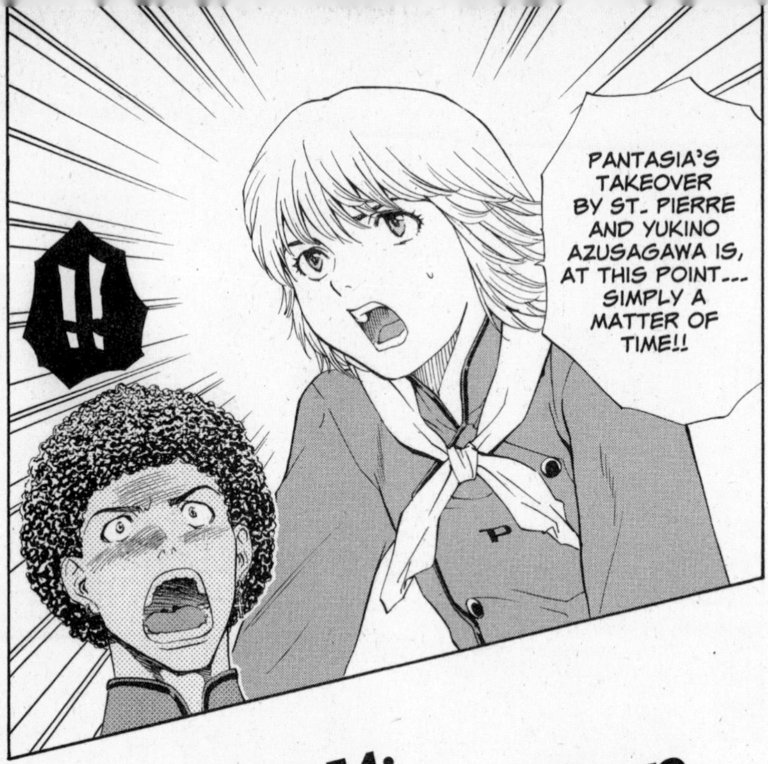
PANTASIA'S TAKEOVER BY ST. PIERRE AND YUKINO AZUSAGAWA IS, AT THIS POINT... SIMPLY A MATTER OF TIME!!
!!

Story 54: 10 Billion Man

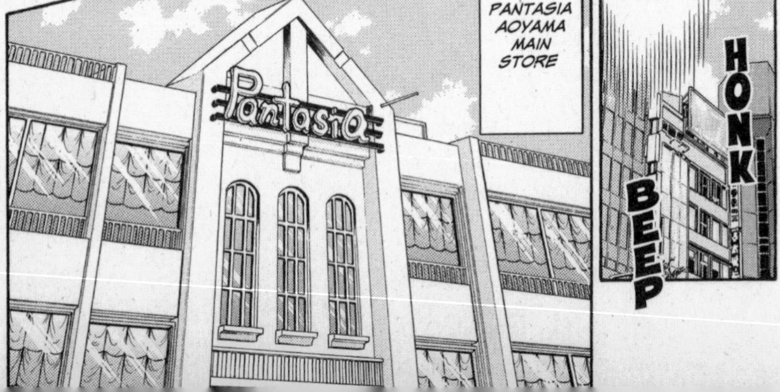
TH... THAT'S THE WORST ...
HONK
BEEP
PANTASIA AOYAMA MAIN STORE
Pantasia

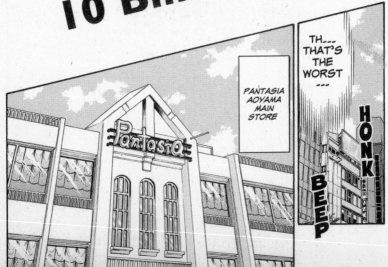

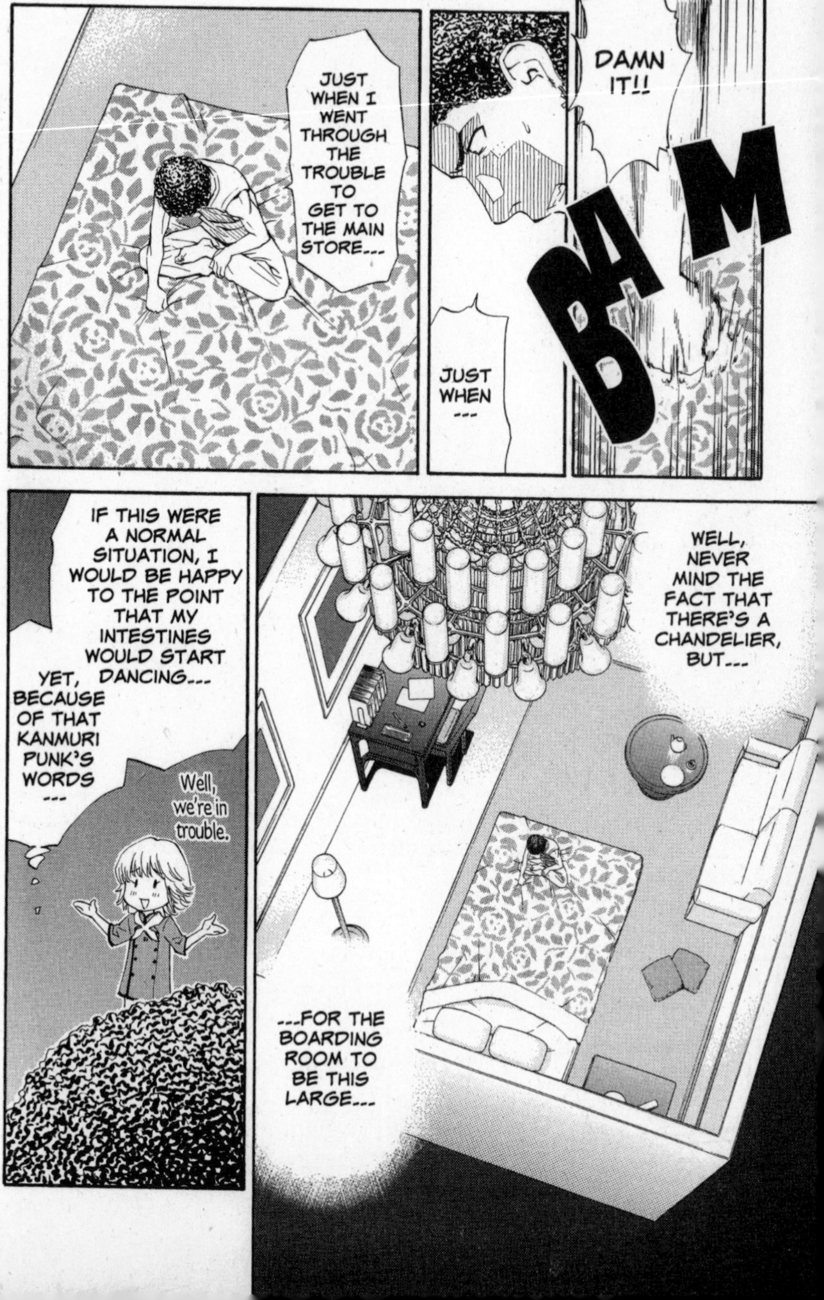
DAMN IT!!
BAM
JUST WHEN ---
JUST WHEN I WENT THROUGH THE TROUBLE TO GET TO THE MAIN STORE---
WELL, NEVER MIND THE FACT THAT THERE'S A CHANDELIER, BUT---
---FOR THE BOARDING ROOM TO BE THIS LARGE---
IF THIS WERE A NORMAL SITUATION, I WOULD BE HAPPY TO THE POINT THAT MY INTESTINES WOULD START DANCING---
YET, BECAUSE OF THAT KANMURI PUNK'S WORDS ---
Well, we're in trouble.

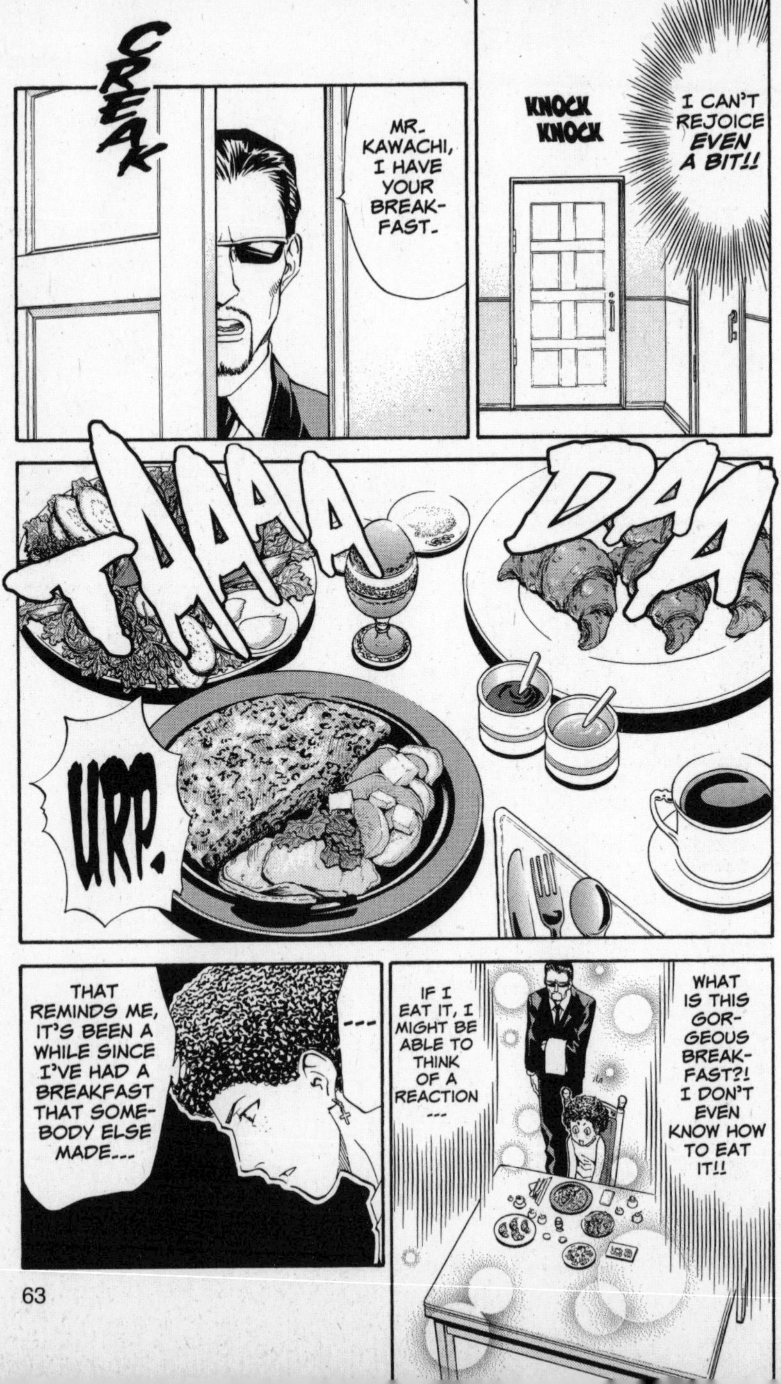
I CAN'T REJOICE EVEN A BIT!!
KNOCK KNOCK
MR. KAWACHI, I HAVE YOUR BREAK-FAST.
CREAK
TAAAA DAA
URP.
WHAT IS THIS GOR-GEOUS BREAK-FAST?! I DON'T EVEN KNOW HOW TO EAT IT!!
IF I EAT IT, I MIGHT BE ABLE TO THINK OF A REACTION ...
...
THAT REMINDS ME, IT'S BEEN A WHILE SINCE I'VE HAD A BREAKFAST THAT SOME-BODY ELSE MADE...

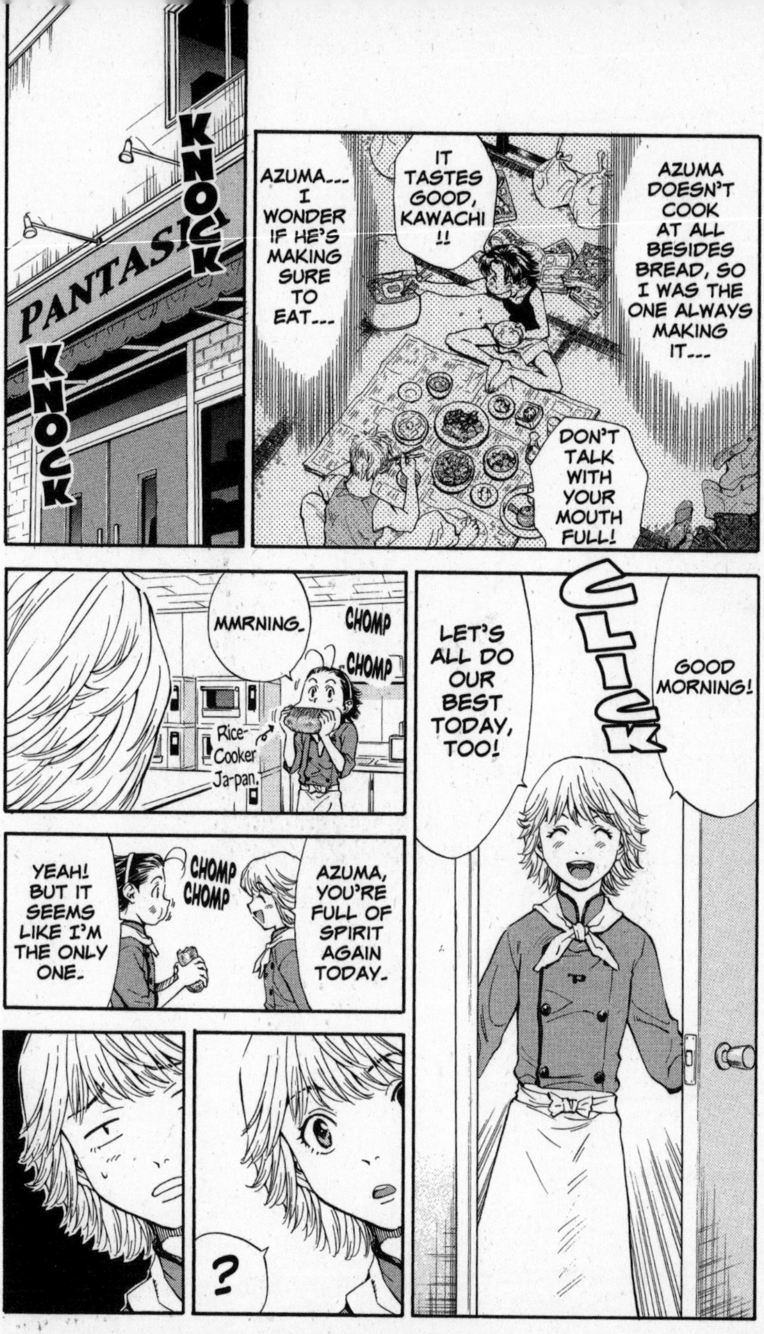
AZUMA DOESN'T COOK AT ALL BESIDES BREAD, SO I WAS THE ONE ALWAYS MAKING IT...
IT TASTES GOOD, KAWACHI!!
AZUMA... I WONDER IF HE'S MAKING SURE TO EAT...
DON'T TALK WITH YOUR MOUTH FULL!
KNOCK
KNOCK
PANTASI
CLICK
GOOD MORNING!
LET'S ALL DO OUR BEST TODAY, TOO!
MMRNING.
CHOMP
CHOMP
Rice-Cooker Ja-pan.
AZUMA, YOU'RE FULL OF SPIRIT AGAIN TODAY.
CHOMP CHOMP
YEAH! BUT IT SEEMS LIKE I'M THE ONLY ONE.
?

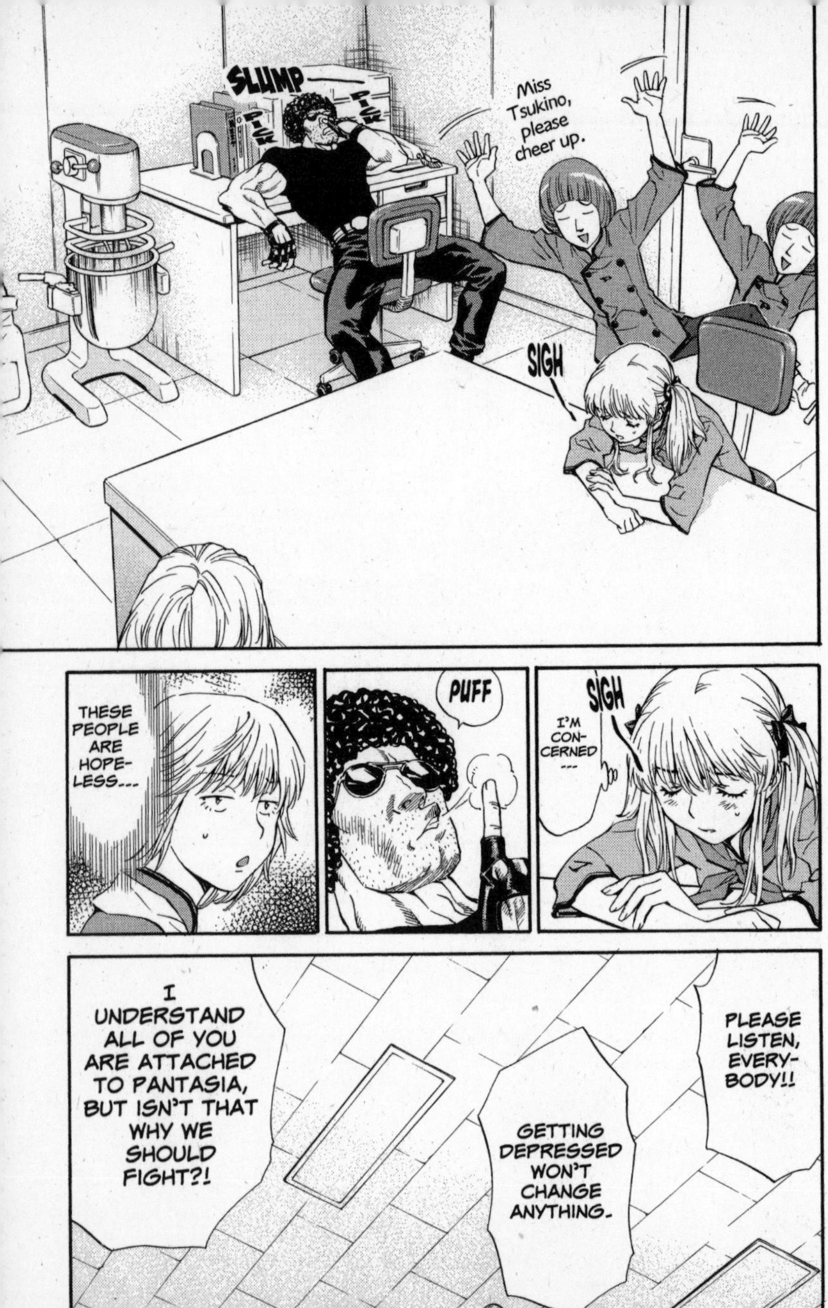
Miss Tsukino, please cheer up.
SLUMP
PICK
PICK
SIGH
SIGH
I'M CONCERNED...
PUFF
THESE PEOPLE ARE HOPELESS...
PLEASE LISTEN, EVERYBODY!!
GETTING DEPRESSED WON'T CHANGE ANYTHING.
I UNDERSTAND ALL OF YOU ARE ATTACHED TO PANTASIA, BUT ISN'T THAT WHY WE SHOULD FIGHT?!

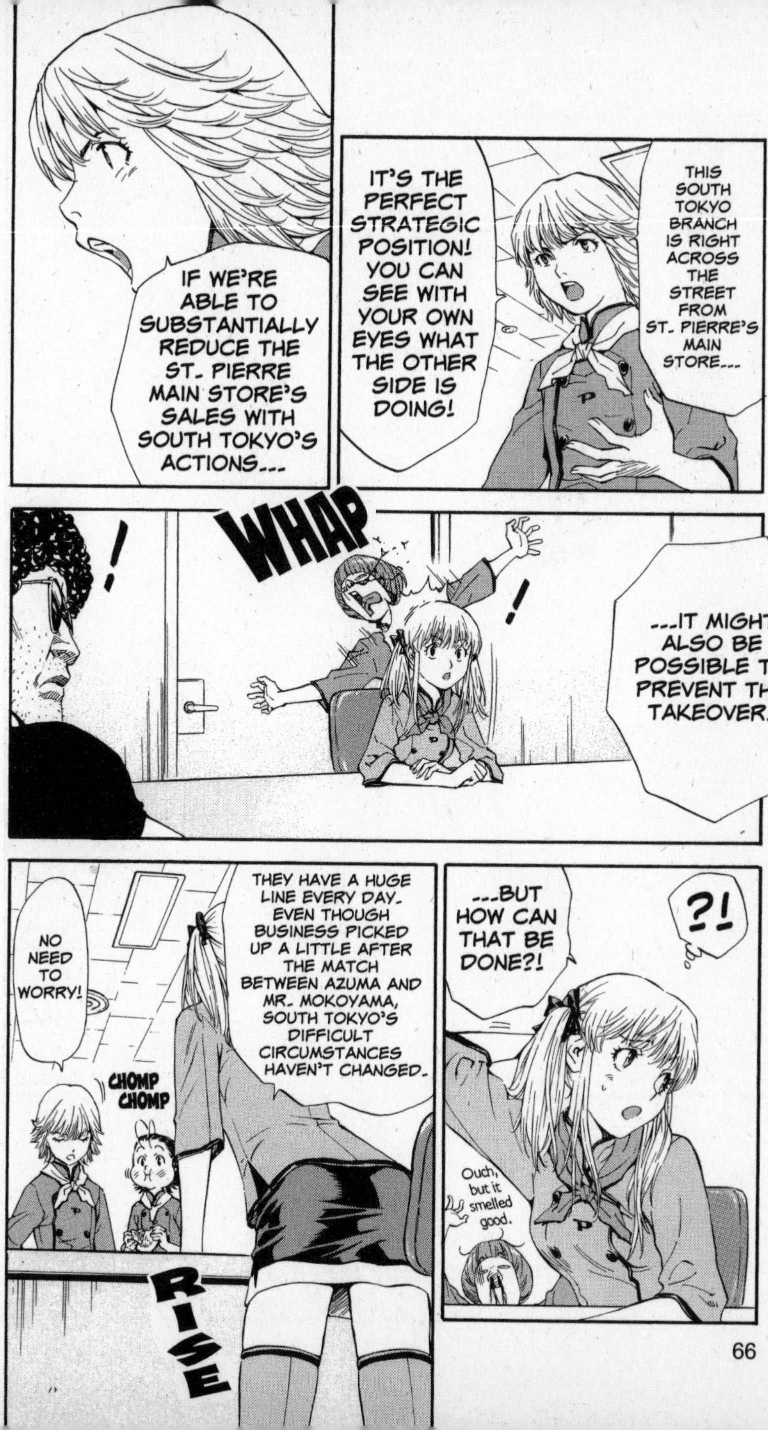
THIS SOUTH TOKYO BRANCH IS RIGHT ACROSS THE STREET FROM ST. PIERRE'S MAIN STORE...
IT'S THE PERFECT STRATEGIC POSITION! YOU CAN SEE WITH YOUR OWN EYES WHAT THE OTHER SIDE IS DOING!
IF WE'RE ABLE TO SUBSTANTIALLY REDUCE THE ST. PIERRE MAIN STORE'S SALES WITH SOUTH TOKYO'S ACTIONS...
...IT MIGHT ALSO BE POSSIBLE TO PREVENT THE TAKEOVER!
!
WHAP
!
?!
...BUT HOW CAN THAT BE DONE?!
Ouch, but it smelled good.
THEY HAVE A HUGE LINE EVERY DAY. EVEN THOUGH BUSINESS PICKED UP A LITTLE AFTER THE MATCH BETWEEN AZUMA AND MR. MOKOYAMA, SOUTH TOKYO'S DIFFICULT CIRCUMSTANCES HAVEN'T CHANGED.
NO NEED TO WORRY!
CHOMP CHOMP
RISE

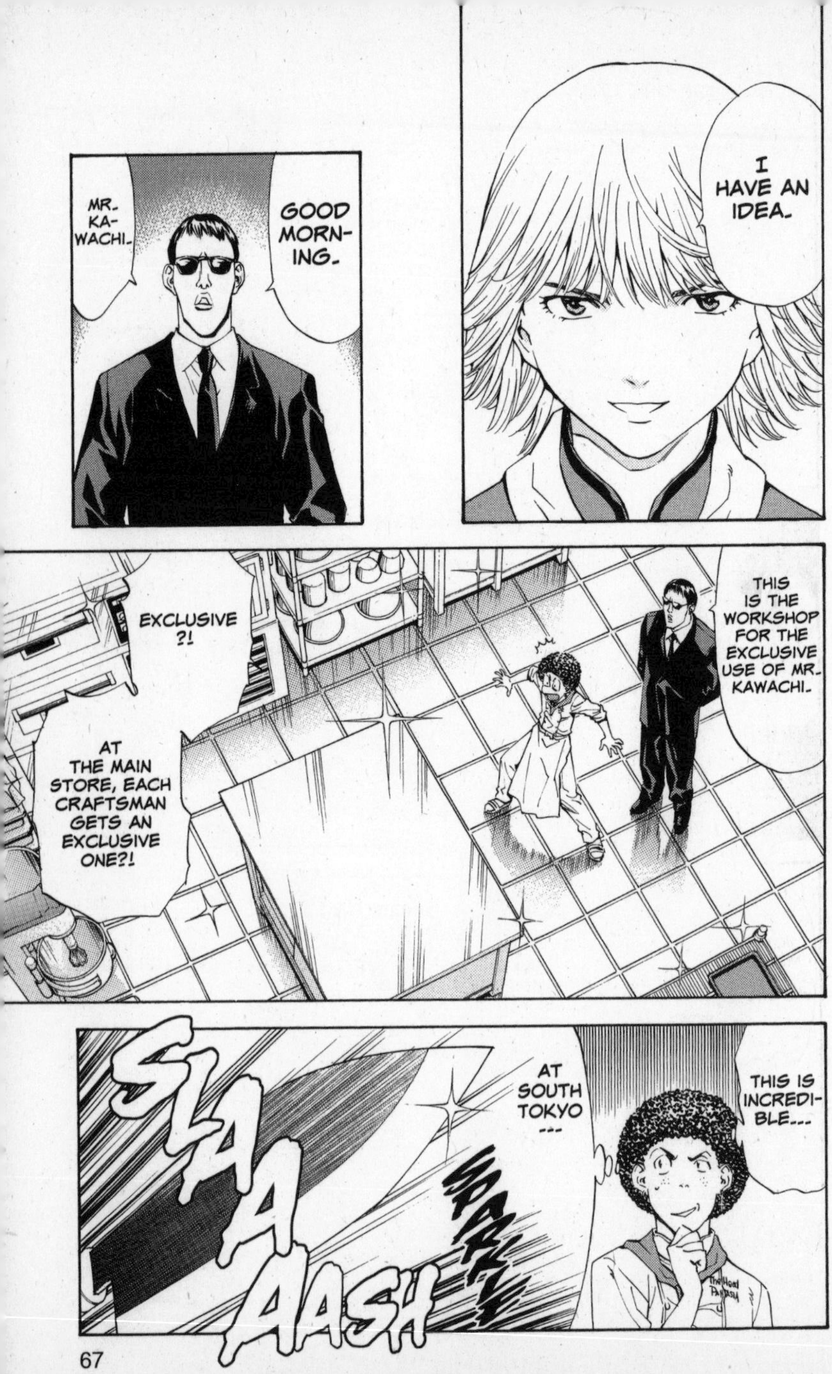
I HAVE AN IDEA.
GOOD MORNING.
MR. KAWACHI.
THIS IS THE WORKSHOP FOR THE EXCLUSIVE USE OF MR. KAWACHI.
EXCLUSIVE?!
AT THE MAIN STORE, EACH CRAFTSMAN GETS AN EXCLUSIVE ONE?!
THIS IS INCREDIBLE...
AT SOUTH TOKYO---
SLAAASH

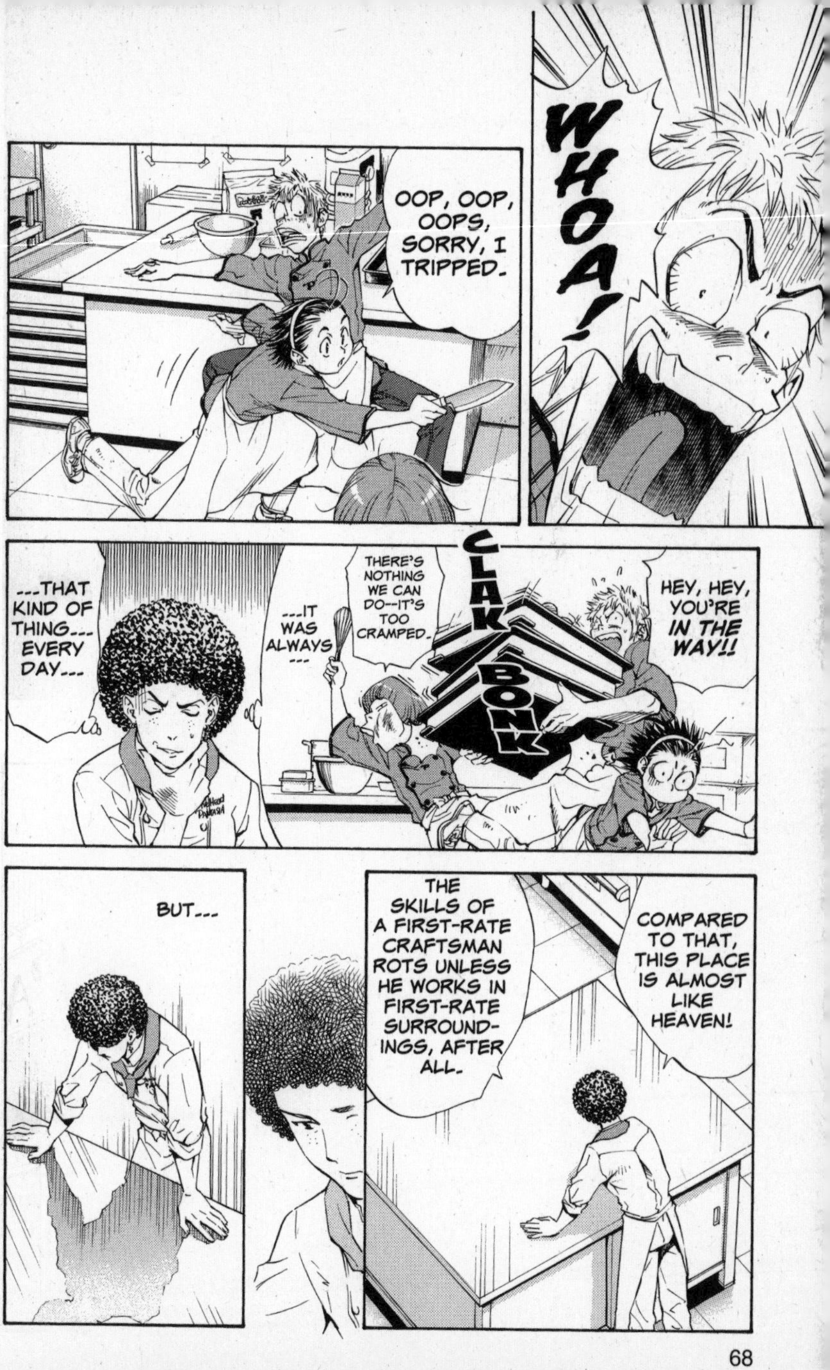
WHOA!
OOP, OOP, OOPS, SORRY, I TRIPPED.
HEY, HEY, YOU'RE *IN THE WAY!!*
CLAK
BONK
THERE'S NOTHING WE CAN DO--IT'S TOO CRAMPED.
...IT WAS ALWAYS...
...THAT KIND OF THING... EVERY DAY...
COMPARED TO THAT, THIS PLACE IS ALMOST LIKE HEAVEN!
THE SKILLS OF A FIRST-RATE CRAFTSMAN ROTS UNLESS HE WORKS IN FIRST-RATE SURROUND-INGS, AFTER ALL.
BUT...

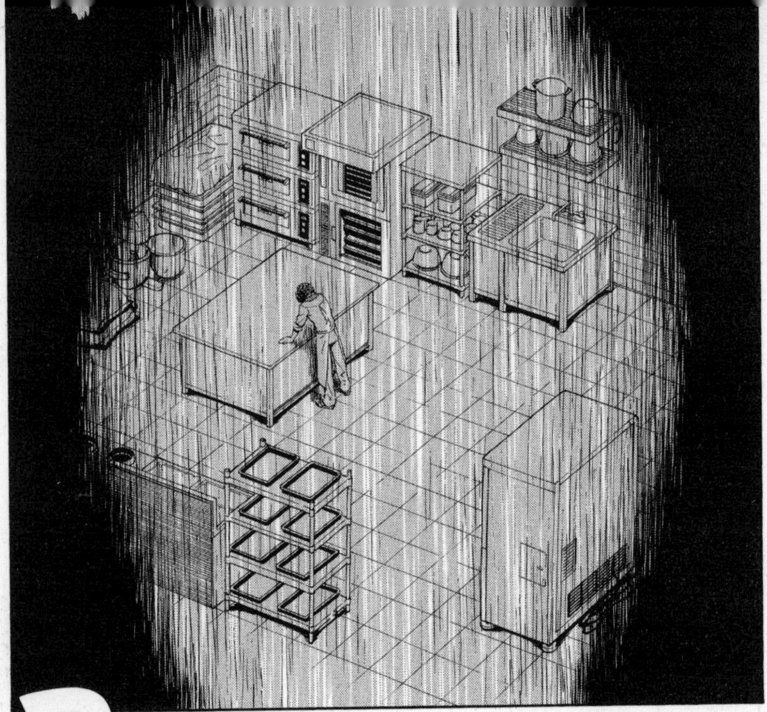

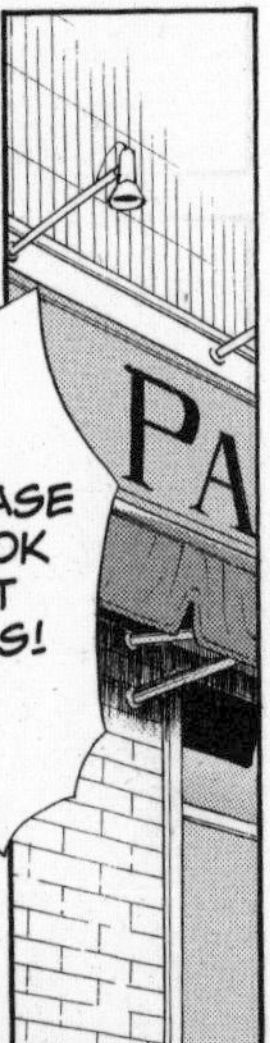
PA

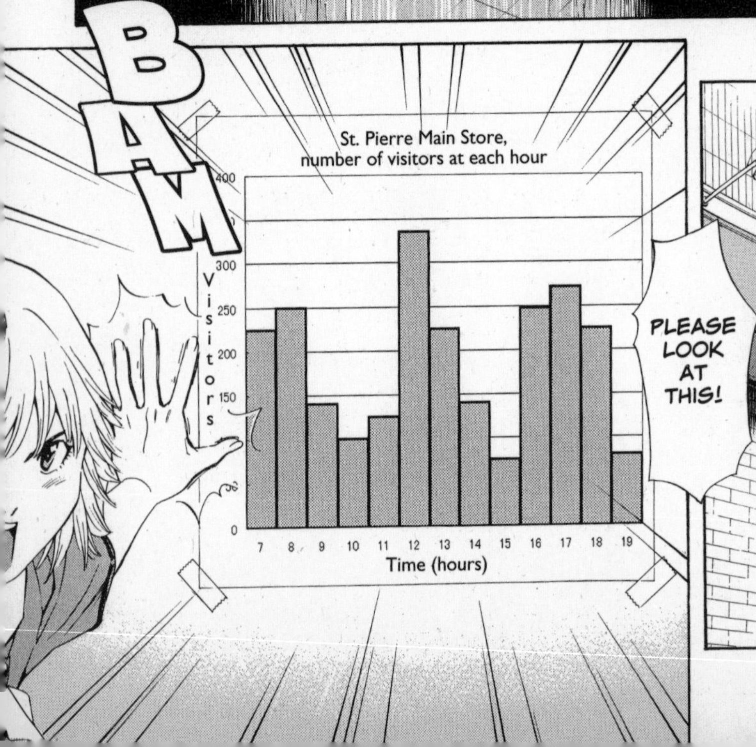
PLEASE LOOK AT THIS!
BAM
St. Pierre Main Store,
number of visitors at each hour
Visitors
400
300
250
200
150
0
7 8 9 10 11 12 13 14 15 16 17 18 19
Time (hours)

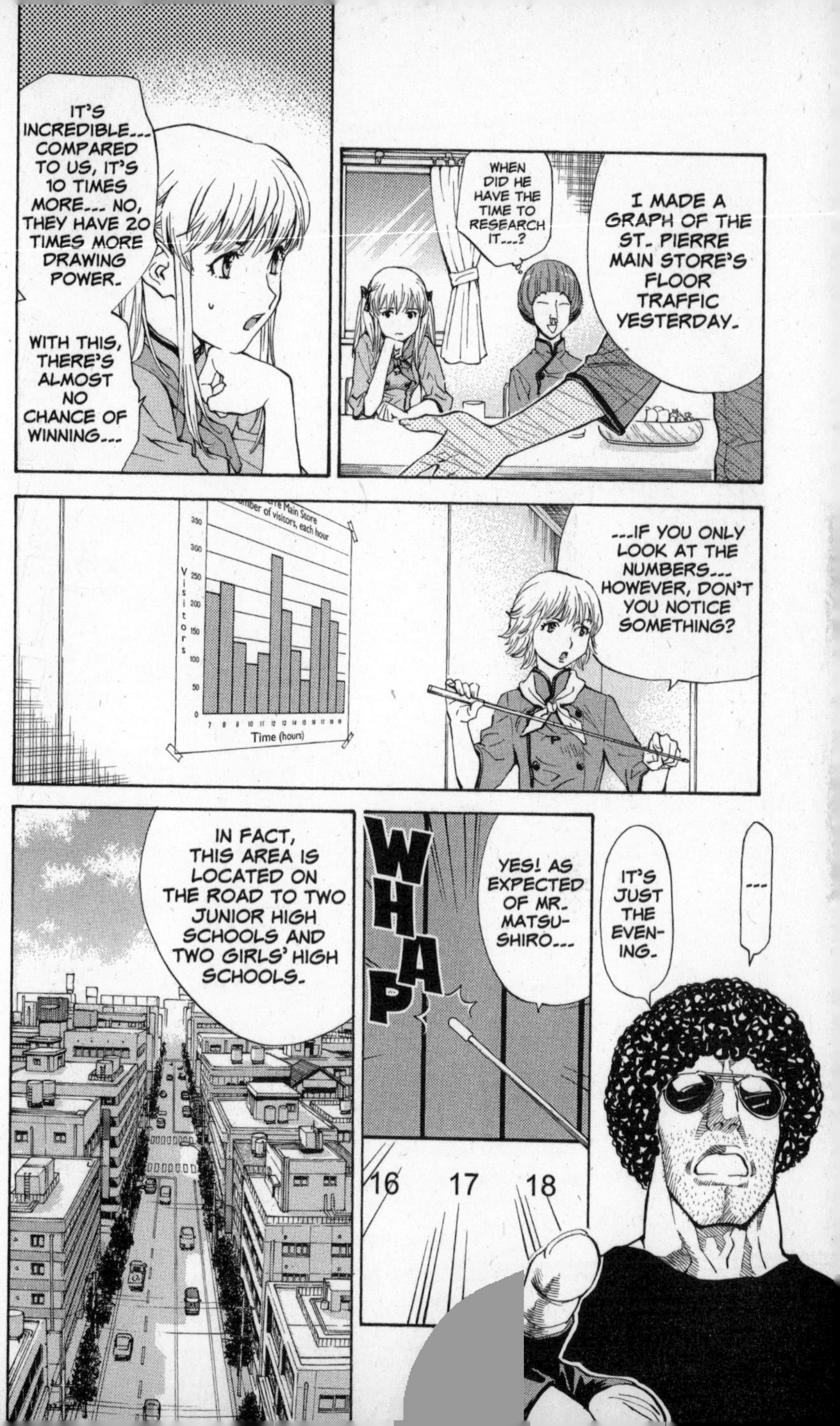
I MADE A GRAPH OF THE ST. PIERRE MAIN STORE'S FLOOR TRAFFIC YESTERDAY.
WHEN DID HE HAVE THE TIME TO RESEARCH IT...?
IT'S INCREDIBLE... COMPARED TO US, IT'S 10 TIMES MORE... NO, THEY HAVE 20 TIMES MORE DRAWING POWER.
WITH THIS, THERE'S ALMOST NO CHANCE OF WINNING...
...IF YOU ONLY LOOK AT THE NUMBERS... HOWEVER, DON'T YOU NOTICE SOMETHING?
Number of visitors, each hour
Visitors
Time (hours)
...
IT'S JUST THE EVEN-ING.
YES! AS EXPECTED OF MR. MATSU-SHIRO...
WHAP
16 17 18
IN FACT, THIS AREA IS LOCATED ON THE ROAD TO TWO JUNIOR HIGH SCHOOLS AND TWO GIRLS' HIGH SCHOOLS.

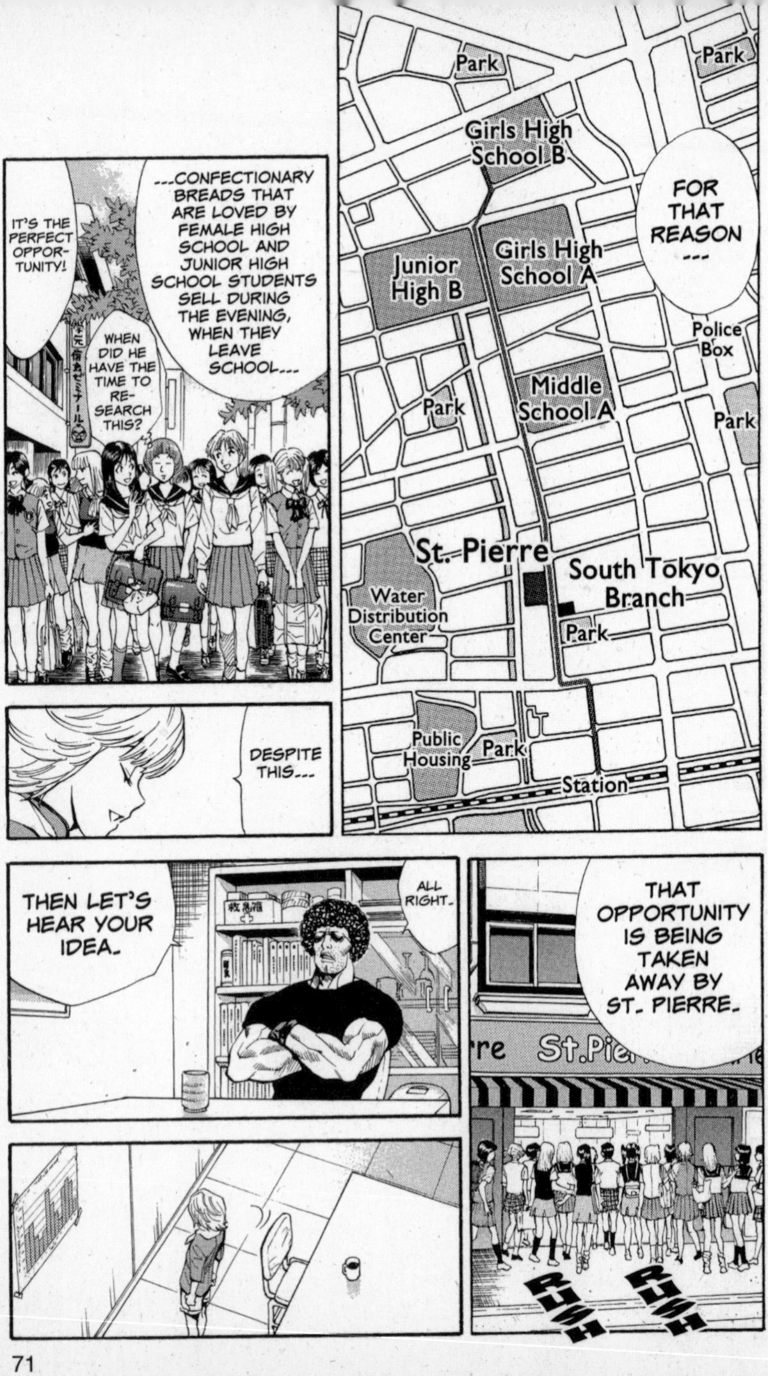
FOR THAT REASON ---
Park
Park
Girls High School B
Girls High School A
Junior High B
Police Box
Middle School A
Park
Park
St. Pierre
South Tokyo Branch
Water Distribution Center
Park
Public Housing
Park
Station
---CONFECTIONARY BREADS THAT ARE LOVED BY FEMALE HIGH SCHOOL AND JUNIOR HIGH SCHOOL STUDENTS SELL DURING THE EVENING, WHEN THEY LEAVE SCHOOL---
IT'S THE PERFECT OPPORTUNITY!
WHEN DID HE HAVE THE TIME TO RESEARCH THIS?
DESPITE THIS---
THAT OPPORTUNITY IS BEING TAKEN AWAY BY ST. PIERRE.
RUSH
RUSH
ALL RIGHT.
THEN LET'S HEAR YOUR IDEA.

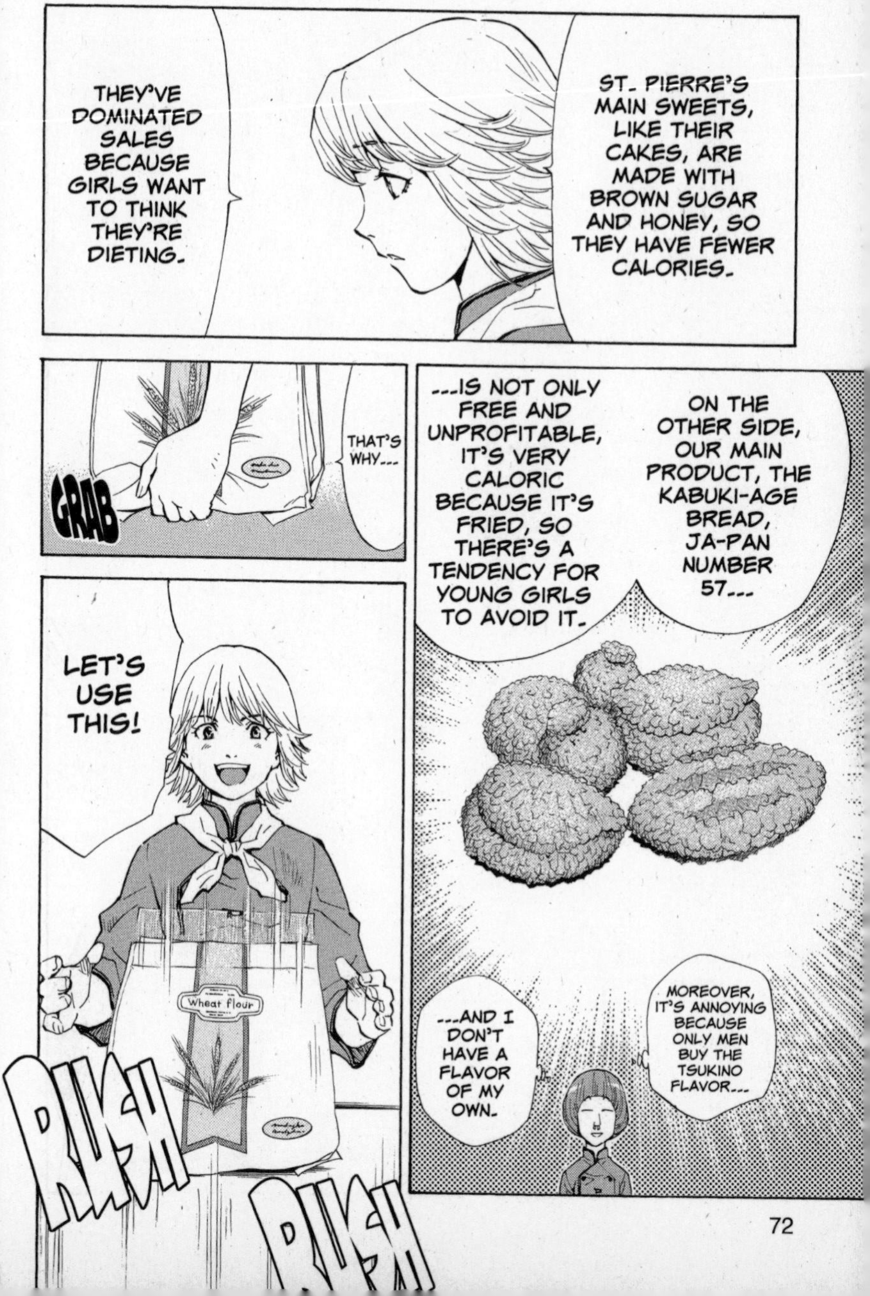
ST. PIERRE'S MAIN SWEETS, LIKE THEIR CAKES, ARE MADE WITH BROWN SUGAR AND HONEY, SO THEY HAVE FEWER CALORIES.
THEY'VE DOMINATED SALES BECAUSE GIRLS WANT TO THINK THEY'RE DIETING.
ON THE OTHER SIDE, OUR MAIN PRODUCT, THE KABUKI-AGE BREAD, JA-PAN NUMBER 57...
...IS NOT ONLY FREE AND UNPROFITABLE, IT'S VERY CALORIC BECAUSE IT'S FRIED, SO THERE'S A TENDENCY FOR YOUNG GIRLS TO AVOID IT.
MOREOVER, IT'S ANNOYING BECAUSE ONLY MEN BUY THE TSUKINO FLAVOR...
...AND I DON'T HAVE A FLAVOR OF MY OWN.
THAT'S WHY...
GRAB
LET'S USE THIS!
Wheat flour
RUSH
RUSH

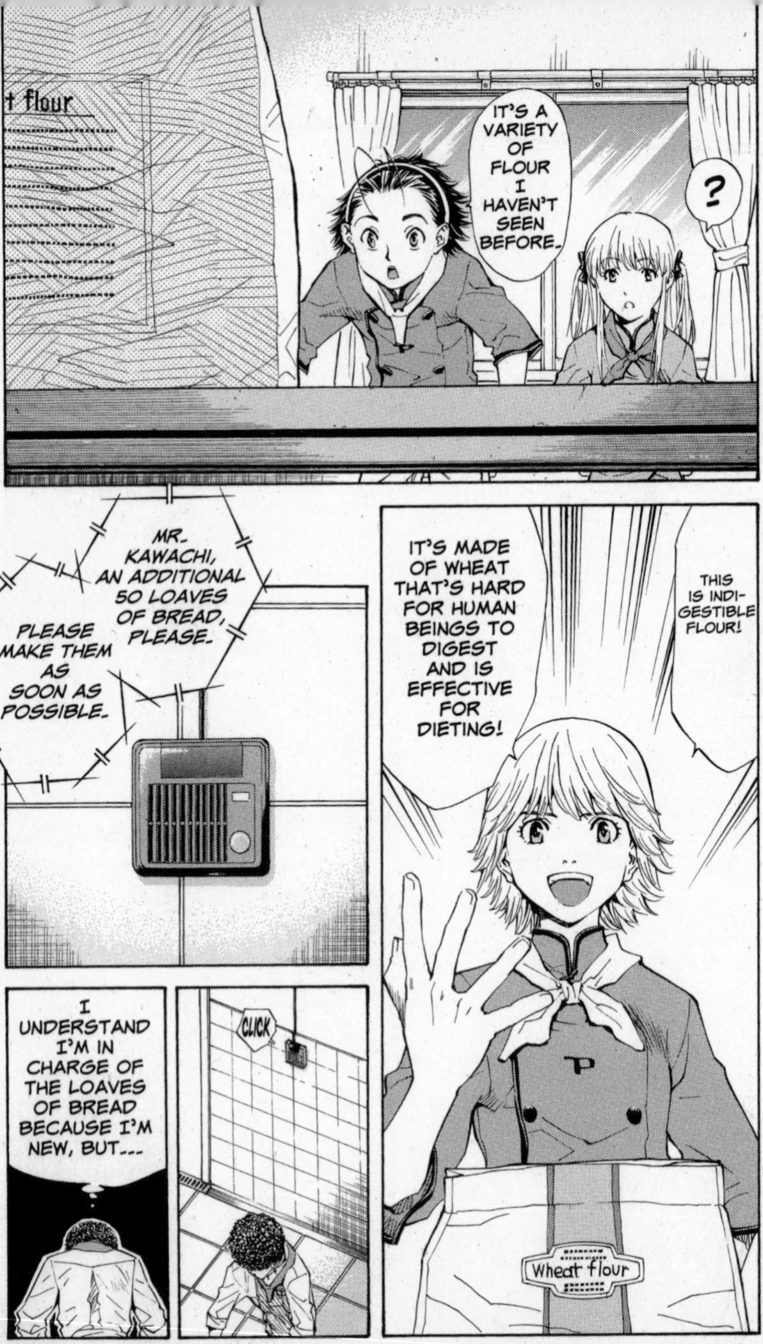
?
IT'S A VARIETY OF FLOUR I HAVEN'T SEEN BEFORE.
t flour
THIS IS INDIGESTIBLE FLOUR!
IT'S MADE OF WHEAT THAT'S HARD FOR HUMAN BEINGS TO DIGEST AND IS EFFECTIVE FOR DIETING!
Wheat flour
MR. KAWACHI, AN ADDITIONAL 50 LOAVES OF BREAD, PLEASE.
PLEASE MAKE THEM AS SOON AS POSSIBLE.
CLICK
I UNDERSTAND I'M IN CHARGE OF THE LOAVES OF BREAD BECAUSE I'M NEW, BUT...

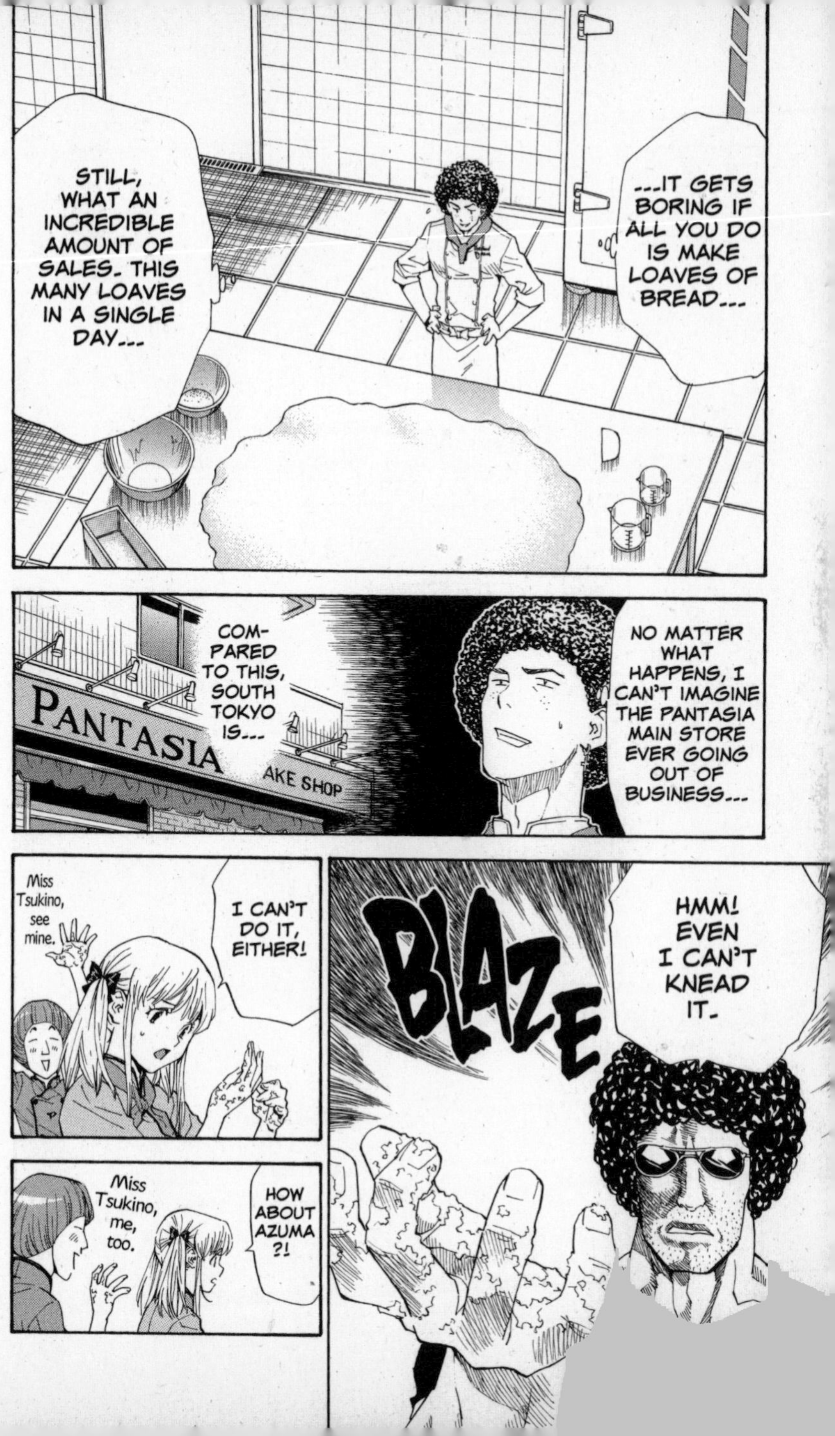
...IT GETS BORING IF ALL YOU DO IS MAKE LOAVES OF BREAD...
STILL, WHAT AN INCREDIBLE AMOUNT OF SALES. THIS MANY LOAVES IN A SINGLE DAY...
NO MATTER WHAT HAPPENS, I CAN'T IMAGINE THE PANTASIA MAIN STORE EVER GOING OUT OF BUSINESS...
COMPARED TO THIS, SOUTH TOKYO IS...
PANTASIA
AKE SHOP
BLAZE
HMM! EVEN I CAN'T KNEAD IT.
I CAN'T DO IT, EITHER!
Miss Tsukino, see mine.
HOW ABOUT AZUMA?!
Miss Tsukino, me, too.

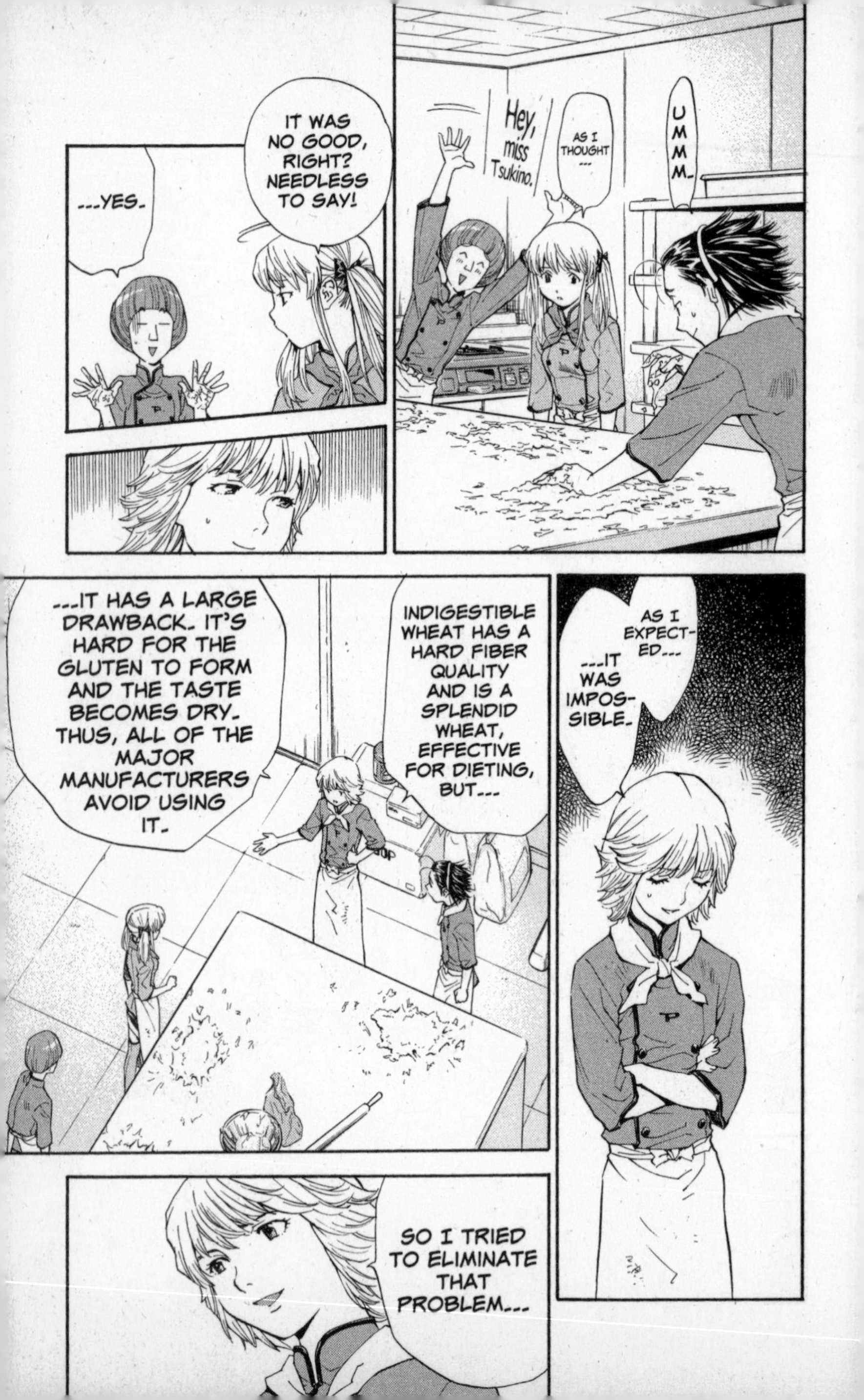
UMMM.
AS I THOUGHT...
Hey, miss Tsukino.
IT WAS NO GOOD, RIGHT? NEEDLESS TO SAY!
...YES.
AS I EXPECTED...
...IT WAS IMPOSSIBLE.
INDIGESTIBLE WHEAT HAS A HARD FIBER QUALITY AND IS A SPLENDID WHEAT, EFFECTIVE FOR DIETING, BUT...
...IT HAS A LARGE DRAWBACK. IT'S HARD FOR THE GLUTEN TO FORM AND THE TASTE BECOMES DRY. THUS, ALL OF THE MAJOR MANUFACTURERS AVOID USING IT.
SO I TRIED TO ELIMINATE THAT PROBLEM...

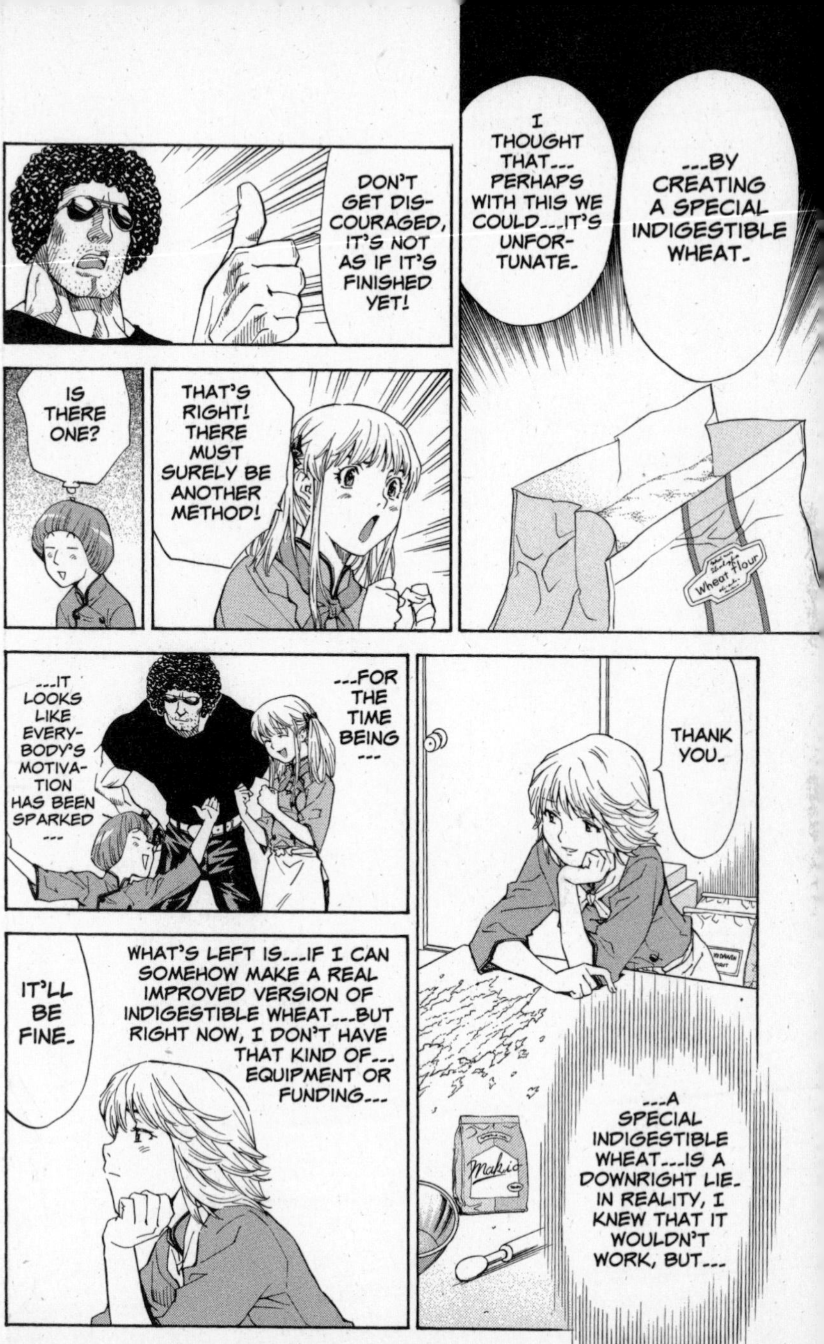
---BY CREATING A SPECIAL INDIGESTIBLE WHEAT.
I THOUGHT THAT... PERHAPS WITH THIS WE COULD... IT'S UNFORTUNATE.
Wheat Flour
DON'T GET DISCOURAGED, IT'S NOT AS IF IT'S FINISHED YET!
THAT'S RIGHT! THERE MUST SURELY BE ANOTHER METHOD!
IS THERE ONE?
THANK YOU.
---A SPECIAL INDIGESTIBLE WHEAT... IS A DOWNRIGHT LIE. IN REALITY, I KNEW THAT IT WOULDN'T WORK, BUT...
---FOR THE TIME BEING---
---IT LOOKS LIKE EVERYBODY'S MOTIVATION HAS BEEN SPARKED---
WHAT'S LEFT IS... IF I CAN SOMEHOW MAKE A REAL IMPROVED VERSION OF INDIGESTIBLE WHEAT... BUT RIGHT NOW, I DON'T HAVE THAT KIND OF... EQUIPMENT OR FUNDING...
IT'LL BE FINE.

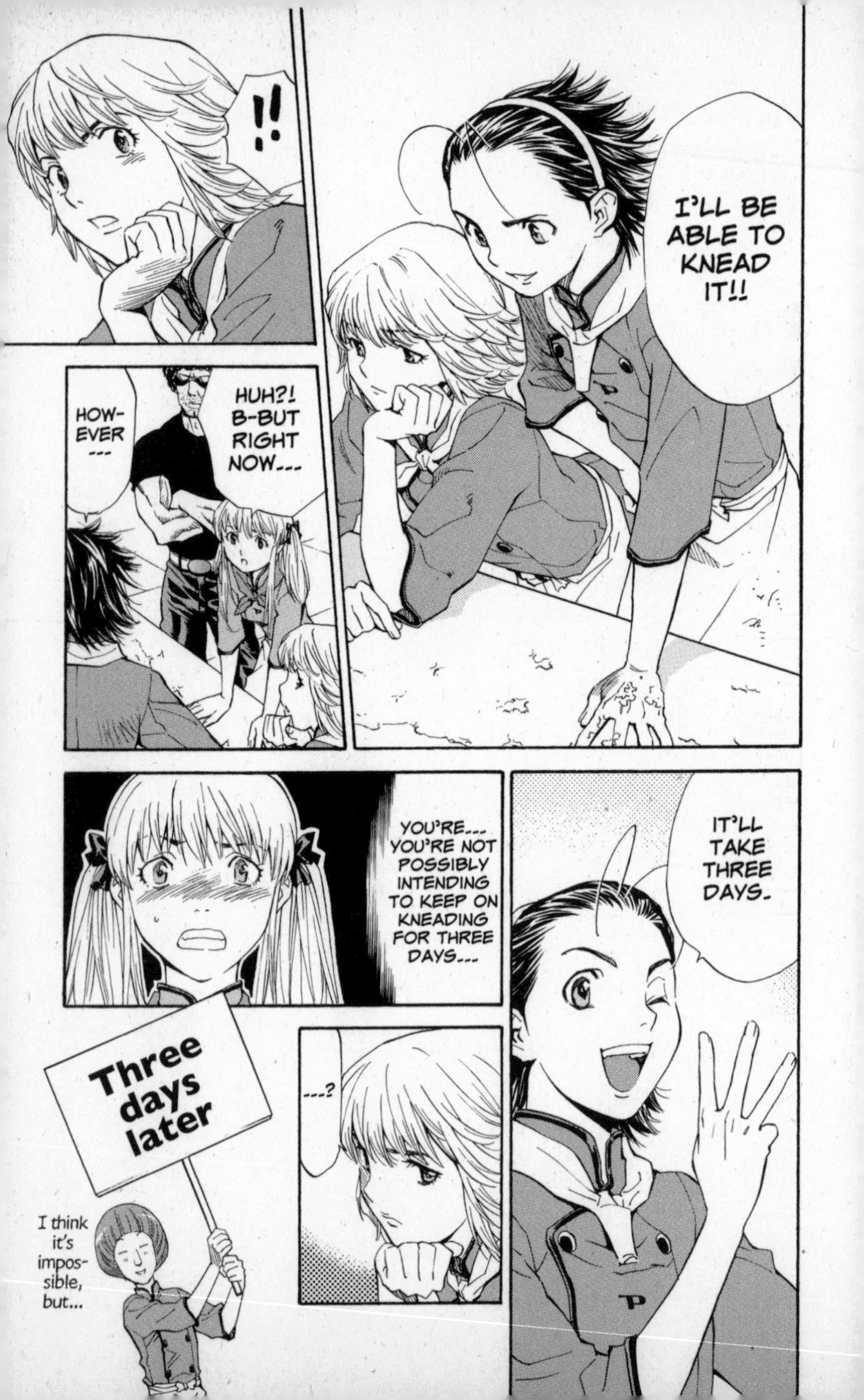

I'LL BE ABLE TO KNEAD IT!!
!!
HUH?! B-BUT RIGHT NOW...
HOW-EVER ---
IT'LL TAKE THREE DAYS.
YOU'RE... YOU'RE NOT POSSIBLY INTENDING TO KEEP ON KNEADING FOR THREE DAYS...
...?
Three days later
I think it's impossible, but...

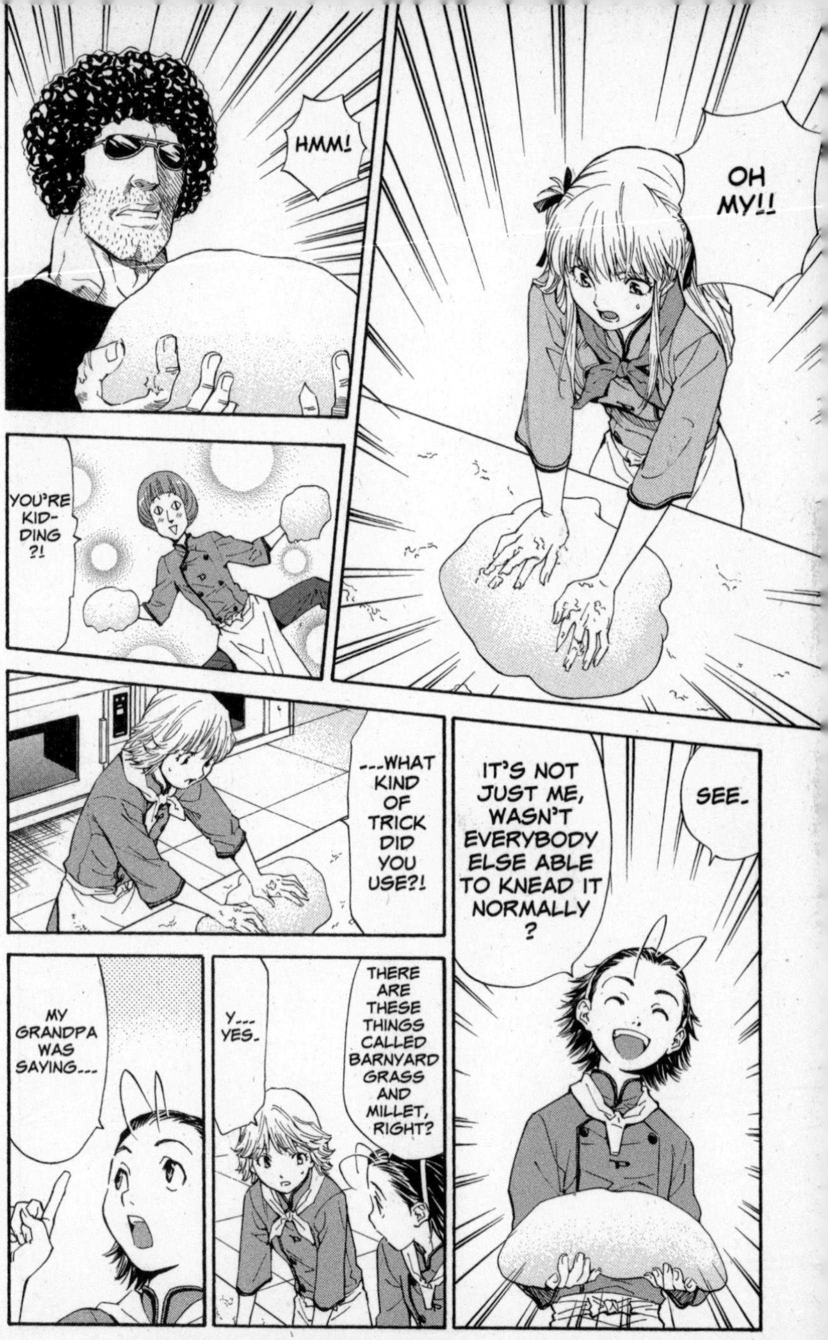
OH MY!!
HMM!
YOU'RE KIDDING?!
SEE.
IT'S NOT JUST ME, WASN'T EVERYBODY ELSE ABLE TO KNEAD IT NORMALLY?
...WHAT KIND OF TRICK DID YOU USE?!
THERE ARE THESE THINGS CALLED BARNYARD GRASS AND MILLET, RIGHT?
Y... YES.
MY GRANDPA WAS SAYING...

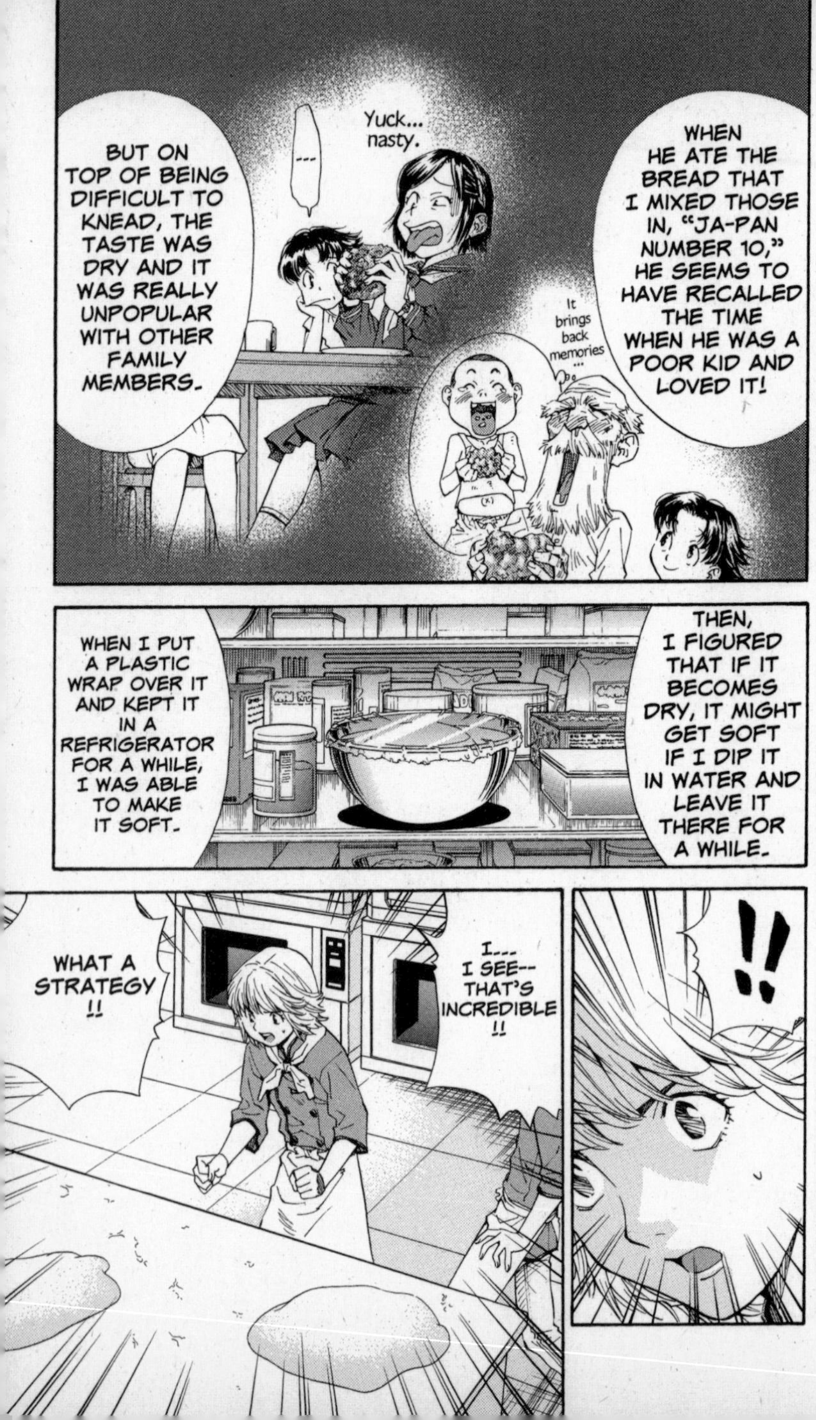
WHEN HE ATE THE BREAD THAT I MIXED THOSE IN, "JA-PAN NUMBER 10," HE SEEMS TO HAVE RECALLED THE TIME WHEN HE WAS A POOR KID AND LOVED IT!
It brings back memories...
Yuck... nasty.
...
BUT ON TOP OF BEING DIFFICULT TO KNEAD, THE TASTE WAS DRY AND IT WAS REALLY UNPOPULAR WITH OTHER FAMILY MEMBERS.
THEN, I FIGURED THAT IF IT BECOMES DRY, IT MIGHT GET SOFT IF I DIP IT IN WATER AND LEAVE IT THERE FOR A WHILE.
WHEN I PUT A PLASTIC WRAP OVER IT AND KEPT IT IN A REFRIGERATOR FOR A WHILE, I WAS ABLE TO MAKE IT SOFT.
!!
I... I SEE-- THAT'S INCREDIBLE !!
WHAT A STRATEGY !!

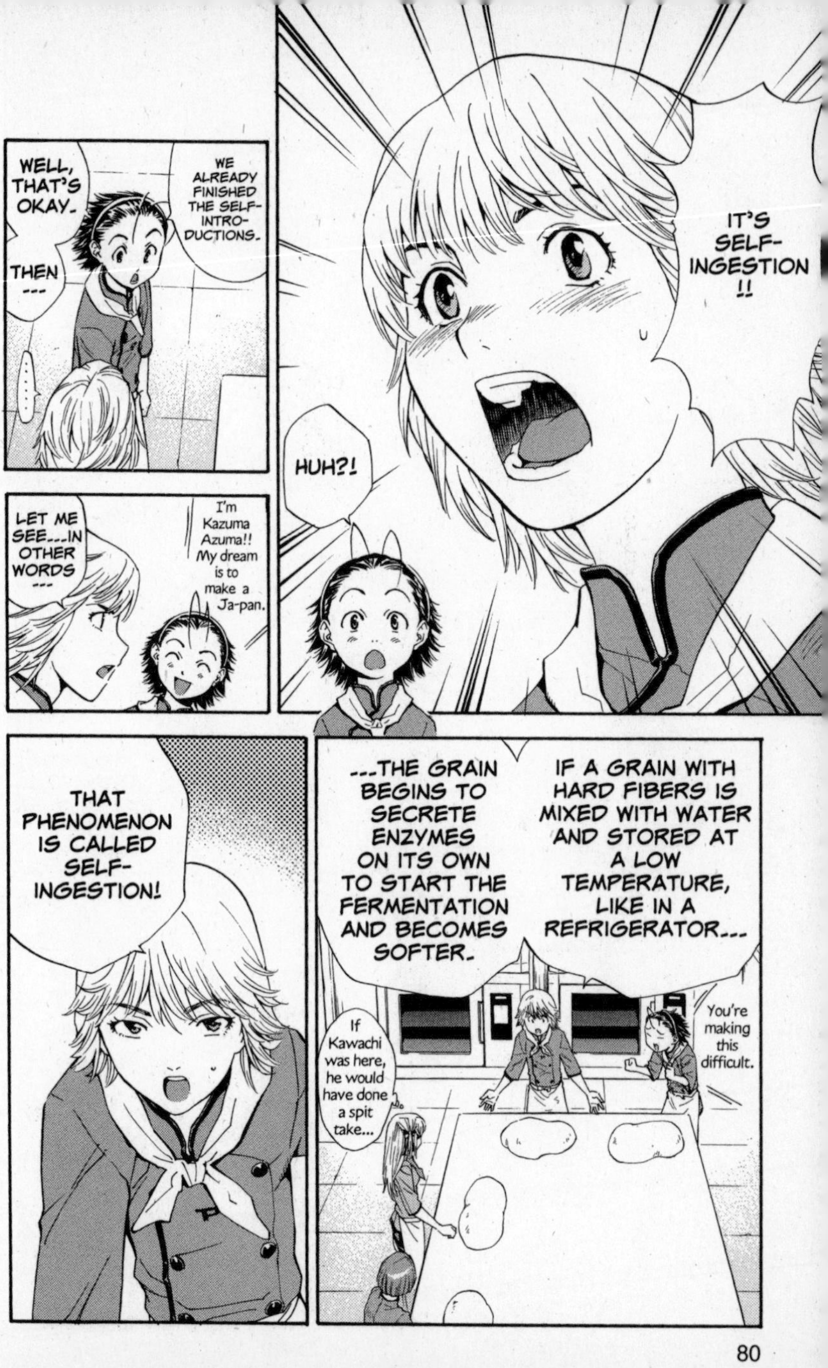
IT'S SELF-INGESTION!!
HUH?!
WE ALREADY FINISHED THE SELF-INTRODUCTIONS.
WELL, THAT'S OKAY.
THEN ---
......
I'm Kazuma Azuma!! My dream is to make a Ja-pan.
LET ME SEE...IN OTHER WORDS ---
IF A GRAIN WITH HARD FIBERS IS MIXED WITH WATER AND STORED AT A LOW TEMPERATURE, LIKE IN A REFRIGERATOR...
---THE GRAIN BEGINS TO SECRETE ENZYMES ON ITS OWN TO START THE FERMENTATION AND BECOMES SOFTER.
You're making this difficult.
If Kawachi was here, he would have done a spit take...
THAT PHENOMENON IS CALLED SELF-INGESTION!

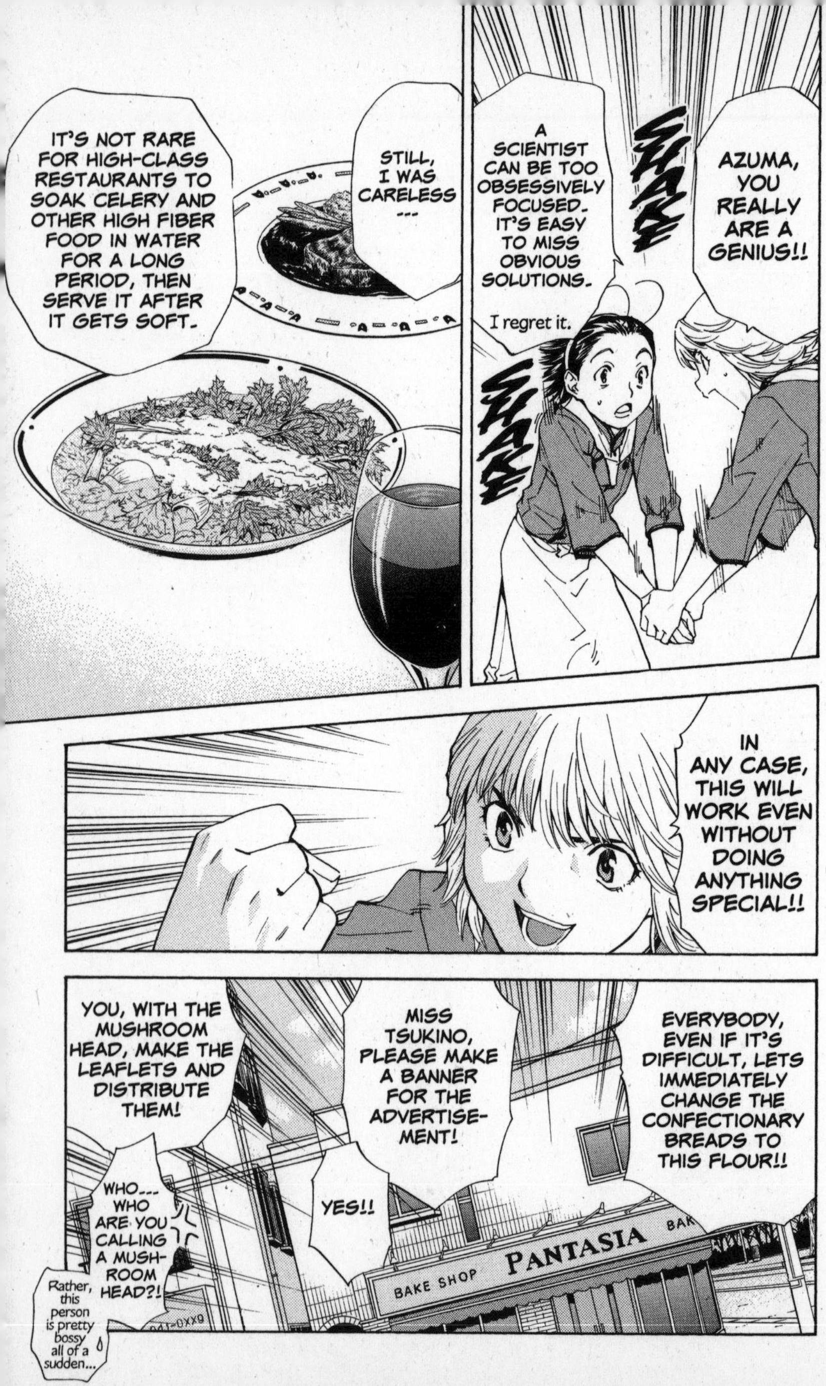
AZUMA, YOU REALLY ARE A GENIUS!!
SHAKE
A SCIENTIST CAN BE TOO OBSESSIVELY FOCUSED. IT'S EASY TO MISS OBVIOUS SOLUTIONS.
I regret it.
SHAKE
STILL, I WAS CARELESS---
IT'S NOT RARE FOR HIGH-CLASS RESTAURANTS TO SOAK CELERY AND OTHER HIGH FIBER FOOD IN WATER FOR A LONG PERIOD, THEN SERVE IT AFTER IT GETS SOFT.
IN ANY CASE, THIS WILL WORK EVEN WITHOUT DOING ANYTHING SPECIAL!!
EVERYBODY, EVEN IF IT'S DIFFICULT, LETS IMMEDIATELY CHANGE THE CONFECTIONARY BREADS TO THIS FLOUR!!
MISS TSUKINO, PLEASE MAKE A BANNER FOR THE ADVERTISE-MENT!
YES!!
YOU, WITH THE MUSHROOM HEAD, MAKE THE LEAFLETS AND DISTRIBUTE THEM!
WHO--- WHO ARE YOU CALLING A MUSH-ROOM HEAD?!
BAK
PANTASIA
BAKE SHOP
041-0XX9
Rather, this person is pretty bossy all of a sudden...

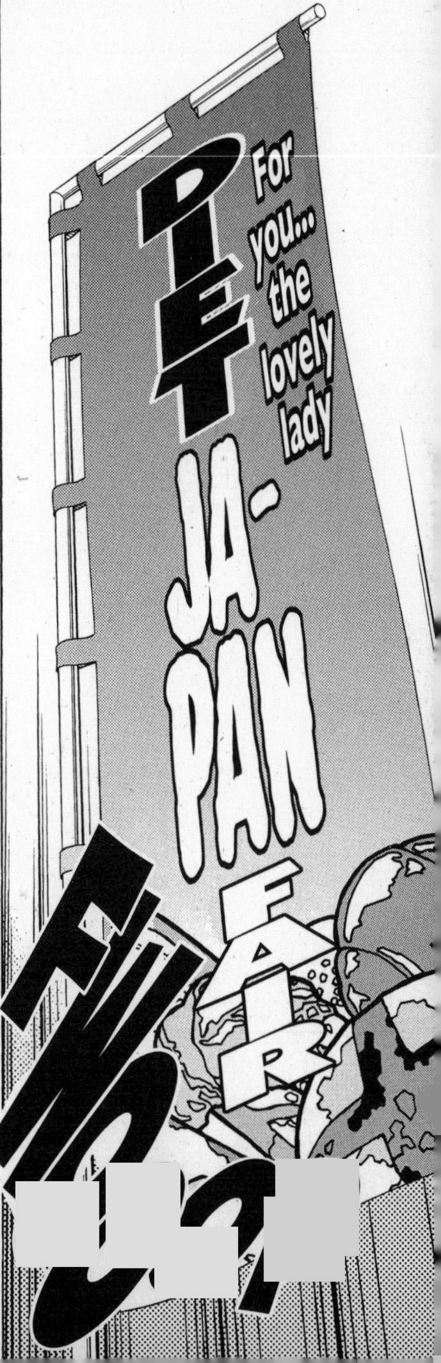
DIET
For you... the lovely lady
JA-PAN
FAIR
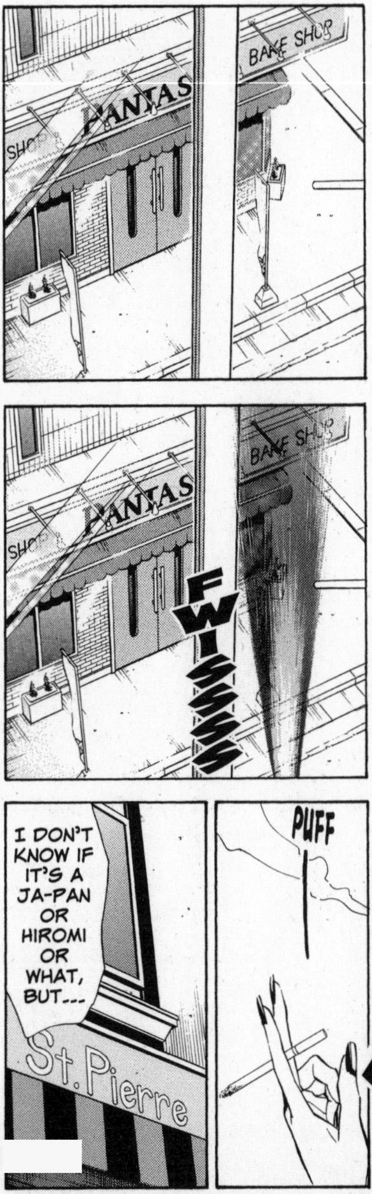
BAKE SHOP
PANTAS
SHOP
BAKE SHOP
PANTAS
SHOP
FWISSSS
PUFF
I DON'T KNOW IF IT'S A JA-PAN OR HIROMI OR WHAT, BUT...
St. Pierre

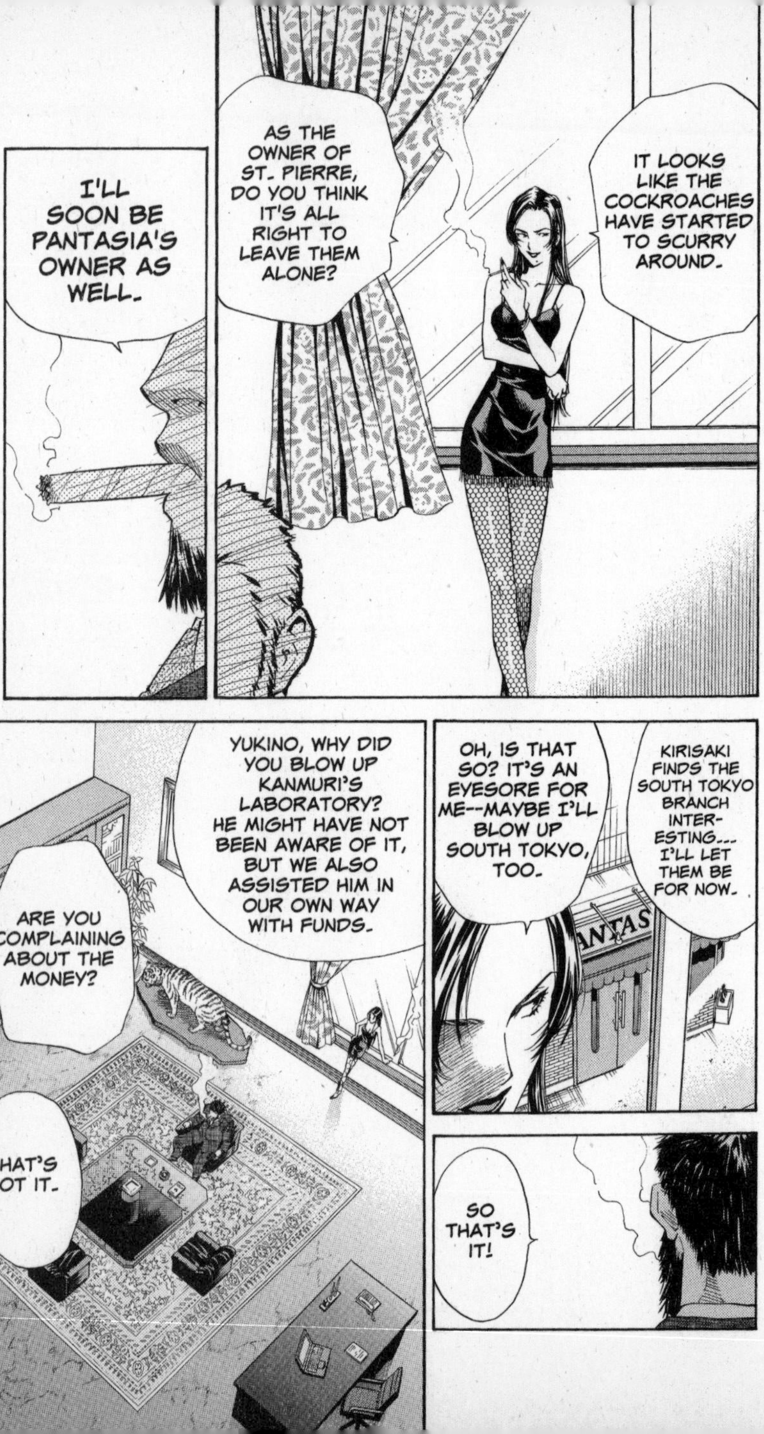
IT LOOKS LIKE THE COCKROACHES HAVE STARTED TO SCURRY AROUND.
AS THE OWNER OF ST. PIERRE, DO YOU THINK IT'S ALL RIGHT TO LEAVE THEM ALONE?
I'LL SOON BE PANTASIA'S OWNER AS WELL.
KIRISAKI FINDS THE SOUTH TOKYO BRANCH INTER-ESTING... I'LL LET THEM BE FOR NOW.
OH, IS THAT SO? IT'S AN EYESORE FOR ME--MAYBE I'LL BLOW UP SOUTH TOKYO, TOO.
SO THAT'S IT!
YUKINO, WHY DID YOU BLOW UP KANMURI'S LABORATORY? HE MIGHT HAVE NOT BEEN AWARE OF IT, BUT WE ALSO ASSISTED HIM IN OUR OWN WAY WITH FUNDS.
ARE YOU COMPLAINING ABOUT THE MONEY?
THAT'S NOT IT.

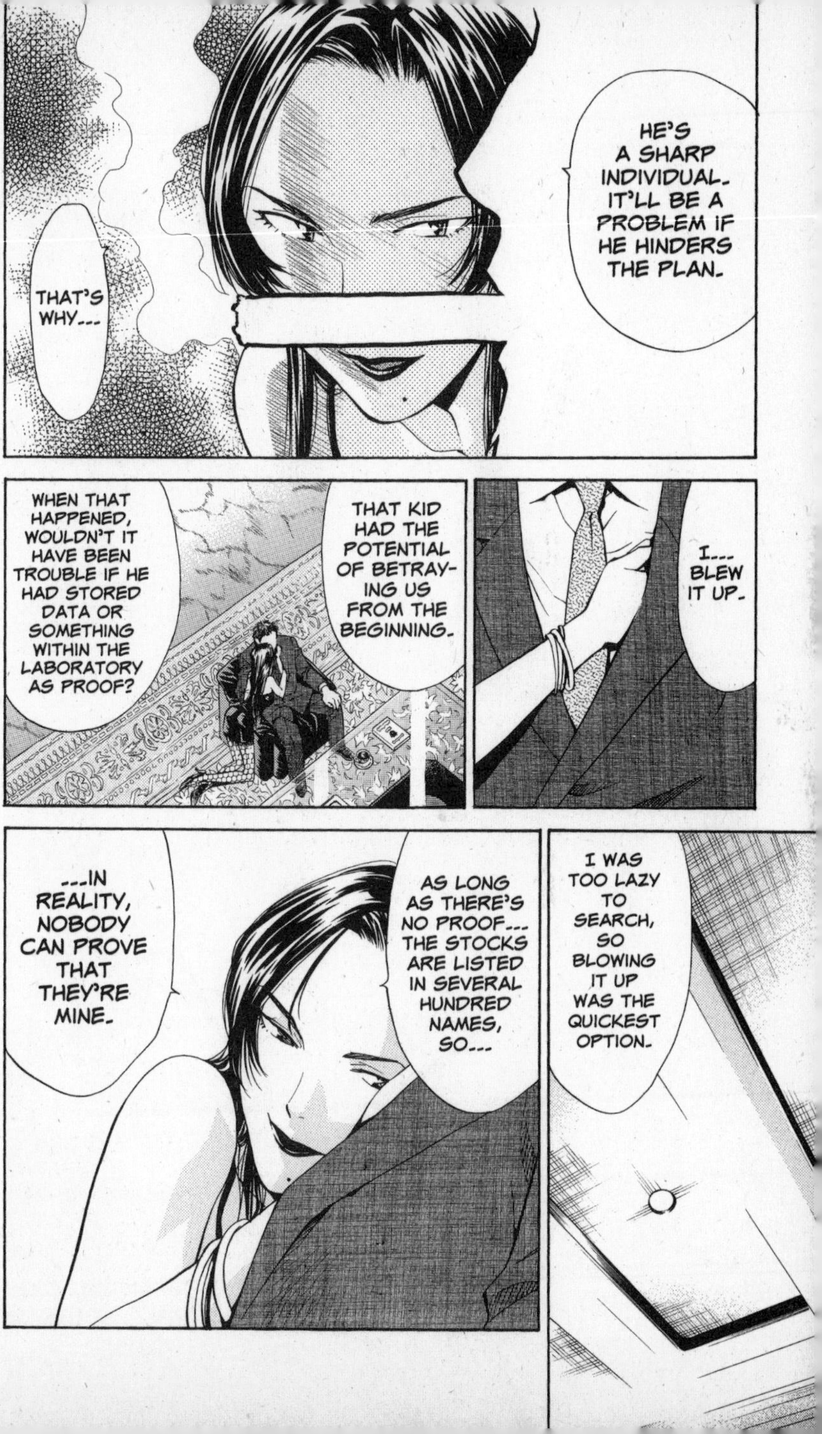
HE'S A SHARP INDIVIDUAL. IT'LL BE A PROBLEM IF HE HINDERS THE PLAN.
THAT'S WHY...
I... BLEW IT UP.
THAT KID HAD THE POTENTIAL OF BETRAYING US FROM THE BEGINNING.
WHEN THAT HAPPENED, WOULDN'T IT HAVE BEEN TROUBLE IF HE HAD STORED DATA OR SOMETHING WITHIN THE LABORATORY AS PROOF?
I WAS TOO LAZY TO SEARCH, SO BLOWING IT UP WAS THE QUICKEST OPTION.
AS LONG AS THERE'S NO PROOF... THE STOCKS ARE LISTED IN SEVERAL HUNDRED NAMES, SO...
...IN REALITY, NOBODY CAN PROVE THAT THEY'RE MINE.

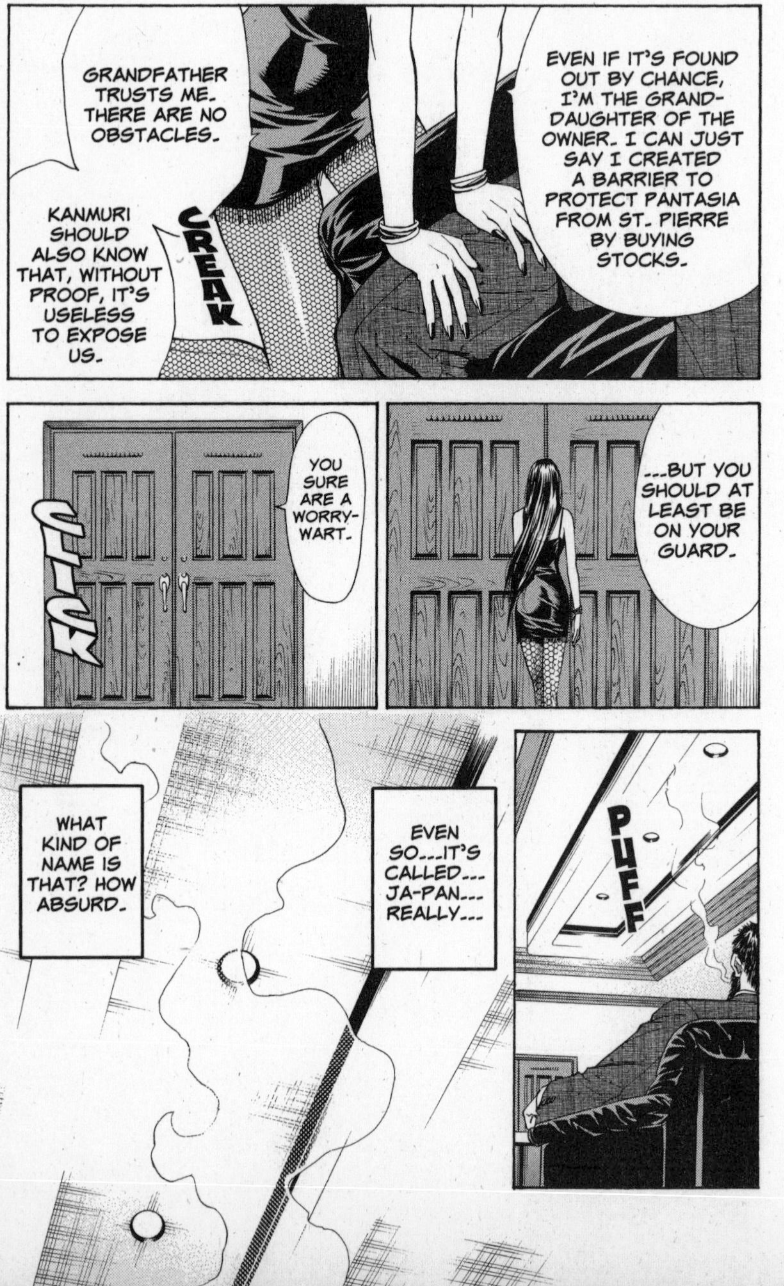
EVEN IF IT'S FOUND OUT BY CHANCE, I'M THE GRAND-DAUGHTER OF THE OWNER. I CAN JUST SAY I CREATED A BARRIER TO PROTECT PANTASIA FROM ST. PIERRE BY BUYING STOCKS.
GRANDFATHER TRUSTS ME. THERE ARE NO OBSTACLES.
CREAK
KANMURI SHOULD ALSO KNOW THAT, WITHOUT PROOF, IT'S USELESS TO EXPOSE US.
...BUT YOU SHOULD AT LEAST BE ON YOUR GUARD.
YOU SURE ARE A WORRY-WART.
CLICK
PUFF
EVEN SO...IT'S CALLED... JA-PAN... REALLY...
WHAT KIND OF NAME IS THAT? HOW ABSURD.

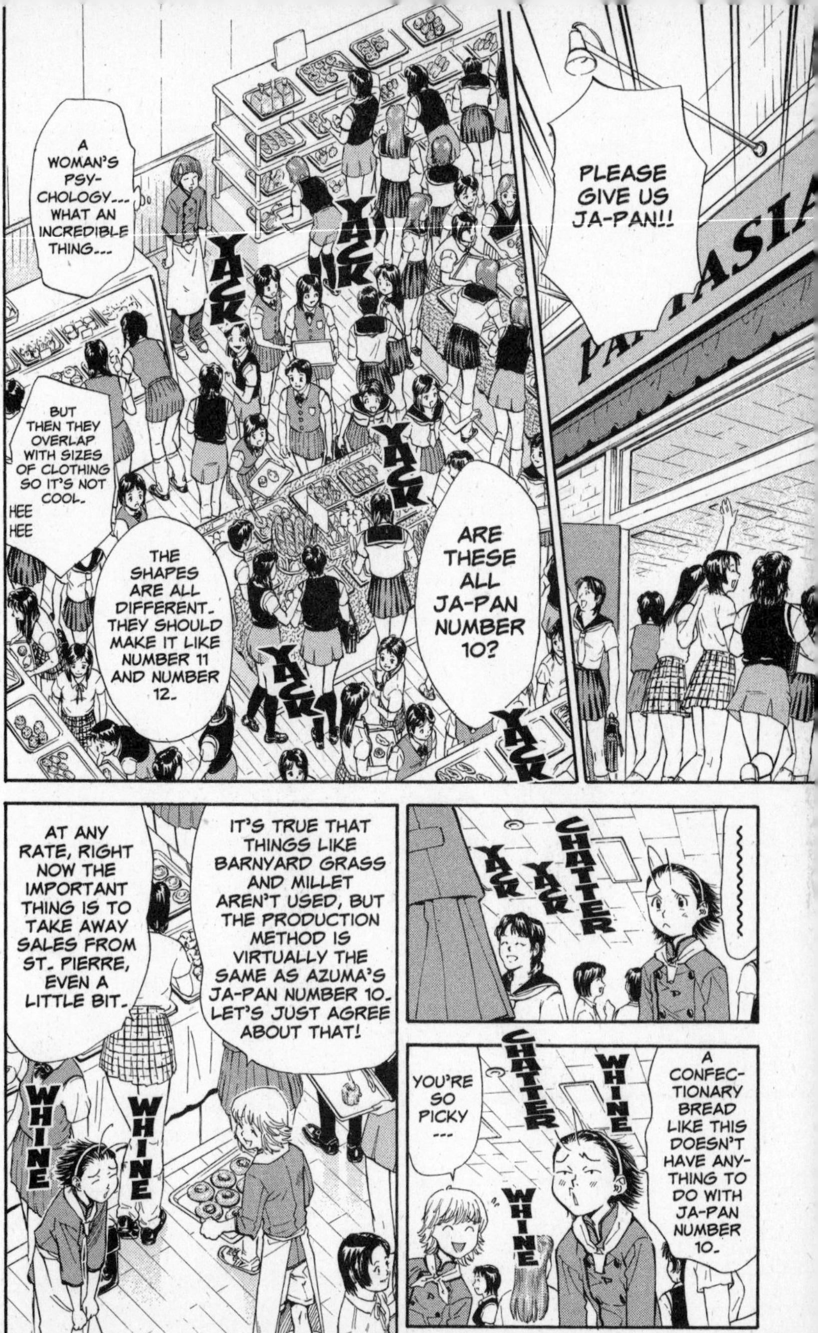
PLEASE GIVE US JA-PAN!!
PANTASIA
YACK
YACK
ARE THESE ALL JA-PAN NUMBER 10?
YACK
THE SHAPES ARE ALL DIFFERENT. THEY SHOULD MAKE IT LIKE NUMBER 11 AND NUMBER 12.
YACK
YACK
A WOMAN'S PSY-CHOLOGY... WHAT AN INCREDIBLE THING...
BUT THEN THEY OVERLAP WITH SIZES OF CLOTHING SO IT'S NOT COOL.
HEE HEE
~~~~~~
CHATTER
YACK
YACK
A CONFECTIONARY BREAD LIKE THIS DOESN'T HAVE ANY-THING TO DO WITH JA-PAN NUMBER 10.
WHINE
CHATTER
YOU'RE SO PICKY...
WHINE
IT'S TRUE THAT THINGS LIKE BARNYARD GRASS AND MILLET AREN'T USED, BUT THE PRODUCTION METHOD IS VIRTUALLY THE SAME AS AZUMA'S JA-PAN NUMBER 10. LET'S JUST AGREE ABOUT THAT!
AT ANY RATE, RIGHT NOW THE IMPORTANT THING IS TO TAKE AWAY SALES FROM ST. PIERRE, EVEN A LITTLE BIT.
WHINE
WHINE
~~~~~~

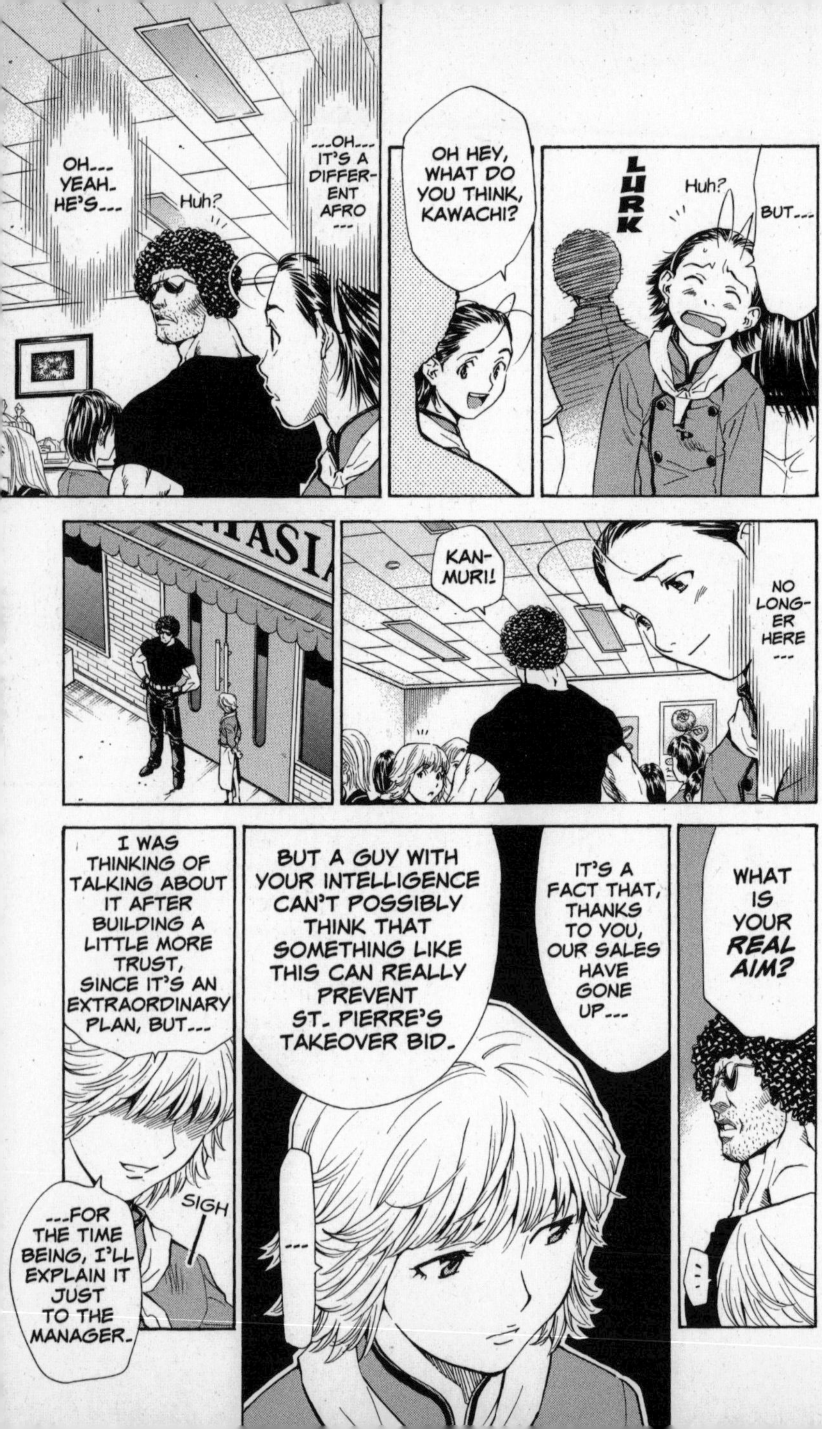

BUT...
Huh?
LURK
OH HEY, WHAT DO YOU THINK, KAWACHI?
...OH... IT'S A DIFFERENT AFRO...
Huh?
OH... YEAH. HE'S...
NO LONGER HERE...
KANMURI!
WHAT IS YOUR REAL AIM?
...
IT'S A FACT THAT, THANKS TO YOU, OUR SALES HAVE GONE UP...
BUT A GUY WITH YOUR INTELLIGENCE CAN'T POSSIBLY THINK THAT SOMETHING LIKE THIS CAN REALLY PREVENT ST. PIERRE'S TAKEOVER BID.
...
I WAS THINKING OF TALKING ABOUT IT AFTER BUILDING A LITTLE MORE TRUST, SINCE IT'S AN EXTRAORDINARY PLAN, BUT...
SIGH
...FOR THE TIME BEING, I'LL EXPLAIN IT JUST TO THE MANAGER.

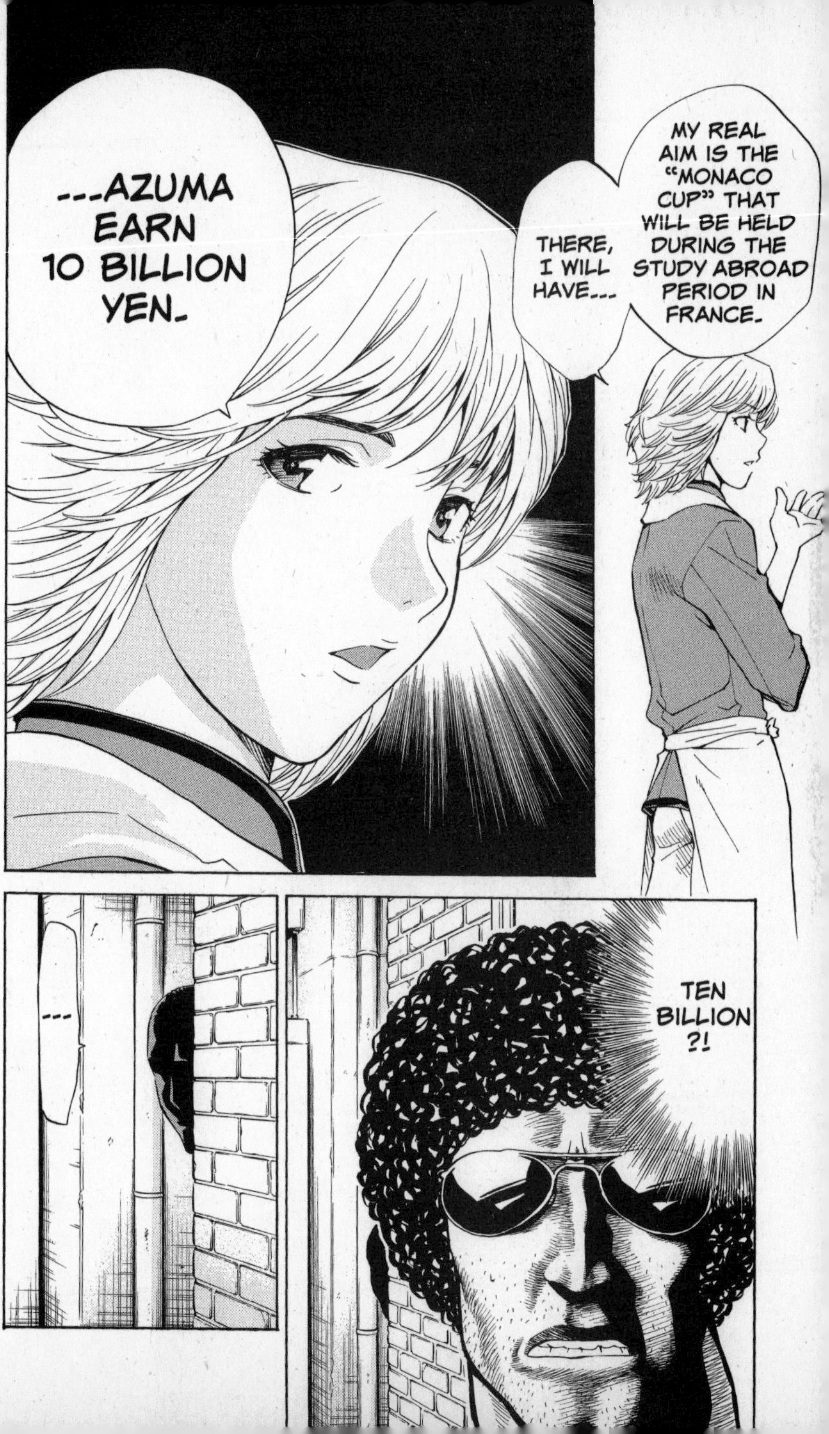
MY REAL AIM IS THE "MONACO CUP" THAT WILL BE HELD DURING THE STUDY ABROAD PERIOD IN FRANCE.
THERE, I WILL HAVE...
...AZUMA EARN 10 BILLION YEN.
TEN BILLION ?!
...

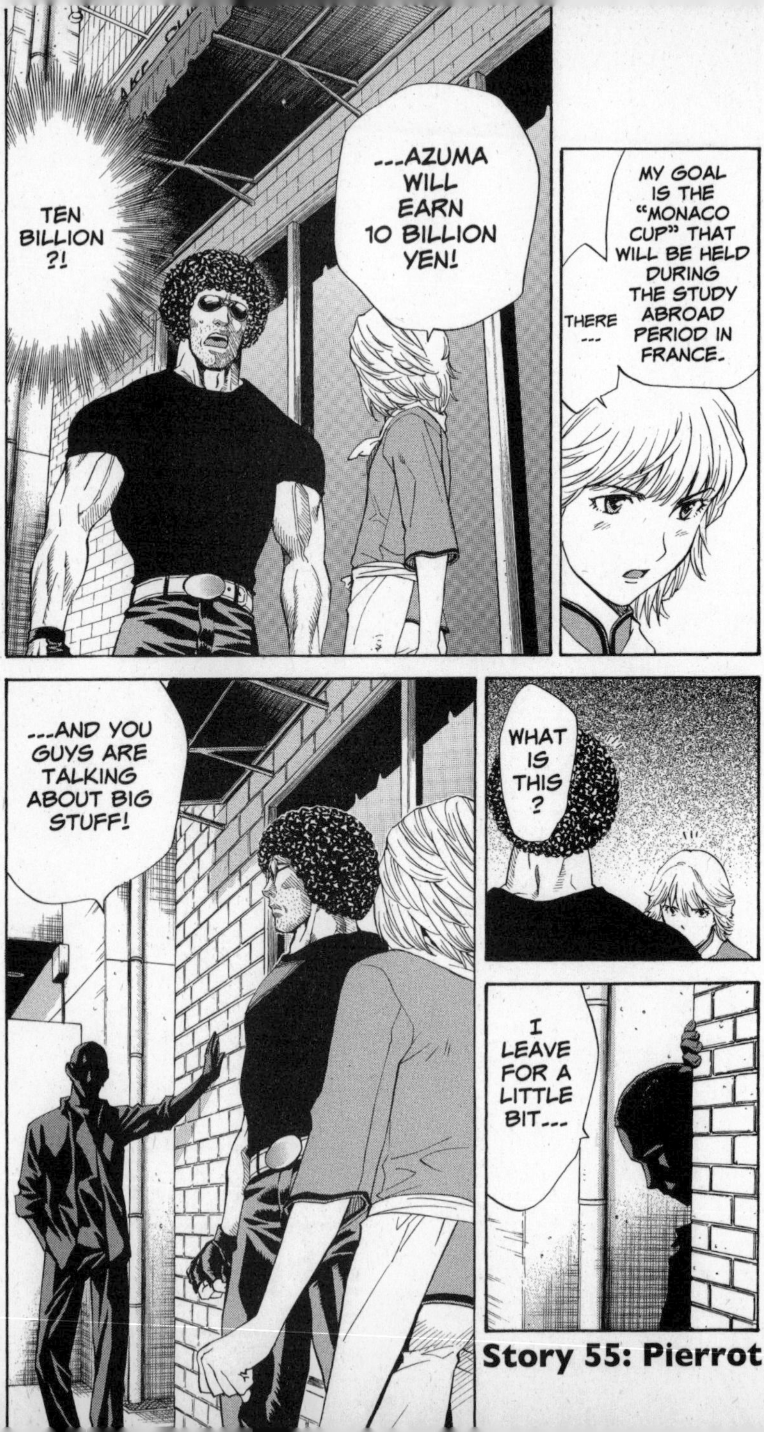
MY GOAL IS THE "MONACO CUP" THAT WILL BE HELD DURING THE STUDY ABROAD PERIOD IN FRANCE.
THERE---
---AZUMA WILL EARN 10 BILLION YEN!
TEN BILLION ?!
WHAT IS THIS ?
I LEAVE FOR A LITTLE BIT...
---AND YOU GUYS ARE TALKING ABOUT BIG STUFF!

Story 55: Pierrot

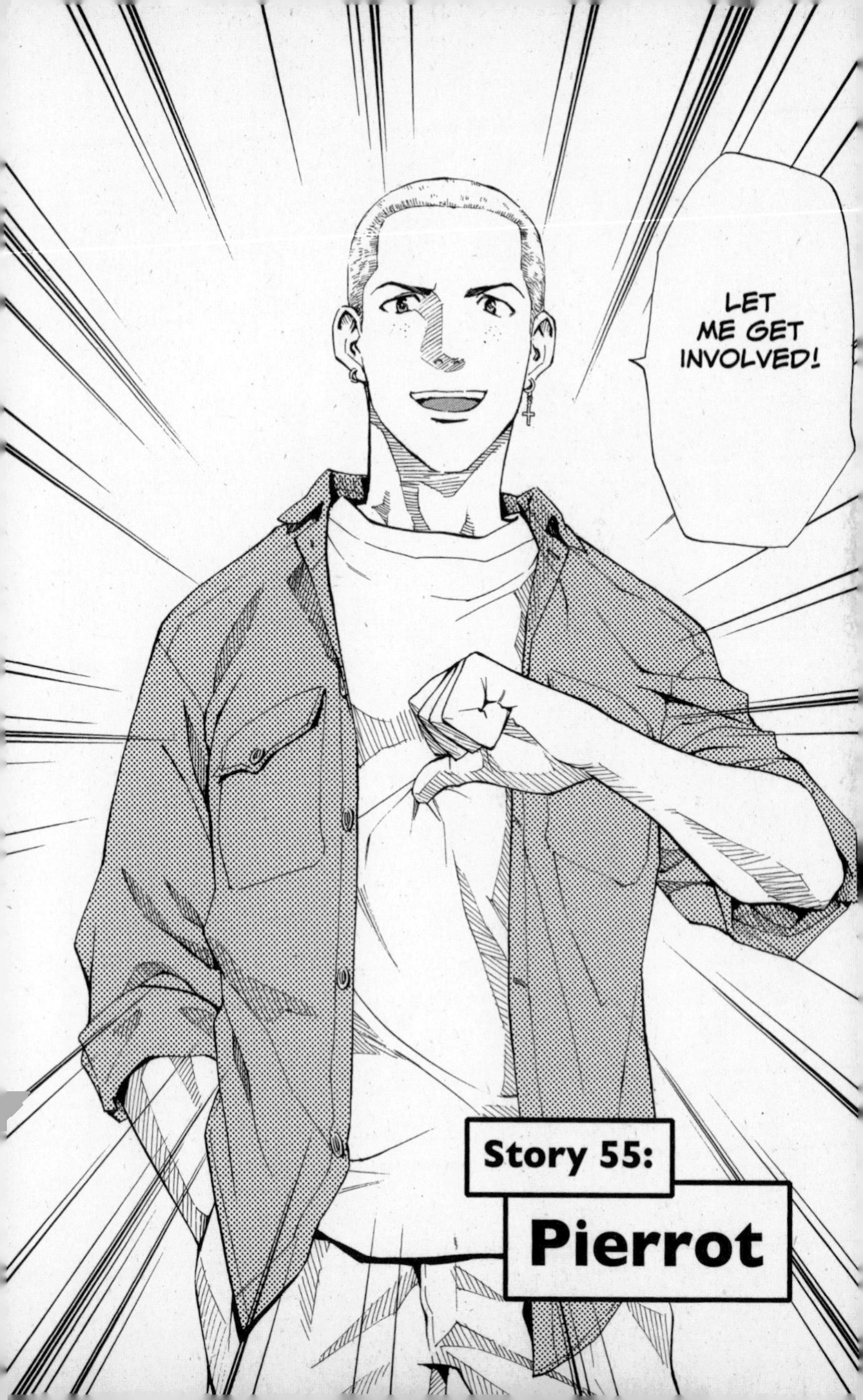
LET ME GET INVOLVED!
Story 55:
Pierrot

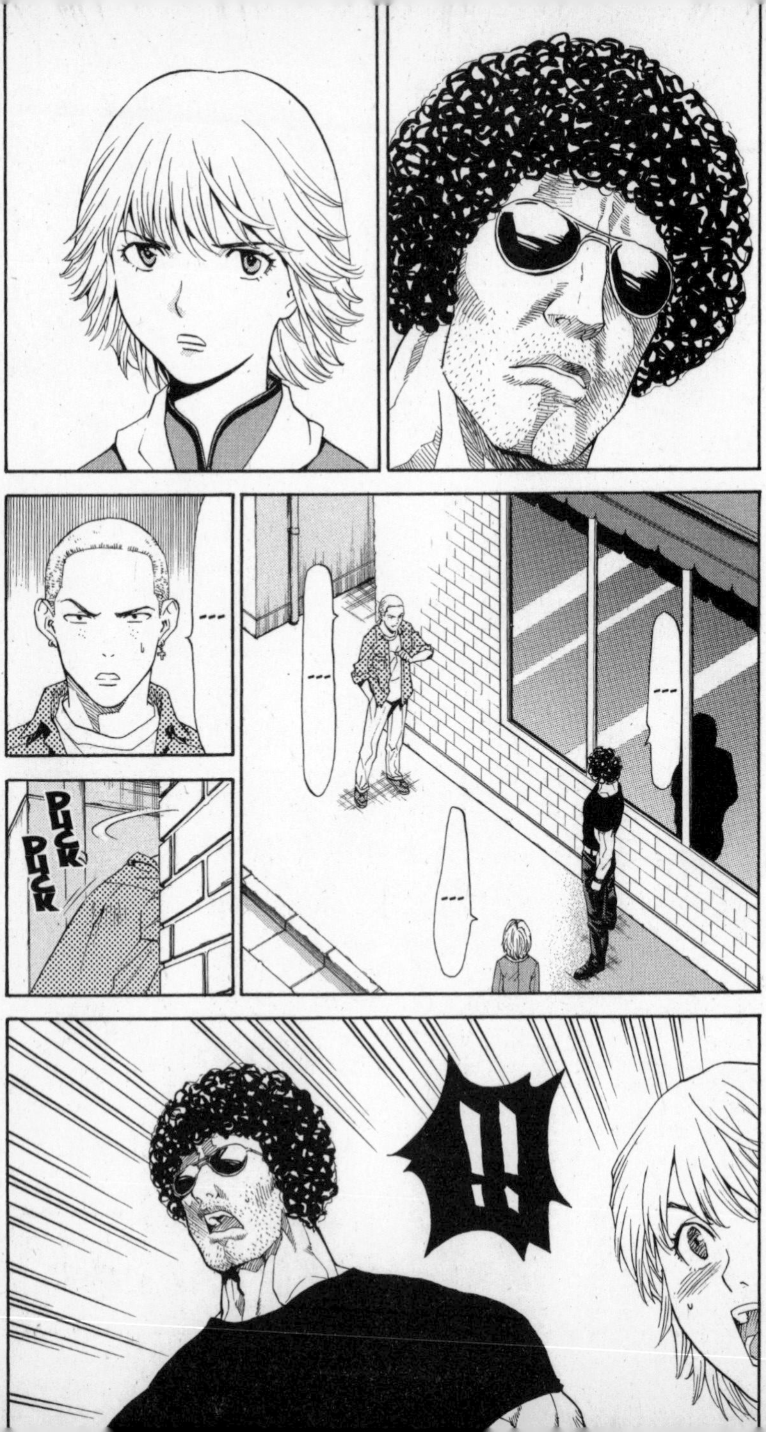
...
...
...
...
PUCK PUCK
!!

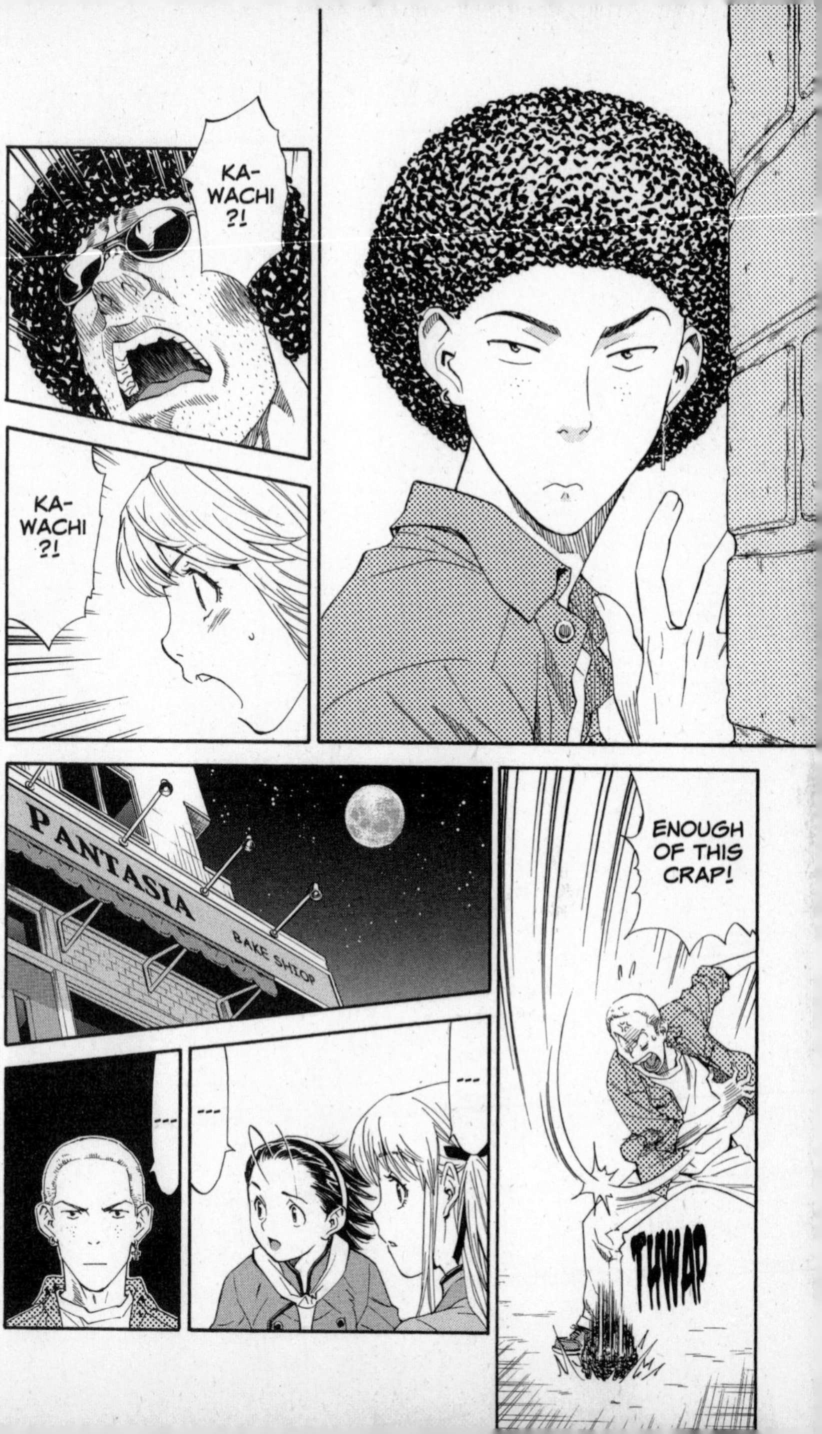
KA-WACHI?!
KA-WACHI?!
ENOUGH OF THIS CRAP!
THWAP
PANTASIA
BAKE SHOP

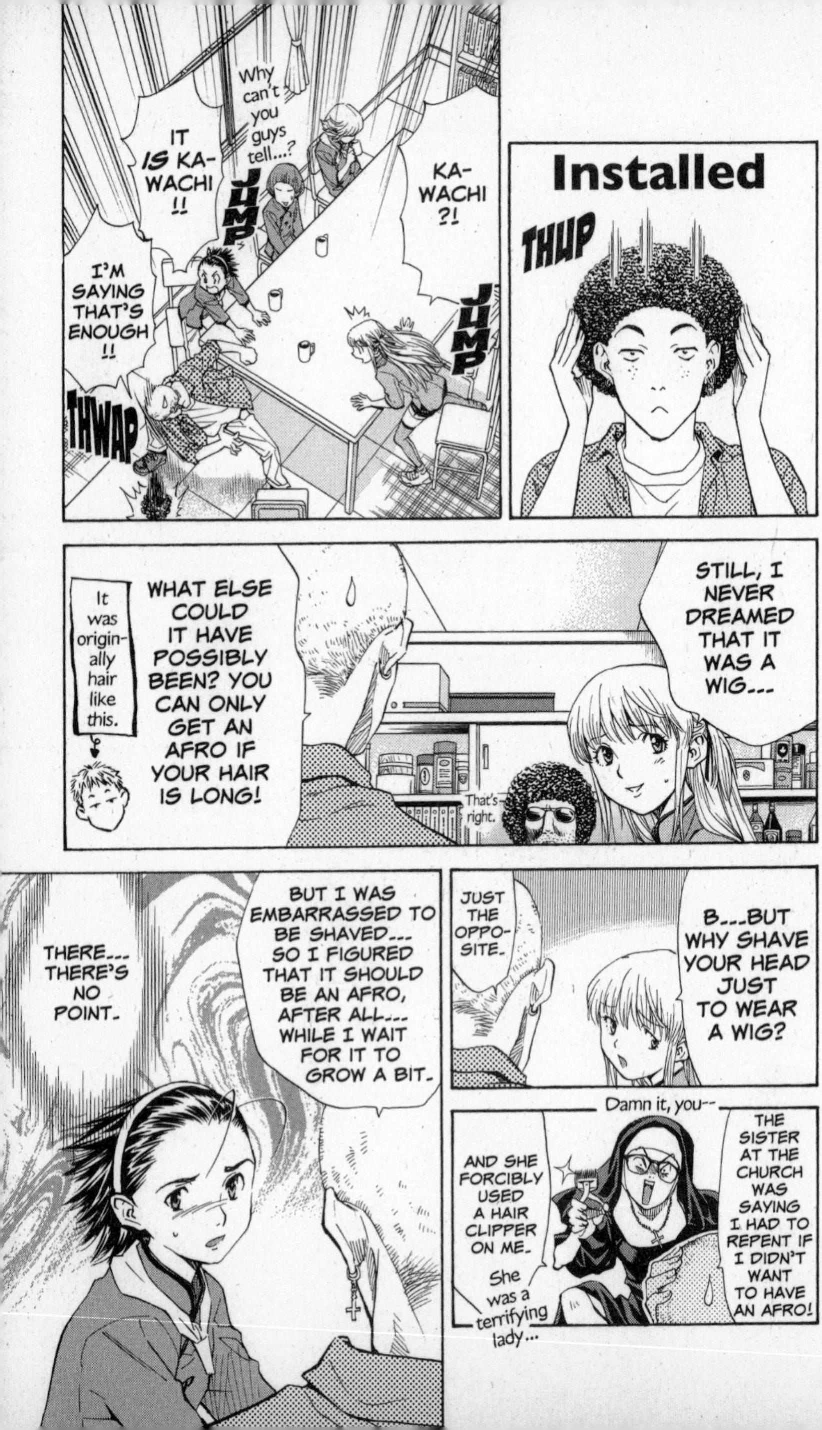
Installed
THUP
KA-WACHI ?!
JUMP
Why can't you guys tell...?
IT IS KA-WACHI !!
JUMP
I'M SAYING THAT'S ENOUGH !!
THWAP
STILL, I NEVER DREAMED THAT IT WAS A WIG...
That's right.
WHAT ELSE COULD IT HAVE POSSIBLY BEEN? YOU CAN ONLY GET AN AFRO IF YOUR HAIR IS LONG!
It was originally hair like this.
B...BUT WHY SHAVE YOUR HEAD JUST TO WEAR A WIG?
JUST THE OPPOSITE.
Damn it, you--
THE SISTER AT THE CHURCH WAS SAYING I HAD TO REPENT IF I DIDN'T WANT TO HAVE AN AFRO!
AND SHE FORCIBLY USED A HAIR CLIPPER ON ME.
She was a terrifying lady...
BUT I WAS EMBARRASSED TO BE SHAVED... SO I FIGURED THAT IT SHOULD BE AN AFRO, AFTER ALL... WHILE I WAIT FOR IT TO GROW A BIT.
THERE... THERE'S NO POINT.

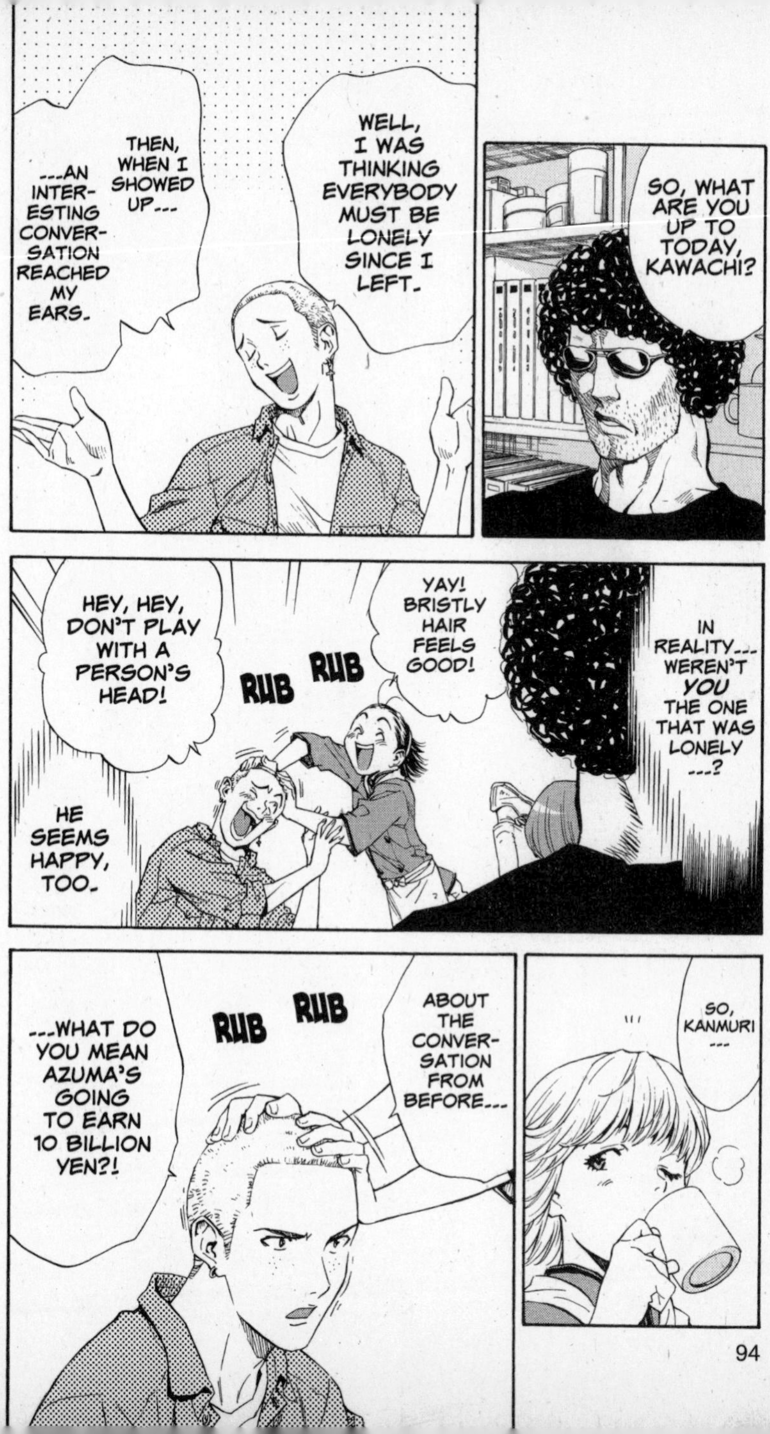
SO, WHAT ARE YOU UP TO TODAY, KAWACHI?
WELL, I WAS THINKING EVERYBODY MUST BE LONELY SINCE I LEFT.
THEN, WHEN I SHOWED UP...
...AN INTERESTING CONVERSATION REACHED MY EARS.
IN REALITY... WEREN'T *YOU* THE ONE THAT WAS LONELY...?
YAY! BRISTLY HAIR FEELS GOOD!
RUB RUB
HEY, HEY, DON'T PLAY WITH A PERSON'S HEAD!
HE SEEMS HAPPY, TOO.
SO, KANMURI...
ABOUT THE CONVERSATION FROM BEFORE...
RUB RUB
...WHAT DO YOU MEAN AZUMA'S GOING TO EARN 10 BILLION YEN?!

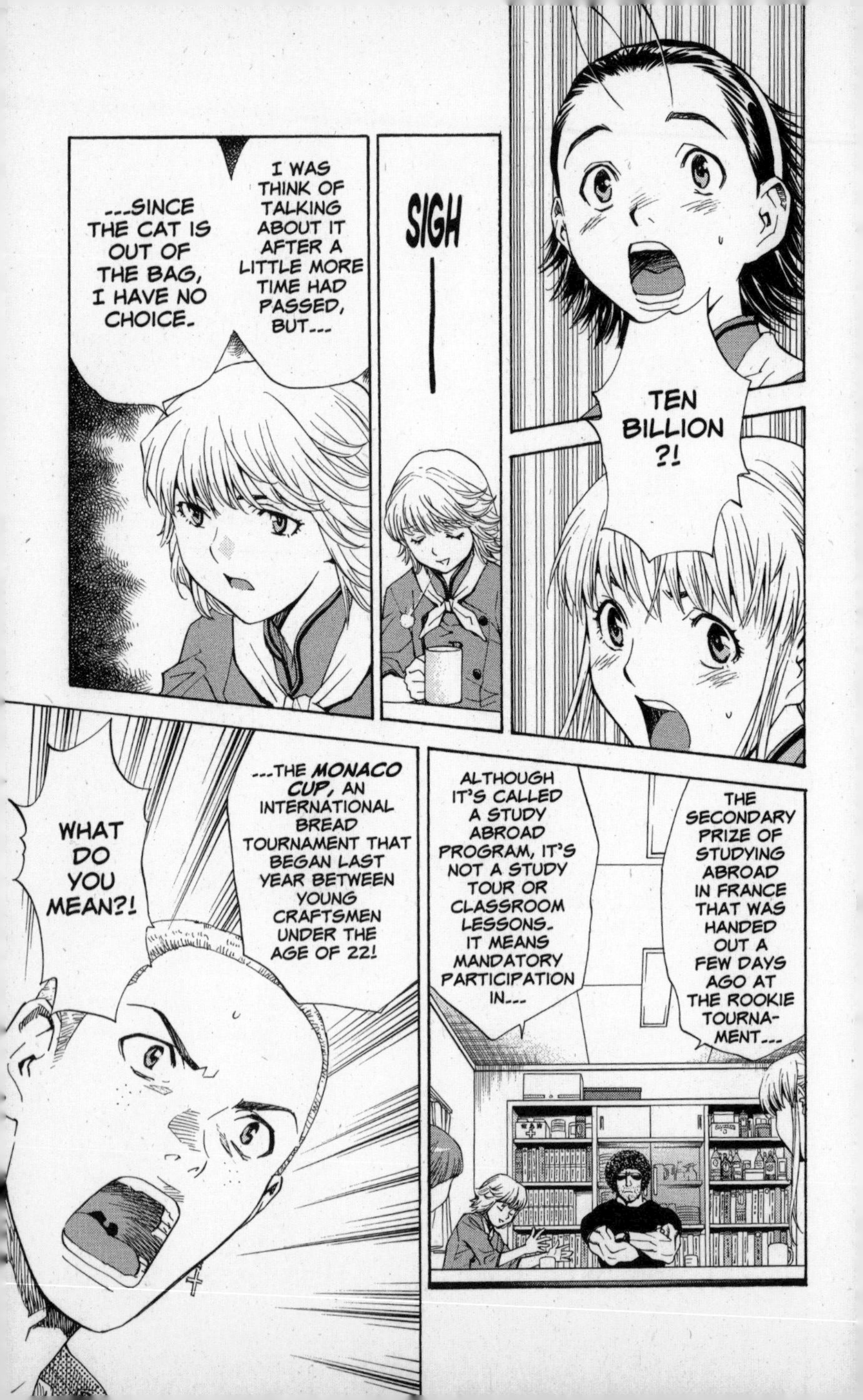
TEN BILLION ?!
SIGH
I WAS THINK OF TALKING ABOUT IT AFTER A LITTLE MORE TIME HAD PASSED, BUT...
...SINCE THE CAT IS OUT OF THE BAG, I HAVE NO CHOICE.
THE SECONDARY PRIZE OF STUDYING ABROAD IN FRANCE THAT WAS HANDED OUT A FEW DAYS AGO AT THE ROOKIE TOURNAMENT...
ALTHOUGH IT'S CALLED A STUDY ABROAD PROGRAM, IT'S NOT A STUDY TOUR OR CLASSROOM LESSONS. IT MEANS MANDATORY PARTICIPATION IN...
...THE MONACO CUP, AN INTERNATIONAL BREAD TOURNAMENT THAT BEGAN LAST YEAR BETWEEN YOUNG CRAFTSMEN UNDER THE AGE OF 22!
WHAT DO YOU MEAN?!

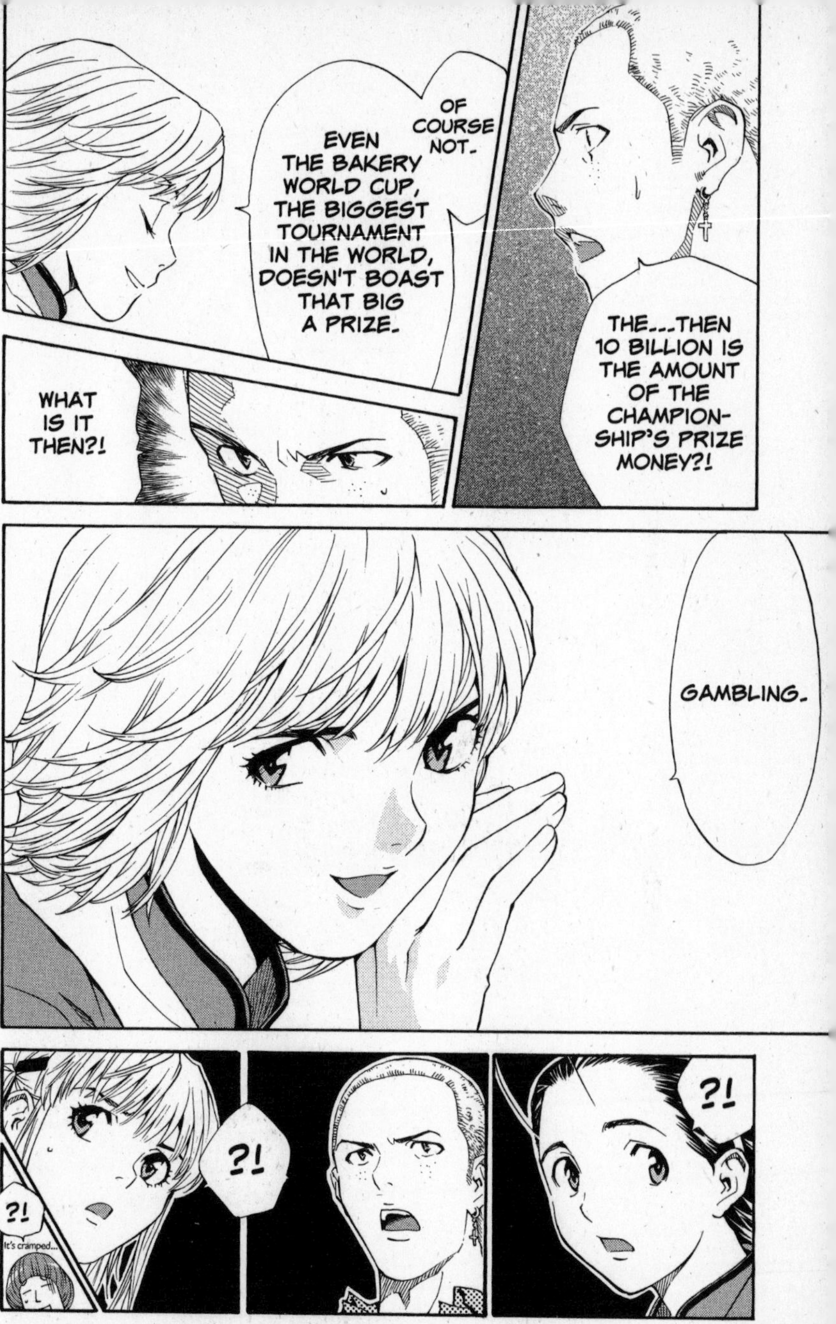
THE...THEN 10 BILLION IS THE AMOUNT OF THE CHAMPIONSHIP'S PRIZE MONEY?!
OF COURSE NOT.
EVEN THE BAKERY WORLD CUP, THE BIGGEST TOURNAMENT IN THE WORLD, DOESN'T BOAST THAT BIG A PRIZE.
WHAT IS IT THEN?!
GAMBLING.
?!
?!
?!
It's cramped...

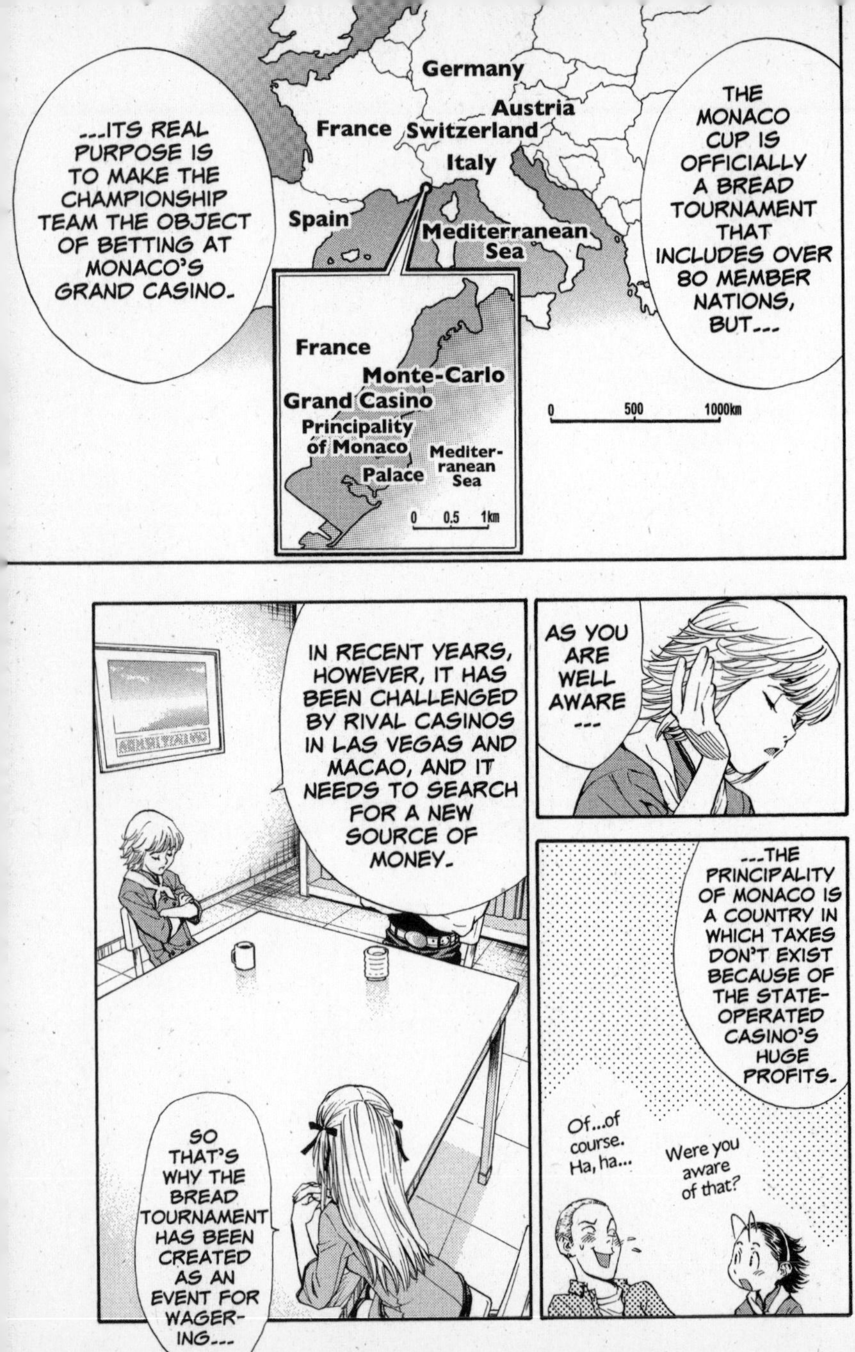
THE MONACO CUP IS OFFICIALLY A BREAD TOURNAMENT THAT INCLUDES OVER 80 MEMBER NATIONS, BUT...
...ITS REAL PURPOSE IS TO MAKE THE CHAMPIONSHIP TEAM THE OBJECT OF BETTING AT MONACO'S GRAND CASINO.
Germany
Austria
France
Switzerland
Italy
Spain
Mediterranean Sea
0 500 1000km
France
Monte-Carlo
Grand Casino
Principality of Monaco
Palace
Mediterranean Sea
0 0.5 1km
AS YOU ARE WELL AWARE...
...THE PRINCIPALITY OF MONACO IS A COUNTRY IN WHICH TAXES DON'T EXIST BECAUSE OF THE STATE-OPERATED CASINO'S HUGE PROFITS.
Were you aware of that?
Of...of course. Ha, ha...
IN RECENT YEARS, HOWEVER, IT HAS BEEN CHALLENGED BY RIVAL CASINOS IN LAS VEGAS AND MACAO, AND IT NEEDS TO SEARCH FOR A NEW SOURCE OF MONEY.
SO THAT'S WHY THE BREAD TOURNAMENT HAS BEEN CREATED AS AN EVENT FOR WAGER-ING...

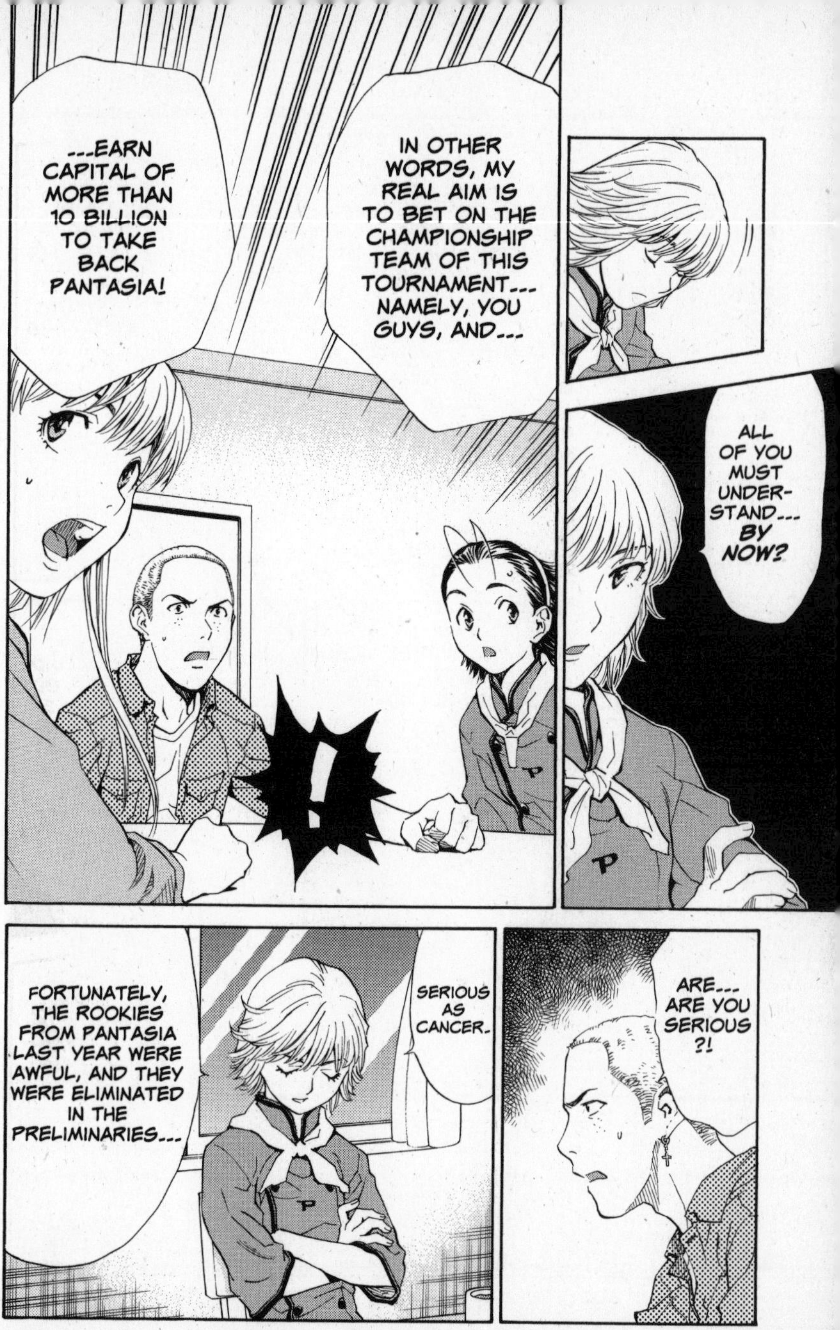
ALL OF YOU MUST UNDER-STAND... BY NOW?
IN OTHER WORDS, MY REAL AIM IS TO BET ON THE CHAMPIONSHIP TEAM OF THIS TOURNAMENT... NAMELY, YOU GUYS, AND...
...EARN CAPITAL OF MORE THAN 10 BILLION TO TAKE BACK PANTASIA!
!
ARE... ARE YOU SERIOUS ?!
SERIOUS AS CANCER.
FORTUNATELY, THE ROOKIES FROM PANTASIA LAST YEAR WERE AWFUL, AND THEY WERE ELIMINATED IN THE PRELIMINARIES...

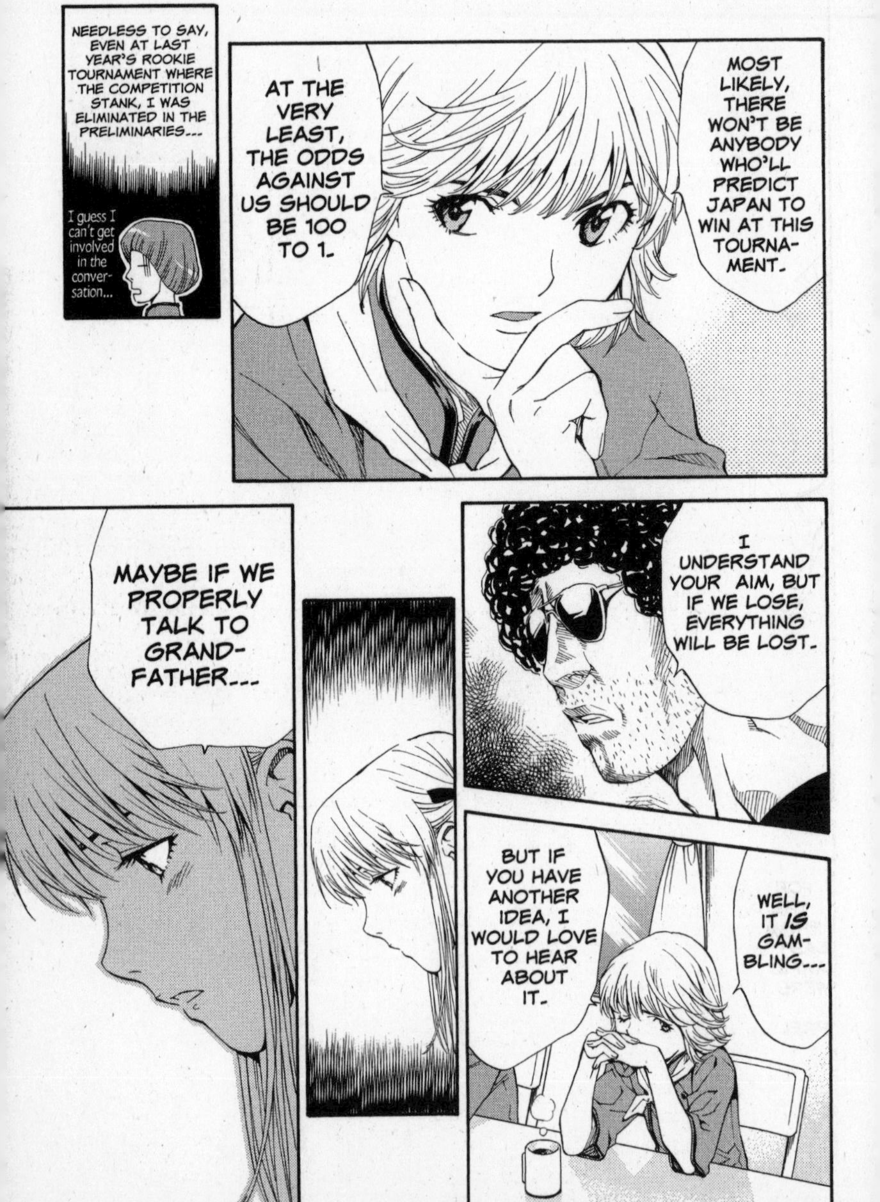
MOST LIKELY, THERE WON'T BE ANYBODY WHO'LL PREDICT JAPAN TO WIN AT THIS TOURNA-MENT.
AT THE VERY LEAST, THE ODDS AGAINST US SHOULD BE 100 TO 1.
NEEDLESS TO SAY, EVEN AT LAST YEAR'S ROOKIE TOURNAMENT WHERE THE COMPETITION STANK, I WAS ELIMINATED IN THE PRELIMINARIES...
I guess I can't get involved in the conver-sation...
I UNDERSTAND YOUR AIM, BUT IF WE LOSE, EVERYTHING WILL BE LOST.
WELL, IT *IS* GAM-BLING...
BUT IF YOU HAVE ANOTHER IDEA, I WOULD LOVE TO HEAR ABOUT IT.
MAYBE IF WE PROPERLY TALK TO GRAND-FATHER...

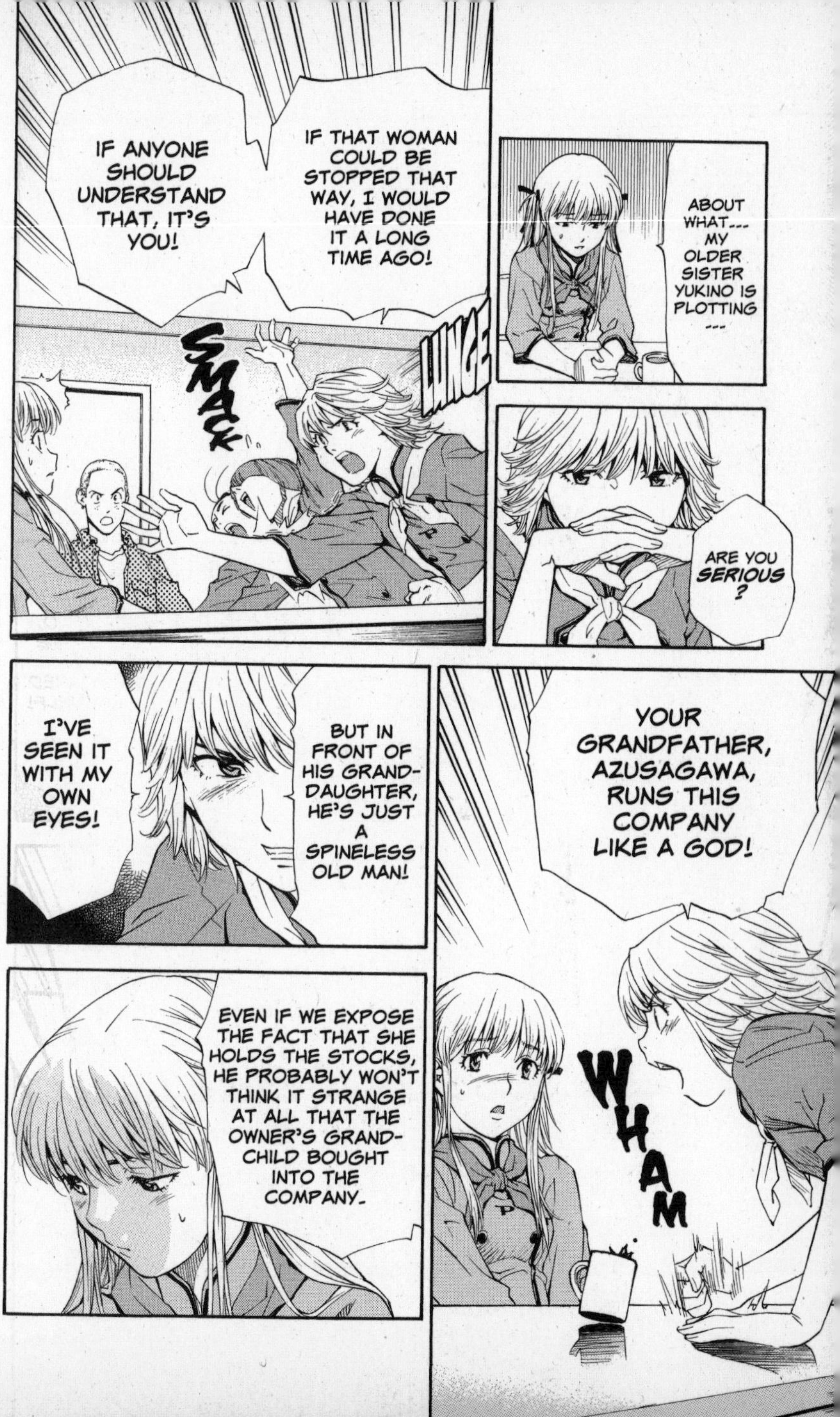
ABOUT WHAT... MY OLDER SISTER YUKINO IS PLOTTING...
ARE YOU SERIOUS?
IF THAT WOMAN COULD BE STOPPED THAT WAY, I WOULD HAVE DONE IT A LONG TIME AGO!
IF ANYONE SHOULD UNDERSTAND THAT, IT'S YOU!
LUNGE
SMACK
YOUR GRANDFATHER, AZUSAGAWA, RUNS THIS COMPANY LIKE A GOD!
WHAM
BUT IN FRONT OF HIS GRAND-DAUGHTER, HE'S JUST A SPINELESS OLD MAN!
I'VE SEEN IT WITH MY OWN EYES!
EVEN IF WE EXPOSE THE FACT THAT SHE HOLDS THE STOCKS, HE PROBABLY WON'T THINK IT STRANGE AT ALL THAT THE OWNER'S GRAND-CHILD BOUGHT INTO THE COMPANY.

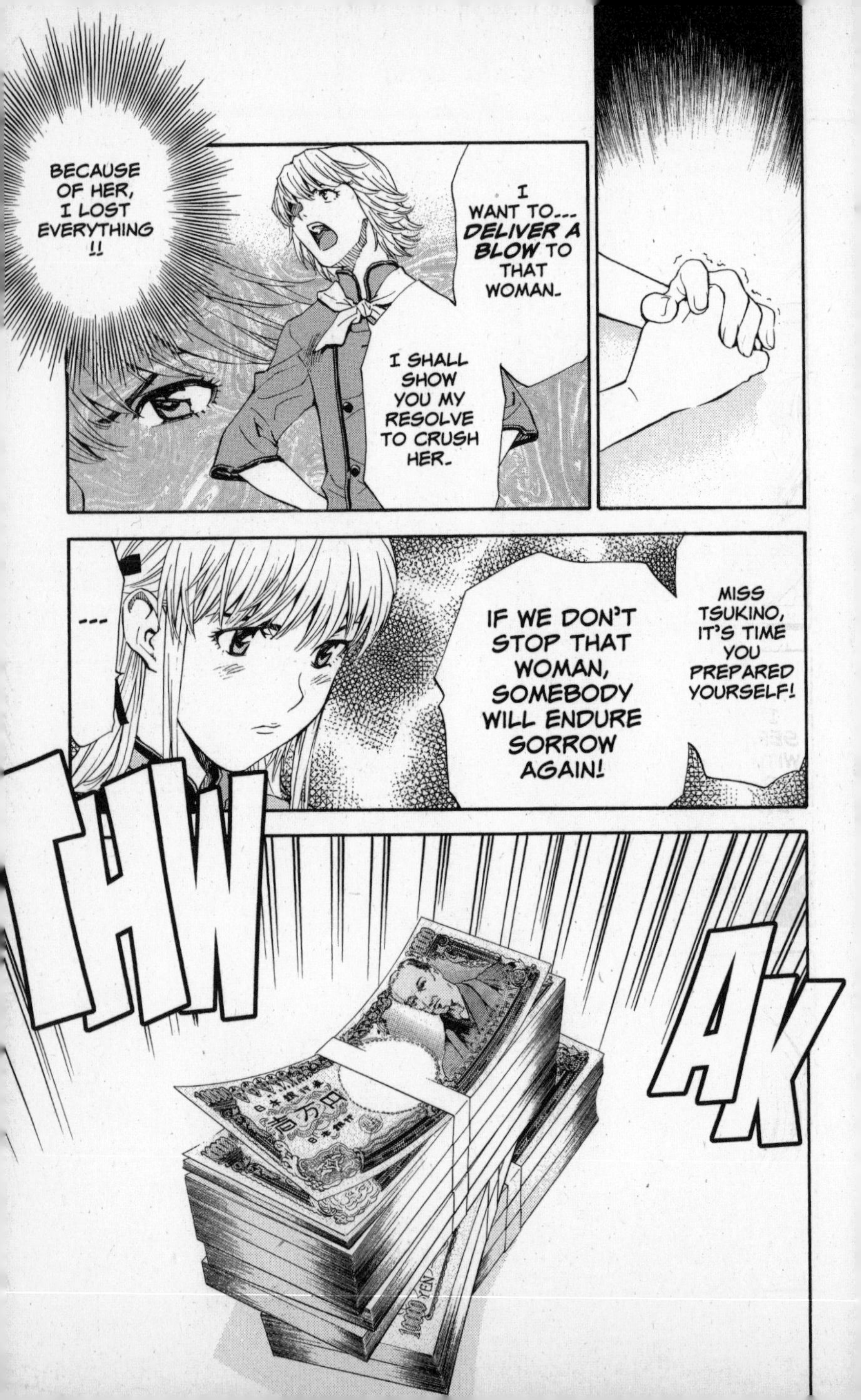

I WANT TO... **DELIVER A BLOW** TO THAT WOMAN.
I SHALL SHOW YOU MY RESOLVE TO CRUSH HER.
BECAUSE OF HER, I LOST EVERYTHING!!
MISS TSUKINO, IT'S TIME YOU PREPARED YOURSELF!
IF WE DON'T STOP THAT WOMAN, SOMEBODY WILL ENDURE SORROW AGAIN!
...
THWAK

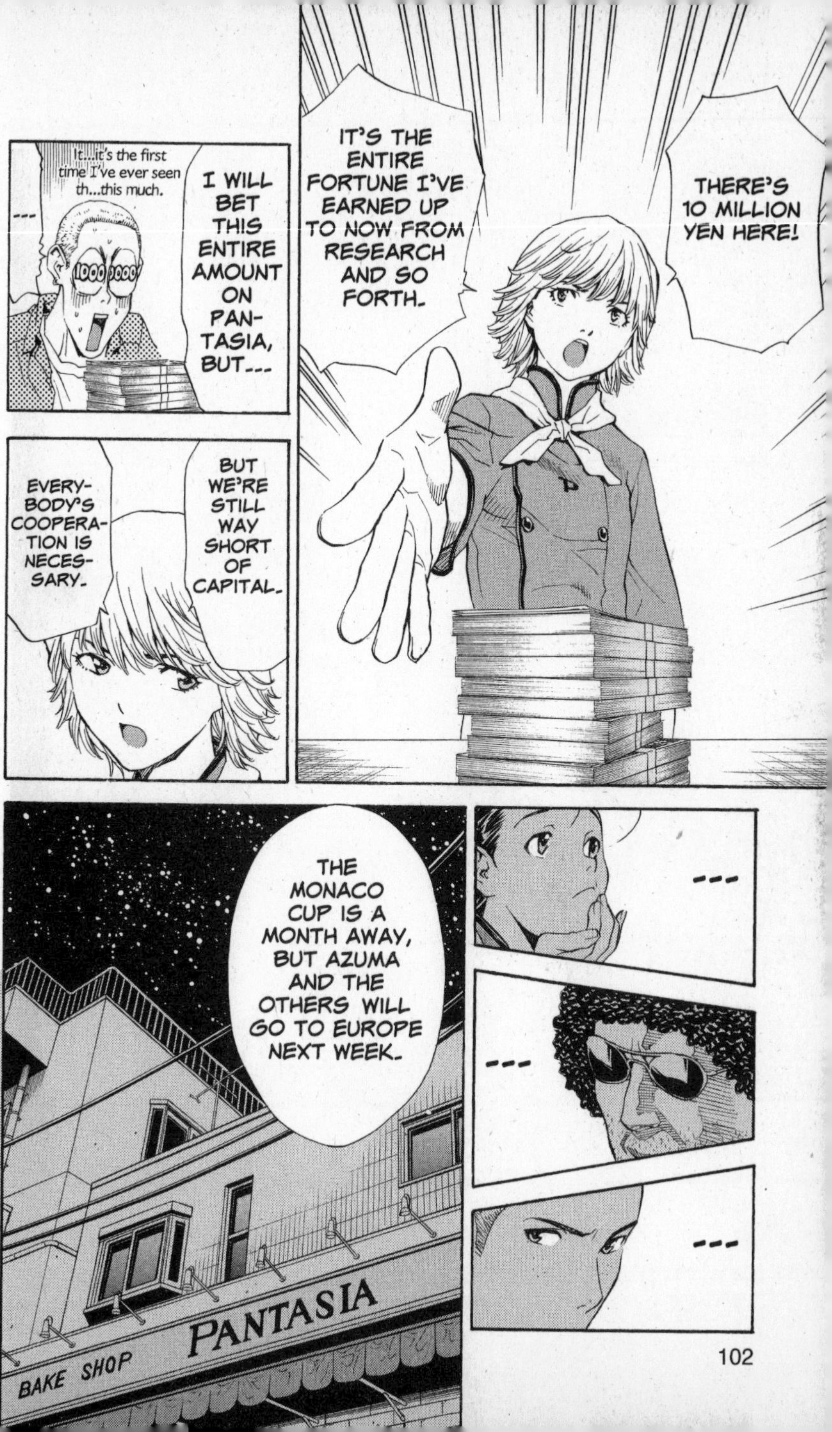
THERE'S 10 MILLION YEN HERE!
IT'S THE ENTIRE FORTUNE I'VE EARNED UP TO NOW FROM RESEARCH AND SO FORTH.
I WILL BET THIS ENTIRE AMOUNT ON PANTASIA, BUT...
It...it's the first time I've ever seen th...this much.
...
1000 0000
BUT WE'RE STILL WAY SHORT OF CAPITAL.
EVERYBODY'S COOPERATION IS NECESSARY.
...
...
...
THE MONACO CUP IS A MONTH AWAY, BUT AZUMA AND THE OTHERS WILL GO TO EUROPE NEXT WEEK.
PANTASIA
BAKE SHOP

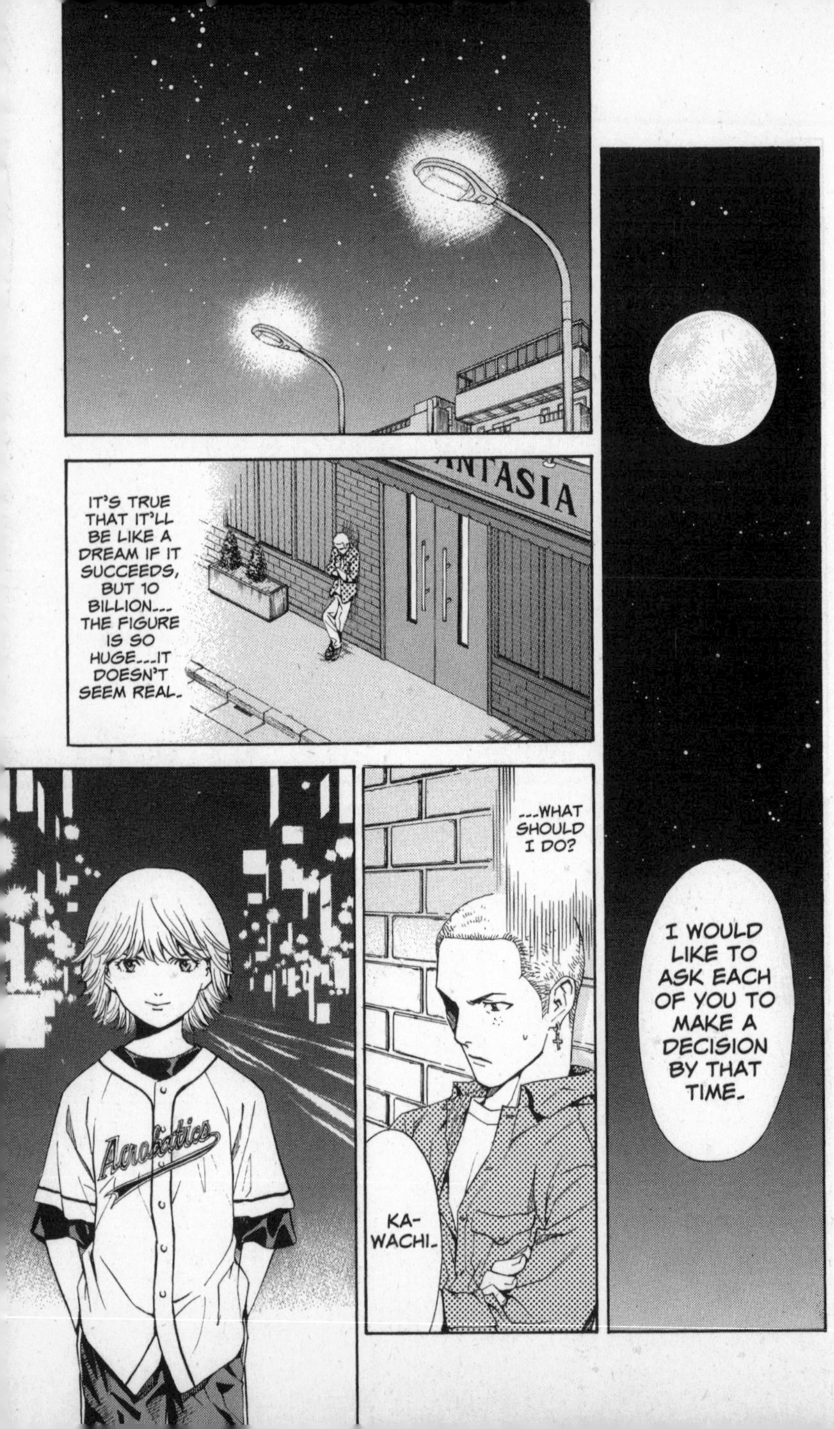
I WOULD LIKE TO ASK EACH OF YOU TO MAKE A DECISION BY THAT TIME.
IT'S TRUE THAT IT'LL BE LIKE A DREAM IF IT SUCCEEDS, BUT 10 BILLION... THE FIGURE IS SO HUGE...IT DOESN'T SEEM REAL.
...WHAT SHOULD I DO?
KA-WACHI.

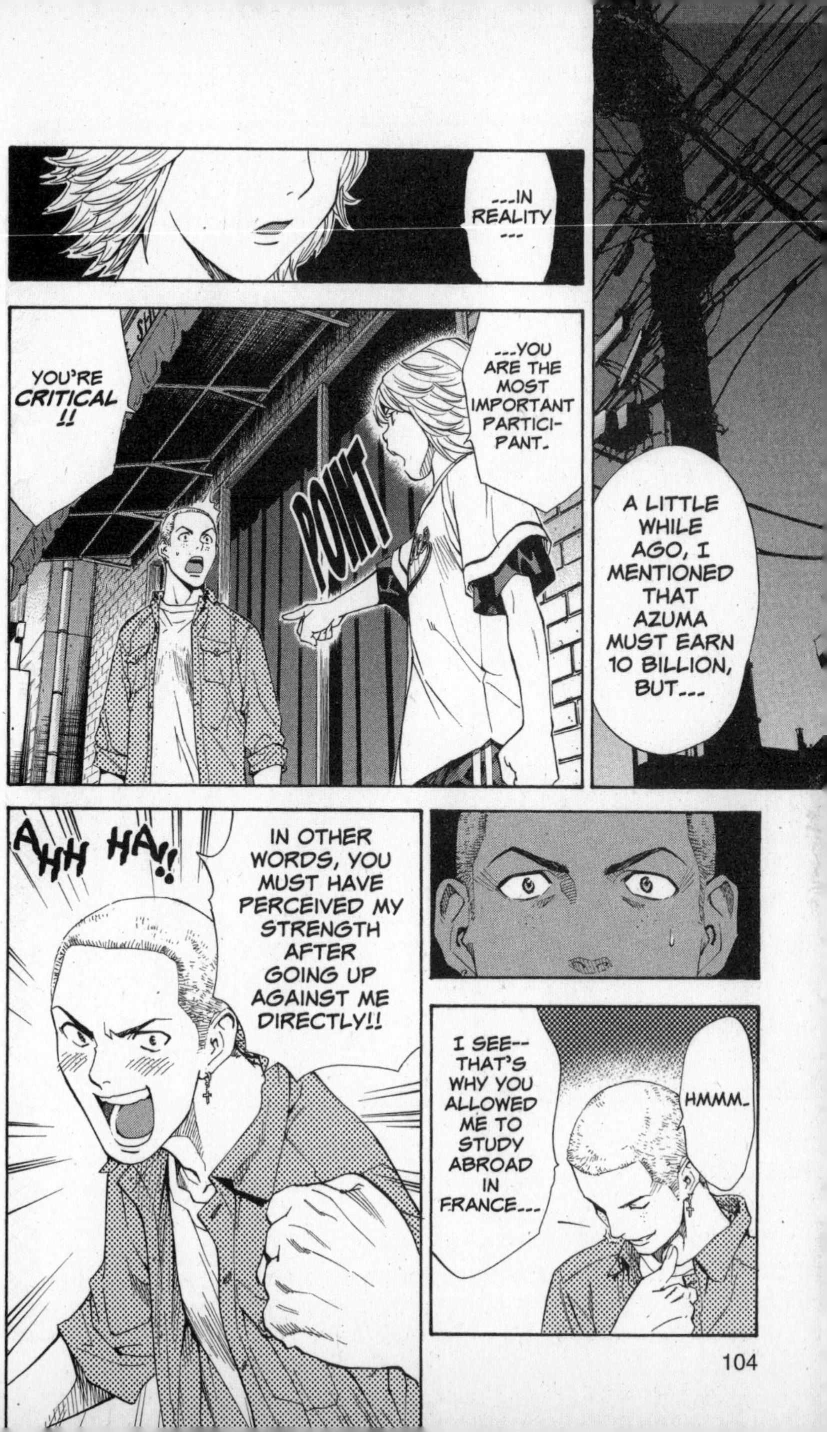
A LITTLE WHILE AGO, I MENTIONED THAT AZUMA MUST EARN 10 BILLION, BUT...
...IN REALITY...
...YOU ARE THE MOST IMPORTANT PARTICI-PANT.
POINT
YOU'RE CRITICAL !!
HMMM.
I SEE-- THAT'S WHY YOU ALLOWED ME TO STUDY ABROAD IN FRANCE...
IN OTHER WORDS, YOU MUST HAVE PERCEIVED MY STRENGTH AFTER GOING UP AGAINST ME DIRECTLY!!
AHH HA!!

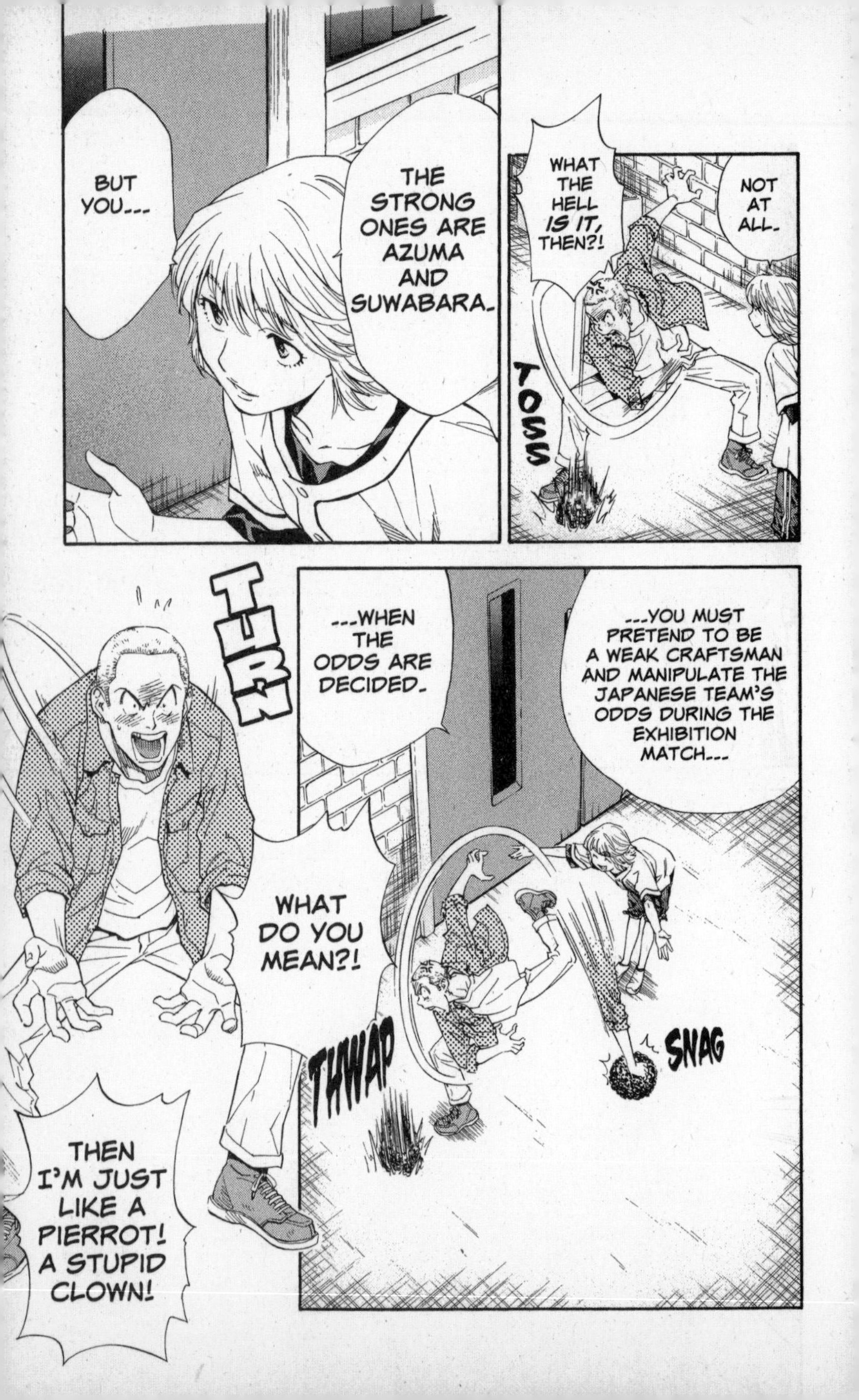
NOT AT ALL.
WHAT THE HELL IS IT, THEN?!
TOSS
THE STRONG ONES ARE AZUMA AND SUWABARA.
BUT YOU...
...YOU MUST PRETEND TO BE A WEAK CRAFTSMAN AND MANIPULATE THE JAPANESE TEAM'S ODDS DURING THE EXHIBITION MATCH...
...WHEN THE ODDS ARE DECIDED.
WHAT DO YOU MEAN?!
SNAG
THWAP
TURN
THEN I'M JUST LIKE A PIERROT! A STUPID CLOWN!

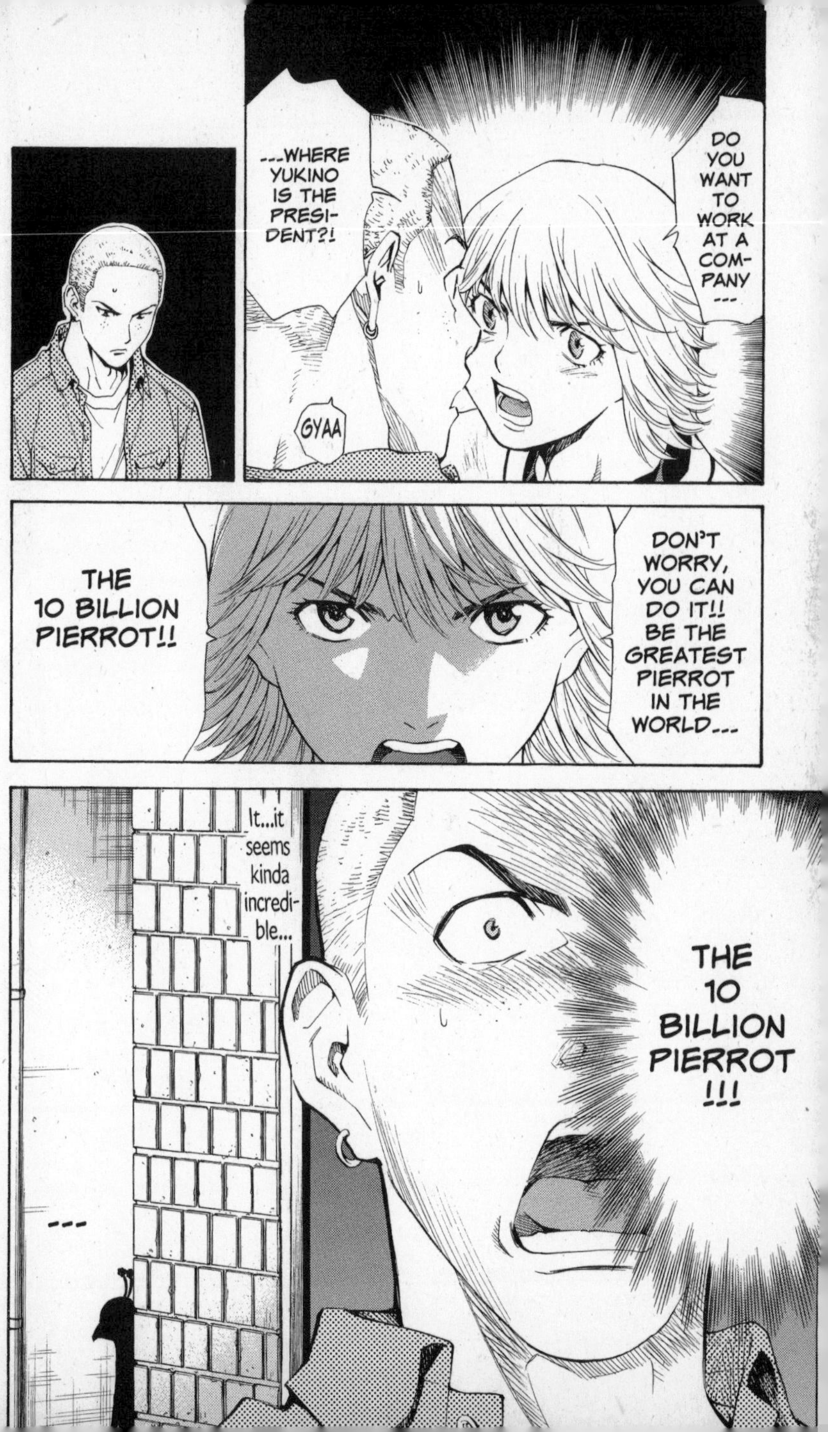
DO YOU WANT TO WORK AT A COMPANY---
---WHERE YUKINO IS THE PRESIDENT?!
GYAA
DON'T WORRY, YOU CAN DO IT!! BE THE GREATEST PIERROT IN THE WORLD---
THE 10 BILLION PIERROT!!
THE 10 BILLION PIERROT!!!
It...it seems kinda incredible...

Story 56: Take-Out

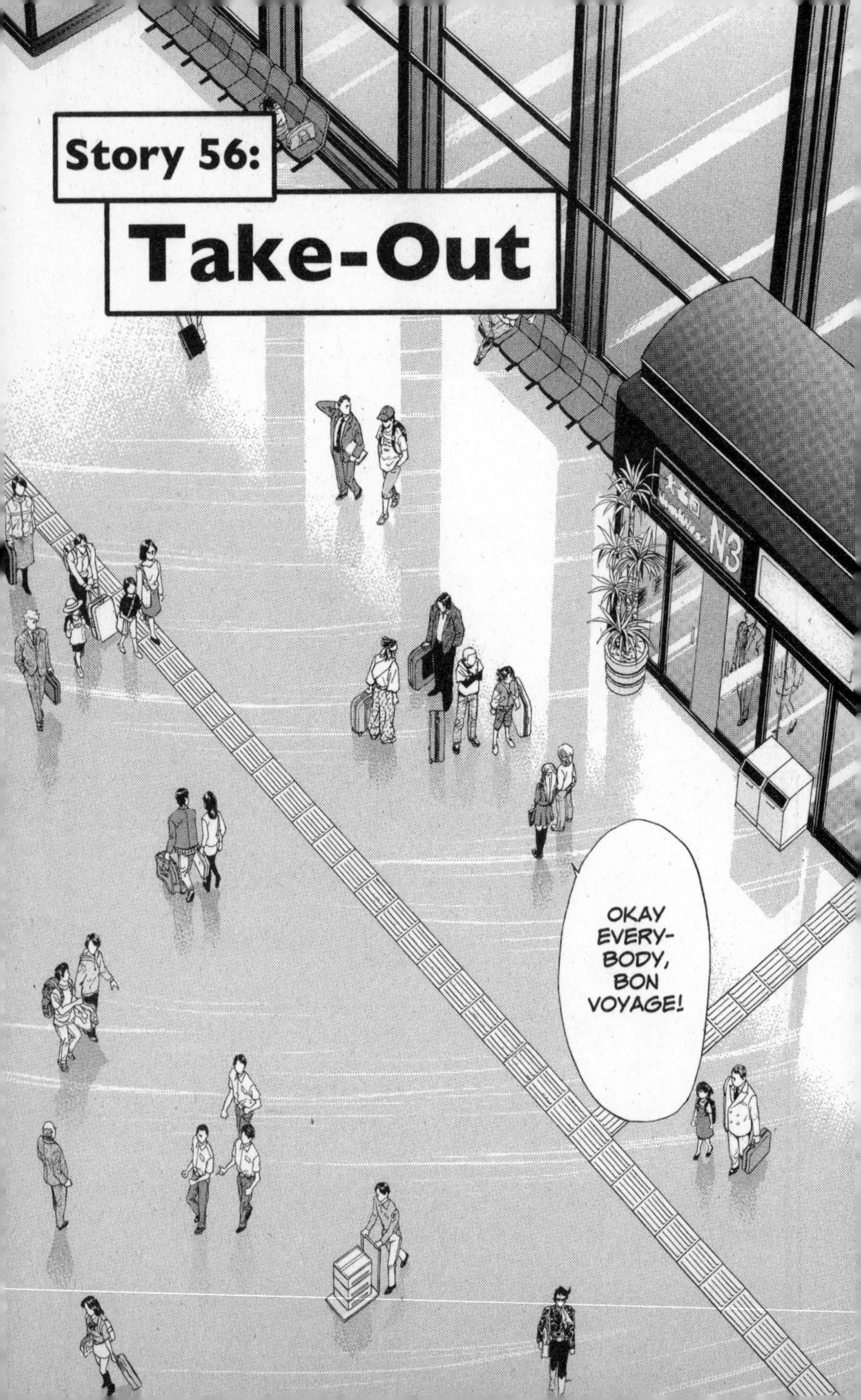
N3
OKAY EVERY-BODY, BON VOYAGE!

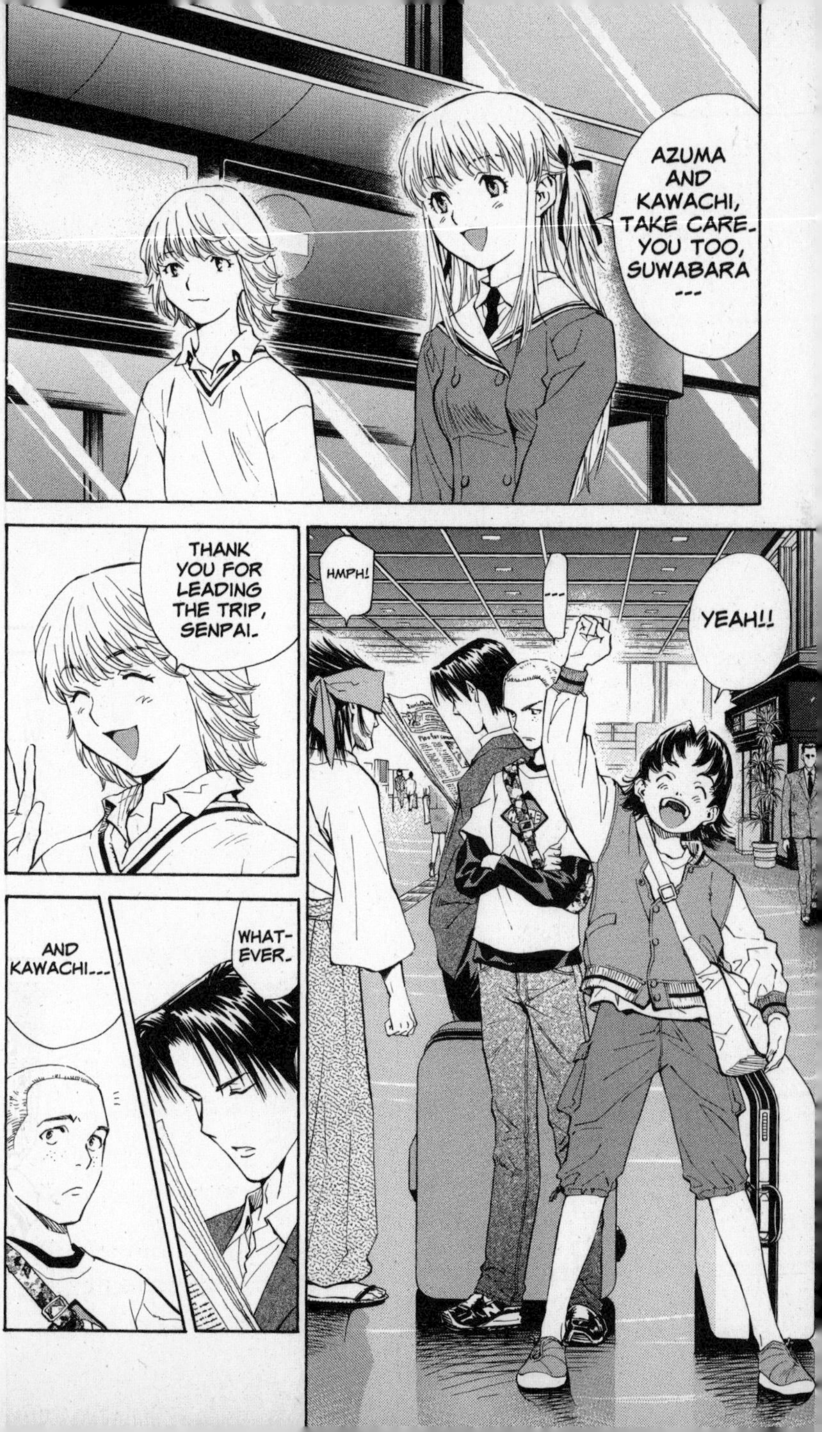
AZUMA AND KAWACHI, TAKE CARE. YOU TOO, SUWABARA...
YEAH!!
...
HMPH!
THANK YOU FOR LEADING THE TRIP, SENPAI.
WHAT-EVER.
AND KAWACHI...

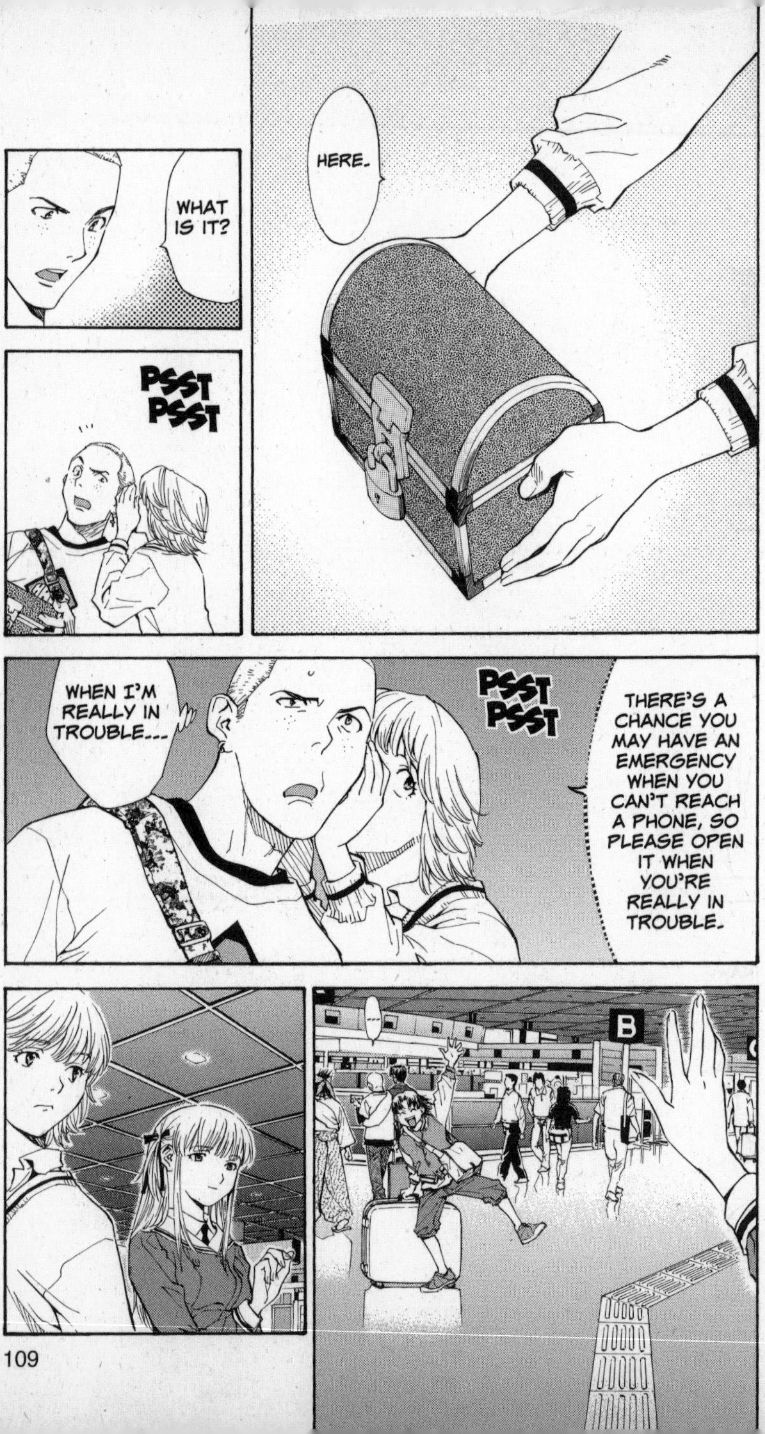
HERE.
WHAT IS IT?
PSST PSST
PSST PSST
THERE'S A CHANCE YOU MAY HAVE AN EMERGENCY WHEN YOU CAN'T REACH A PHONE, SO PLEASE OPEN IT WHEN YOU'RE REALLY IN TROUBLE.
WHEN I'M REALLY IN TROUBLE...
...
B

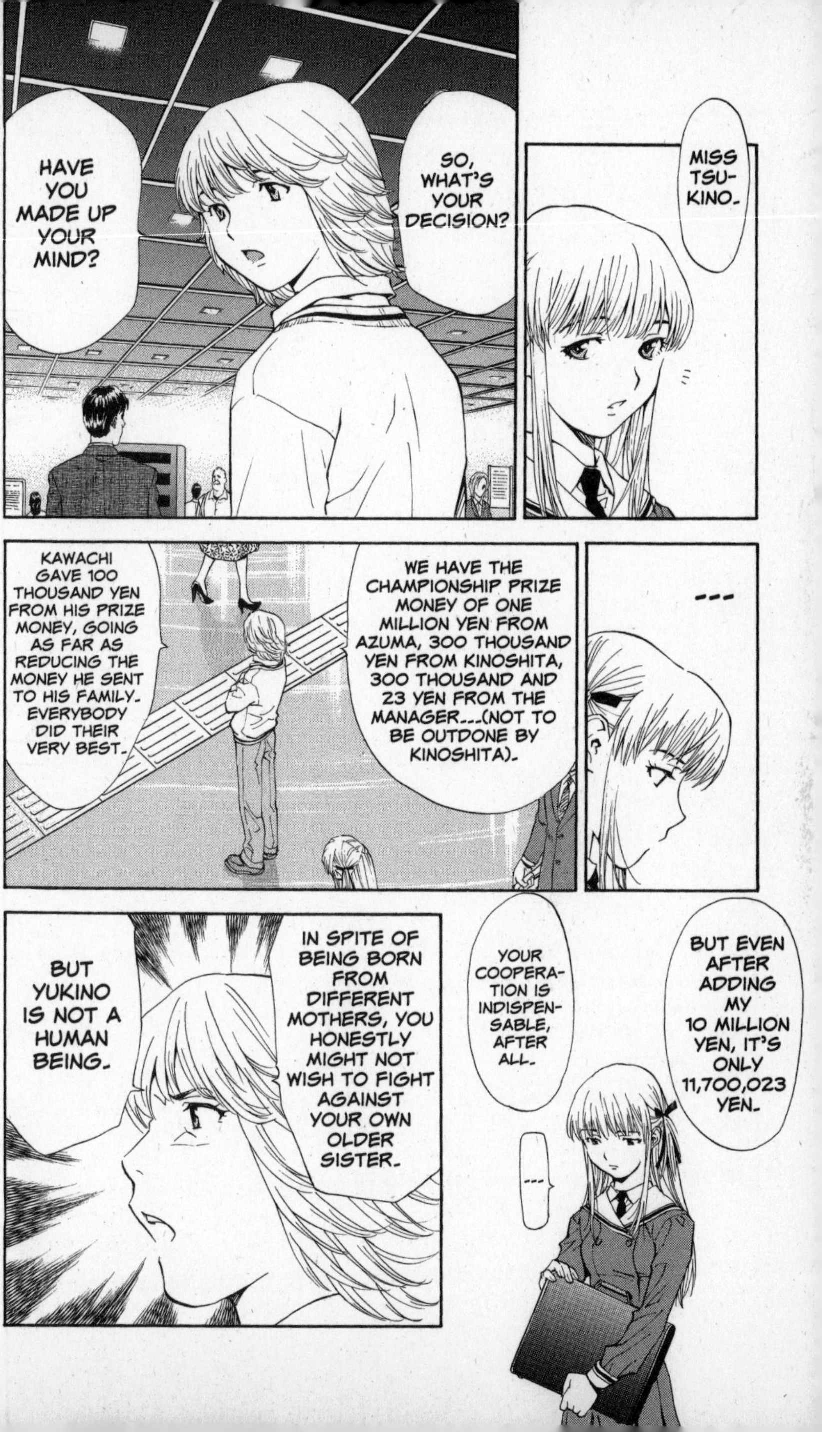
MISS TSU-KINO.
SO, WHAT'S YOUR DECISION?
HAVE YOU MADE UP YOUR MIND?
...
WE HAVE THE CHAMPIONSHIP PRIZE MONEY OF ONE MILLION YEN FROM AZUMA, 300 THOUSAND YEN FROM KINOSHITA, 300 THOUSAND AND 23 YEN FROM THE MANAGER...(NOT TO BE OUTDONE BY KINOSHITA).
KAWACHI GAVE 100 THOUSAND YEN FROM HIS PRIZE MONEY, GOING AS FAR AS REDUCING THE MONEY HE SENT TO HIS FAMILY. EVERYBODY DID THEIR VERY BEST.
BUT EVEN AFTER ADDING MY 10 MILLION YEN, IT'S ONLY 11,700,023 YEN.
YOUR COOPERATION IS INDISPENSABLE, AFTER ALL.
...
IN SPITE OF BEING BORN FROM DIFFERENT MOTHERS, YOU HONESTLY MIGHT NOT WISH TO FIGHT AGAINST YOUR OWN OLDER SISTER.
BUT YUKINO IS NOT A HUMAN BEING.

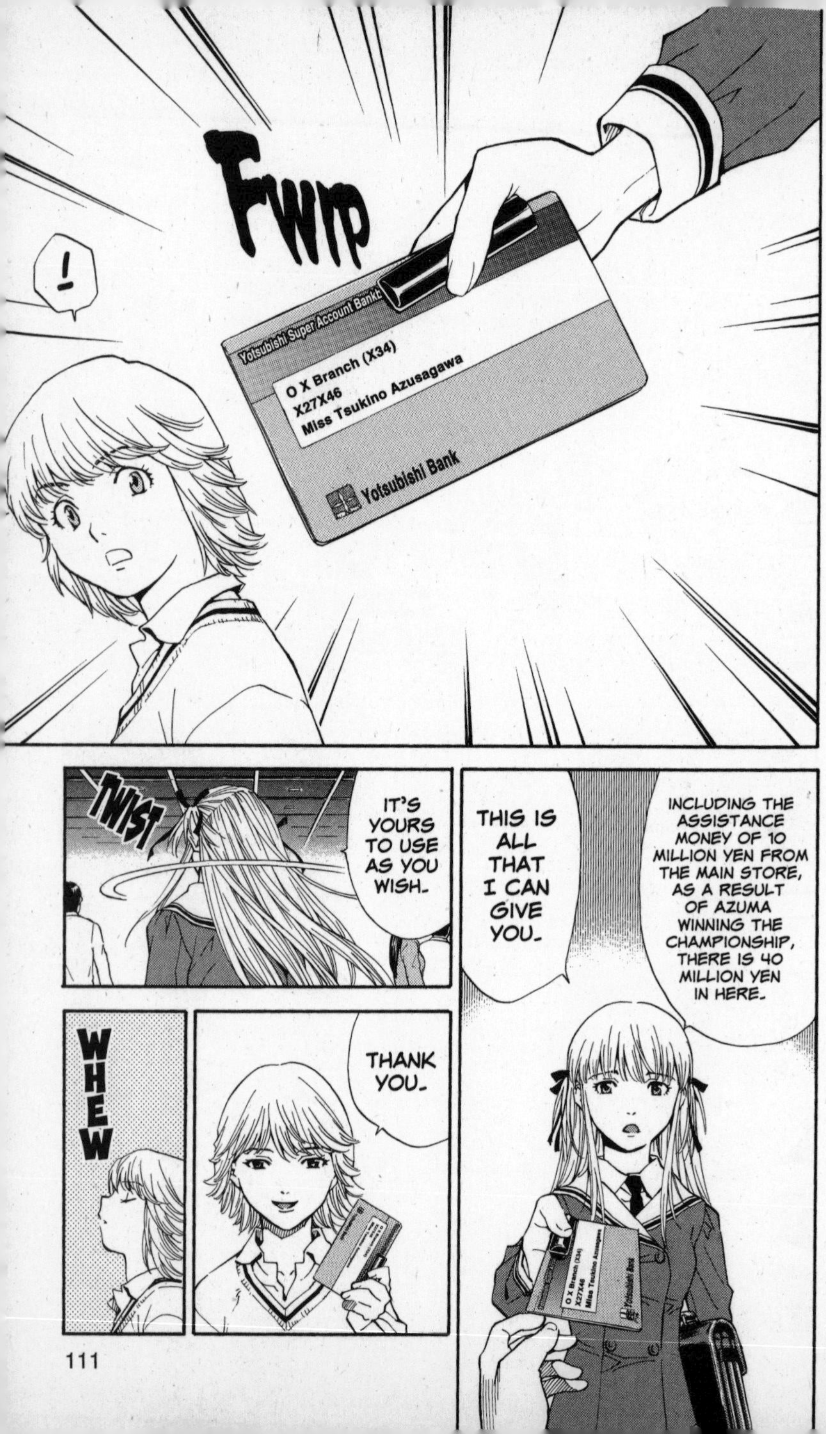

FWIP
!
Yotsubishi Super Account Bankb
O X Branch (X34)
X27X46
Miss Tsukino Azusagawa
Yotsubishi Bank
INCLUDING THE ASSISTANCE MONEY OF 10 MILLION YEN FROM THE MAIN STORE, AS A RESULT OF AZUMA WINNING THE CHAMPIONSHIP, THERE IS 40 MILLION YEN IN HERE.
THIS IS ALL THAT I CAN GIVE YOU.
TWIST
IT'S YOURS TO USE AS YOU WISH.
THANK YOU.
WHEW

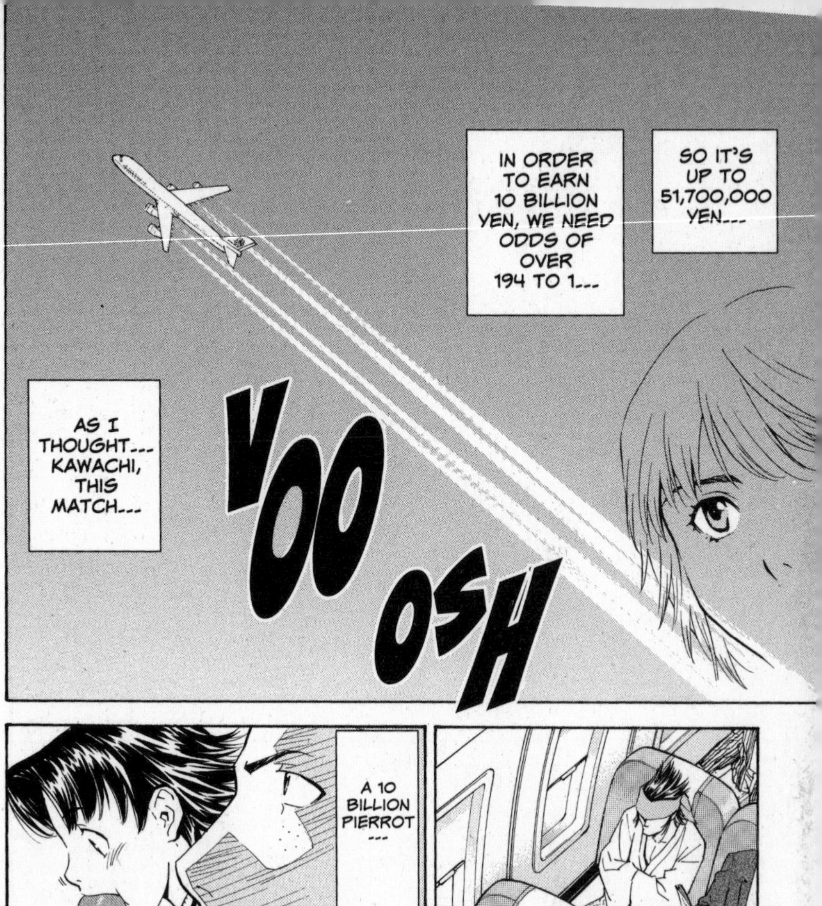
SO IT'S UP TO 51,700,000 YEN...
IN ORDER TO EARN 10 BILLION YEN, WE NEED ODDS OF OVER 194 TO 1...
VOOOSH
AS I THOUGHT... KAWACHI, THIS MATCH...
...DEPENDS ON HOW GOOD OF AN ACTOR YOU CAN BE!!
A 10 BILLION PIERROT ...
I UNDERSTAND IT'S MY ROLE TO MAKE IT APPEAR THAT THE JAPANESE TEAM IS WEAK...SO WE CAN MANIPULATE THE ODDS AT THE CASINO, BUT...
...WHY DOES IT HAVE TO BE ME?
MEE MEE FRANCE

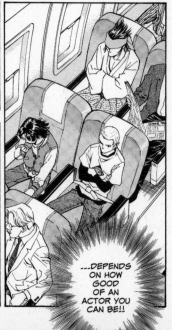

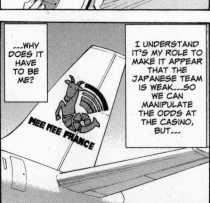

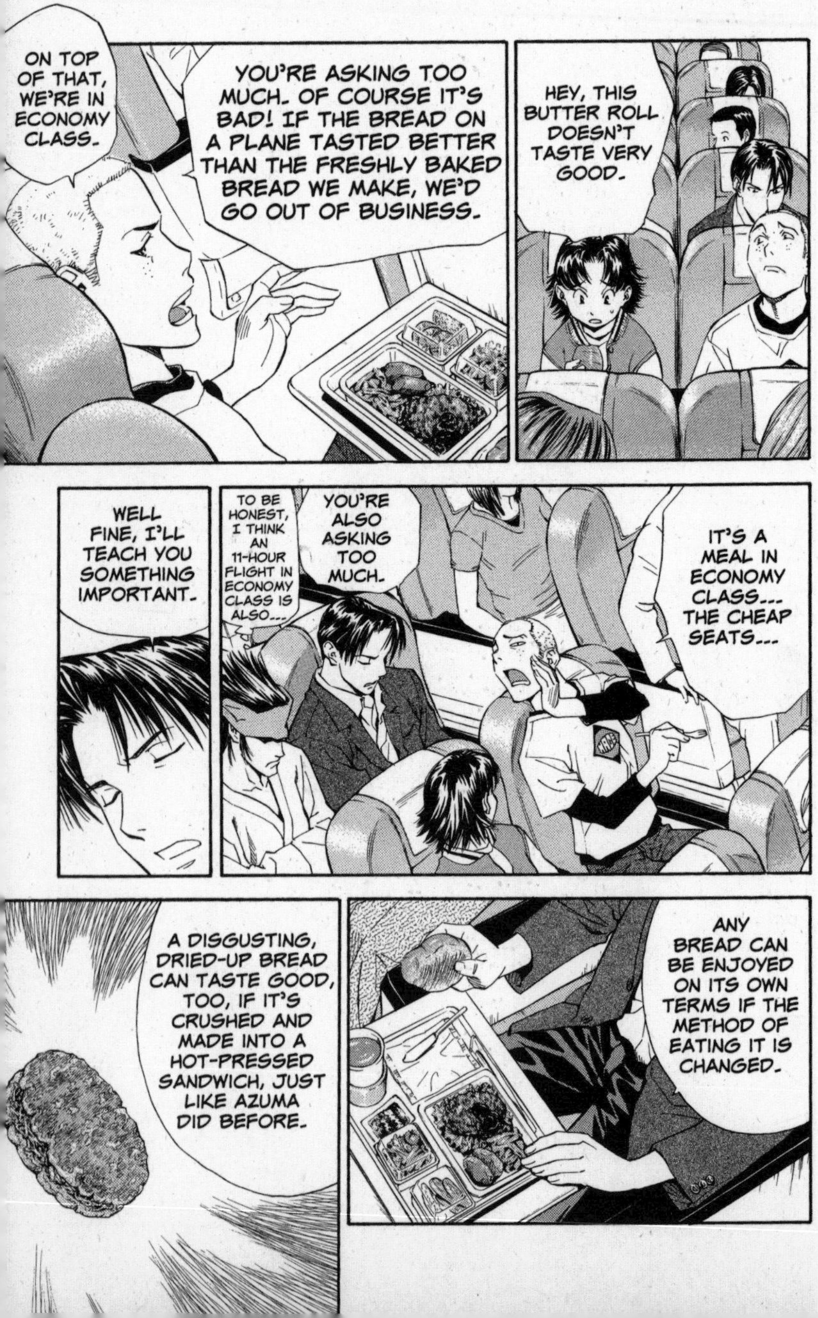
HEY, THIS BUTTER ROLL DOESN'T TASTE VERY GOOD.
YOU'RE ASKING TOO MUCH. OF COURSE IT'S BAD! IF THE BREAD ON A PLANE TASTED BETTER THAN THE FRESHLY BAKED BREAD WE MAKE, WE'D GO OUT OF BUSINESS.
ON TOP OF THAT, WE'RE IN ECONOMY CLASS.
IT'S A MEAL IN ECONOMY CLASS... THE CHEAP SEATS...
YOU'RE ALSO ASKING TOO MUCH.
TO BE HONEST, I THINK AN 11-HOUR FLIGHT IN ECONOMY CLASS IS ALSO...
WELL FINE, I'LL TEACH YOU SOMETHING IMPORTANT.
ANY BREAD CAN BE ENJOYED ON ITS OWN TERMS IF THE METHOD OF EATING IT IS CHANGED.
A DISGUSTING, DRIED-UP BREAD CAN TASTE GOOD, TOO, IF IT'S CRUSHED AND MADE INTO A HOT-PRESSED SANDWICH, JUST LIKE AZUMA DID BEFORE.

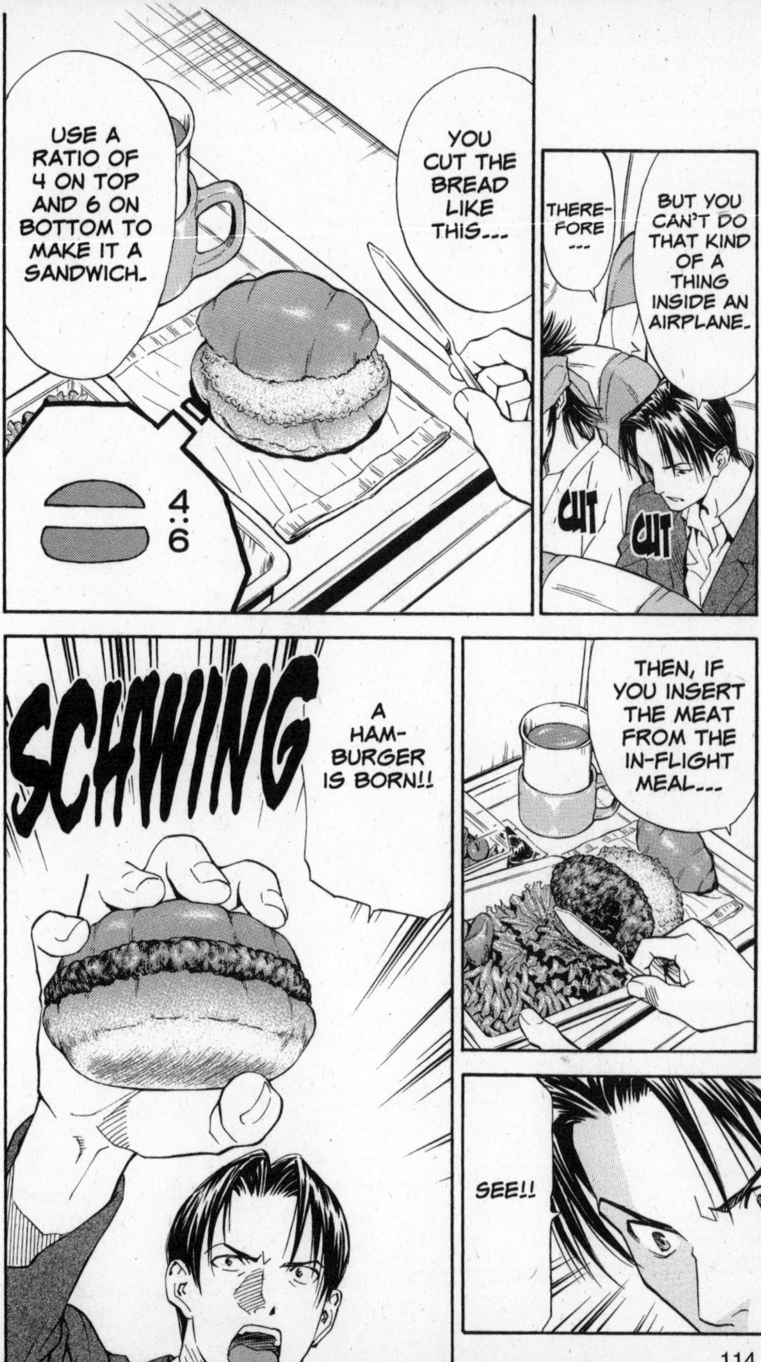
BUT YOU CAN'T DO THAT KIND OF A THING INSIDE AN AIRPLANE.
THERE-FORE ---
CUT
CUT
YOU CUT THE BREAD LIKE THIS---
USE A RATIO OF 4 ON TOP AND 6 ON BOTTOM TO MAKE IT A SANDWICH.
4:6
THEN, IF YOU INSERT THE MEAT FROM THE IN-FLIGHT MEAL---
SEE!!
A HAM-BURGER IS BORN!!
SCHWING

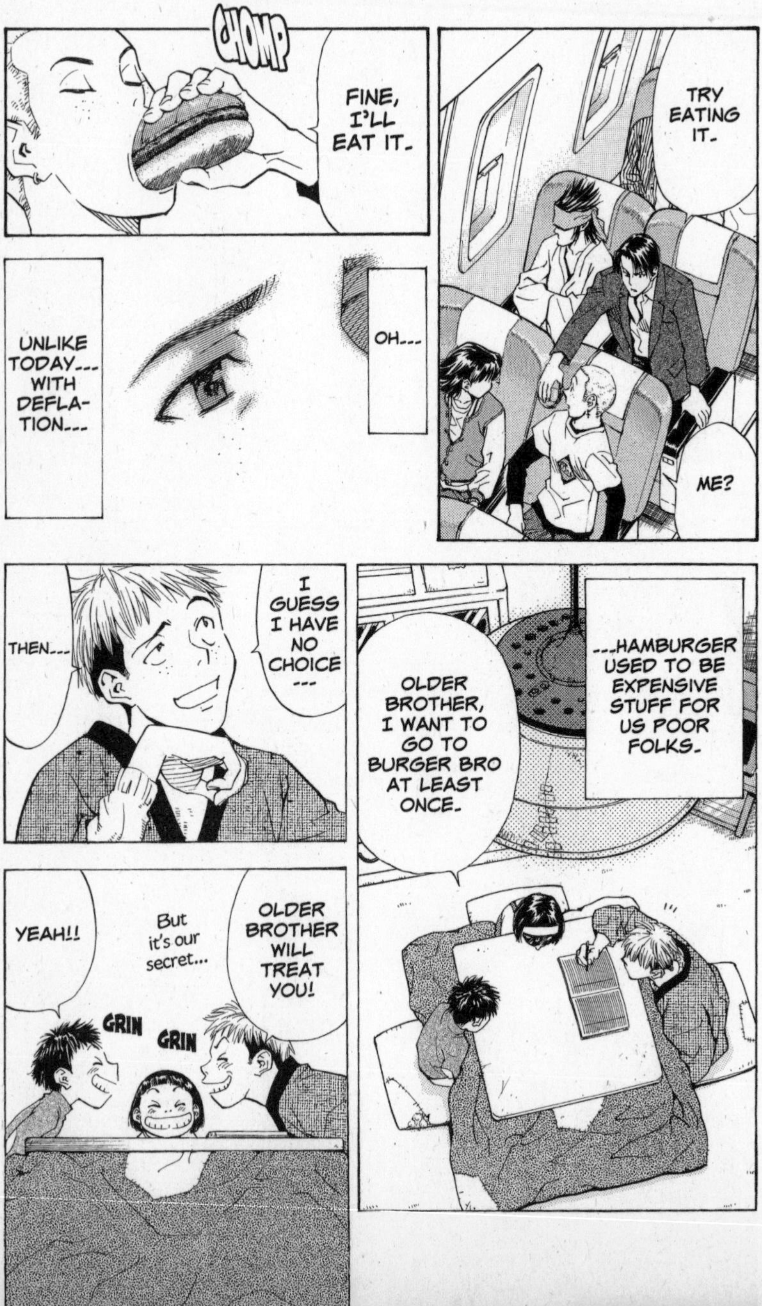
TRY EATING IT.
ME?
CHOMP
FINE, I'LL EAT IT.
OH...
UNLIKE TODAY... WITH DEFLA-TION...
...HAMBURGER USED TO BE EXPENSIVE STUFF FOR US POOR FOLKS.
OLDER BROTHER, I WANT TO GO TO BURGER BRO AT LEAST ONCE.
I GUESS I HAVE NO CHOICE...
THEN...
OLDER BROTHER WILL TREAT YOU!
But it's our secret...
GRIN
GRIN
YEAH!!

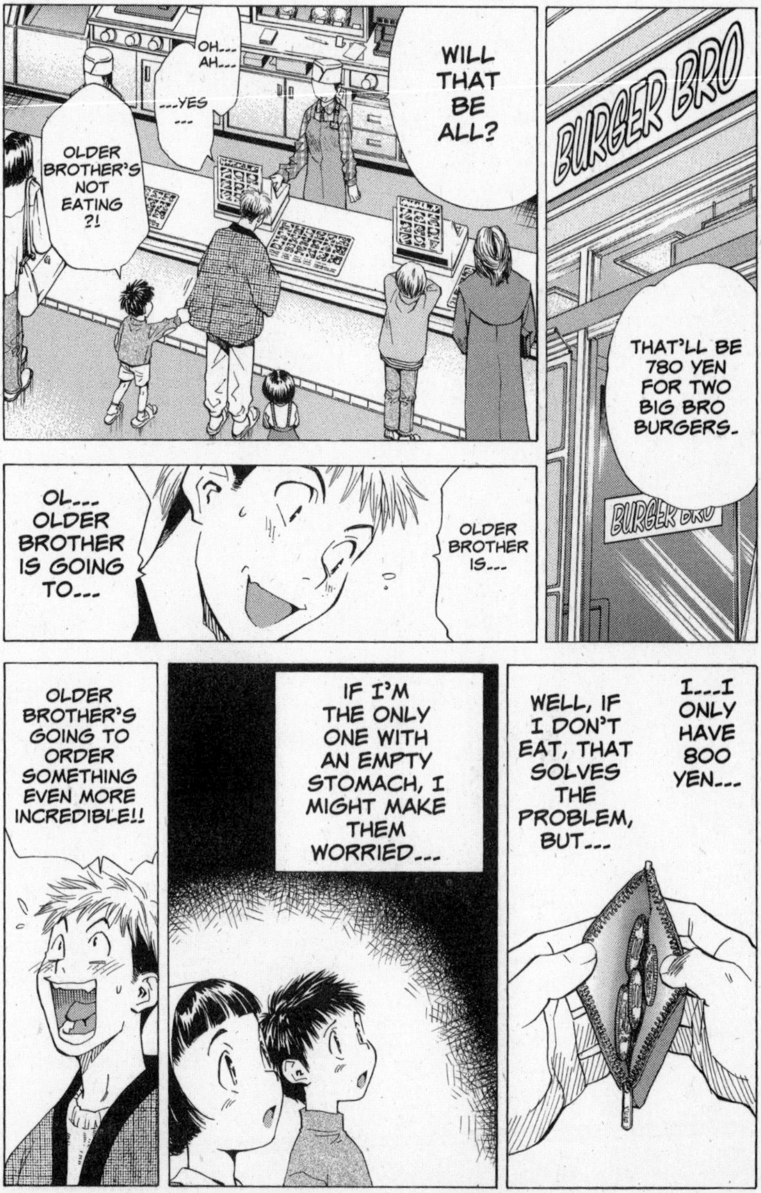

BURGER BRO
THAT'LL BE 780 YEN FOR TWO BIG BRO BURGERS.
BURGER BRO
WILL THAT BE ALL?
OH... AH...
...YES ...
OLDER BROTHER'S NOT EATING ?!
OLDER BROTHER IS...
OL... OLDER BROTHER IS GOING TO...
I...I ONLY HAVE 800 YEN...
WELL, IF I DON'T EAT, THAT SOLVES THE PROBLEM, BUT...
IF I'M THE ONLY ONE WITH AN EMPTY STOMACH, I MIGHT MAKE THEM WORRIED...
OLDER BROTHER'S GOING TO ORDER SOMETHING EVEN MORE INCREDIBLE!!

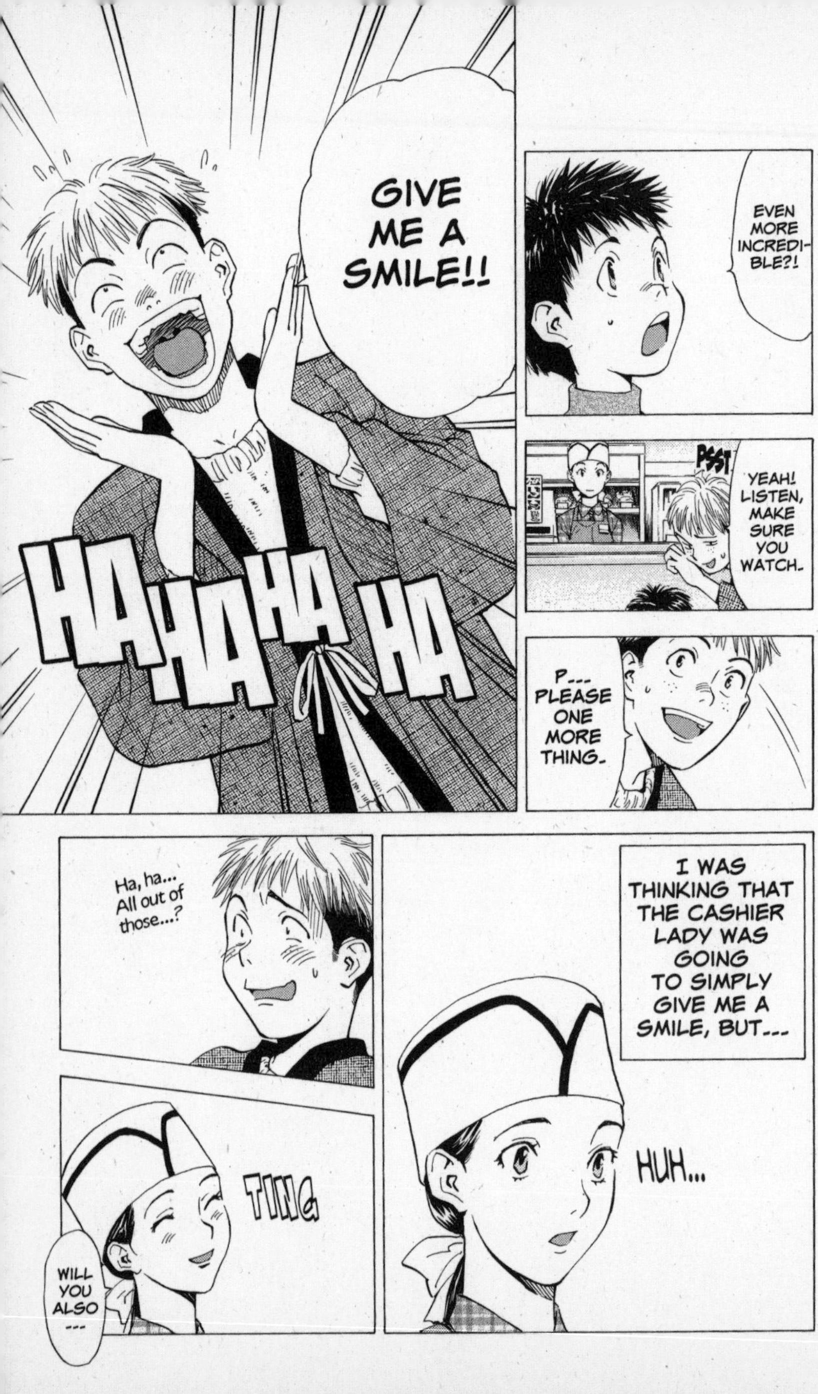
EVEN MORE INCREDI-BLE?!
PSST
YEAH! LISTEN, MAKE SURE YOU WATCH.
P... PLEASE ONE MORE THING.
GIVE ME A SMILE!!
HA HA HA HA HA HA
I WAS THINKING THAT THE CASHIER LADY WAS GOING TO SIMPLY GIVE ME A SMILE, BUT...
HUH...
Ha, ha... All out of those...?
TING
WILL YOU ALSO ---

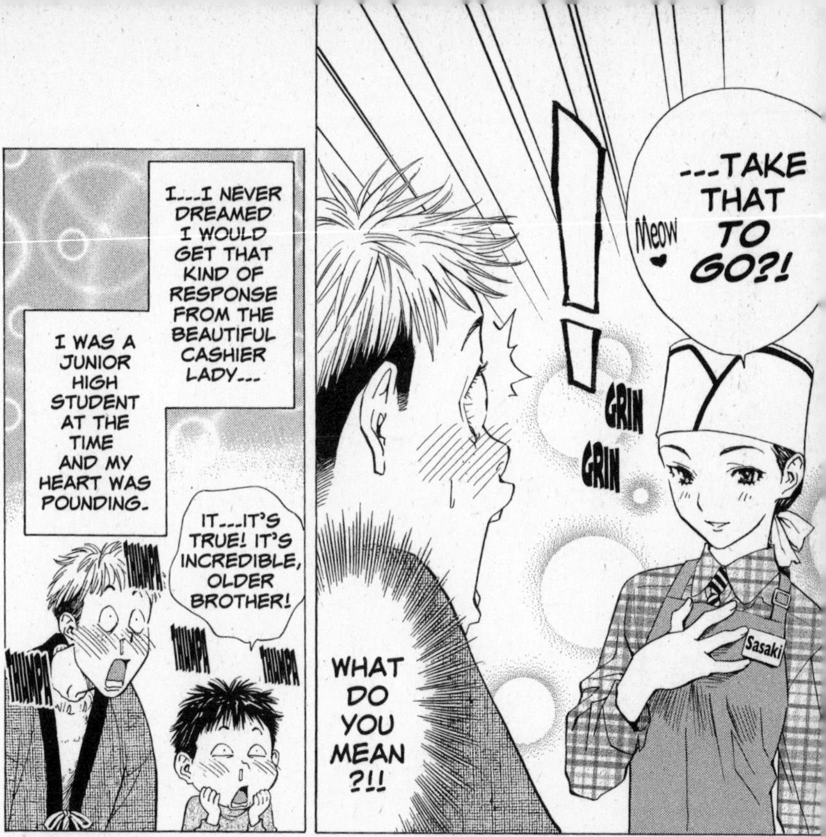
...TAKE THAT TO GO?!
Meow ♥
!
GRIN
GRIN
WHAT DO YOU MEAN ?!!
I...I NEVER DREAMED I WOULD GET THAT KIND OF RESPONSE FROM THE BEAUTIFUL CASHIER LADY...
I WAS A JUNIOR HIGH STUDENT AT THE TIME AND MY HEART WAS POUNDING.
IT...IT'S TRUE! IT'S INCREDIBLE, OLDER BROTHER!
THUMPA
THUMPA
THUMPA
THUMPA

*PART OF THIS WAS BASED ON THE TRUE EXPERIENCES OF THE AUTHOR AS WELL AS THE EDITOR IN CHARGE.

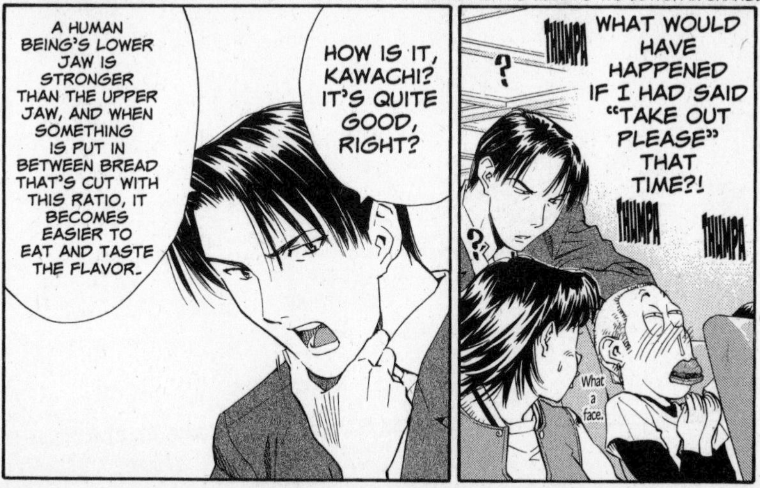
WHAT WOULD HAVE HAPPENED IF I HAD SAID "TAKE OUT PLEASE" THAT TIME?!
THUMPA
?
?
THUMPA
THUMPA
What a face.
HOW IS IT, KAWACHI? IT'S QUITE GOOD, RIGHT?
A HUMAN BEING'S LOWER JAW IS STRONGER THAN THE UPPER JAW, AND WHEN SOMETHING IS PUT IN BETWEEN BREAD THAT'S CUT WITH THIS RATIO, IT BECOMES EASIER TO EAT AND TASTE THE FLAVOR.

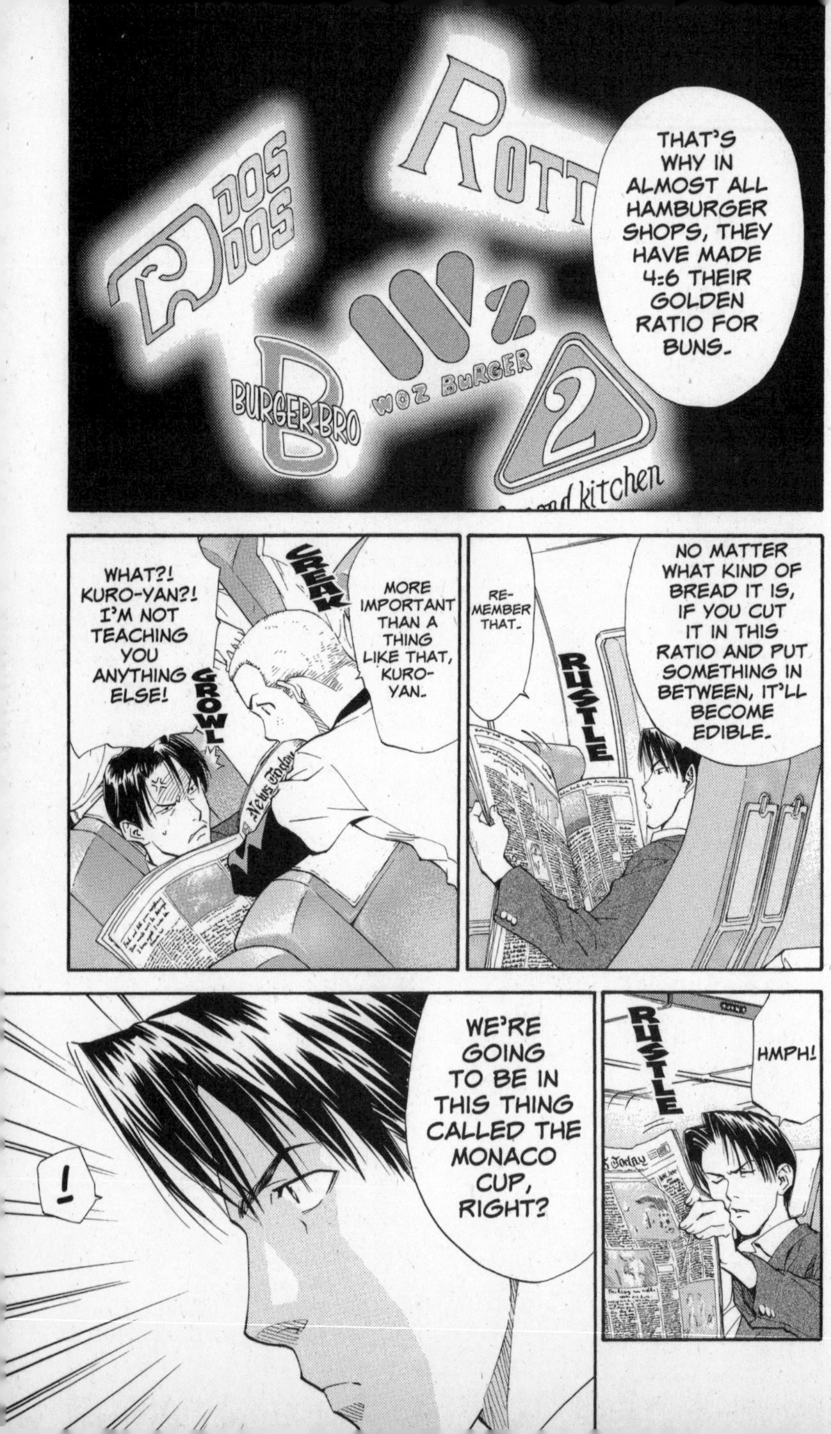
THAT'S WHY IN ALMOST ALL HAMBURGER SHOPS, THEY HAVE MADE 4:6 THEIR GOLDEN RATIO FOR BUNS.
ROTT
DOS DOS
WOZ BURGER
BURGER BRO
2
NO MATTER WHAT KIND OF BREAD IT IS, IF YOU CUT IT IN THIS RATIO AND PUT SOMETHING IN BETWEEN, IT'LL BECOME EDIBLE.
RE-MEMBER THAT.
RUSTLE
MORE IMPORTANT THAN A THING LIKE THAT, KURO-YAN.
CREAK
WHAT?! KURO-YAN?! I'M NOT TEACHING YOU ANYTHING ELSE!
GROWL
RUSTLE
HMPH!
WE'RE GOING TO BE IN THIS THING CALLED THE MONACO CUP, RIGHT?
!

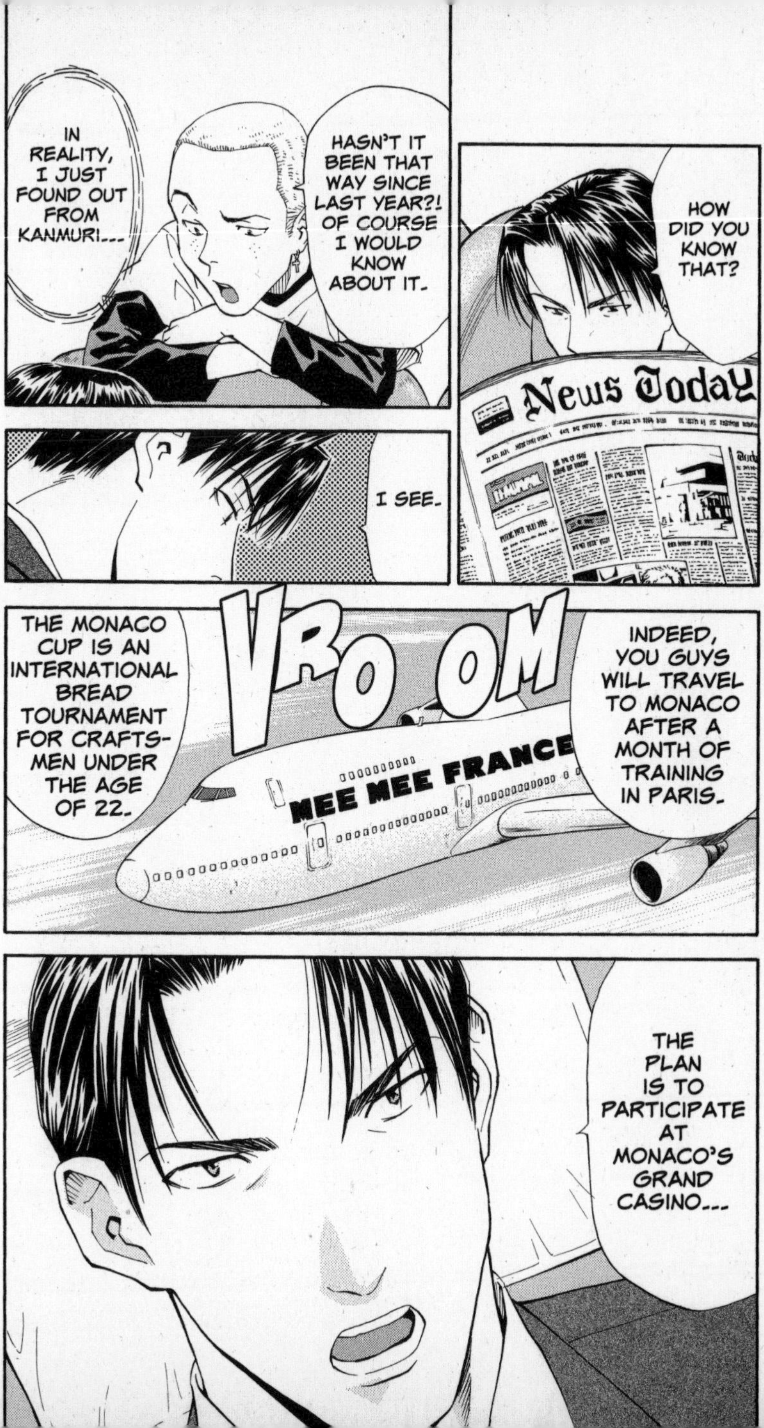
HOW DID YOU KNOW THAT?
News Today
HASN'T IT BEEN THAT WAY SINCE LAST YEAR?! OF COURSE I WOULD KNOW ABOUT IT.
IN REALITY, I JUST FOUND OUT FROM KANMURI...
I SEE.
INDEED, YOU GUYS WILL TRAVEL TO MONACO AFTER A MONTH OF TRAINING IN PARIS.
VROOM
MEE MEE FRANCE
THE MONACO CUP IS AN INTERNATIONAL BREAD TOURNAMENT FOR CRAFTS-MEN UNDER THE AGE OF 22.
THE PLAN IS TO PARTICIPATE AT MONACO'S GRAND CASINO...

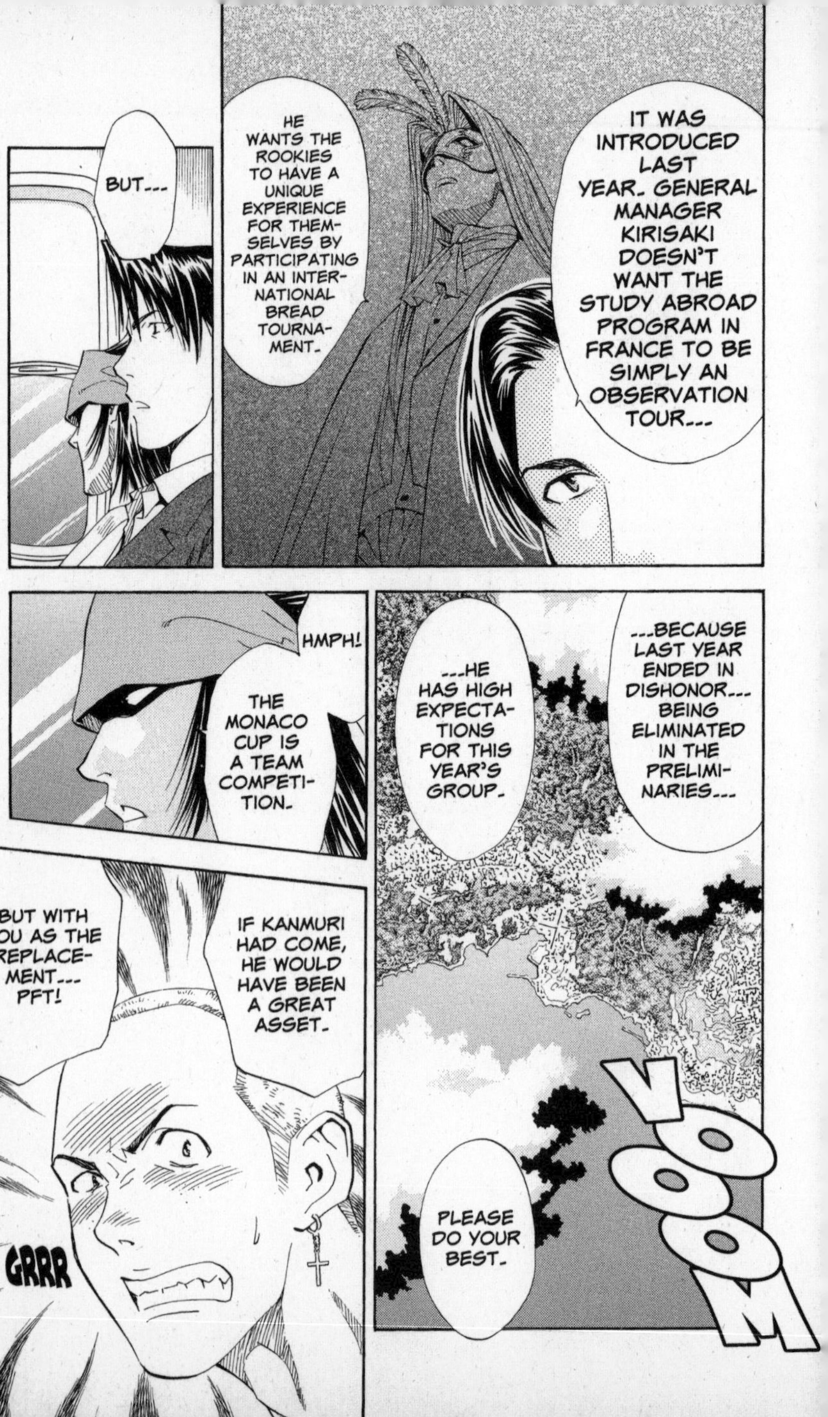
IT WAS INTRODUCED LAST YEAR. GENERAL MANAGER KIRISAKI DOESN'T WANT THE STUDY ABROAD PROGRAM IN FRANCE TO BE SIMPLY AN OBSERVATION TOUR...
HE WANTS THE ROOKIES TO HAVE A UNIQUE EXPERIENCE FOR THEMSELVES BY PARTICIPATING IN AN INTERNATIONAL BREAD TOURNAMENT.
BUT...
...BECAUSE LAST YEAR ENDED IN DISHONOR... BEING ELIMINATED IN THE PRELIMINARIES...
...HE HAS HIGH EXPECTATIONS FOR THIS YEAR'S GROUP.
VOOOOM
PLEASE DO YOUR BEST.
HMPH!
THE MONACO CUP IS A TEAM COMPETITION.
IF KANMURI HAD COME, HE WOULD HAVE BEEN A GREAT ASSET.
BUT WITH YOU AS THE REPLACEMENT... PFT!
GRRR

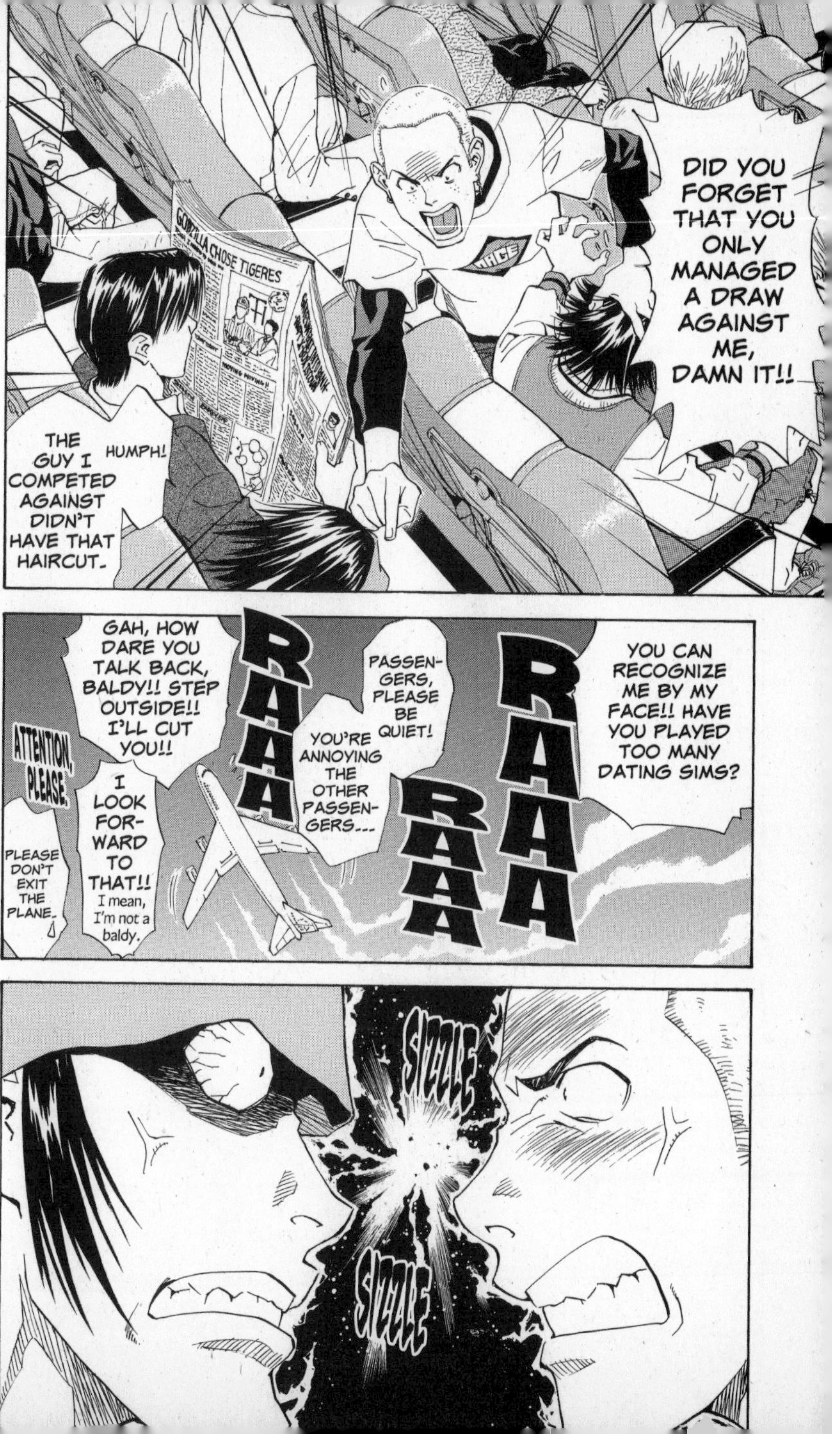
DID YOU FORGET THAT YOU ONLY MANAGED A DRAW AGAINST ME, DAMN IT!!
HAGE
GODZILLA CHOSE TIGERES
HUMPH!
THE GUY I COMPETED AGAINST DIDN'T HAVE THAT HAIRCUT.
YOU CAN RECOGNIZE ME BY MY FACE!! HAVE YOU PLAYED TOO MANY DATING SIMS?
RAAA
RAAA
PASSEN-GERS, PLEASE BE QUIET!
YOU'RE ANNOYING THE OTHER PASSEN-GERS...
RAAA
GAH, HOW DARE YOU TALK BACK, BALDY!! STEP OUTSIDE!! I'LL CUT YOU!!
I LOOK FOR-WARD TO THAT!!
I mean, I'm not a baldy.
ATTENTION, PLEASE.
PLEASE DON'T EXIT THE PLANE.
SIZZLE
SIZZLE

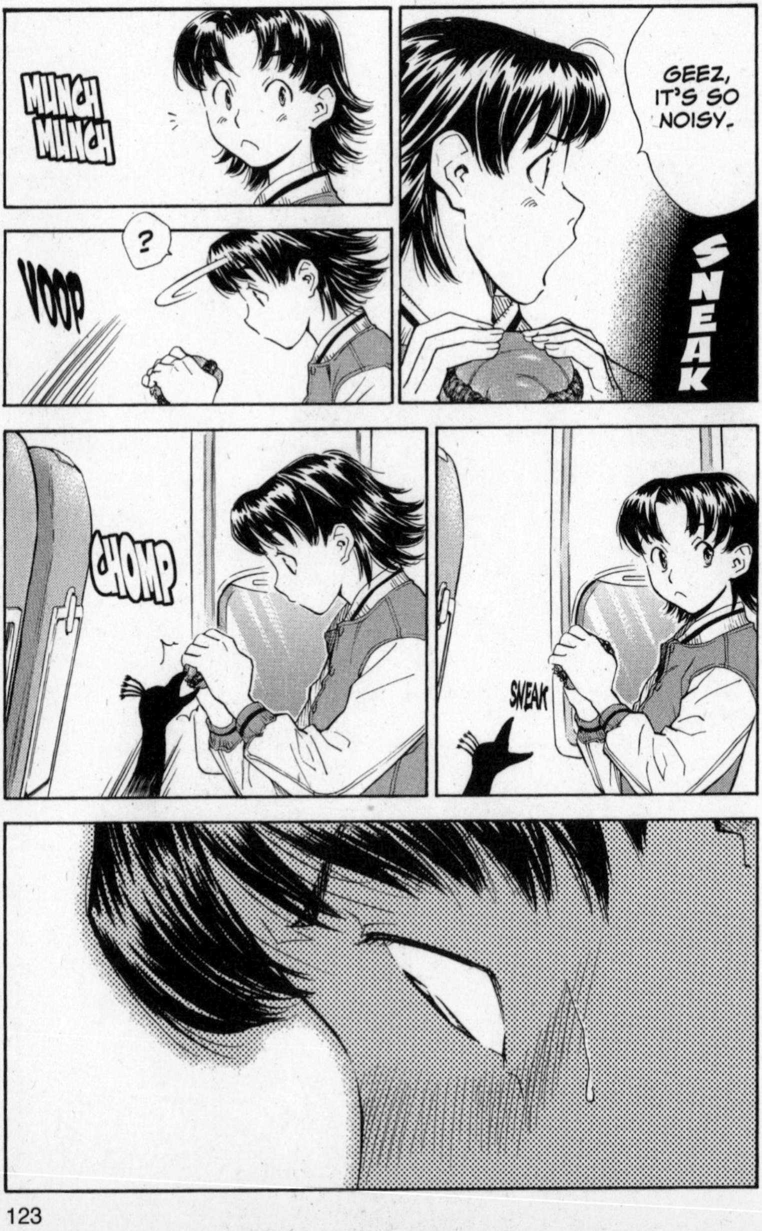
GEEZ, IT'S SO NOISY.
SNEAK
MUNCH MUNCH
?
VOOP
SNEAK
CHOMP

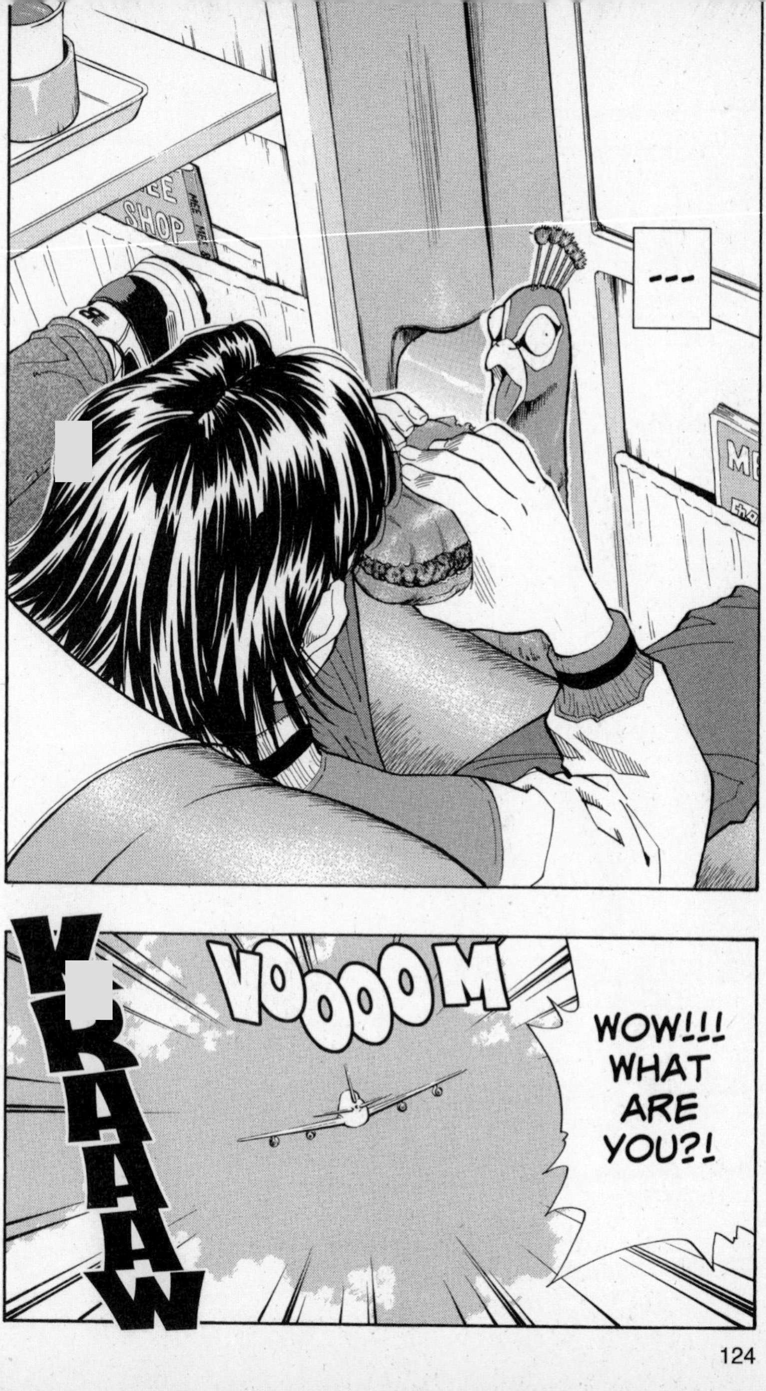

WOW!!!
WHAT
ARE
YOU?!
VOOOOM

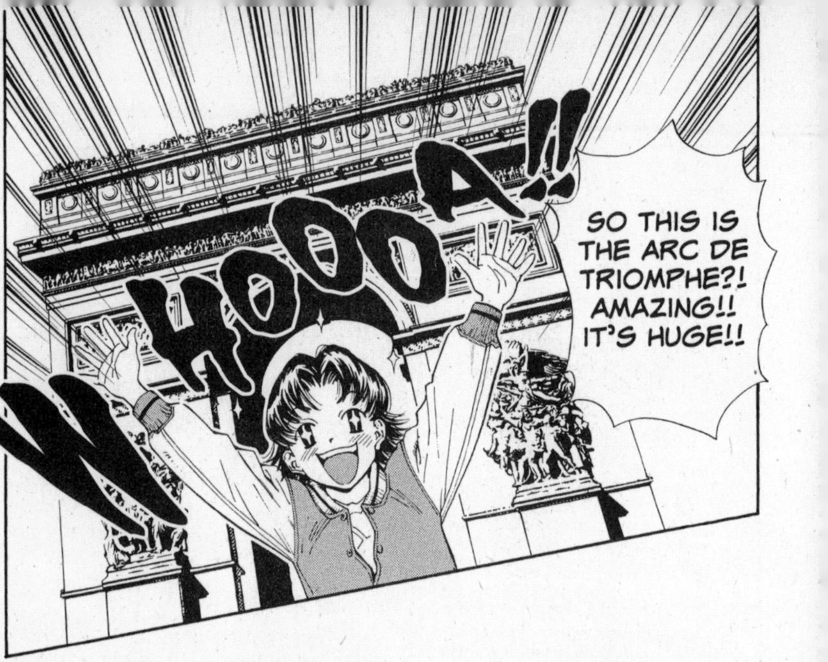
WHOOOA!!
SO THIS IS THE ARC DE TRIOMPHE?! AMAZING!! IT'S HUGE!!

Story 57: Who Are You?

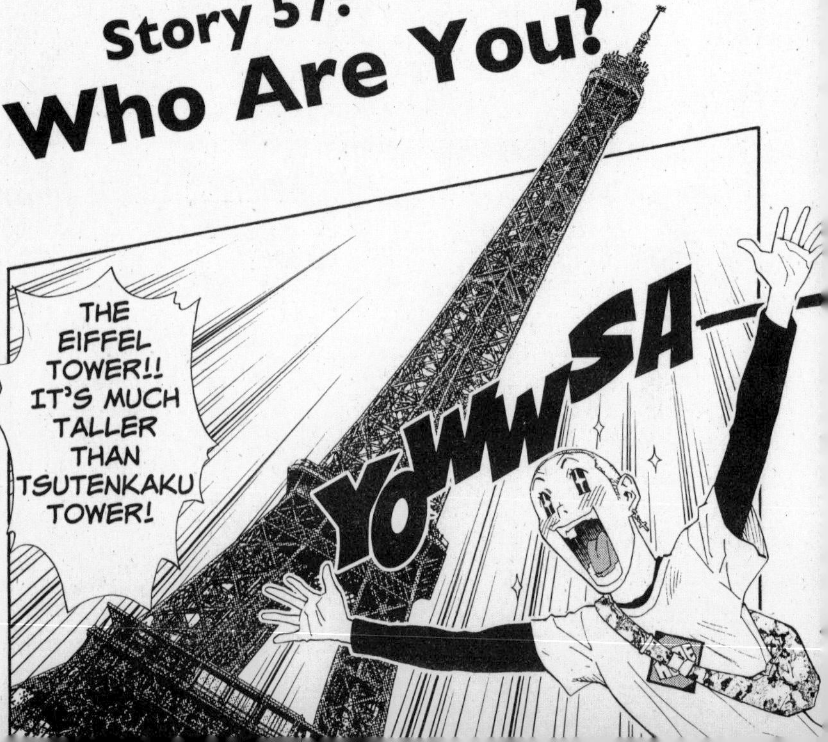
YOWWSA—!
THE EIFFEL TOWER!! IT'S MUCH TALLER THAN TSUTENKAKU TOWER!

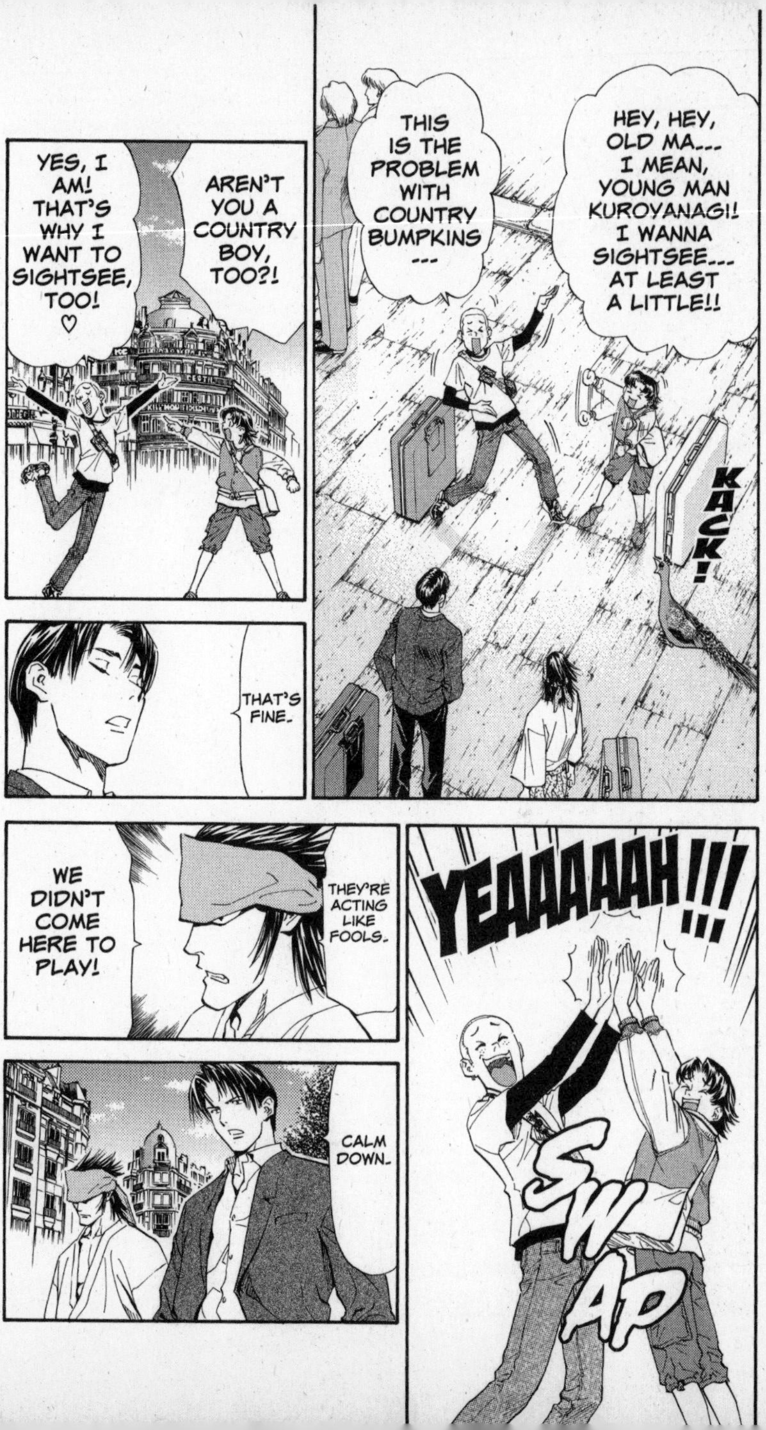
HEY, HEY, OLD MA... I MEAN, YOUNG MAN KUROYANAGI!! I WANNA SIGHTSEE... AT LEAST A LITTLE!!
THIS IS THE PROBLEM WITH COUNTRY BUMPKINS...
KACK!
AREN'T YOU A COUNTRY BOY, TOO?!
YES, I AM! THAT'S WHY I WANT TO SIGHTSEE, TOO! ♡
THAT'S FINE.
YEAAAAAH!!!
SWAP
THEY'RE ACTING LIKE FOOLS.
WE DIDN'T COME HERE TO PLAY!
CALM DOWN.

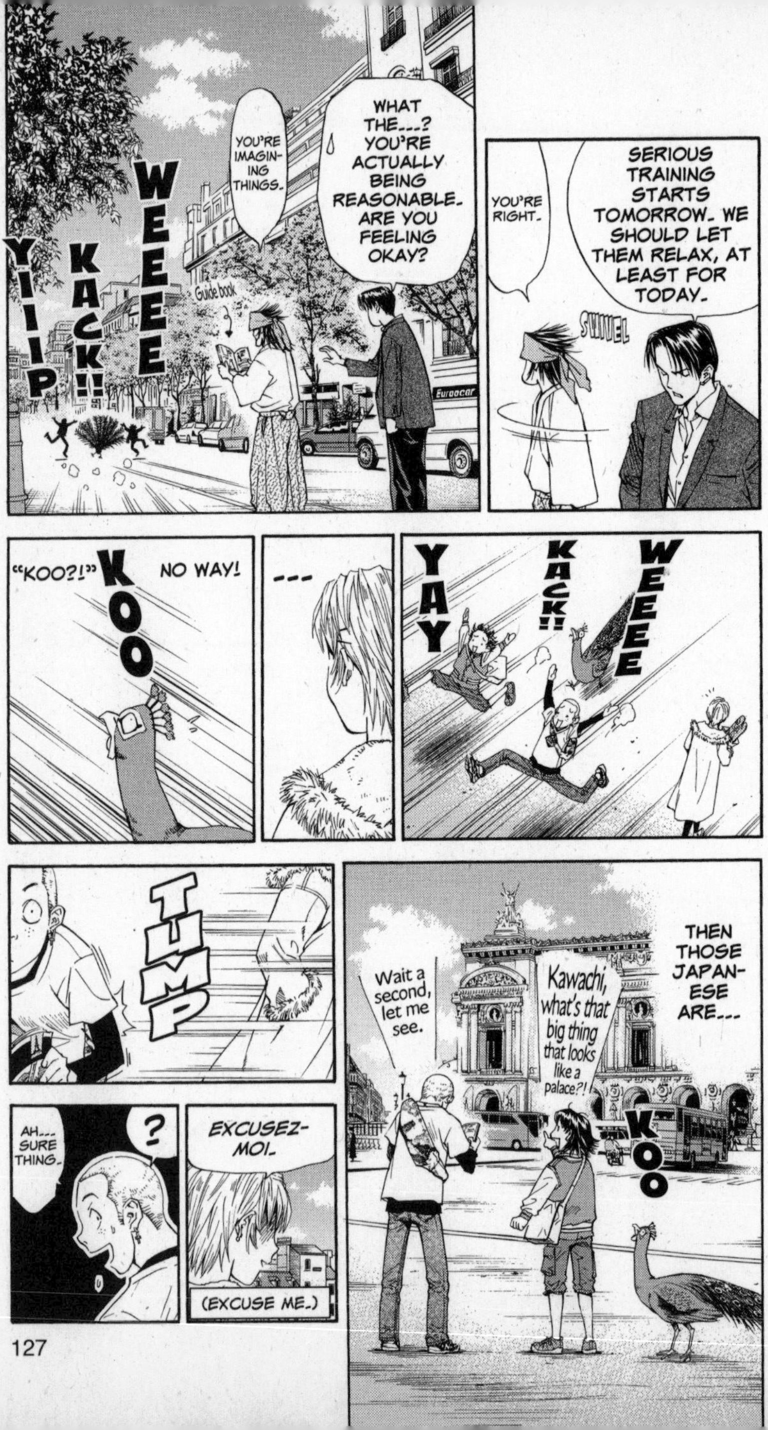
SERIOUS TRAINING STARTS TOMORROW. WE SHOULD LET THEM RELAX, AT LEAST FOR TODAY.
YOU'RE RIGHT.
SWIVEL
WHAT THE...? YOU'RE ACTUALLY BEING REASONABLE. ARE YOU FEELING OKAY?
YOU'RE IMAGINING THINGS.
Guide book
Euroocar
WEEEE
KACK!!
YIIIP
WEEEE
KACK!!
YAY
...
NO WAY!
"KOO?!"
KOO
THEN THOSE JAPANESE ARE...
Kawachi, what's that big thing that looks like a palace?!
Wait a second, let me see.
KOO
TUMP
EXCUSEZ-MOI.
(EXCUSE ME.)
?
AH... SURE THING.

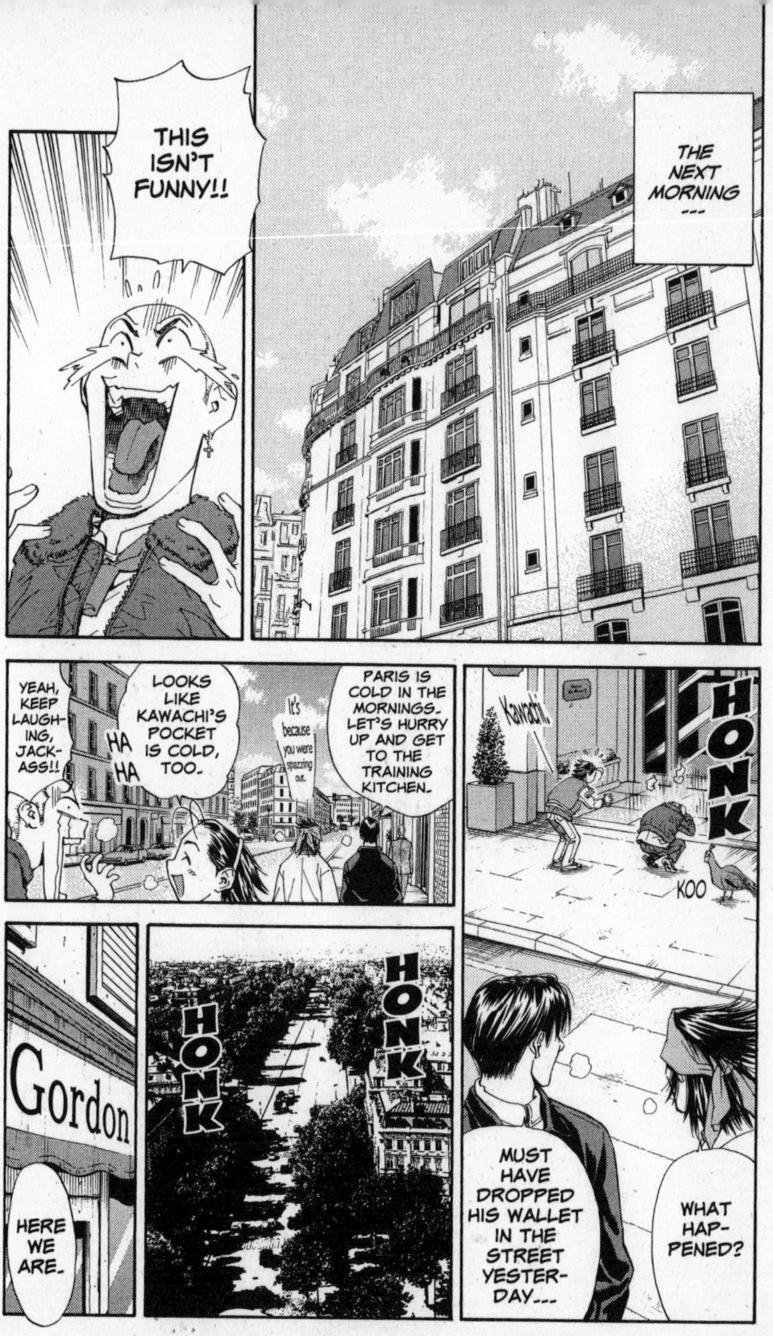
THE NEXT MORNING ---
THIS ISN'T FUNNY!!
Kawachi.
HONK
KOO
PARIS IS COLD IN THE MORNINGS. LET'S HURRY UP AND GET TO THE TRAINING KITCHEN.
It's because you were spazzing out.
LOOKS LIKE KAWACHI'S POCKET IS COLD, TOO.
HA HA
YEAH, KEEP LAUGHING, JACKASS!!
WHAT HAPPENED?
MUST HAVE DROPPED HIS WALLET IN THE STREET YESTERDAY...
HONK
HONK
Gordon
HERE WE ARE.

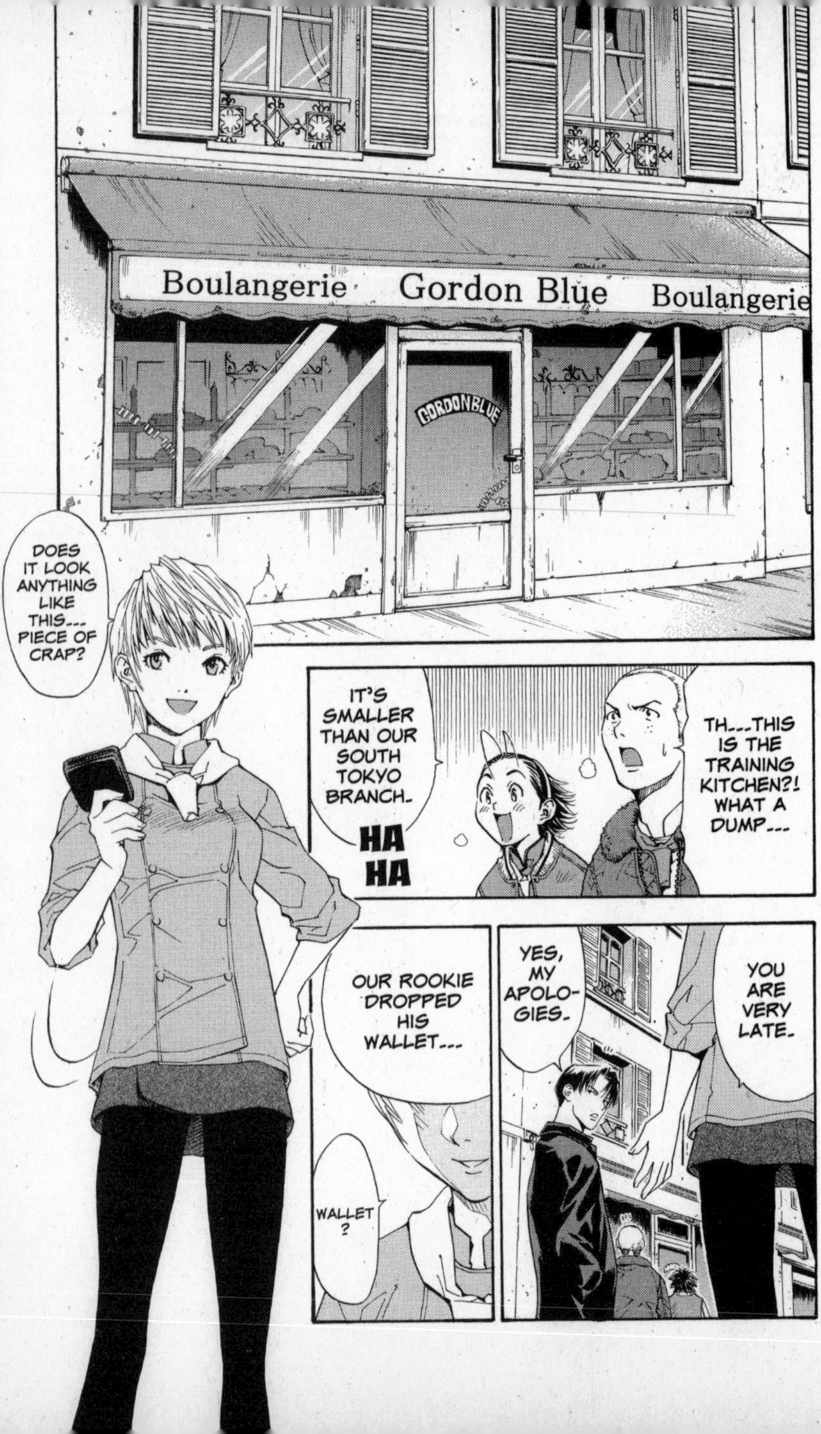
Boulangerie Gordon Blue Boulangerie
GORDONBLUE
DOES IT LOOK ANYTHING LIKE THIS... PIECE OF CRAP?
TH...THIS IS THE TRAINING KITCHEN?! WHAT A DUMP...
IT'S SMALLER THAN OUR SOUTH TOKYO BRANCH.
HA HA
YOU ARE VERY LATE.
YES, MY APOLOGIES.
OUR ROOKIE DROPPED HIS WALLET...
WALLET?

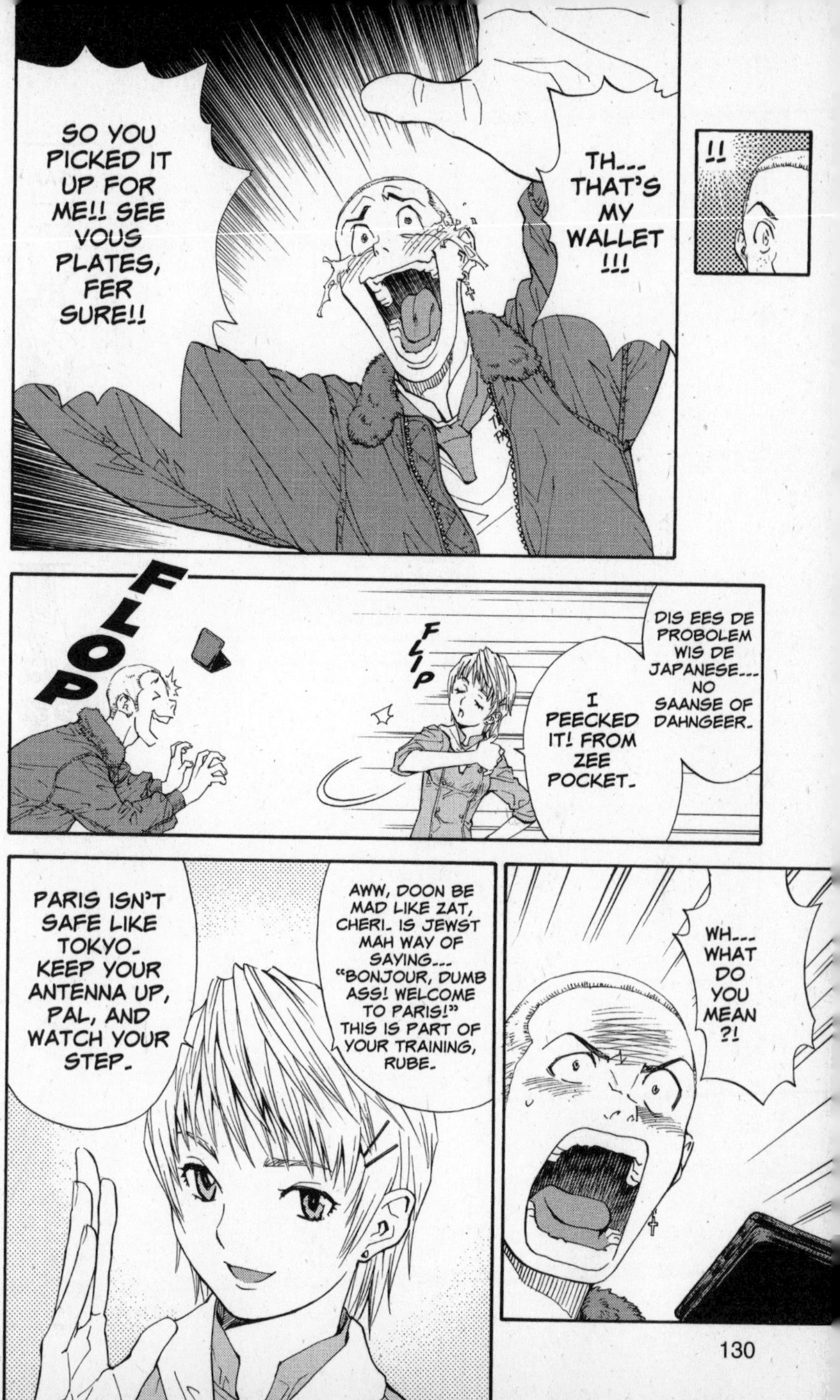
!!
TH... THAT'S MY WALLET!!!
SO YOU PICKED IT UP FOR ME!! SEE VOUS PLATES, FER SURE!!
DIS EES DE PROBOLEM WIS DE JAPANESE... NO SAANSE OF DAHNGEER.
I PEECKED IT! FROM ZEE POCKET.
FLIP
FLOP
WH... WHAT DO YOU MEAN?!
AWW, DOON BE MAD LIKE ZAT, CHERI. IS JEWST MAH WAY OF SAYING... "BONJOUR, DUMB ASS! WELCOME TO PARIS!" THIS IS PART OF YOUR TRAINING, RUBE.
PARIS ISN'T SAFE LIKE TOKYO. KEEP YOUR ANTENNA UP, PAL, AND WATCH YOUR STEP.

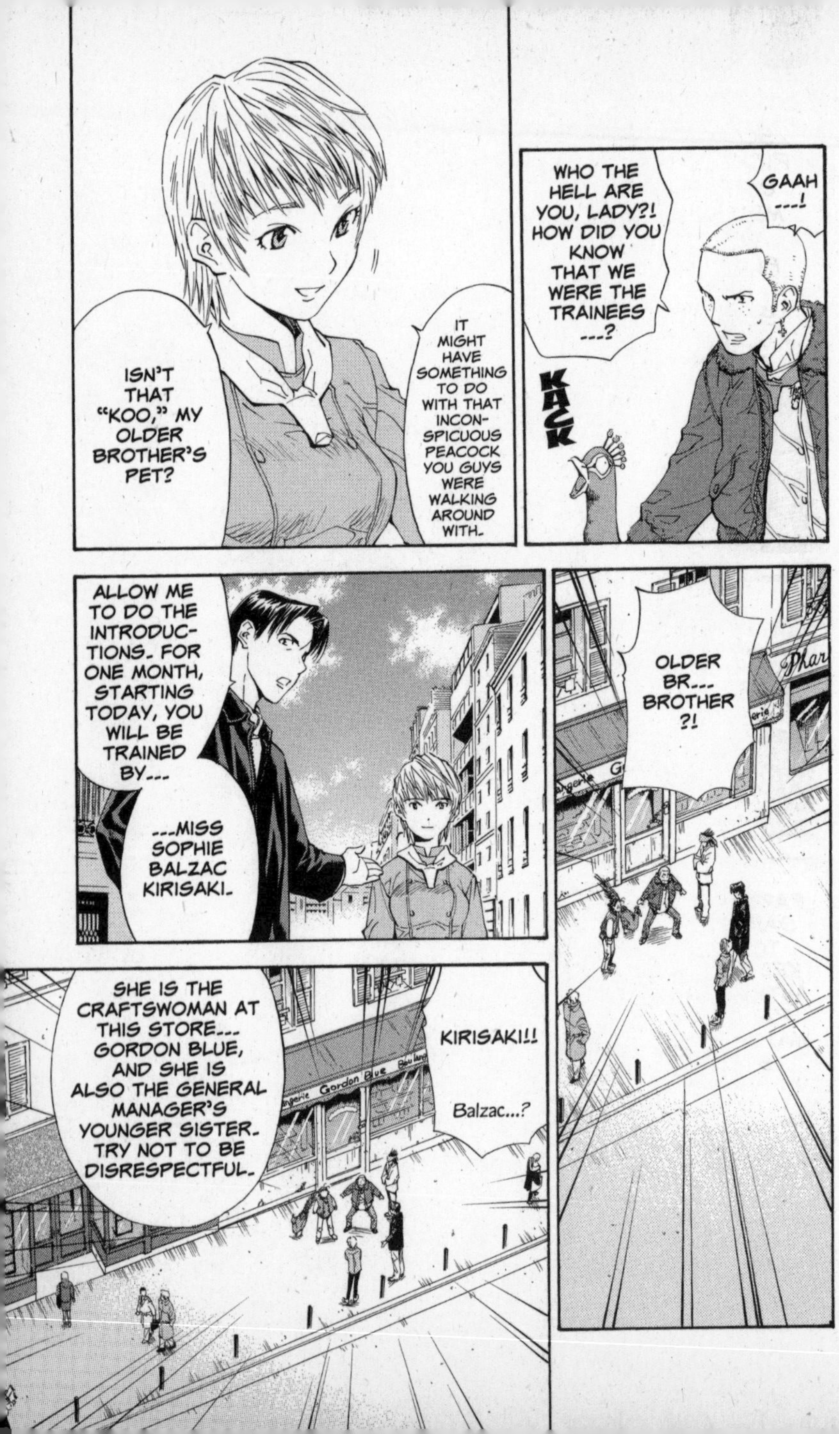
GAAH---!
WHO THE HELL ARE YOU, LADY?! HOW DID YOU KNOW THAT WE WERE THE TRAINEES---?
KACK
IT MIGHT HAVE SOMETHING TO DO WITH THAT INCON-SPICUOUS PEACOCK YOU GUYS WERE WALKING AROUND WITH.
ISN'T THAT "KOO," MY OLDER BROTHER'S PET?
OLDER BR--- BROTHER?!
ALLOW ME TO DO THE INTRODUC-TIONS. FOR ONE MONTH, STARTING TODAY, YOU WILL BE TRAINED BY---
---MISS SOPHIE BALZAC KIRISAKI.
SHE IS THE CRAFTSWOMAN AT THIS STORE--- GORDON BLUE, AND SHE IS ALSO THE GENERAL MANAGER'S YOUNGER SISTER. TRY NOT TO BE DISRESPECTFUL.
KIRISAKI!!
Balzac...?

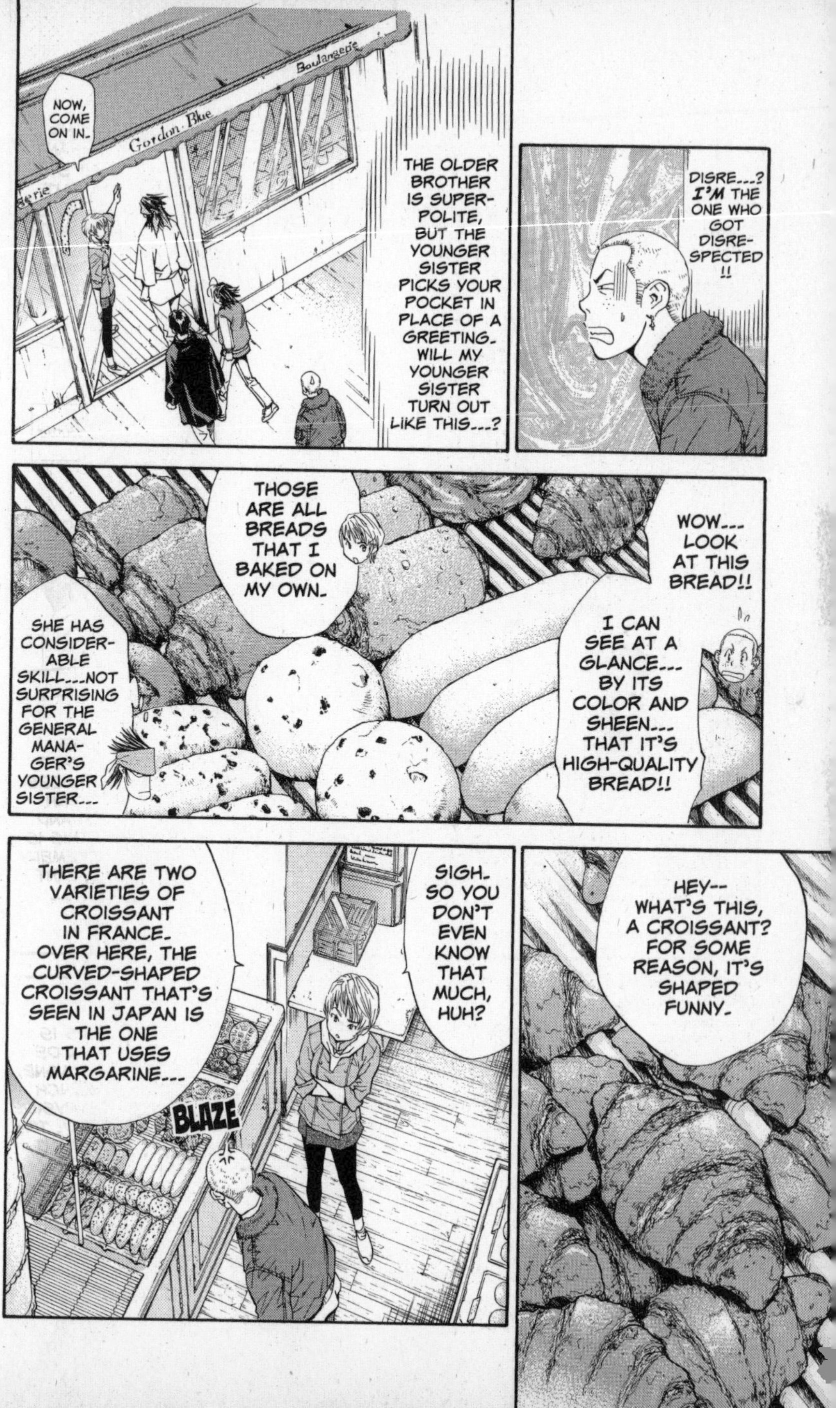
DISRE...? *I'M* THE ONE WHO GOT DISRESPECTED!!
NOW, COME IN.
Boulangerie
Gordon Blue
THE OLDER BROTHER IS SUPER-POLITE, BUT THE YOUNGER SISTER PICKS YOUR POCKET IN PLACE OF A GREETING. WILL MY YOUNGER SISTER TURN OUT LIKE THIS...?
WOW... LOOK AT THIS BREAD!!
I CAN SEE AT A GLANCE... BY ITS COLOR AND SHEEN... THAT IT'S HIGH-QUALITY BREAD!!
THOSE ARE ALL BREADS THAT I BAKED ON MY OWN.
SHE HAS CONSIDERABLE SKILL...NOT SURPRISING FOR THE GENERAL MANAGER'S YOUNGER SISTER...
HEY-- WHAT'S THIS, A CROISSANT? FOR SOME REASON, IT'S SHAPED FUNNY.
SIGH. SO YOU DON'T EVEN KNOW THAT MUCH, HUH?
THERE ARE TWO VARIETIES OF CROISSANT IN FRANCE. OVER HERE, THE CURVED-SHAPED CROISSANT THAT'S SEEN IN JAPAN IS THE ONE THAT USES MARGARINE...
BLAZE

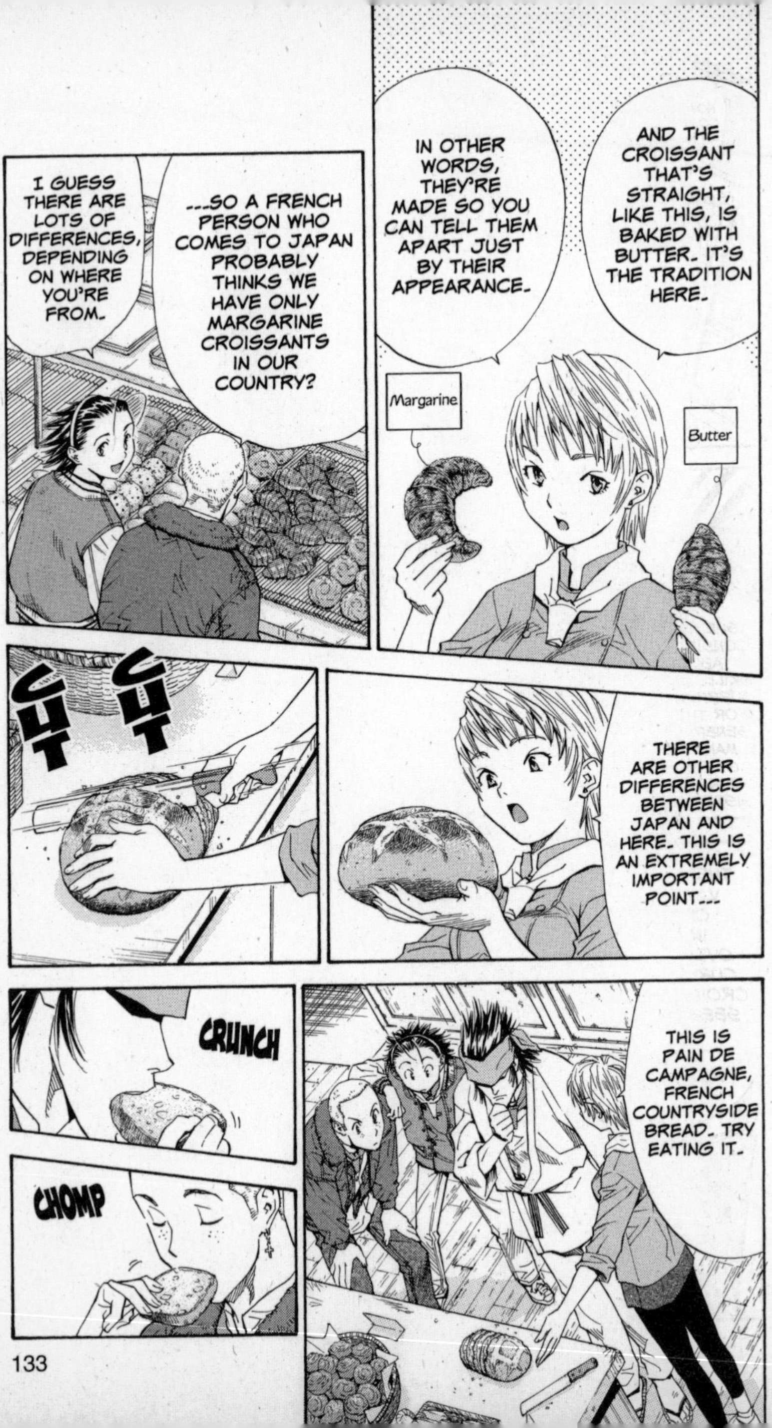
AND THE CROISSANT THAT'S STRAIGHT, LIKE THIS, IS BAKED WITH BUTTER. IT'S THE TRADITION HERE.
IN OTHER WORDS, THEY'RE MADE SO YOU CAN TELL THEM APART JUST BY THEIR APPEARANCE.
Butter
Margarine
...SO A FRENCH PERSON WHO COMES TO JAPAN PROBABLY THINKS WE HAVE ONLY MARGARINE CROISSANTS IN OUR COUNTRY?
I GUESS THERE ARE LOTS OF DIFFERENCES, DEPENDING ON WHERE YOU'RE FROM.
THERE ARE OTHER DIFFERENCES BETWEEN JAPAN AND HERE. THIS IS AN EXTREMELY IMPORTANT POINT...
CUT
CUT
THIS IS PAIN DE CAMPAGNE, FRENCH COUNTRYSIDE BREAD. TRY EATING IT.
CRUNCH
CHOMP

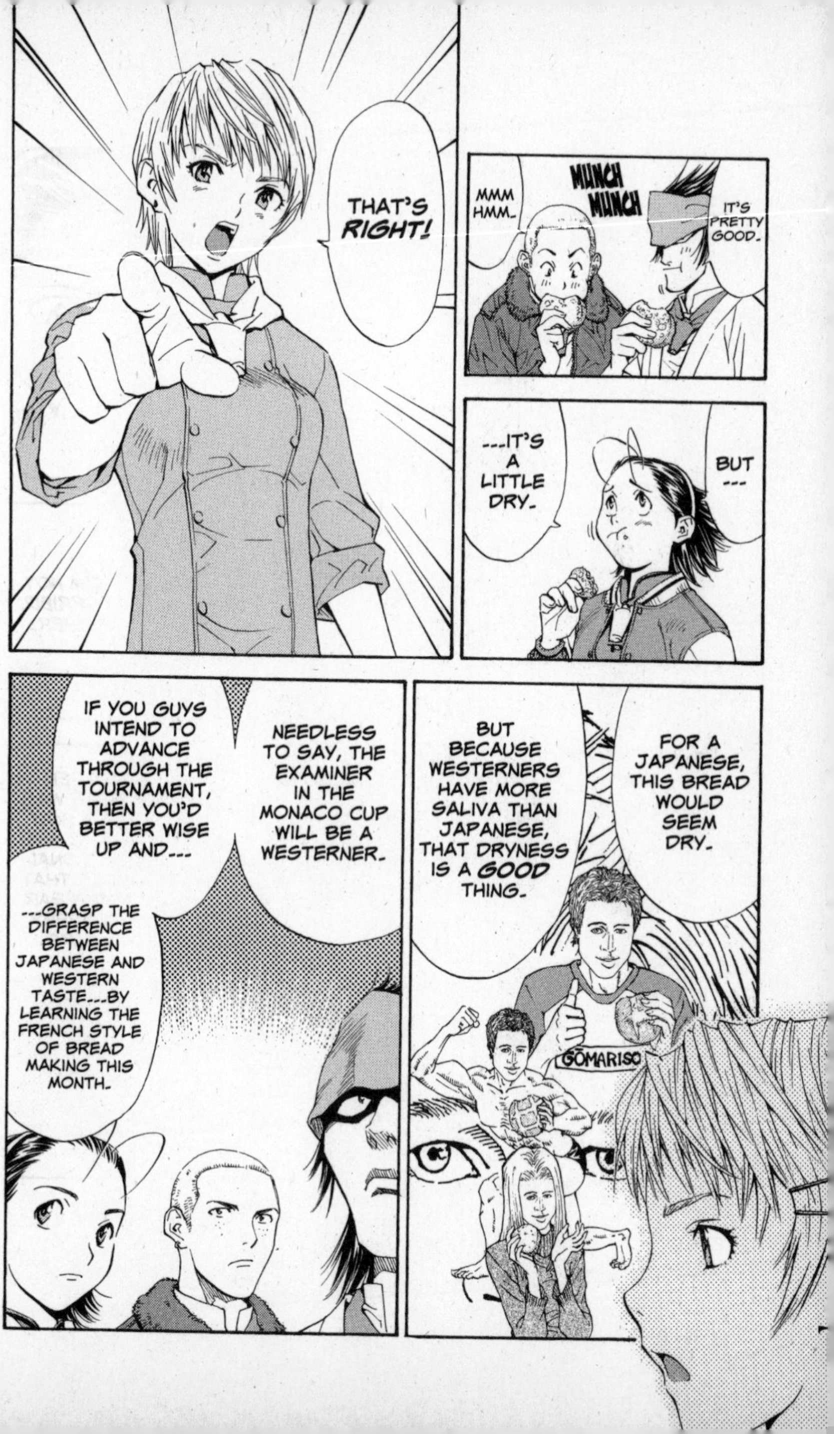
IT'S PRETTY GOOD.
MUNCH MUNCH
MMM HMM...
BUT ---
---IT'S A LITTLE DRY.
THAT'S *RIGHT!*
FOR A JAPANESE, THIS BREAD WOULD SEEM DRY.
BUT BECAUSE WESTERNERS HAVE MORE SALIVA THAN JAPANESE, THAT DRYNESS IS A *GOOD* THING.
GOMARISO
NEEDLESS TO SAY, THE EXAMINER IN THE MONACO CUP WILL BE A WESTERNER.
IF YOU GUYS INTEND TO ADVANCE THROUGH THE TOURNAMENT, THEN YOU'D BETTER WISE UP AND---
---GRASP THE DIFFERENCE BETWEEN JAPANESE AND WESTERN TASTE---BY LEARNING THE FRENCH STYLE OF BREAD MAKING THIS MONTH.

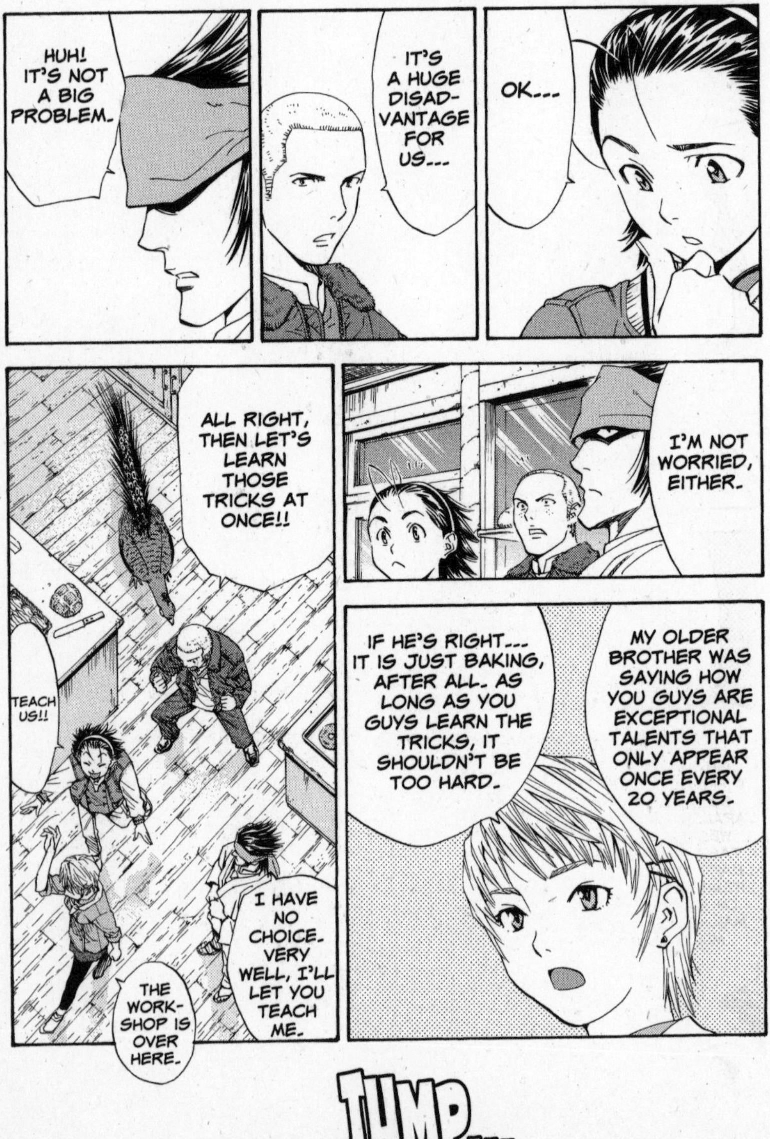
OK...
IT'S A HUGE DISAD-VANTAGE FOR US...
HUH! IT'S NOT A BIG PROBLEM.
I'M NOT WORRIED, EITHER.
MY OLDER BROTHER WAS SAYING HOW YOU GUYS ARE EXCEPTIONAL TALENTS THAT ONLY APPEAR ONCE EVERY 20 YEARS.
IF HE'S RIGHT... IT IS JUST BAKING, AFTER ALL. AS LONG AS YOU GUYS LEARN THE TRICKS, IT SHOULDN'T BE TOO HARD.
ALL RIGHT, THEN LET'S LEARN THOSE TRICKS AT ONCE!!
TEACH US!!
I HAVE NO CHOICE. VERY WELL, I'LL LET YOU TEACH ME.
THE WORK-SHOP IS OVER HERE.
TUMP...

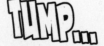

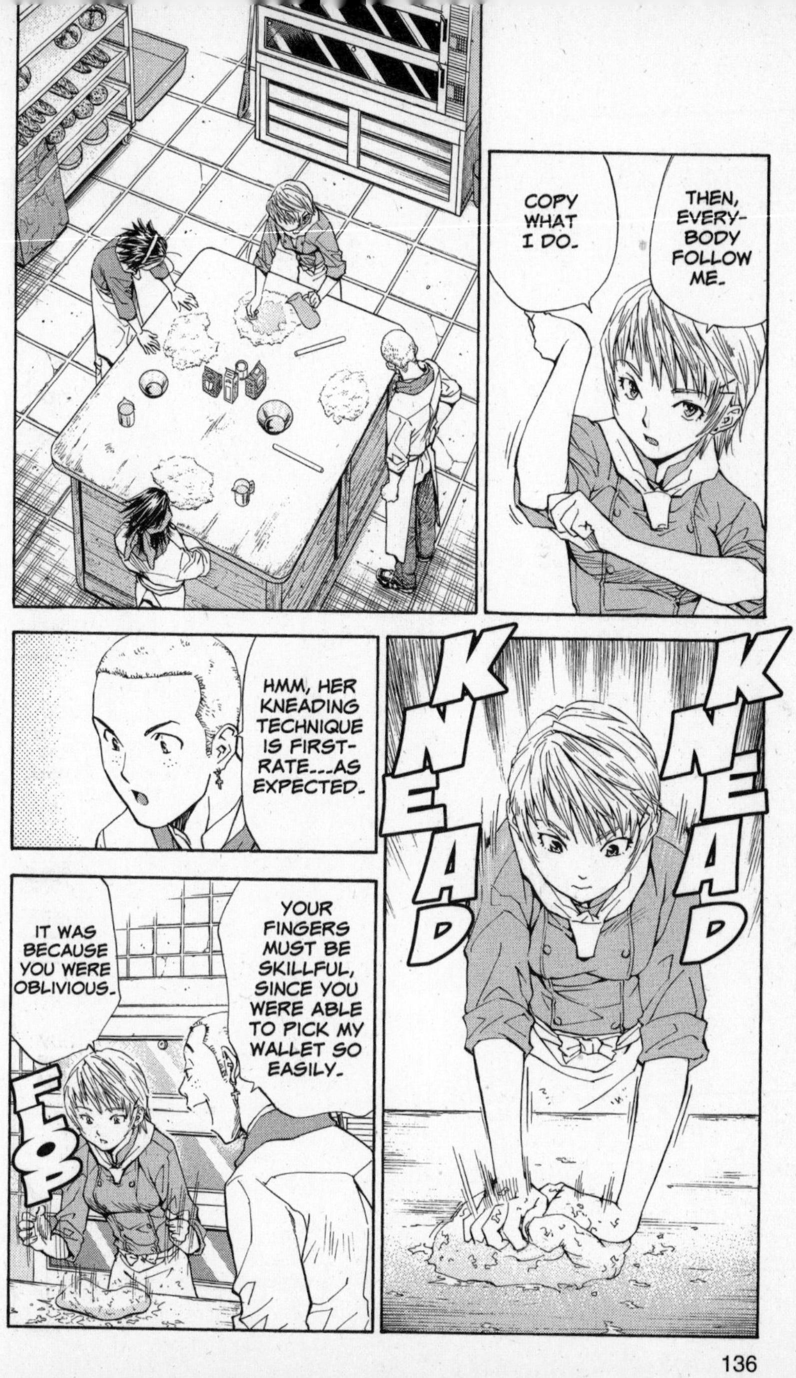
THEN, EVERY-BODY FOLLOW ME.
COPY WHAT I DO.
KNEAD
KNEAD
HMM, HER KNEADING TECHNIQUE IS FIRST-RATE...AS EXPECTED.
YOUR FINGERS MUST BE SKILLFUL, SINCE YOU WERE ABLE TO PICK MY WALLET SO EASILY.
IT WAS BECAUSE YOU WERE OBLIVIOUS.
FLOP

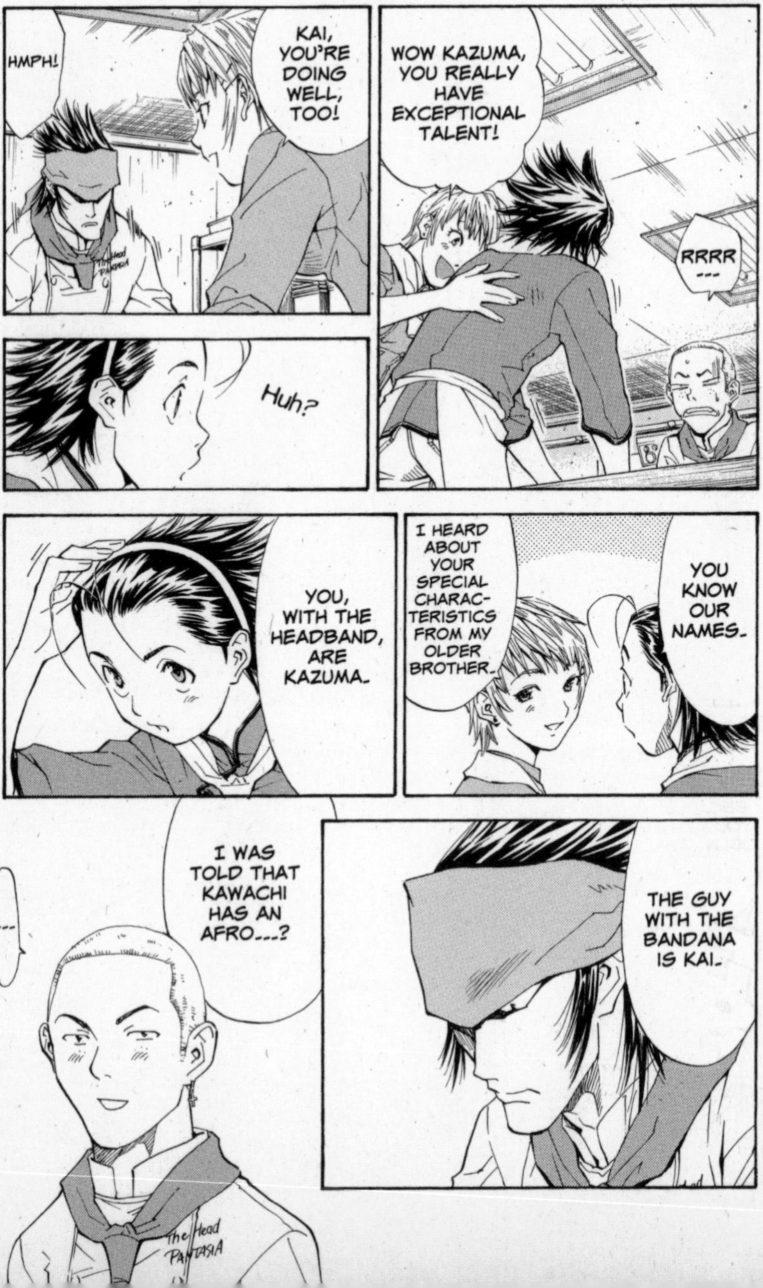
WOW KAZUMA, YOU REALLY HAVE EXCEPTIONAL TALENT!
RRRR ---
KAI, YOU'RE DOING WELL, TOO!
HMPH!
Huh?
YOU KNOW OUR NAMES.
I HEARD ABOUT YOUR SPECIAL CHARAC-TERISTICS FROM MY OLDER BROTHER.
YOU, WITH THE HEADBAND, ARE KAZUMA.
THE GUY WITH THE BANDANA IS KAI.
I WAS TOLD THAT KAWACHI HAS AN AFRO...?

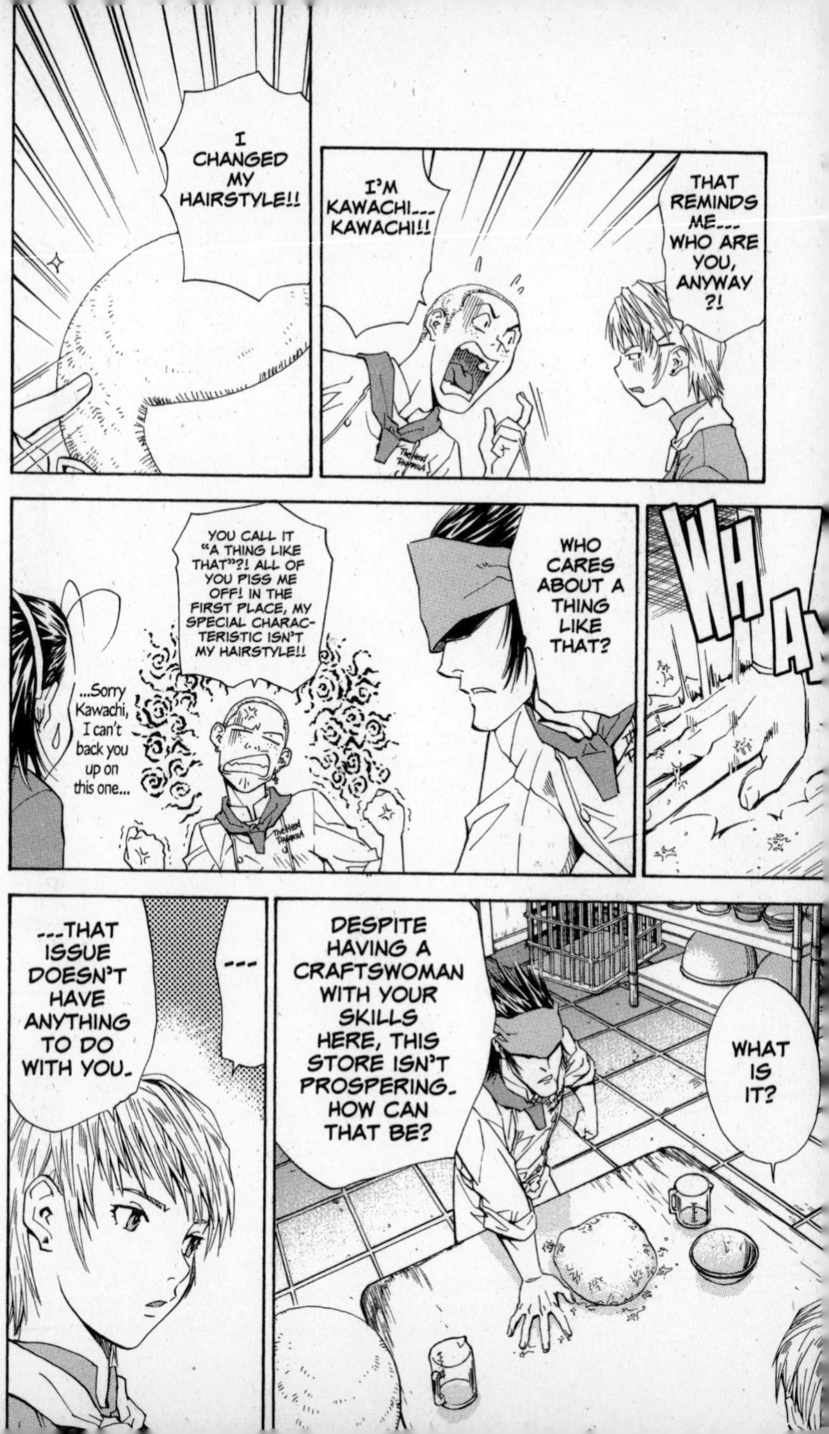
THAT REMINDS ME... WHO ARE YOU, ANYWAY?!
I'M KAWACHI... KAWACHI!!
I CHANGED MY HAIRSTYLE!!
WHA
WHO CARES ABOUT A THING LIKE THAT?
YOU CALL IT "A THING LIKE THAT"?! ALL OF YOU PISS ME OFF! IN THE FIRST PLACE, MY SPECIAL CHARACTERISTIC ISN'T MY HAIRSTYLE!!
...Sorry Kawachi, I can't back you up on this one...
WHAT IS IT?
DESPITE HAVING A CRAFTSWOMAN WITH YOUR SKILLS HERE, THIS STORE ISN'T PROSPERING. HOW CAN THAT BE?
...
...THAT ISSUE DOESN'T HAVE ANYTHING TO DO WITH YOU.

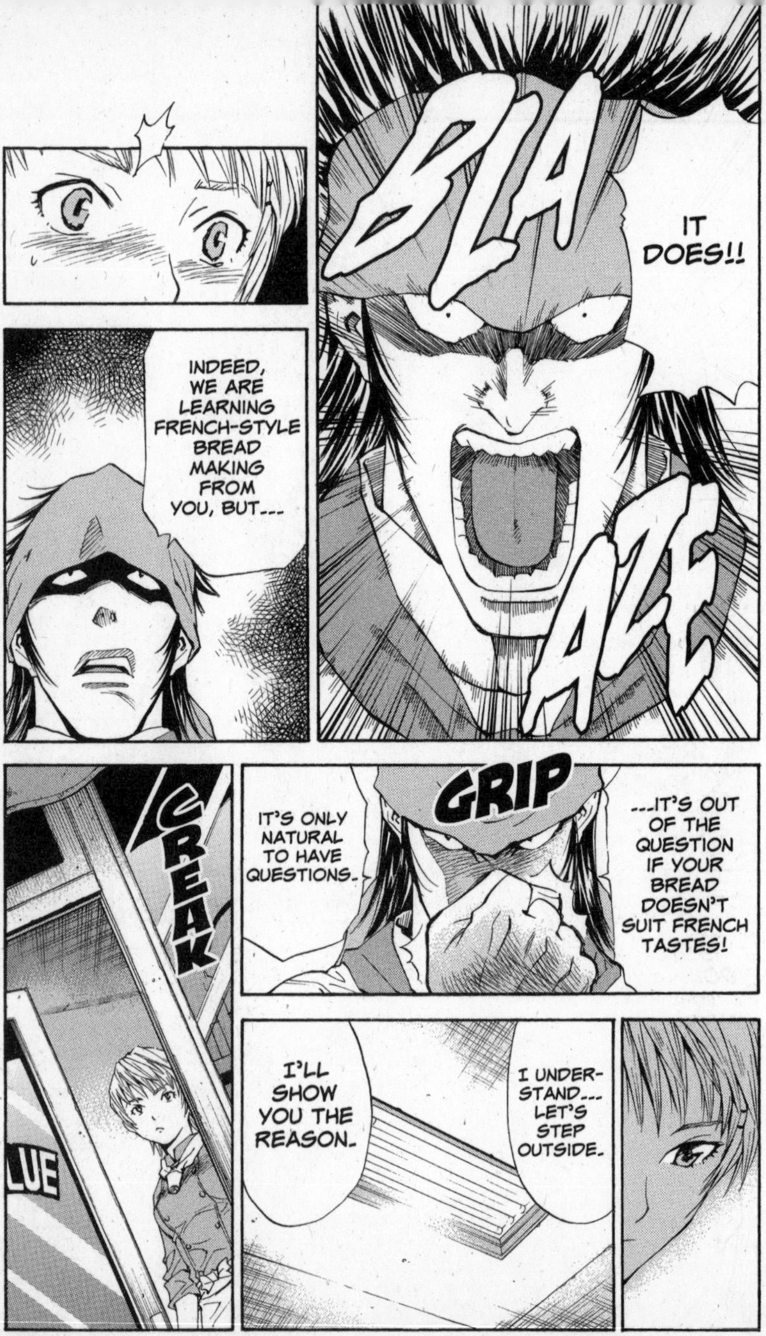
IT DOES!!
BLAZE
INDEED, WE ARE LEARNING FRENCH-STYLE BREAD MAKING FROM YOU, BUT---
GRIP
---IT'S OUT OF THE QUESTION IF YOUR BREAD DOESN'T SUIT FRENCH TASTES!
IT'S ONLY NATURAL TO HAVE QUESTIONS.
I UNDER-STAND--- LET'S STEP OUTSIDE.
I'LL SHOW YOU THE REASON.
CREAK
LUE

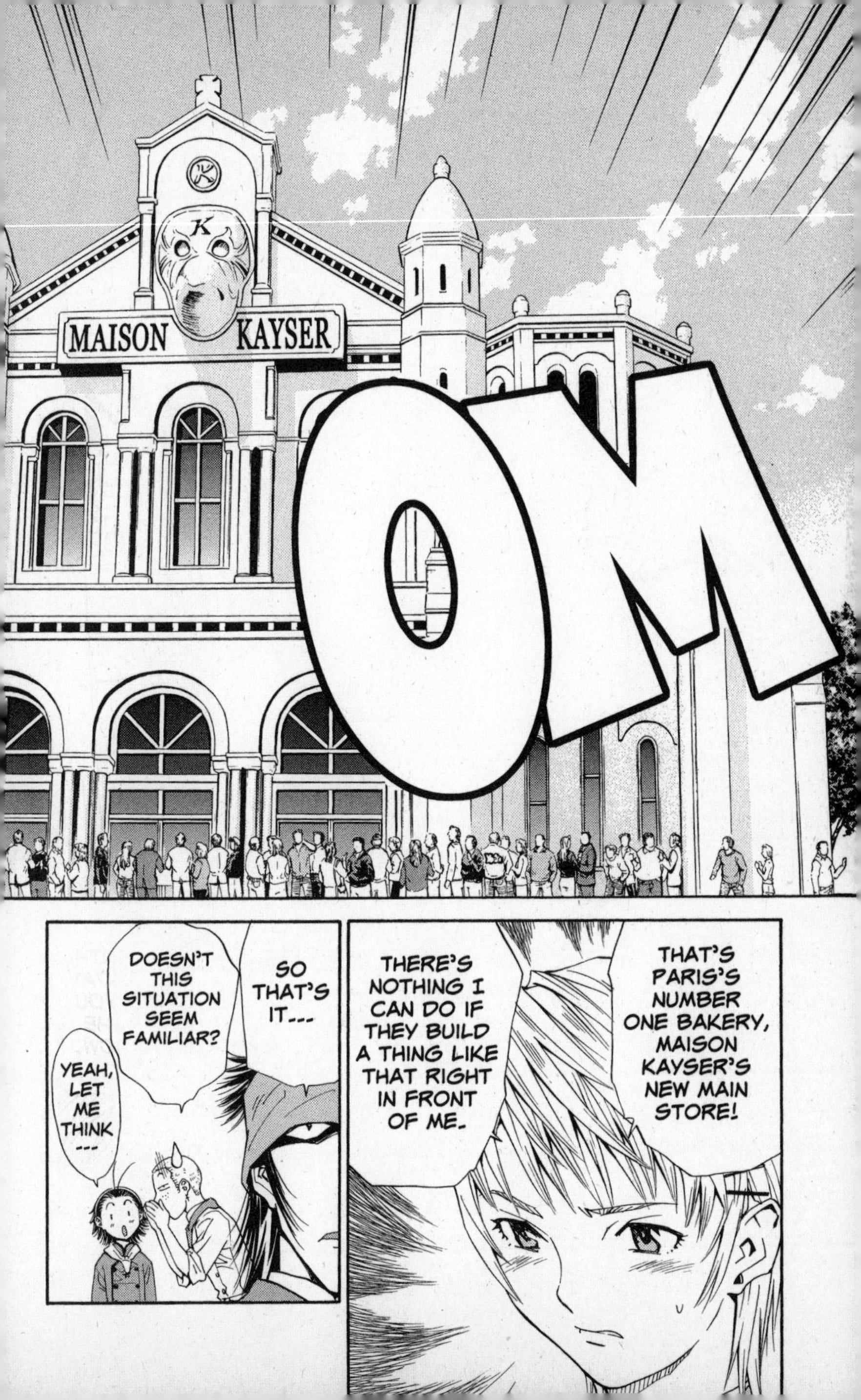
MAISON KAYSER
OM
THAT'S PARIS'S NUMBER ONE BAKERY, MAISON KAYSER'S NEW MAIN STORE!
THERE'S NOTHING I CAN DO IF THEY BUILD A THING LIKE THAT RIGHT IN FRONT OF ME.
SO THAT'S IT...
DOESN'T THIS SITUATION SEEM FAMILIAR?
YEAH, LET ME THINK...

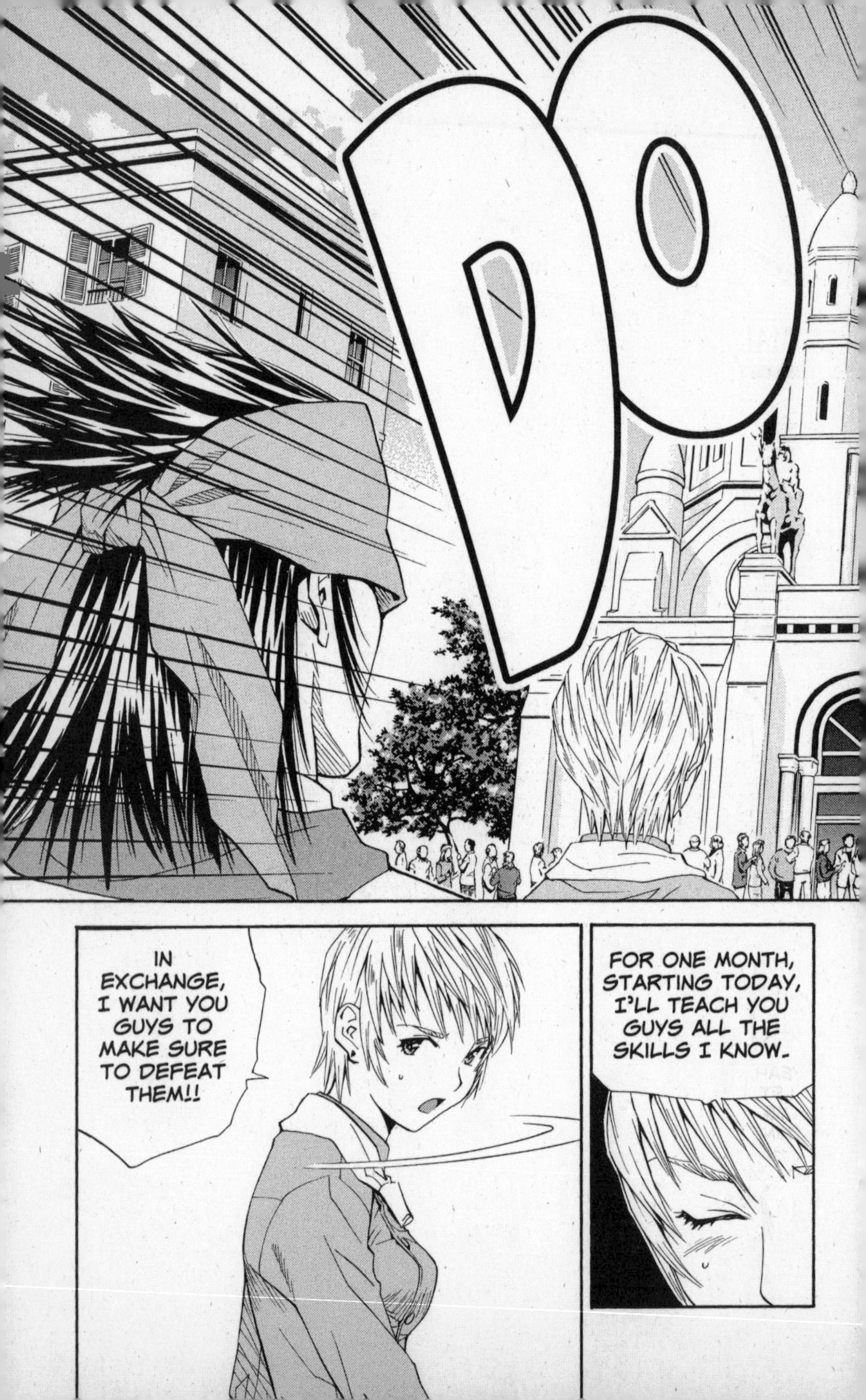
DO
FOR ONE MONTH, STARTING TODAY, I'LL TEACH YOU GUYS ALL THE SKILLS I KNOW.
IN EXCHANGE, I WANT YOU GUYS TO MAKE SURE TO DEFEAT THEM!!

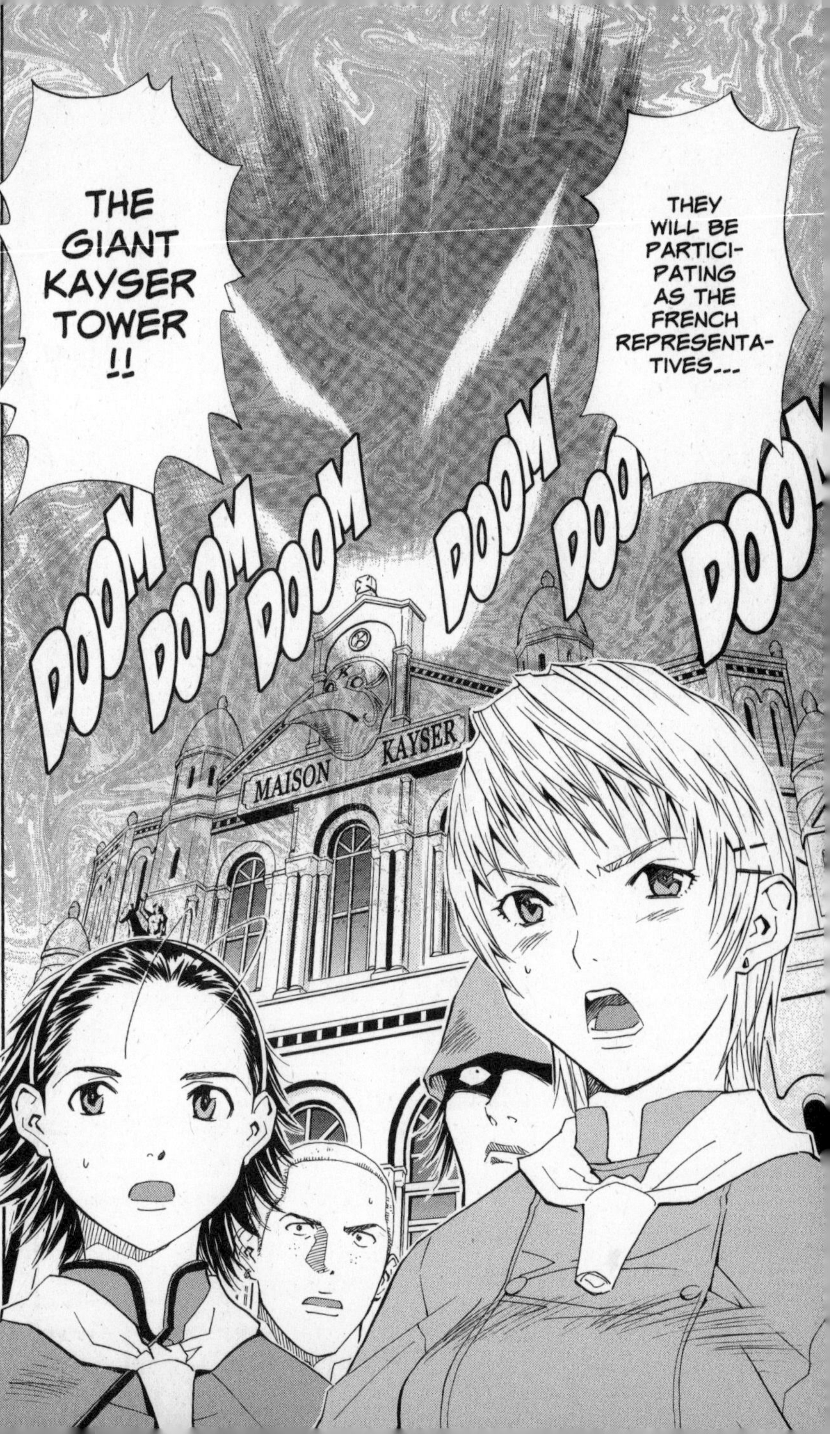
THEY WILL BE PARTICI-PATING AS THE FRENCH REPRESENTA-TIVES...
THE GIANT KAYSER TOWER !!
DOO
DOO
DOOM
DOOM
DOOM
DOOM
MAISON KAYSER

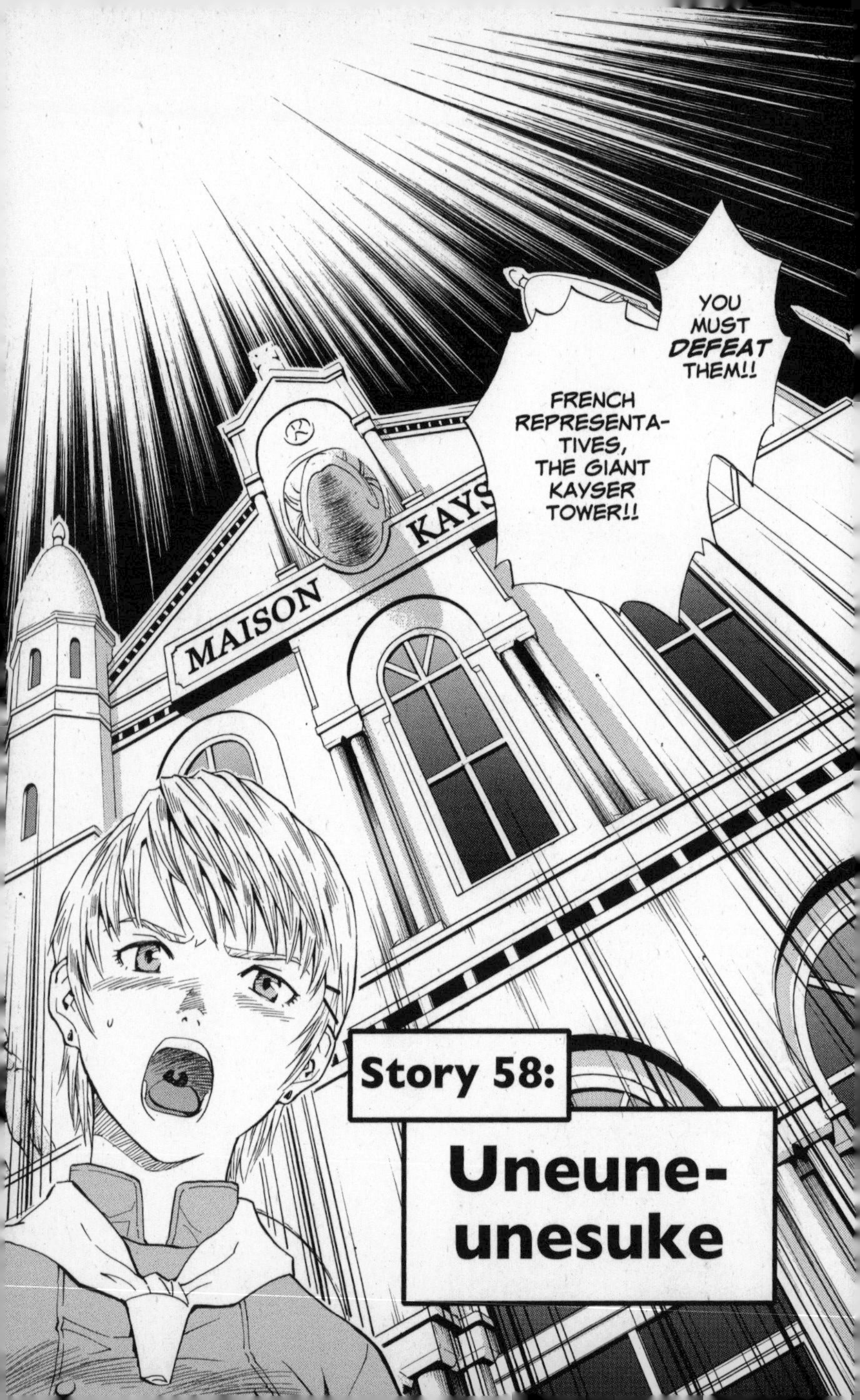
YOU MUST DEFEAT THEM!!
FRENCH REPRESENTA-TIVES, THE GIANT KAYSER TOWER!!
MAISON KAYS
Story 58:
Uneune-unesuke

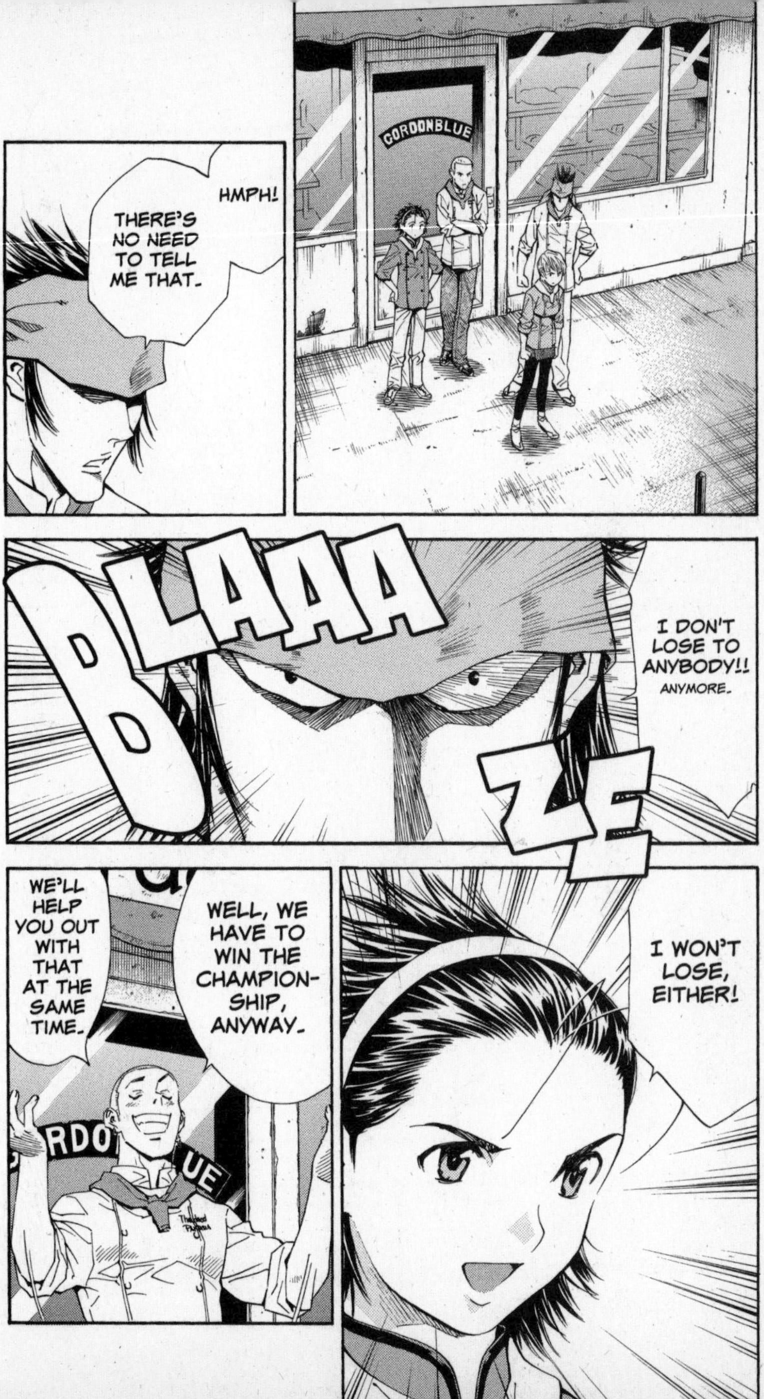
CORDONBLUE
HMPH!
THERE'S NO NEED TO TELL ME THAT...
BLAAAZE
I DON'T LOSE TO ANYBODY!! ANYMORE...
I WON'T LOSE, EITHER!
WELL, WE HAVE TO WIN THE CHAMPIONSHIP, ANYWAY...
WE'LL HELP YOU OUT WITH THAT AT THE SAME TIME...

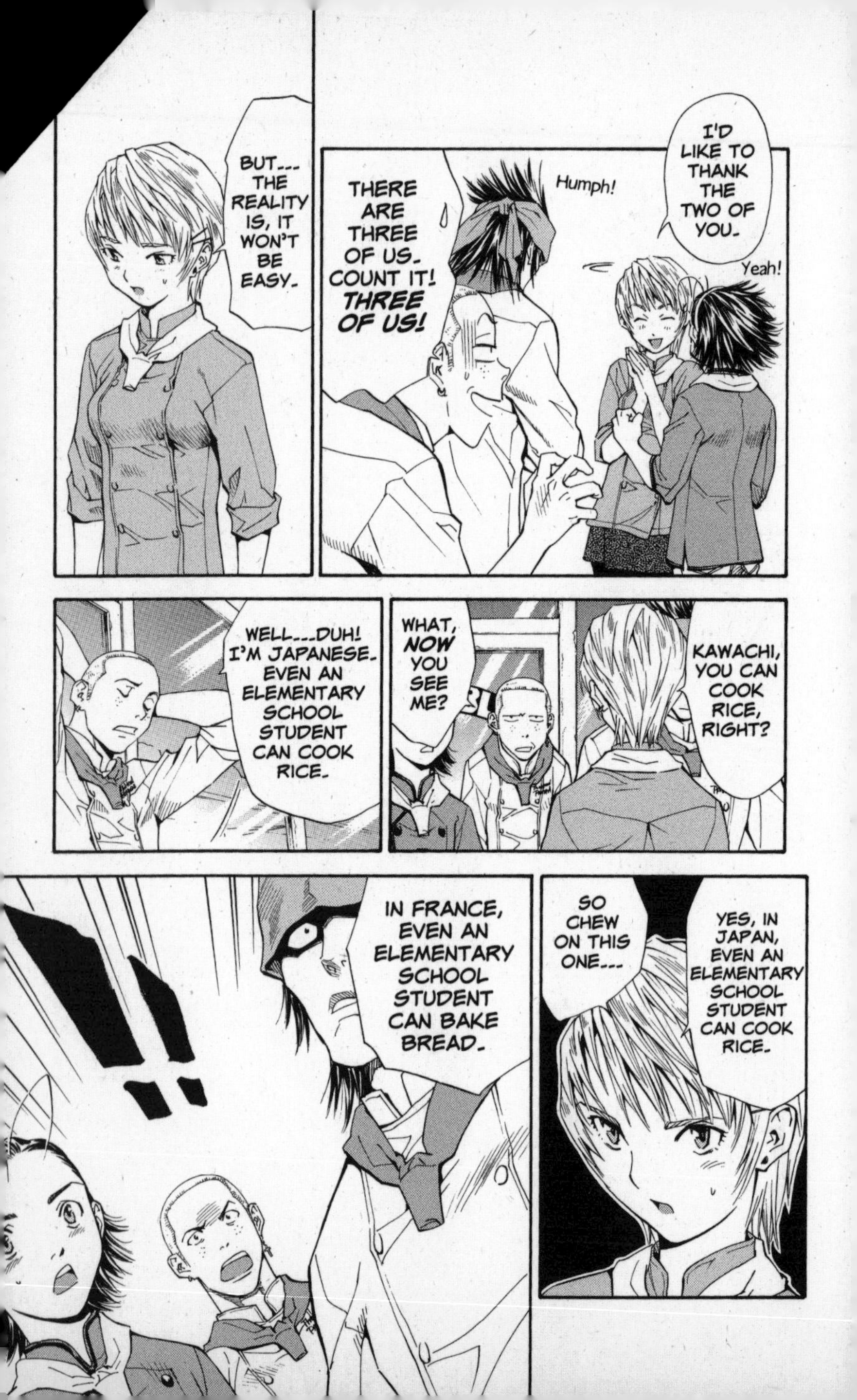
I'D LIKE TO THANK THE TWO OF YOU.
Humph!
Yeah!
THERE ARE THREE OF US. COUNT IT! *THREE OF US!*
BUT... THE REALITY IS, IT WON'T BE EASY.
KAWACHI, YOU CAN COOK RICE, RIGHT?
WHAT, *NOW* YOU SEE ME?
WELL...DUH! I'M JAPANESE. EVEN AN ELEMENTARY SCHOOL STUDENT CAN COOK RICE.
YES, IN JAPAN, EVEN AN ELEMENTARY SCHOOL STUDENT CAN COOK RICE.
SO CHEW ON THIS ONE...
IN FRANCE, EVEN AN ELEMENTARY SCHOOL STUDENT CAN BAKE BREAD.

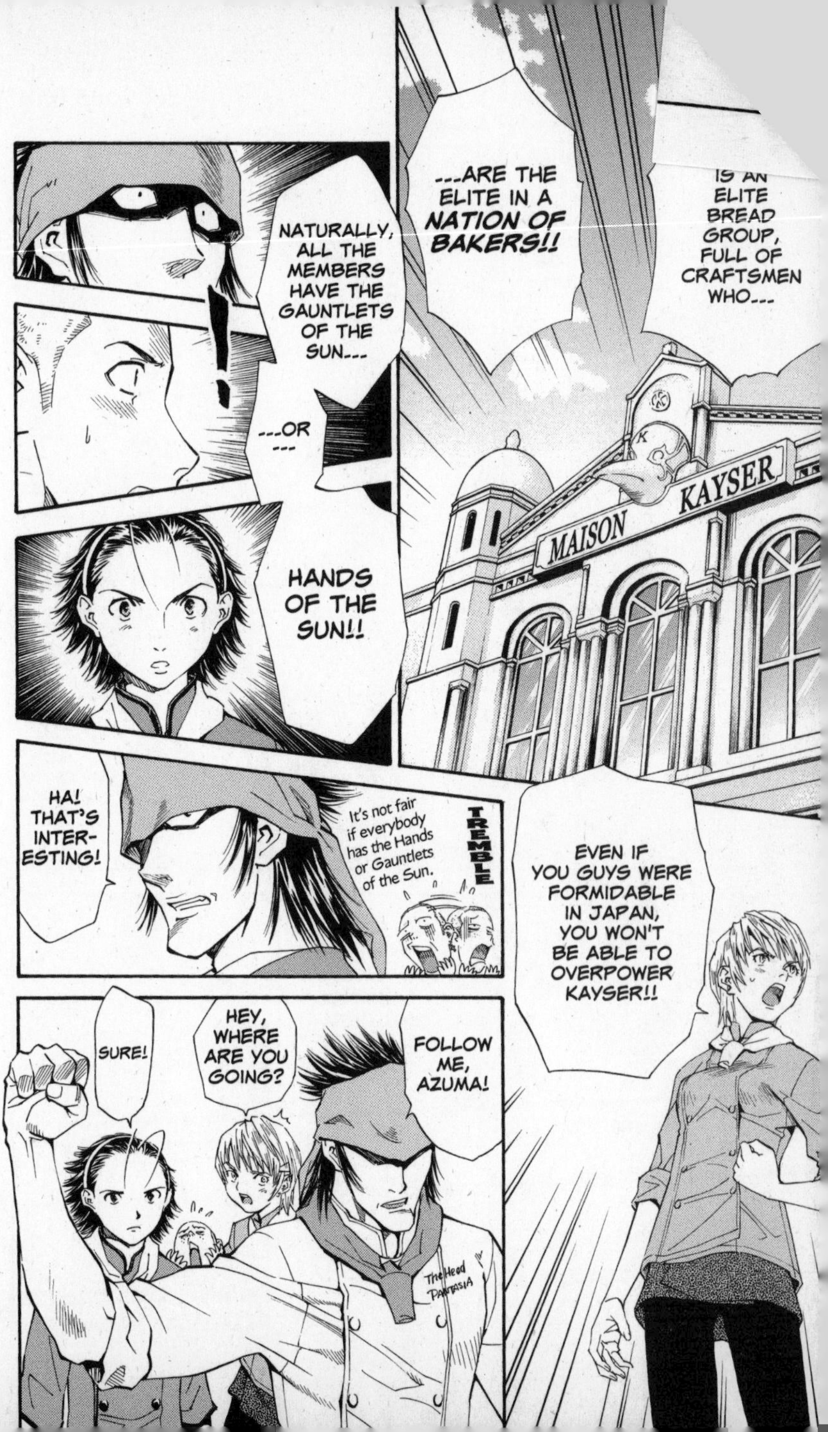
IS AN ELITE BREAD GROUP, FULL OF CRAFTSMEN WHO...
...ARE THE ELITE IN A NATION OF BAKERS!!
MAISON KAYSER
!
NATURALLY, ALL THE MEMBERS HAVE THE GAUNTLETS OF THE SUN...
...OR ...
HANDS OF THE SUN!!
EVEN IF YOU GUYS WERE FORMIDABLE IN JAPAN, YOU WON'T BE ABLE TO OVERPOWER KAYSER!!
TREMBLE
It's not fair if everybody has the Hands or Gauntlets of the Sun.
HA! THAT'S INTER-ESTING!
FOLLOW ME, AZUMA!
HEY, WHERE ARE YOU GOING?
SURE!
The Head PANTASIA

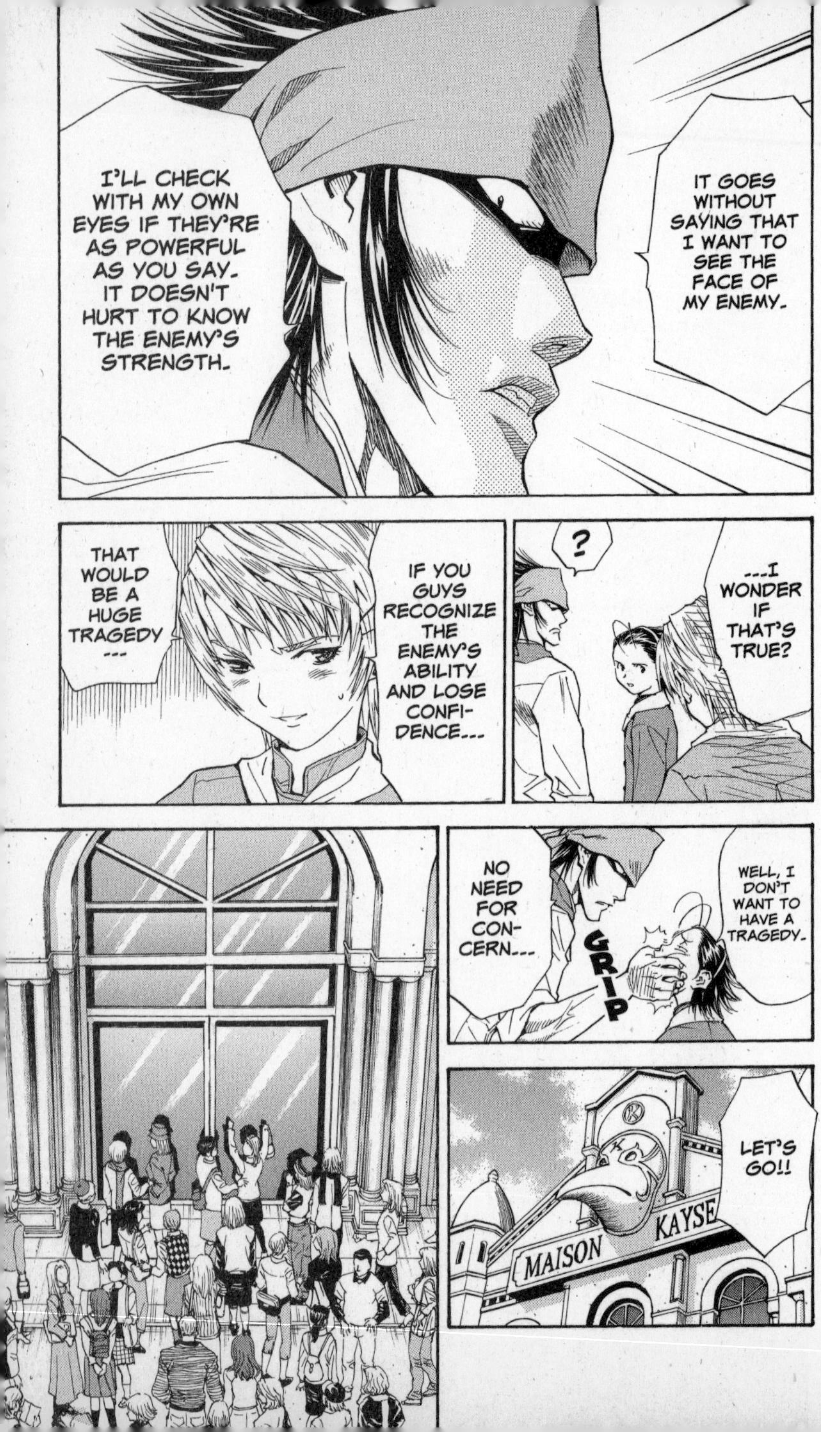
IT GOES WITHOUT SAYING THAT I WANT TO SEE THE FACE OF MY ENEMY.
I'LL CHECK WITH MY OWN EYES IF THEY'RE AS POWERFUL AS YOU SAY. IT DOESN'T HURT TO KNOW THE ENEMY'S STRENGTH.
?
...I WONDER IF THAT'S TRUE?
IF YOU GUYS RECOGNIZE THE ENEMY'S ABILITY AND LOSE CONFIDENCE...
THAT WOULD BE A HUGE TRAGEDY...
WELL, I DON'T WANT TO HAVE A TRAGEDY.
NO NEED FOR CONCERN...
GRIP
LET'S GO!!
MAISON KAYSE

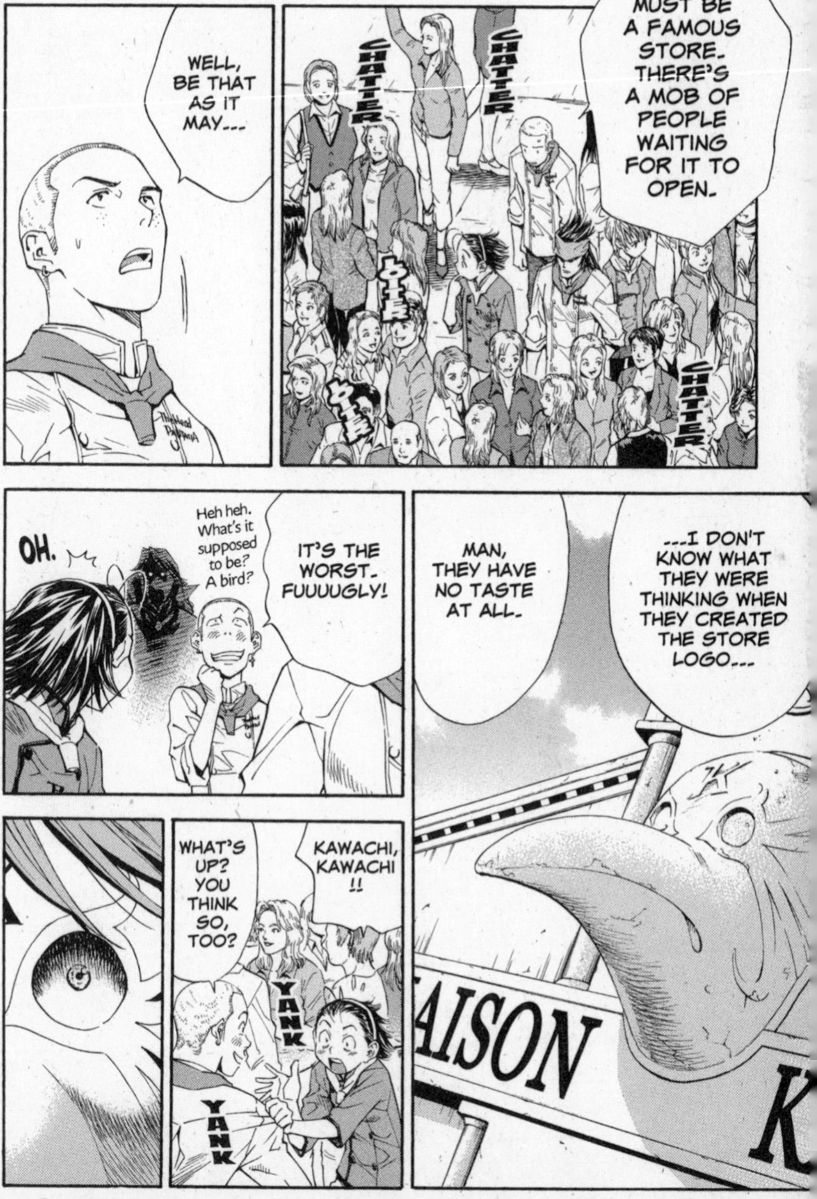
MUST BE A FAMOUS STORE. THERE'S A MOB OF PEOPLE WAITING FOR IT TO OPEN.
CHATTER
CHATTER
CHATTER
WELL, BE THAT AS IT MAY...
...I DON'T KNOW WHAT THEY WERE THINKING WHEN THEY CREATED THE STORE LOGO...
MAN, THEY HAVE NO TASTE AT ALL.
AISON
K
IT'S THE WORST. FUUUUGLY!
Heh heh. What's it supposed to be? A bird?
OH.
KAWACHI, KAWACHI !!
WHAT'S UP? YOU THINK SO, TOO?
YANK
YANK

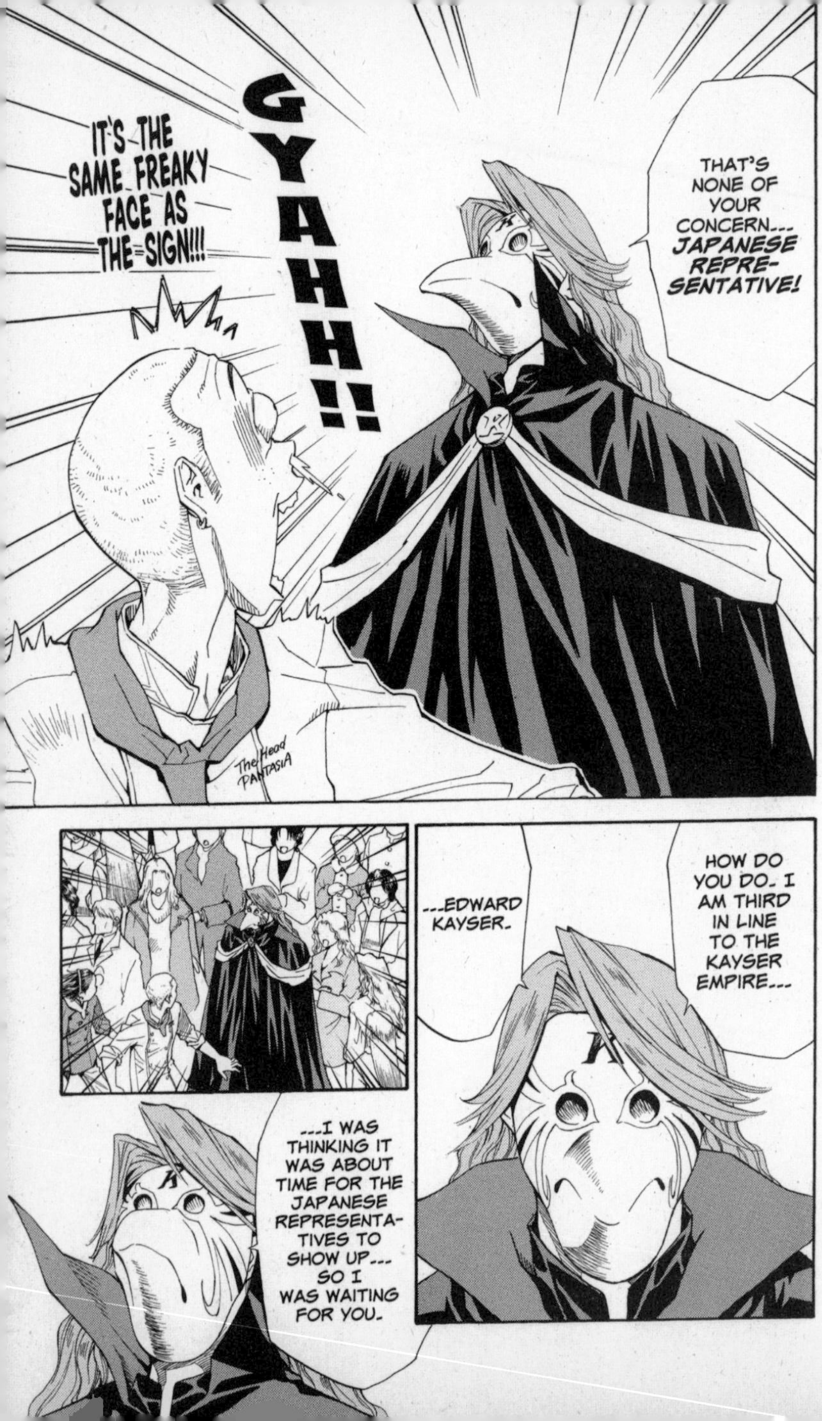
THAT'S NONE OF YOUR CONCERN... JAPANESE REPRESENTATIVE!
GYAHH!!
IT'S THE SAME FREAKY FACE AS THE SIGN!!!
The Head PANTASIA
HOW DO YOU DO. I AM THIRD IN LINE TO THE KAYSER EMPIRE...
...EDWARD KAYSER.
...I WAS THINKING IT WAS ABOUT TIME FOR THE JAPANESE REPRESENTATIVES TO SHOW UP... SO I WAS WAITING FOR YOU.

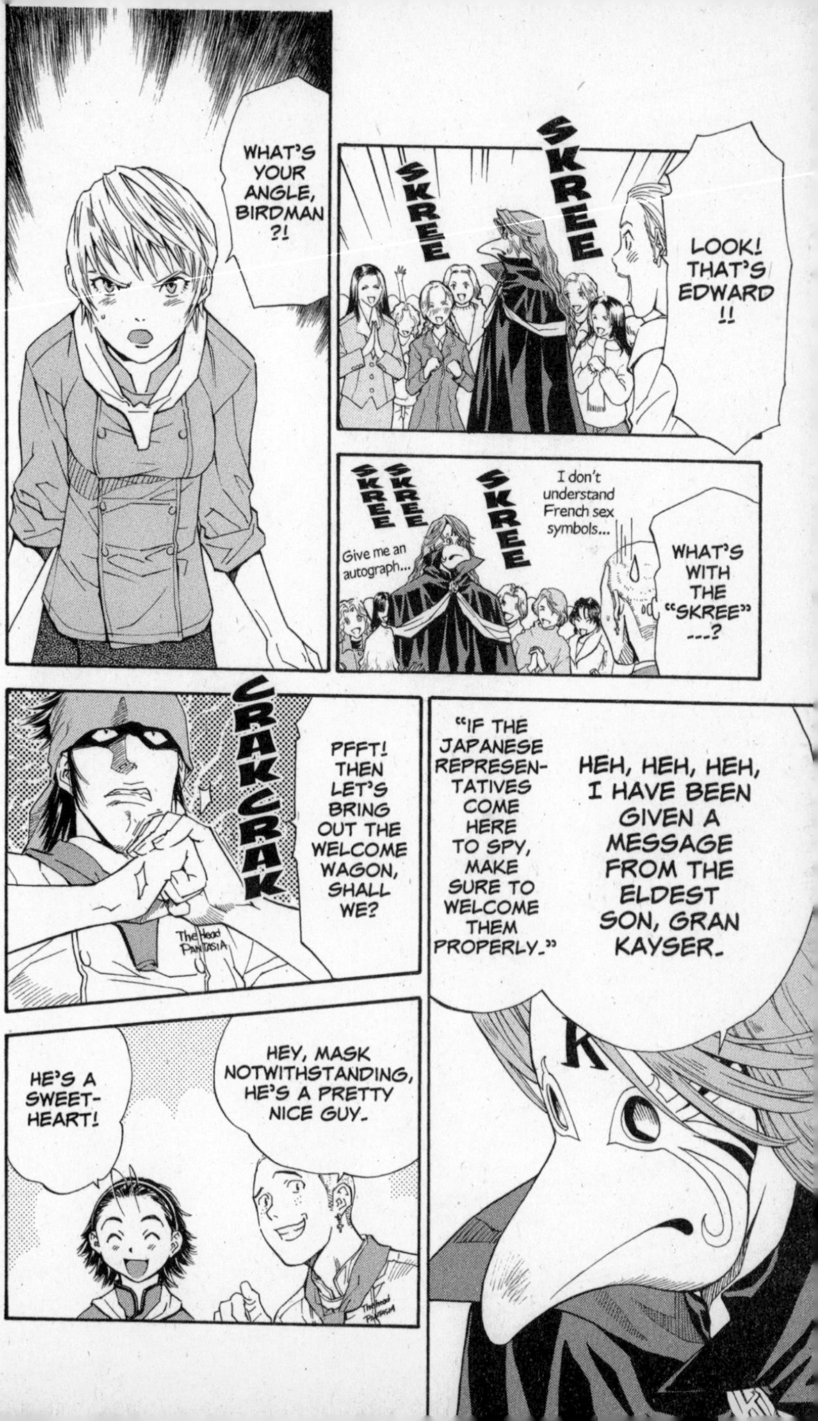
SKREE
SKREE
LOOK! THAT'S EDWARD!!
SKREE
SKREE
SKREE
WHAT'S WITH THE "SKREE"---?
I don't understand French sex symbols...
Give me an autograph...
WHAT'S YOUR ANGLE, BIRDMAN?!
HEH, HEH, HEH, I HAVE BEEN GIVEN A MESSAGE FROM THE ELDEST SON, GRAN KAYSER.
"IF THE JAPANESE REPRESENTATIVES COME HERE TO SPY, MAKE SURE TO WELCOME THEM PROPERLY."
CRAKCRAK
PFFT! THEN LET'S BRING OUT THE WELCOME WAGON, SHALL WE?
HEY, MASK NOTWITHSTANDING, HE'S A PRETTY NICE GUY.
HE'S A SWEETHEART!

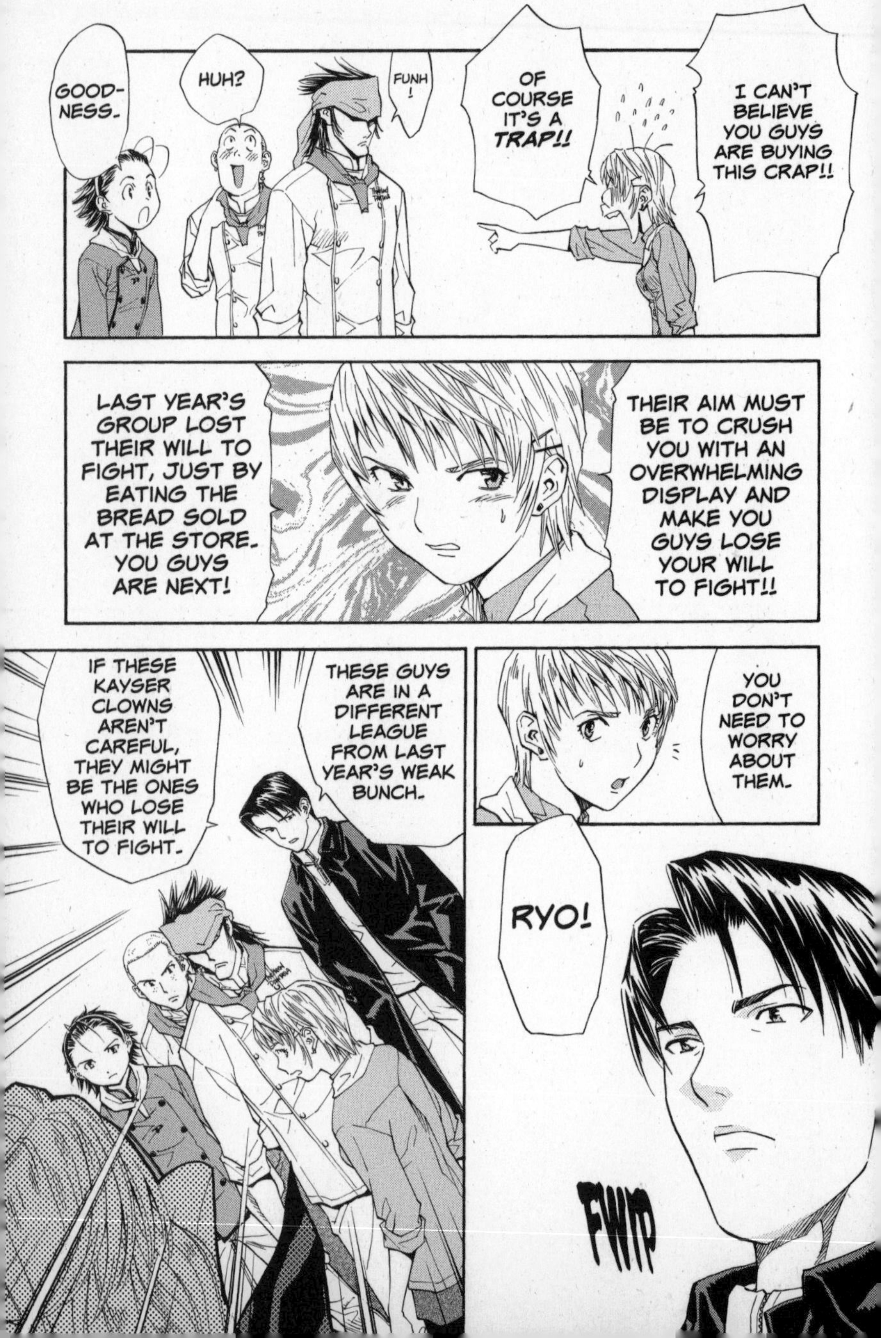
I CAN'T BELIEVE YOU GUYS ARE BUYING THIS CRAP!!
OF COURSE IT'S A TRAP!!
FUNH!
HUH?
GOODNESS.
THEIR AIM MUST BE TO CRUSH YOU WITH AN OVERWHELMING DISPLAY AND MAKE YOU GUYS LOSE YOUR WILL TO FIGHT!!
LAST YEAR'S GROUP LOST THEIR WILL TO FIGHT, JUST BY EATING THE BREAD SOLD AT THE STORE. YOU GUYS ARE NEXT!
YOU DON'T NEED TO WORRY ABOUT THEM.
RYO!
FWIP
THESE GUYS ARE IN A DIFFERENT LEAGUE FROM LAST YEAR'S WEAK BUNCH.
IF THESE KAYSER CLOWNS AREN'T CAREFUL, THEY MIGHT BE THE ONES WHO LOSE THEIR WILL TO FIGHT.

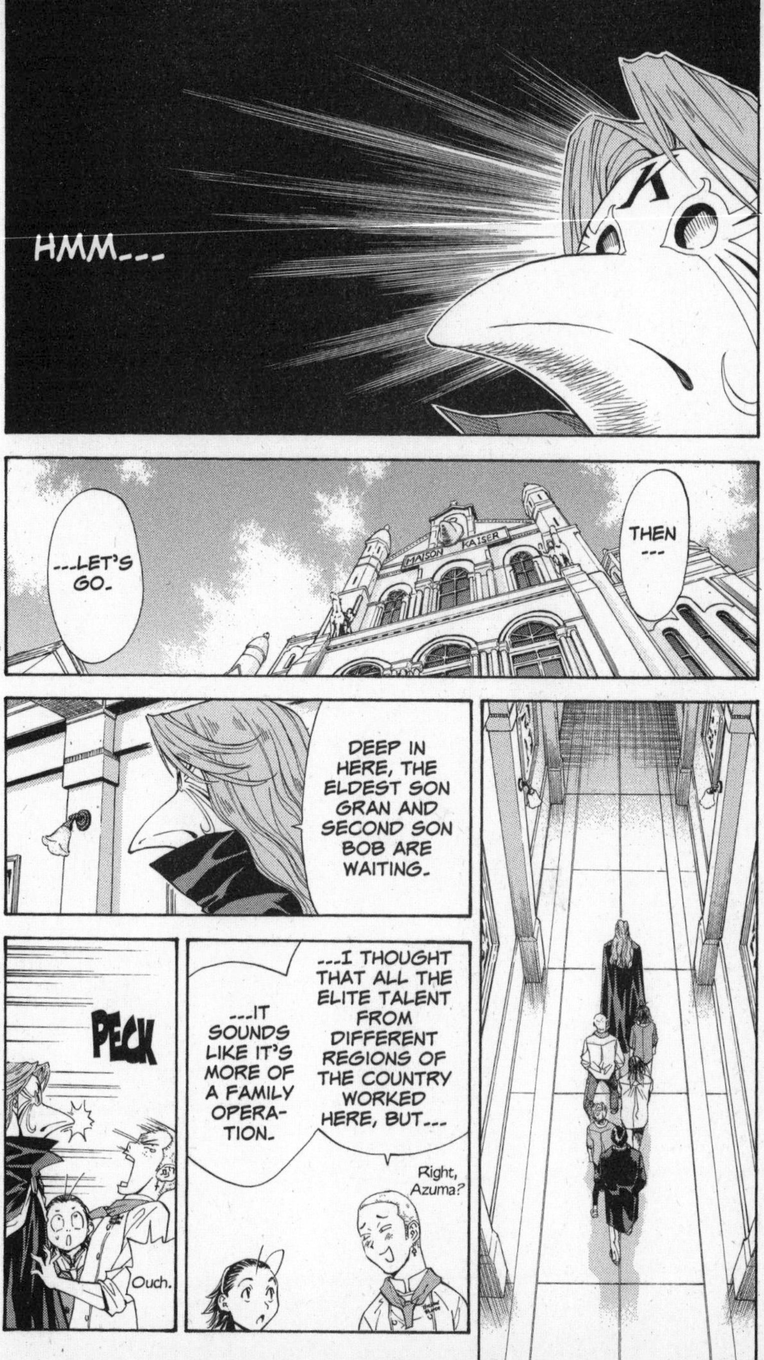
HMM...
THEN ---
---LET'S GO.
DEEP IN HERE, THE ELDEST SON GRAN AND SECOND SON BOB ARE WAITING.
---I THOUGHT THAT ALL THE ELITE TALENT FROM DIFFERENT REGIONS OF THE COUNTRY WORKED HERE, BUT---
---IT SOUNDS LIKE IT'S MORE OF A FAMILY OPERATION.
Right, Azuma?
PECK
Ouch.

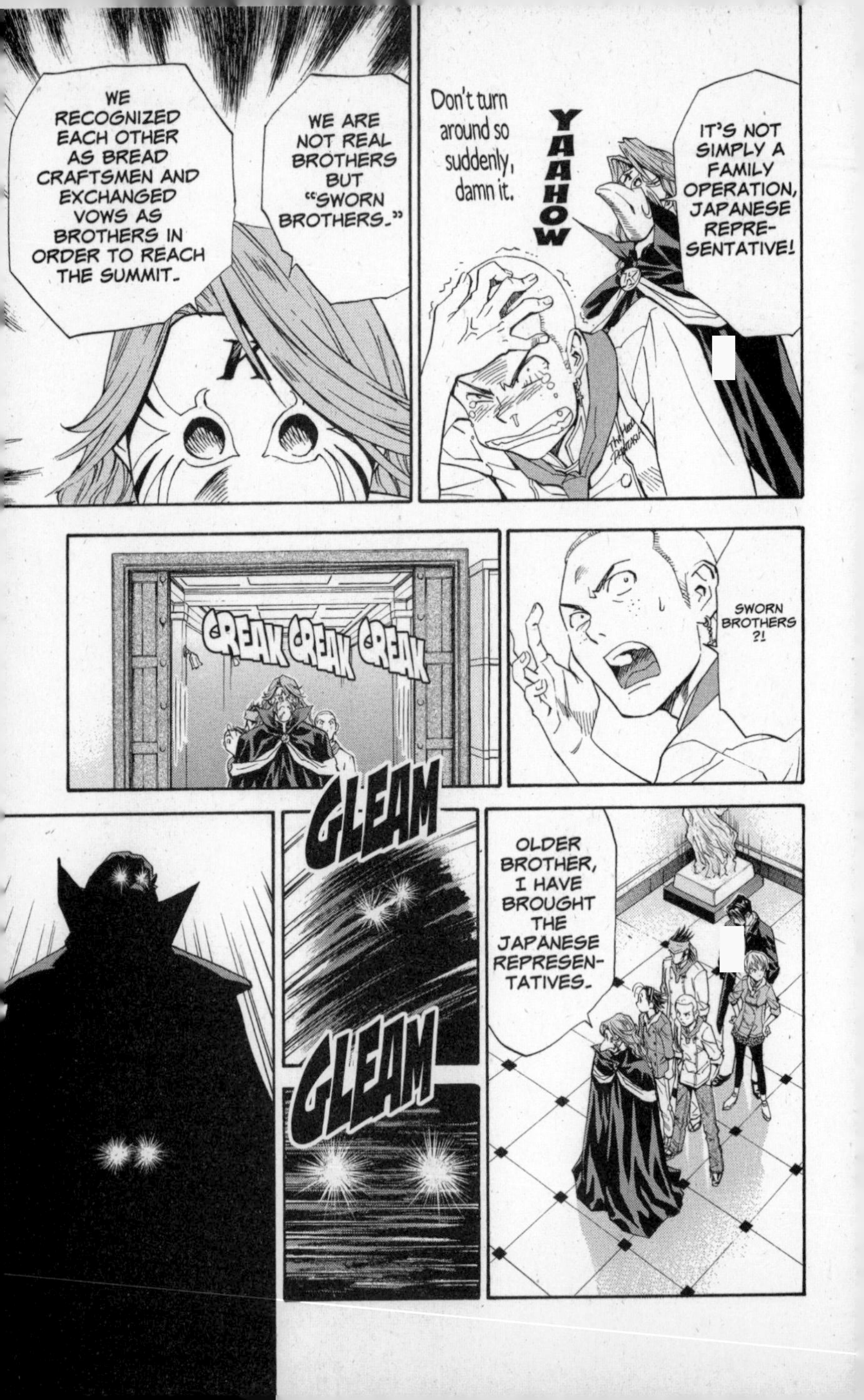
IT'S NOT SIMPLY A FAMILY OPERATION, JAPANESE REPRE-SENTATIVE!
YAAHOW
Don't turn around so suddenly, damn it.
WE ARE NOT REAL BROTHERS BUT "SWORN BROTHERS."
WE RECOGNIZED EACH OTHER AS BREAD CRAFTSMEN AND EXCHANGED VOWS AS BROTHERS IN ORDER TO REACH THE SUMMIT.
SWORN BROTHERS?!
CREAK CREAK CREAK
OLDER BROTHER, I HAVE BROUGHT THE JAPANESE REPRESEN-TATIVES.
GLEAM
GLEAM

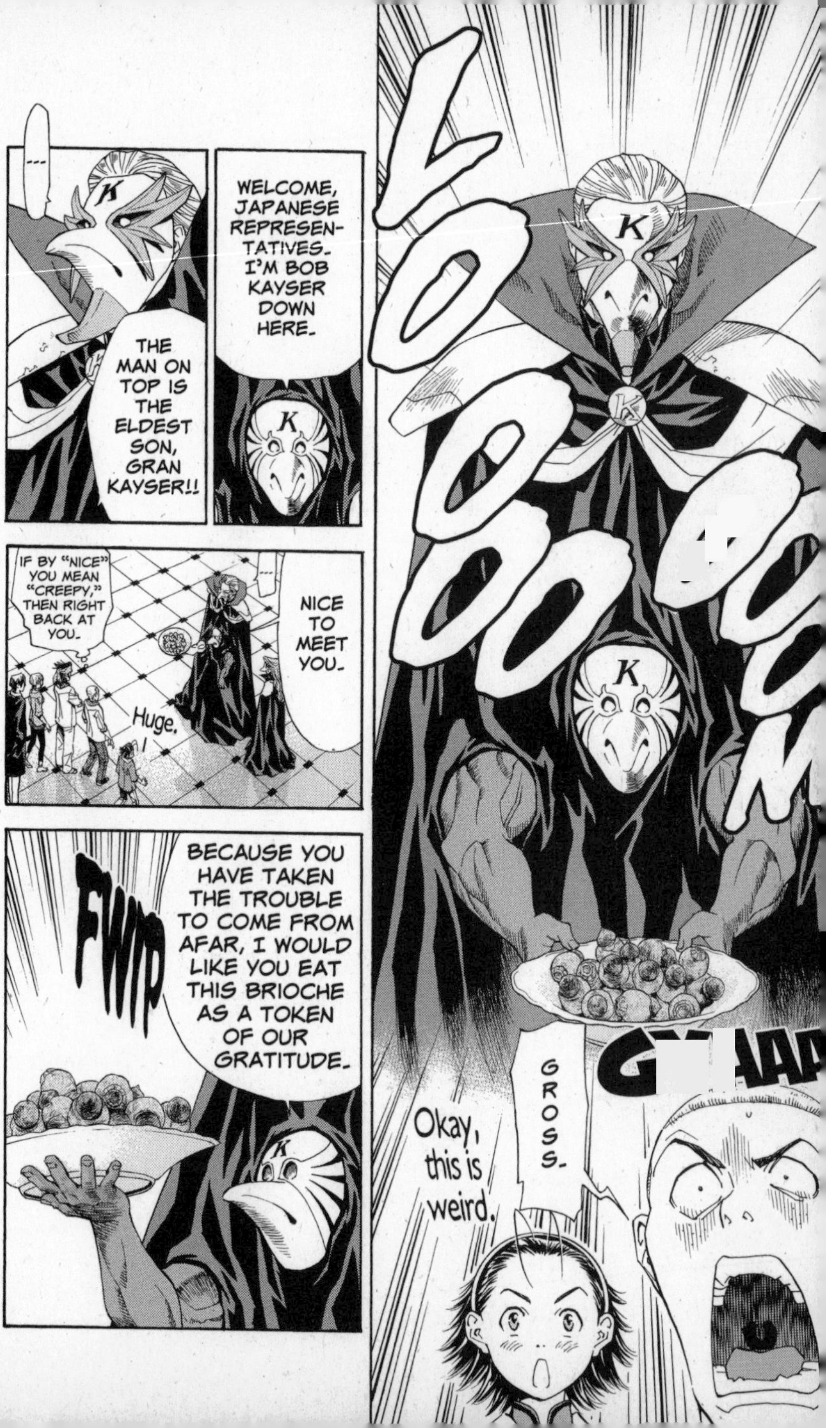
LOOOOOM
GROSS.
Okay, this is weird.
WELCOME, JAPANESE REPRESEN-TATIVES. I'M BOB KAYSER DOWN HERE.
...
THE MAN ON TOP IS THE ELDEST SON, GRAN KAYSER!!
...
NICE TO MEET YOU.
IF BY "NICE" YOU MEAN "CREEPY," THEN RIGHT BACK AT YOU.
Huge.
BECAUSE YOU HAVE TAKEN THE TROUBLE TO COME FROM AFAR, I WOULD LIKE YOU EAT THIS BRIOCHE AS A TOKEN OF OUR GRATITUDE.
FWIP

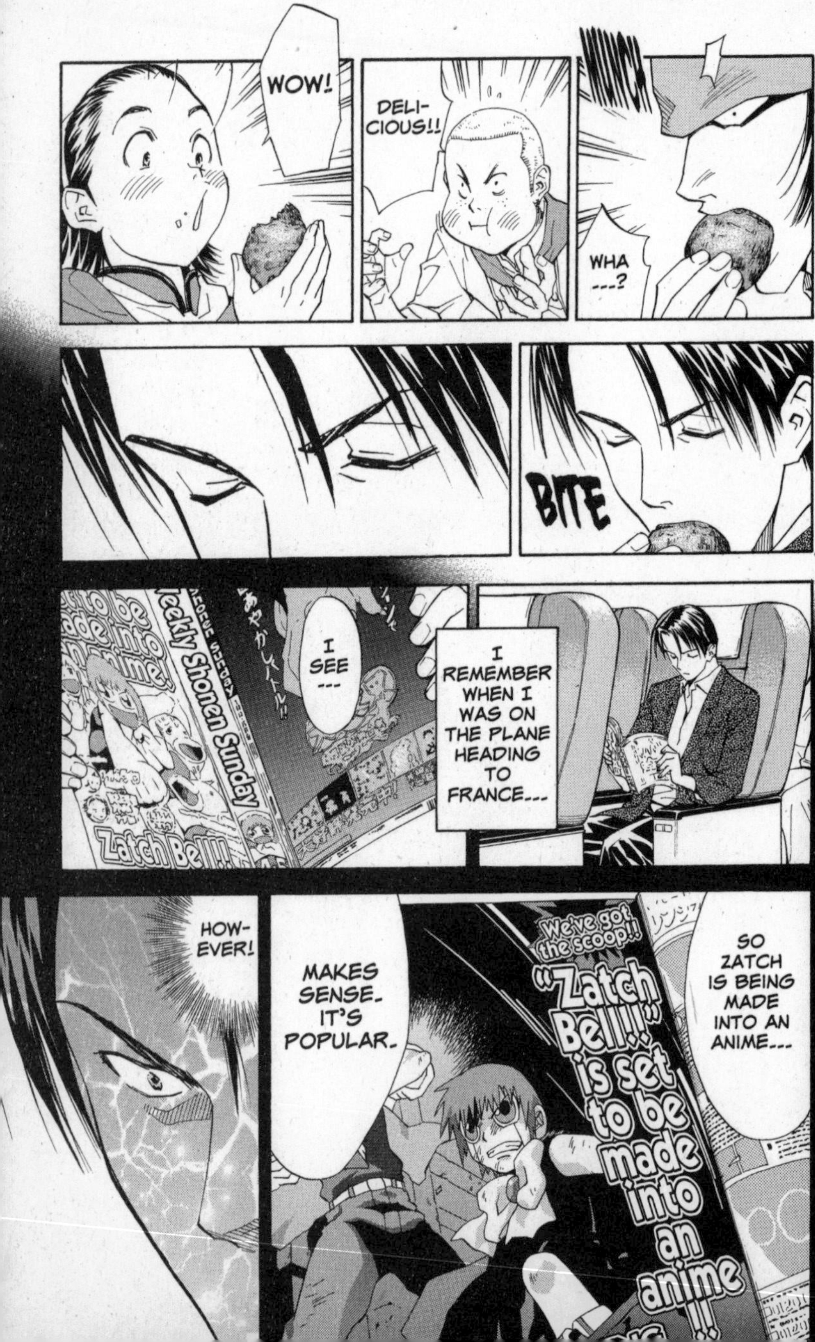
MUNCH
WHA ---?
DELI-CIOUS!!
WOW!
BITE
I REMEMBER WHEN I WAS ON THE PLANE HEADING TO FRANCE...
I SEE ---
Weekly Shonen Sunday
Zatch Bell!!
SO ZATCH IS BEING MADE INTO AN ANIME...
We've got the scoop!!
"Zatch Bell!!" is set to be made into an anime!!
MAKES SENSE. IT'S POPULAR.
HOW-EVER!

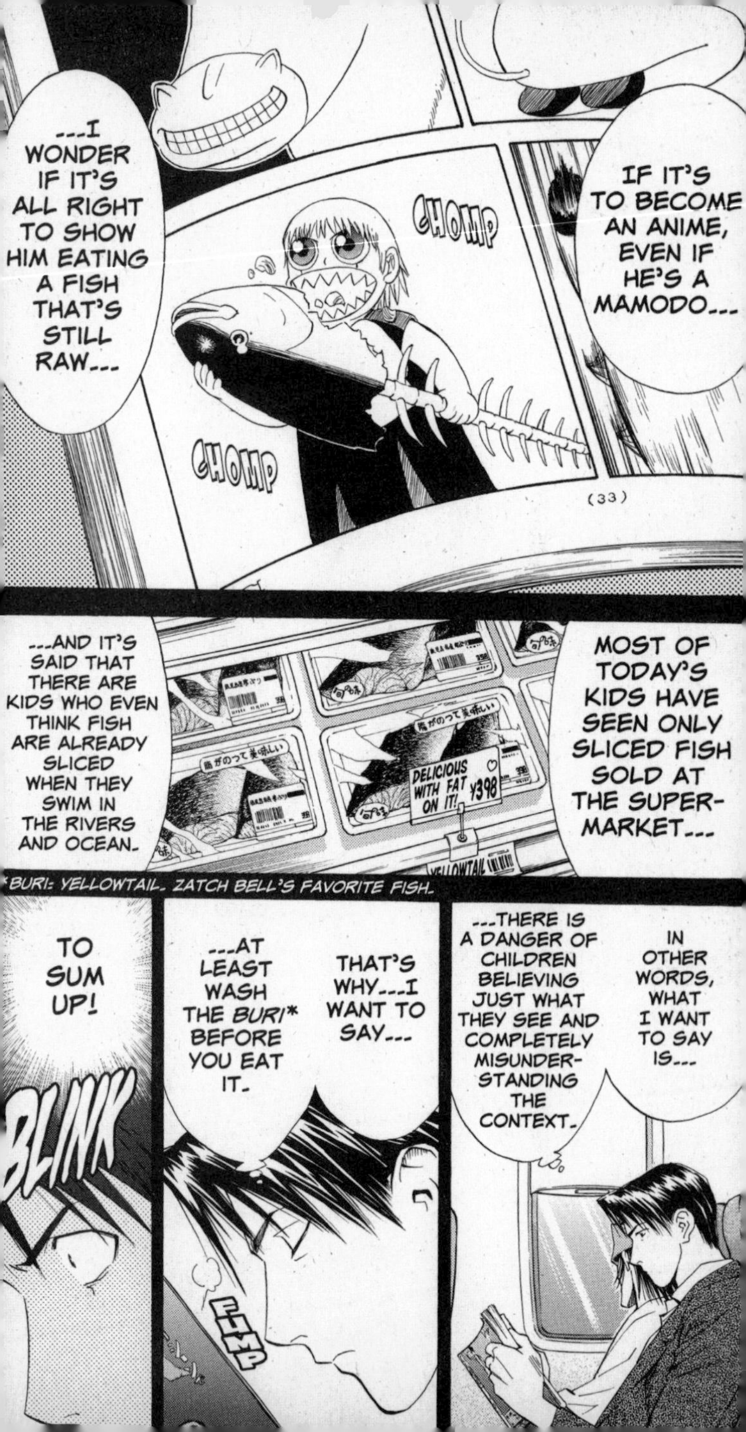
IF IT'S TO BECOME AN ANIME, EVEN IF HE'S A MAMODO...
...I WONDER IF IT'S ALL RIGHT TO SHOW HIM EATING A FISH THAT'S STILL RAW...
CHOMP
CHOMP
(33)
MOST OF TODAY'S KIDS HAVE SEEN ONLY SLICED FISH SOLD AT THE SUPER-MARKET...
...AND IT'S SAID THAT THERE ARE KIDS WHO EVEN THINK FISH ARE ALREADY SLICED WHEN THEY SWIM IN THE RIVERS AND OCEAN.
DELICIOUS WITH FAT ON IT! ¥398
YELLOWTAIL
IN OTHER WORDS, WHAT I WANT TO SAY IS...
...THERE IS A DANGER OF CHILDREN BELIEVING JUST WHAT THEY SEE AND COMPLETELY MISUNDER-STANDING THE CONTEXT.
THAT'S WHY...I WANT TO SAY...
...AT LEAST WASH THE *BURI** BEFORE YOU EAT IT.
FLUMP
TO SUM UP!
BLINK
*BURI: YELLOWTAIL. ZATCH BELL'S FAVORITE FISH.

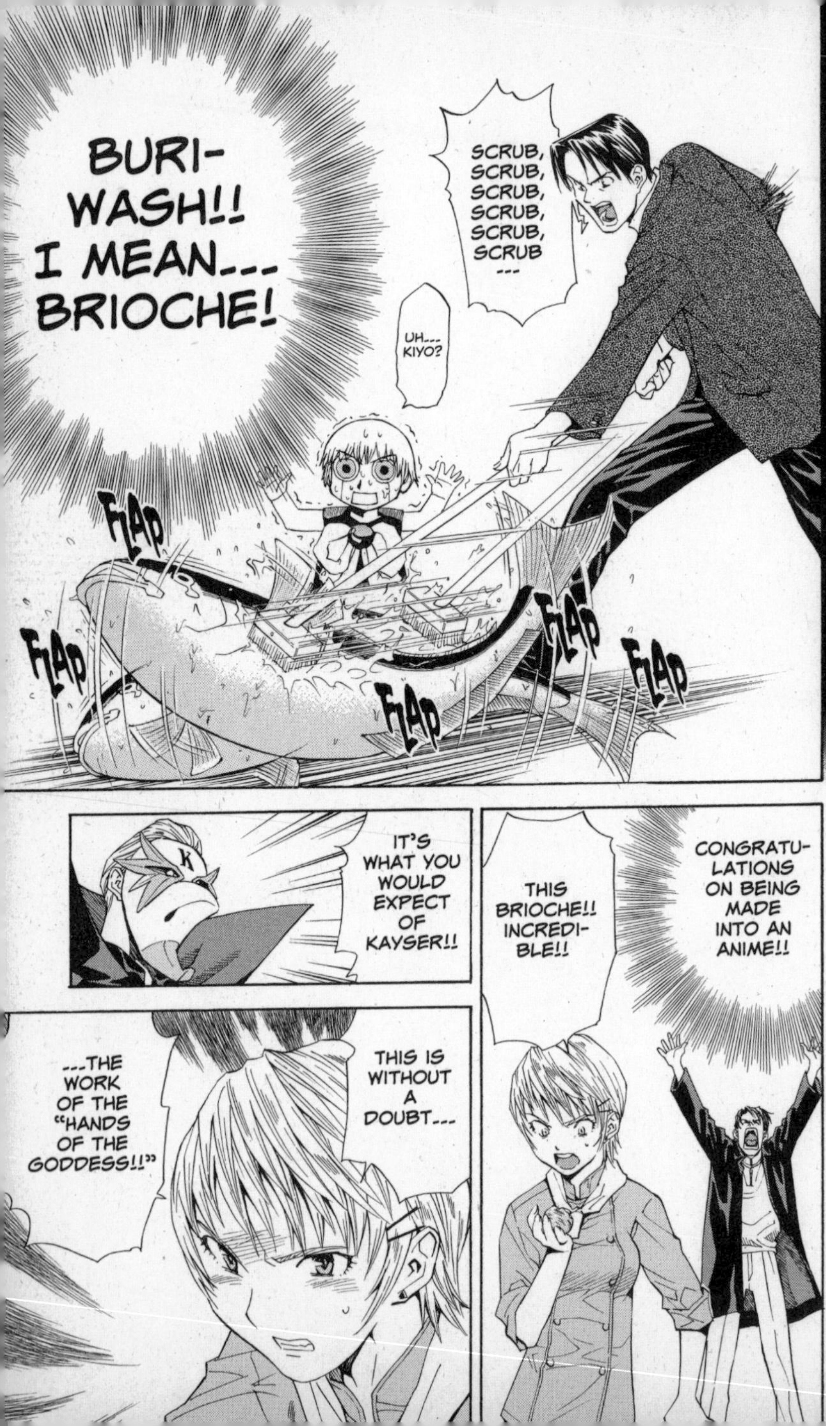
SCRUB, SCRUB, SCRUB, SCRUB, SCRUB, SCRUB---
UH--- KIYO?
BURI-WASH!! I MEAN--- BRIOCHE!
FLAP
FLAP
FLAP
FLAP
FLAP
CONGRATULATIONS ON BEING MADE INTO AN ANIME!!
THIS BRIOCHE!! INCREDIBLE!!
IT'S WHAT YOU WOULD EXPECT OF KAYSER!!
THIS IS WITHOUT A DOUBT---
---THE WORK OF THE "HANDS OF THE GODDESS!!"

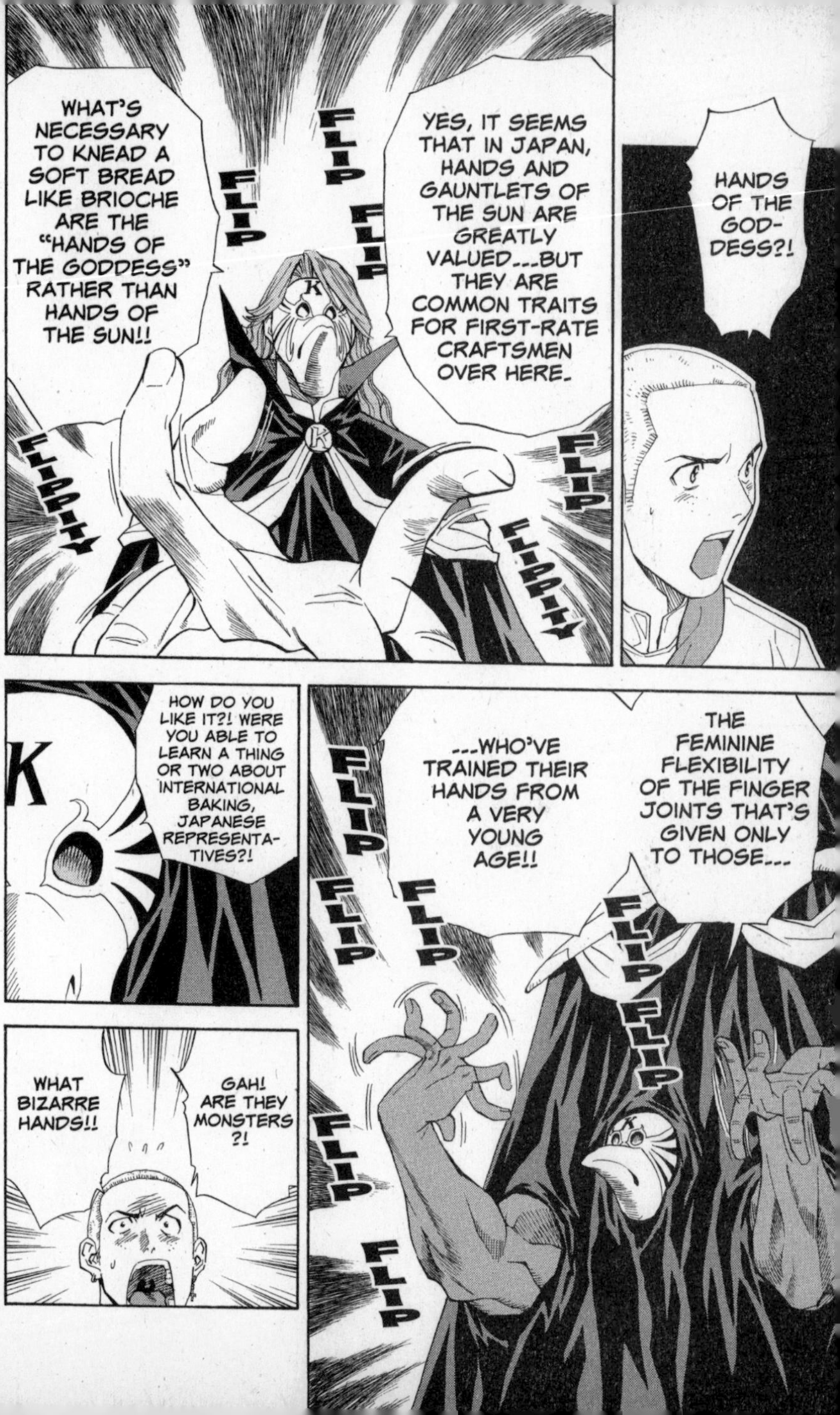
HANDS OF THE GOD-DESS?!
YES, IT SEEMS THAT IN JAPAN, HANDS AND GAUNTLETS OF THE SUN ARE GREATLY VALUED...BUT THEY ARE COMMON TRAITS FOR FIRST-RATE CRAFTSMEN OVER HERE.
FLIP
FLIP
FLIPPITY
FLIP
FLIP
WHAT'S NECESSARY TO KNEAD A SOFT BREAD LIKE BRIOCHE ARE THE "HANDS OF THE GODDESS" RATHER THAN HANDS OF THE SUN!!
FLIPPITY
THE FEMININE FLEXIBILITY OF THE FINGER JOINTS THAT'S GIVEN ONLY TO THOSE...
...WHO'VE TRAINED THEIR HANDS FROM A VERY YOUNG AGE!!
FLIP
FLIP
FLIP
FLIP
FLIP
FLIP
FLIP
FLIP
K
HOW DO YOU LIKE IT?! WERE YOU ABLE TO LEARN A THING OR TWO ABOUT INTERNATIONAL BAKING, JAPANESE REPRESENTA-TIVES?!
GAH! ARE THEY MONSTERS ?!
WHAT BIZARRE HANDS!!

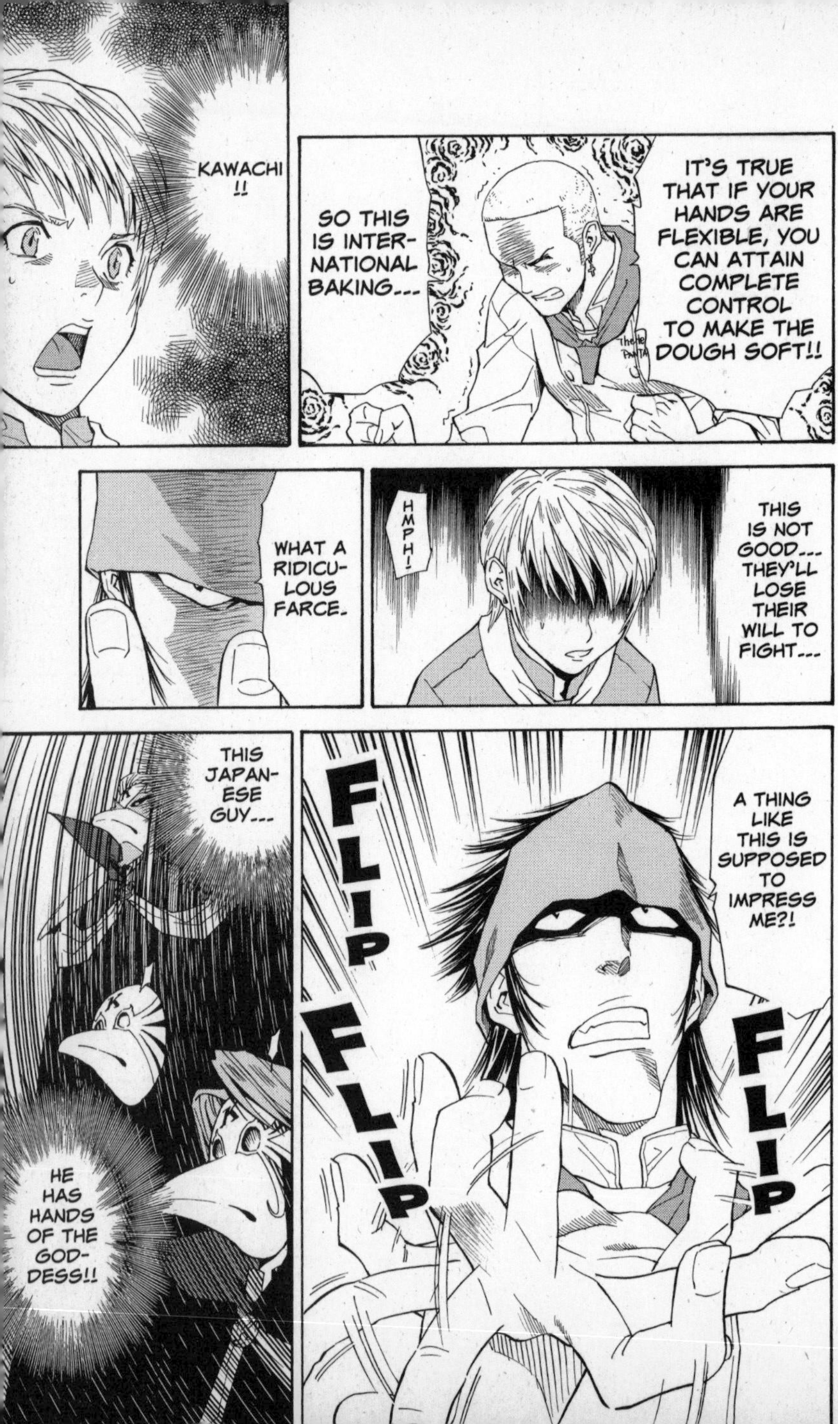
IT'S TRUE THAT IF YOUR HANDS ARE FLEXIBLE, YOU CAN ATTAIN COMPLETE CONTROL TO MAKE THE DOUGH SOFT!!
SO THIS IS INTERNATIONAL BAKING...
KAWACHI!!
THIS IS NOT GOOD... THEY'LL LOSE THEIR WILL TO FIGHT...
HMPH!
WHAT A RIDICULOUS FARCE.
A THING LIKE THIS IS SUPPOSED TO IMPRESS ME?!
FLIP FLIP
FLIP FLIP
THIS JAPANESE GUY...
HE HAS HANDS OF THE GODDESS!!

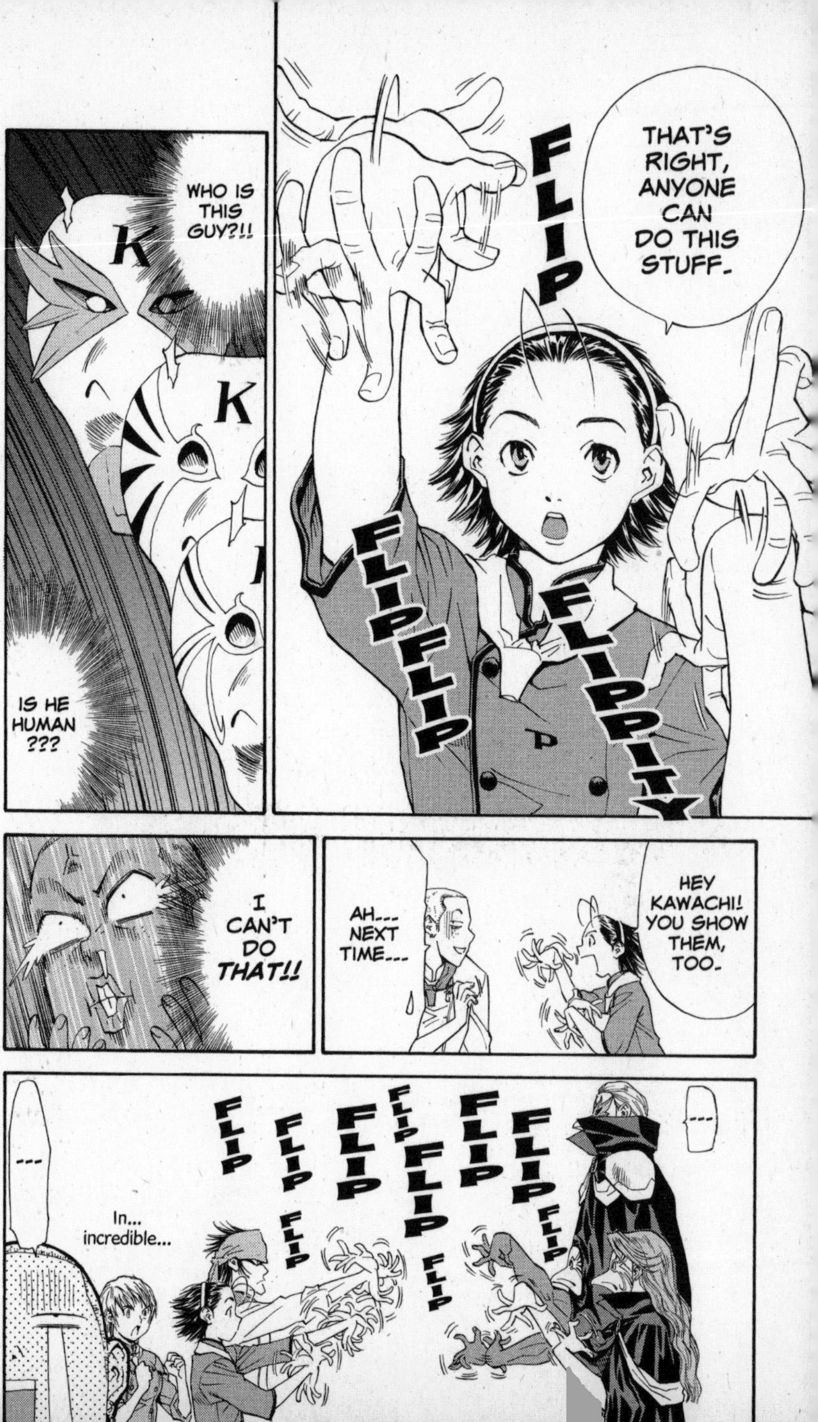
FLIP
THAT'S RIGHT, ANYONE CAN DO THIS STUFF.
FLIPPITY
FLIPFLIP
WHO IS THIS GUY?!!
K
K
K
IS HE HUMAN???
HEY KAWACHI! YOU SHOW THEM, TOO.
AH... NEXT TIME...
I CAN'T DO THAT!!
...
FLIP
FLIP
FLIP
FLIP
FLIP
FLIP
FLIP
FLIP
FLIP
FLIP
FLIP
In... incredible...
...

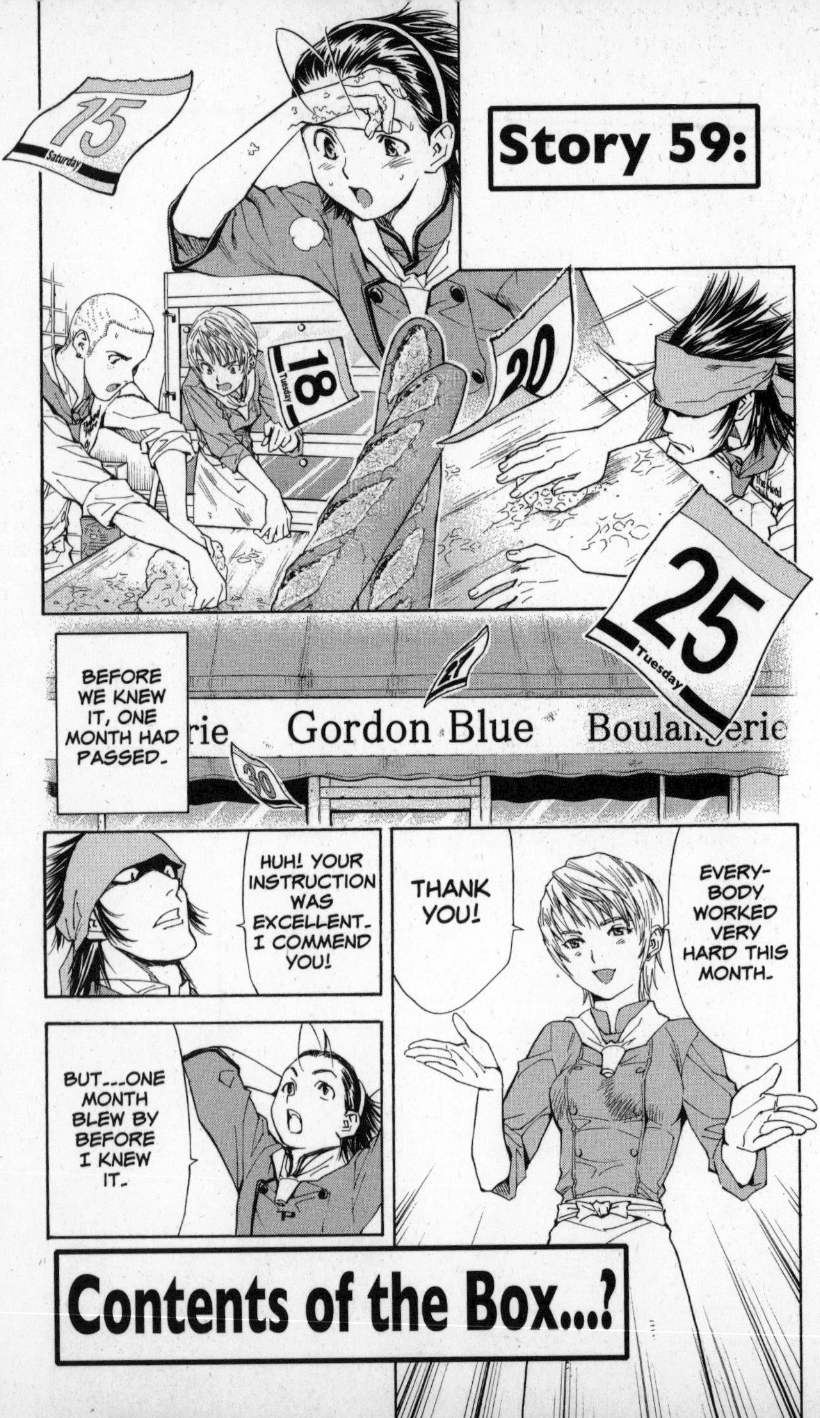
Story 59:
15 Saturday
18 Tuesday
20
25 Tuesday
Gordon Blue
BEFORE WE KNEW IT, ONE MONTH HAD PASSED.
EVERY-BODY WORKED VERY HARD THIS MONTH.
THANK YOU!
HUH! YOUR INSTRUCTION WAS EXCELLENT. I COMMEND YOU!
BUT...ONE MONTH BLEW BY BEFORE I KNEW IT.
Contents of the Box...?

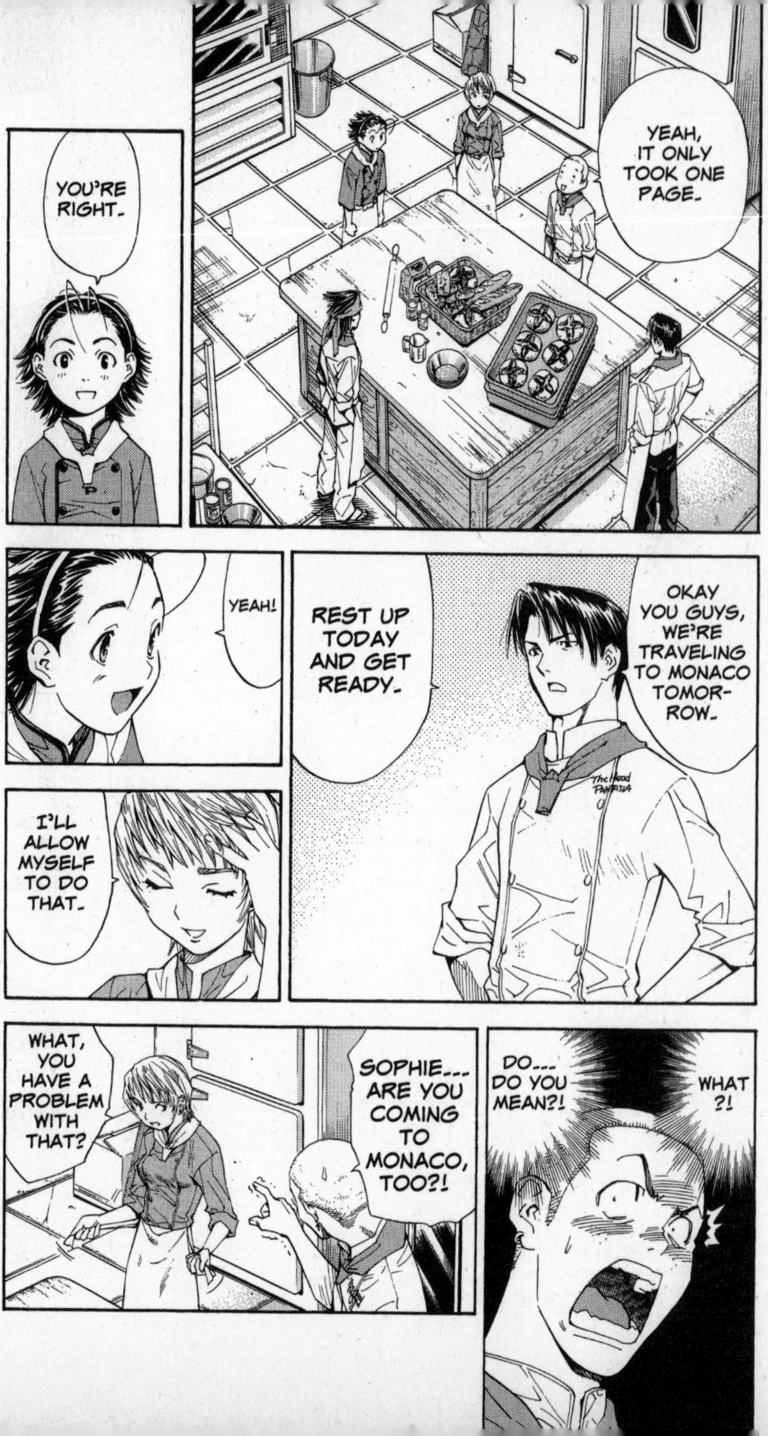
YEAH, IT ONLY TOOK ONE PAGE.
YOU'RE RIGHT.
OKAY YOU GUYS, WE'RE TRAVELING TO MONACO TOMORROW.
REST UP TODAY AND GET READY.
YEAH!
I'LL ALLOW MYSELF TO DO THAT.
WHAT?!
DO... DO YOU MEAN?!
SOPHIE... ARE YOU COMING TO MONACO, TOO?!
WHAT, YOU HAVE A PROBLEM WITH THAT?

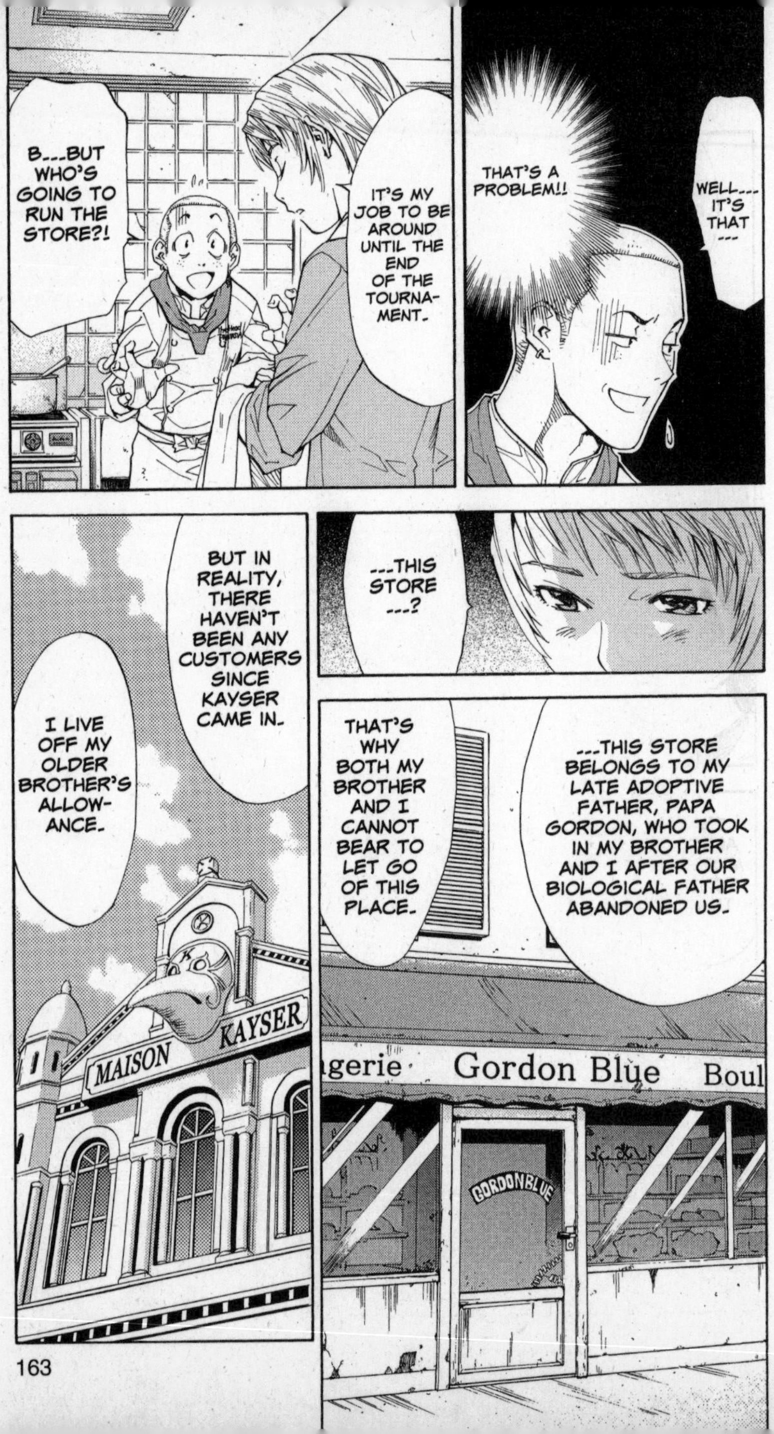
WELL... IT'S THAT ---
THAT'S A PROBLEM!!
IT'S MY JOB TO BE AROUND UNTIL THE END OF THE TOURNAMENT.
B...BUT WHO'S GOING TO RUN THE STORE?!
---THIS STORE ---?
---THIS STORE BELONGS TO MY LATE ADOPTIVE FATHER, PAPA GORDON, WHO TOOK IN MY BROTHER AND I AFTER OUR BIOLOGICAL FATHER ABANDONED US.
THAT'S WHY BOTH MY BROTHER AND I CANNOT BEAR TO LET GO OF THIS PLACE.
agerie Gordon Blue Boul
GORDON BLUE
BUT IN REALITY, THERE HAVEN'T BEEN ANY CUSTOMERS SINCE KAYSER CAME IN.
I LIVE OFF MY OLDER BROTHER'S ALLOW-ANCE.
MAISON KAYSER

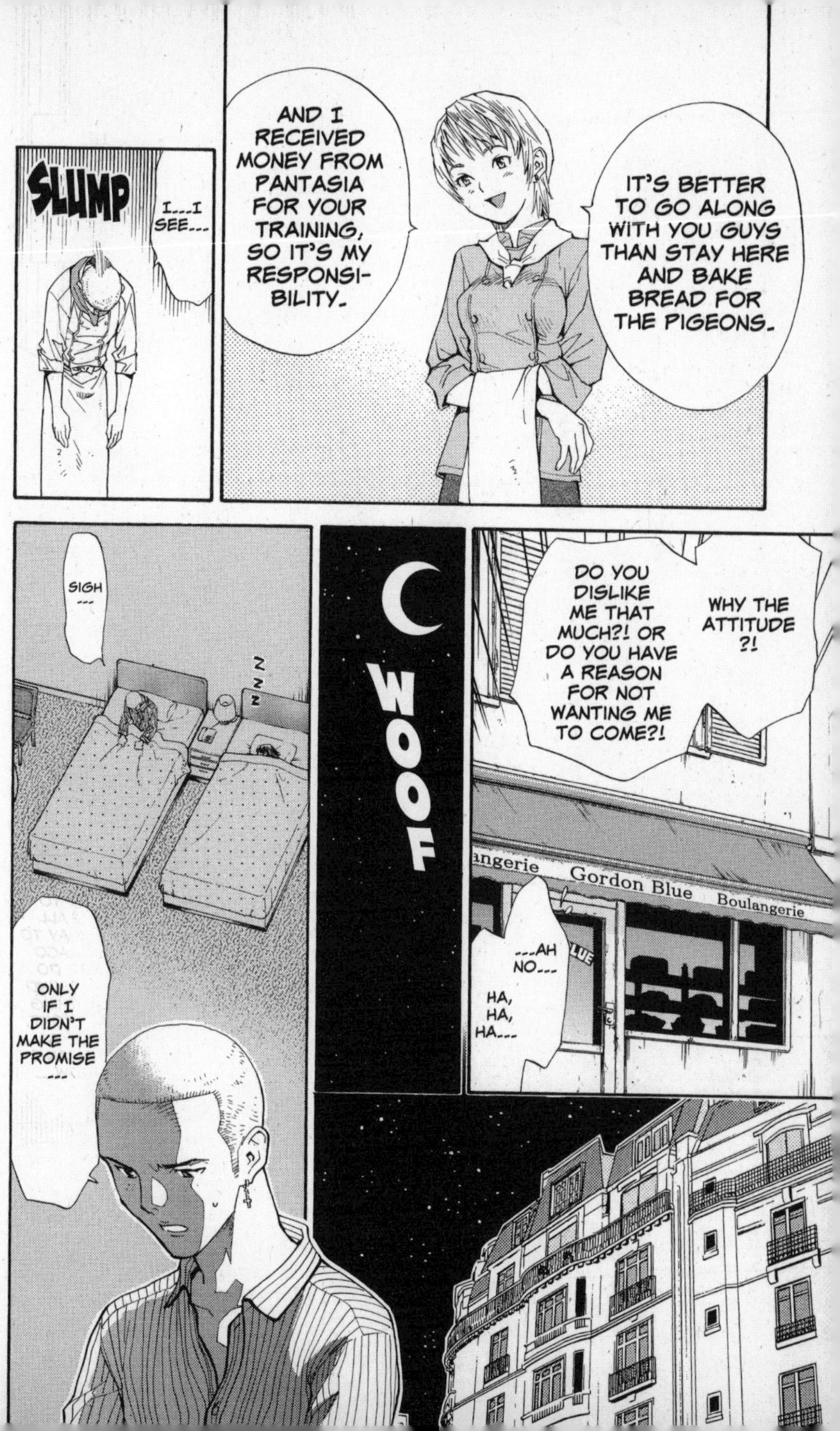
IT'S BETTER TO GO ALONG WITH YOU GUYS THAN STAY HERE AND BAKE BREAD FOR THE PIGEONS.
AND I RECEIVED MONEY FROM PANTASIA FOR YOUR TRAINING, SO IT'S MY RESPONSIBILITY.
SLUMP
I...I SEE...
WHY THE ATTITUDE?!
DO YOU DISLIKE ME THAT MUCH?! OR DO YOU HAVE A REASON FOR NOT WANTING ME TO COME?!
angerie Gordon Blue Boulangerie
...AH NO...
HA, HA, HA...
WOOF
SIGH...
Z Z Z
ONLY IF I DIDN'T MAKE THE PROMISE...

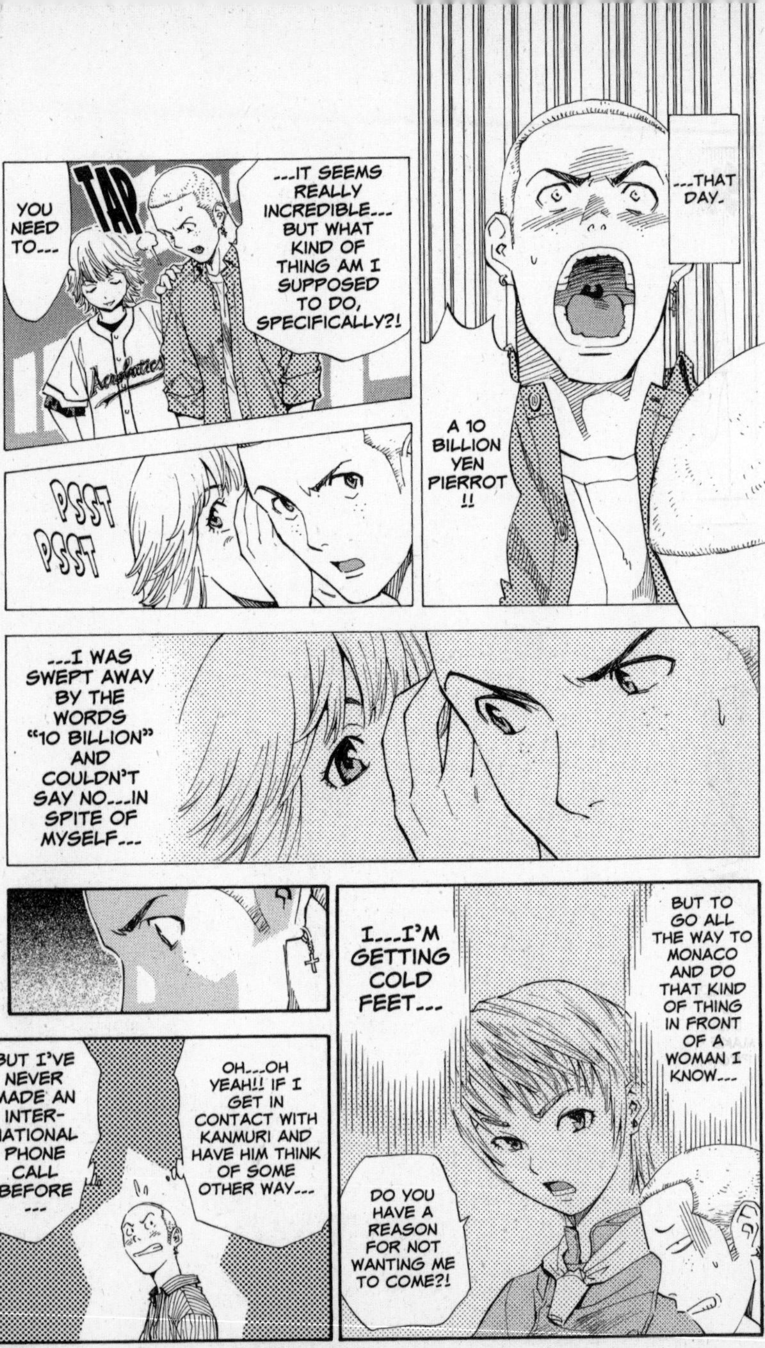
...THAT DAY.
A 10 BILLION YEN PIERROT!!
...IT SEEMS REALLY INCREDIBLE... BUT WHAT KIND OF THING AM I SUPPOSED TO DO, SPECIFICALLY?!
TAP
YOU NEED TO...
PSST PSST
...I WAS SWEPT AWAY BY THE WORDS "10 BILLION" AND COULDN'T SAY NO...IN SPITE OF MYSELF...
BUT TO GO ALL THE WAY TO MONACO AND DO THAT KIND OF THING IN FRONT OF A WOMAN I KNOW...
I...I'M GETTING COLD FEET...
DO YOU HAVE A REASON FOR NOT WANTING ME TO COME?!
OH...OH YEAH!! IF I GET IN CONTACT WITH KANMURI AND HAVE HIM THINK OF SOME OTHER WAY...
BUT I'VE NEVER MADE AN INTER-NATIONAL PHONE CALL BEFORE ...

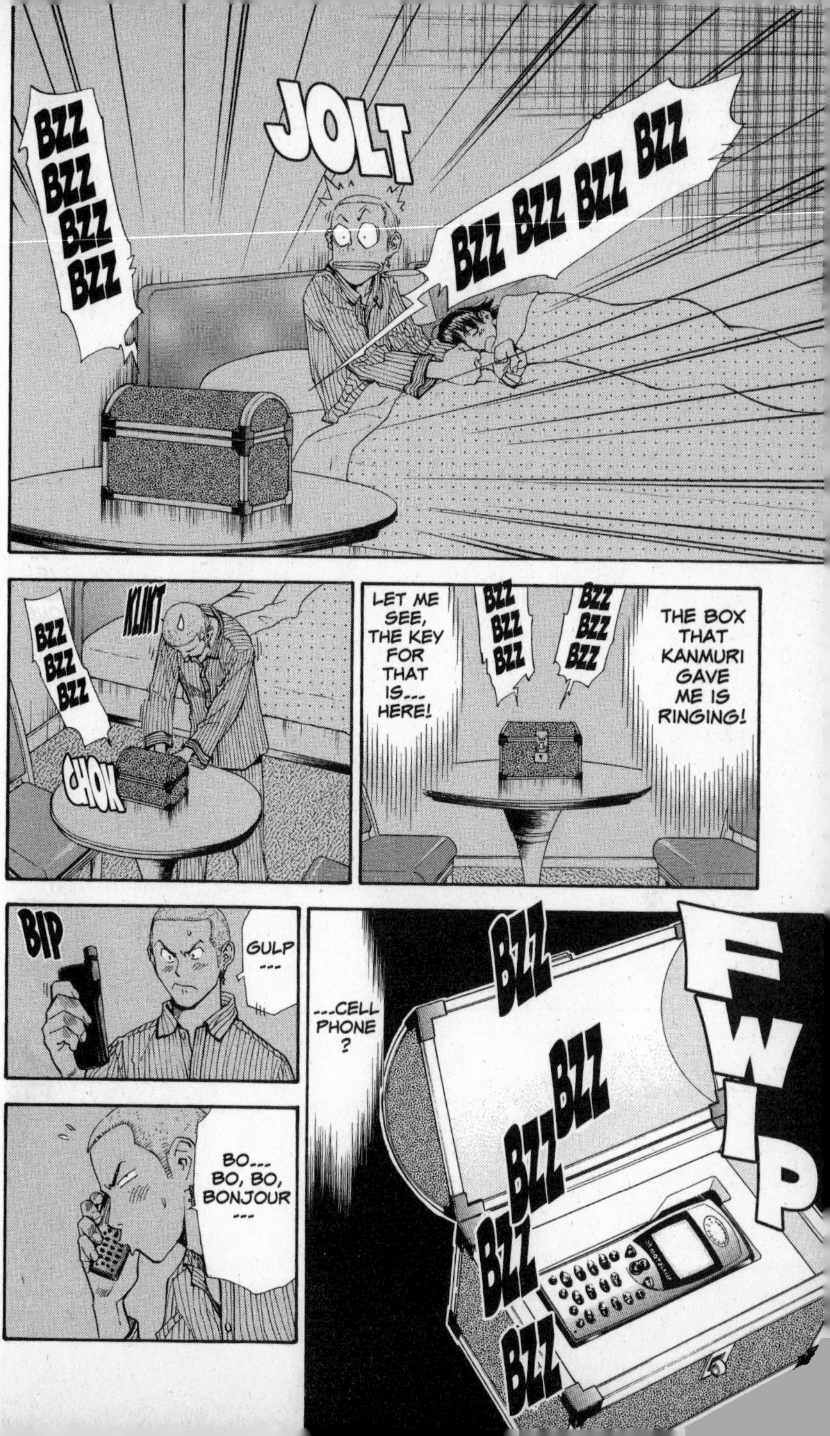
BZZ BZZ BZZ BZZ
JOLT
BZZ BZZ BZZ BZZ
THE BOX THAT KANMURI GAVE ME IS RINGING!
BZZ BZZ BZZ
BZZ BZZ BZZ
LET ME SEE, THE KEY FOR THAT IS... HERE!
KLIKT
BZZ BZZ BZZ
CHOK
FWIP
BZZ
BZZ BZZ
BZZ BZZ
BZZ
...CELL PHONE?
BIP
GULP...
BO... BO, BO, BONJOUR...

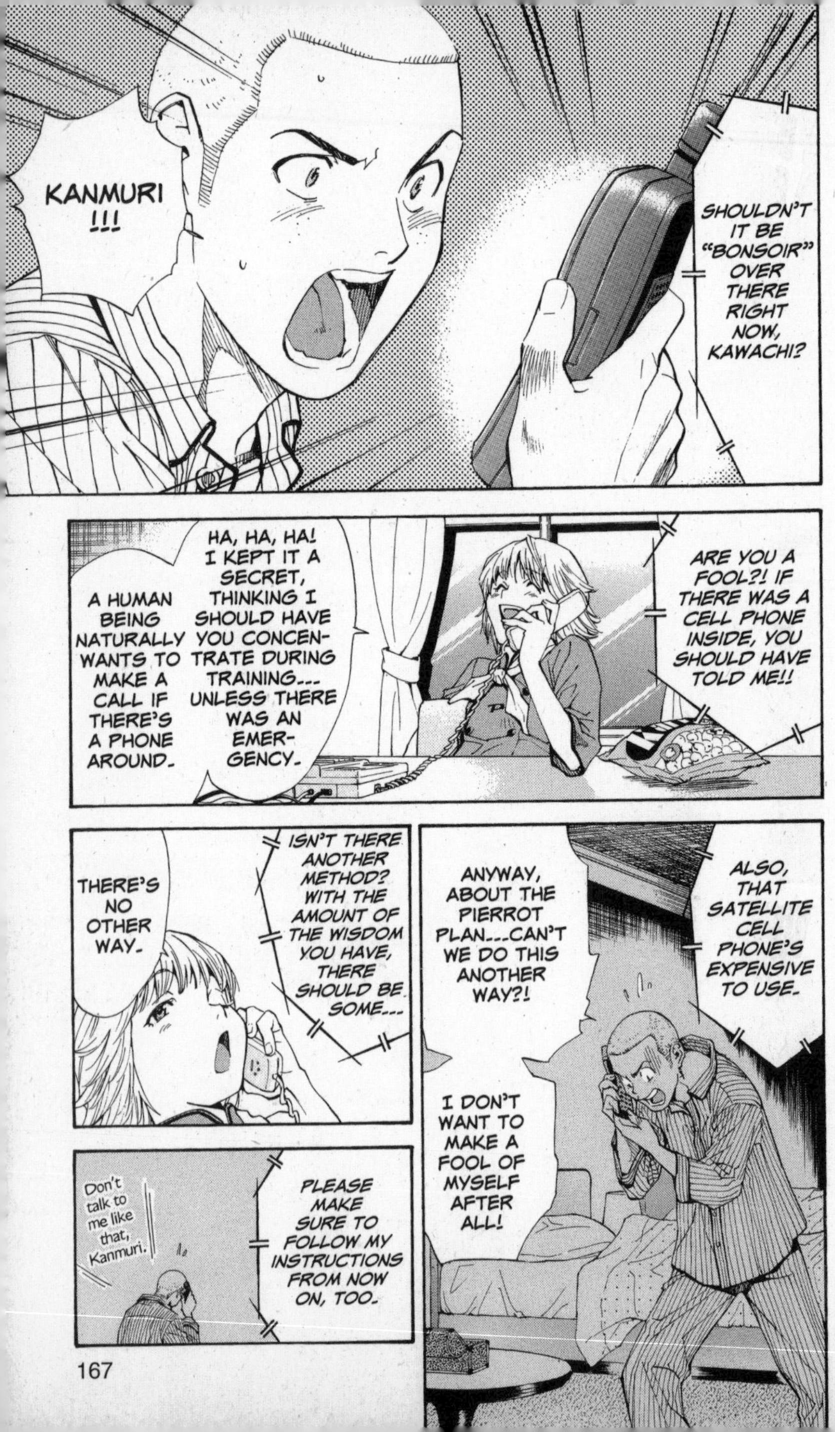
SHOULDN'T IT BE "BONSOIR" OVER THERE RIGHT NOW, KAWACHI?
KANMURI !!!
ARE YOU A FOOL?! IF THERE WAS A CELL PHONE INSIDE, YOU SHOULD HAVE TOLD ME!!
HA, HA, HA! I KEPT IT A SECRET, THINKING I SHOULD HAVE YOU CONCEN-TRATE DURING TRAINING... UNLESS THERE WAS AN EMER-GENCY.
A HUMAN BEING NATURALLY WANTS TO MAKE A CALL IF THERE'S A PHONE AROUND.
ALSO, THAT SATELLITE CELL PHONE'S EXPENSIVE TO USE.
ANYWAY, ABOUT THE PIERROT PLAN... CAN'T WE DO THIS ANOTHER WAY?!
I DON'T WANT TO MAKE A FOOL OF MYSELF AFTER ALL!
ISN'T THERE ANOTHER METHOD? WITH THE AMOUNT OF THE WISDOM YOU HAVE, THERE SHOULD BE SOME...
THERE'S NO OTHER WAY.
PLEASE MAKE SURE TO FOLLOW MY INSTRUCTIONS FROM NOW ON, TOO.
Don't talk to me like that, Kanmuri.

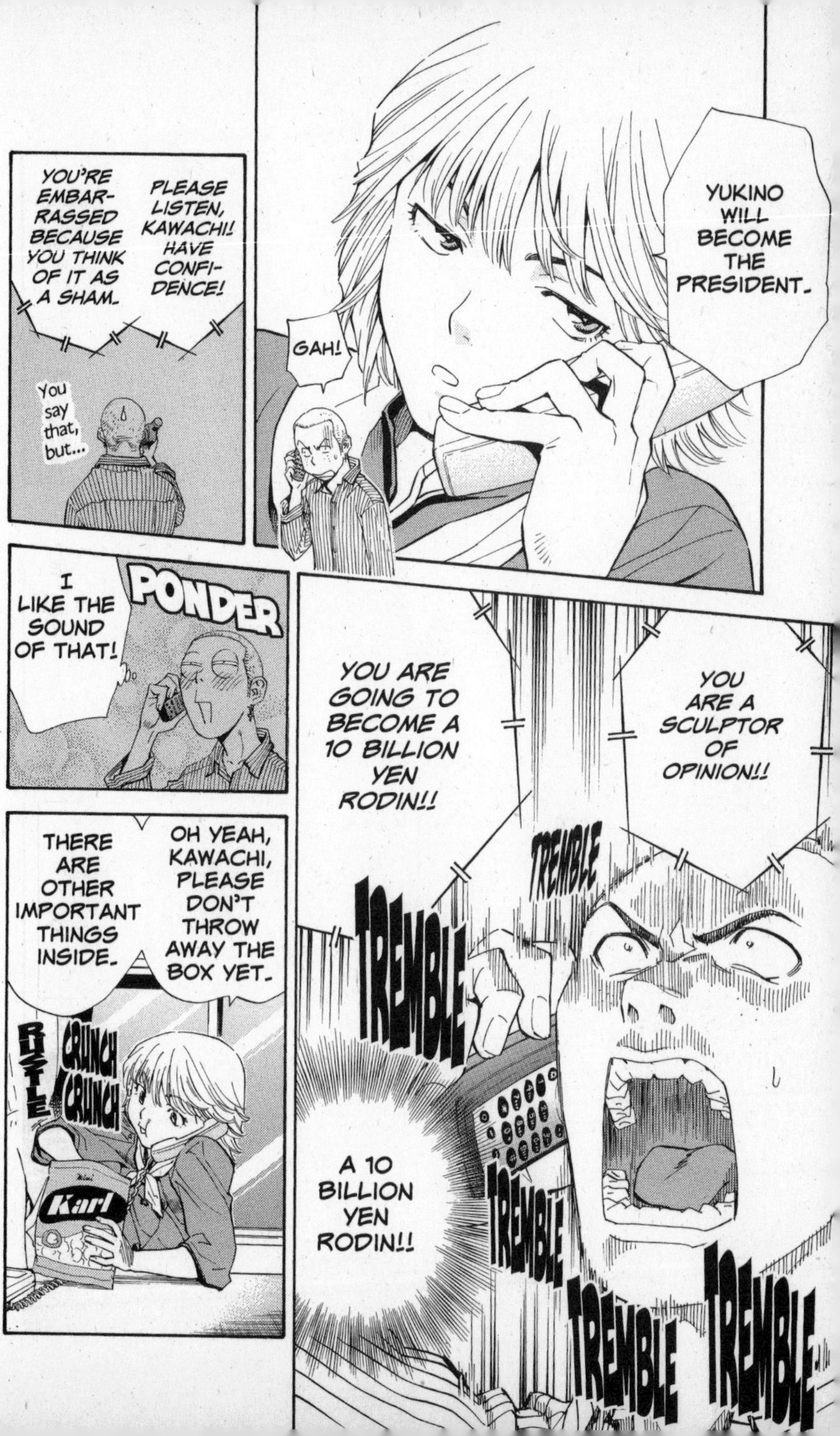
YUKINO WILL BECOME THE PRESIDENT…
GAH!
PLEASE LISTEN, KAWACHI! HAVE CONFIDENCE!
YOU'RE EMBARRASSED BECAUSE YOU THINK OF IT AS A SHAM…
You say that, but…
YOU ARE A SCULPTOR OF OPINION!!
YOU ARE GOING TO BECOME A 10 BILLION YEN RODIN!!
TREMBLE
TREMBLE
A 10 BILLION YEN RODIN!!
TREMBLE
TREMBLE
TREMBLE
PONDER
I LIKE THE SOUND OF THAT!
OH YEAH, KAWACHI, PLEASE DON'T THROW AWAY THE BOX YET…
THERE ARE OTHER IMPORTANT THINGS INSIDE…
CRUNCH CRUNCH
RUSTLE
Karl

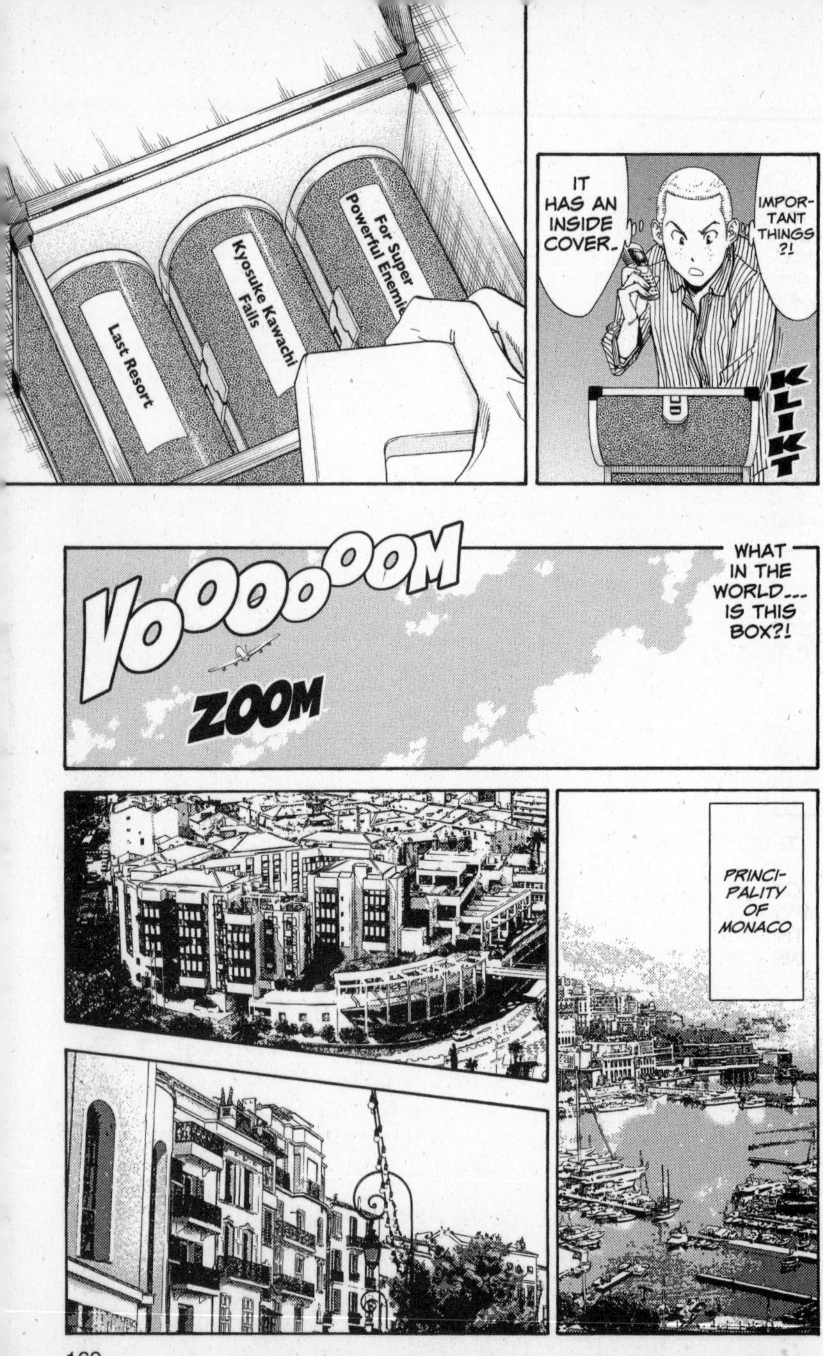
IMPOR-TANT THINGS?!
IT HAS AN INSIDE COVER...
KLIKT
For Super Powerful Enemie
Kyosuke Kawachi Fails
Last Resort
WHAT IN THE WORLD... IS THIS BOX?!
VOOOOOOM
ZOOM
PRINCI-PALITY OF MONACO

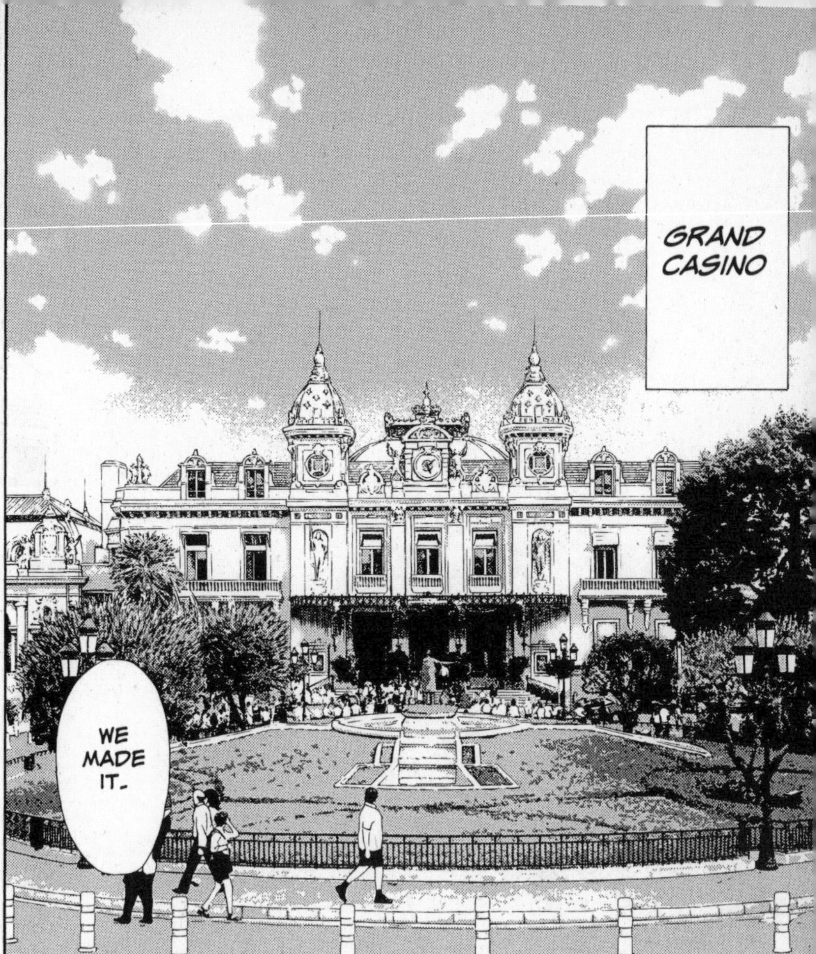
GRAND CASINO
WE MADE IT.

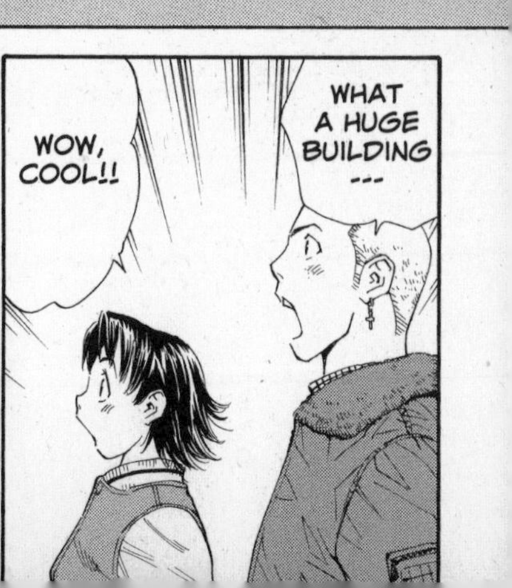
WHAT A HUGE BUILDING ---
WOW, COOL!!

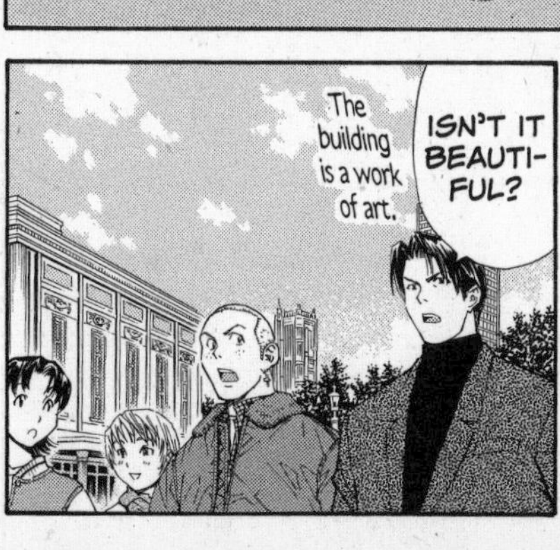
ISN'T IT BEAUTIFUL?
The building is a work of art.

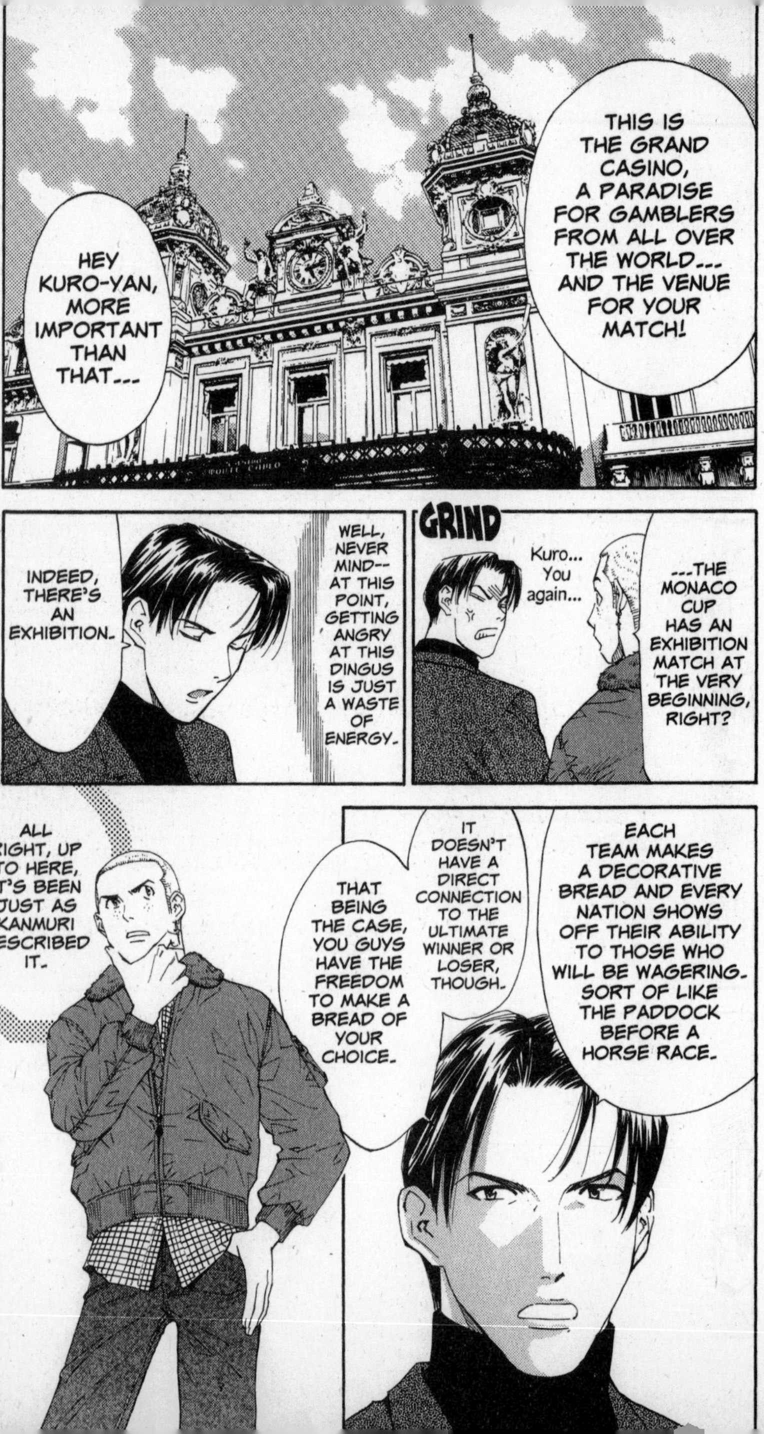
THIS IS THE GRAND CASINO, A PARADISE FOR GAMBLERS FROM ALL OVER THE WORLD... AND THE VENUE FOR YOUR MATCH!
HEY KURO-YAN, MORE IMPORTANT THAN THAT...
...THE MONACO CUP HAS AN EXHIBITION MATCH AT THE VERY BEGINNING, RIGHT?
GRIND
Kuro... You again...
WELL, NEVER MIND--AT THIS POINT, GETTING ANGRY AT THIS DINGUS IS JUST A WASTE OF ENERGY.
INDEED, THERE'S AN EXHIBITION.
EACH TEAM MAKES A DECORATIVE BREAD AND EVERY NATION SHOWS OFF THEIR ABILITY TO THOSE WHO WILL BE WAGERING. SORT OF LIKE THE PADDOCK BEFORE A HORSE RACE.
IT DOESN'T HAVE A DIRECT CONNECTION TO THE ULTIMATE WINNER OR LOSER, THOUGH.
THAT BEING THE CASE, YOU GUYS HAVE THE FREEDOM TO MAKE A BREAD OF YOUR CHOICE.
ALL RIGHT, UP TO HERE, IT'S BEEN JUST AS KANMURI DESCRIBED IT.

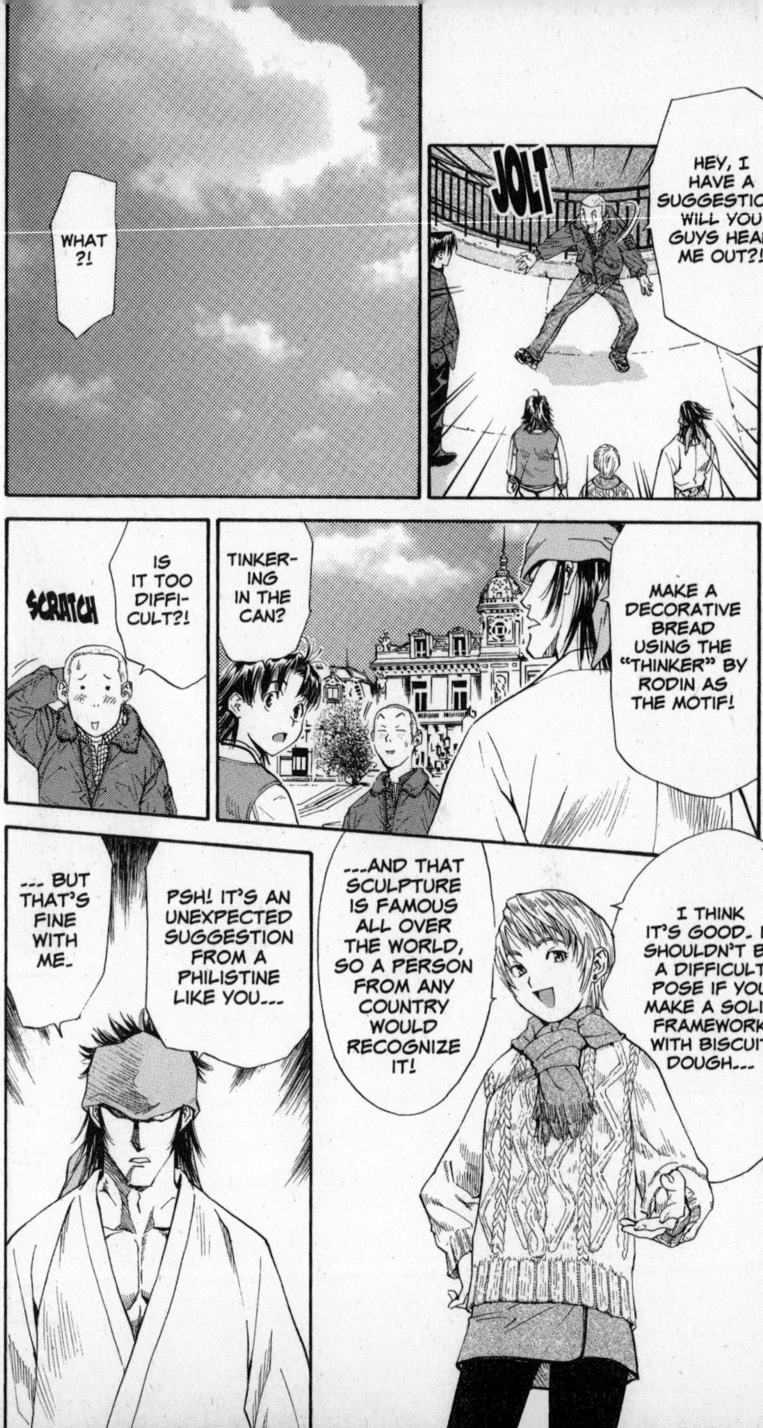
HEY, I HAVE A SUGGESTION. WILL YOU GUYS HEAR ME OUT?!
JOLT
WHAT?!
MAKE A DECORATIVE BREAD USING THE "THINKER" BY RODIN AS THE MOTIF!
TINKERING IN THE CAN?
IS IT TOO DIFFICULT?!
SCRATCH
I THINK IT'S GOOD. IT SHOULDN'T BE A DIFFICULT POSE IF YOU MAKE A SOLID FRAMEWORK WITH BISCUIT DOUGH...
...AND THAT SCULPTURE IS FAMOUS ALL OVER THE WORLD, SO A PERSON FROM ANY COUNTRY WOULD RECOGNIZE IT!
PSH! IT'S AN UNEXPECTED SUGGESTION FROM A PHILISTINE LIKE YOU...
... BUT THAT'S FINE WITH ME.

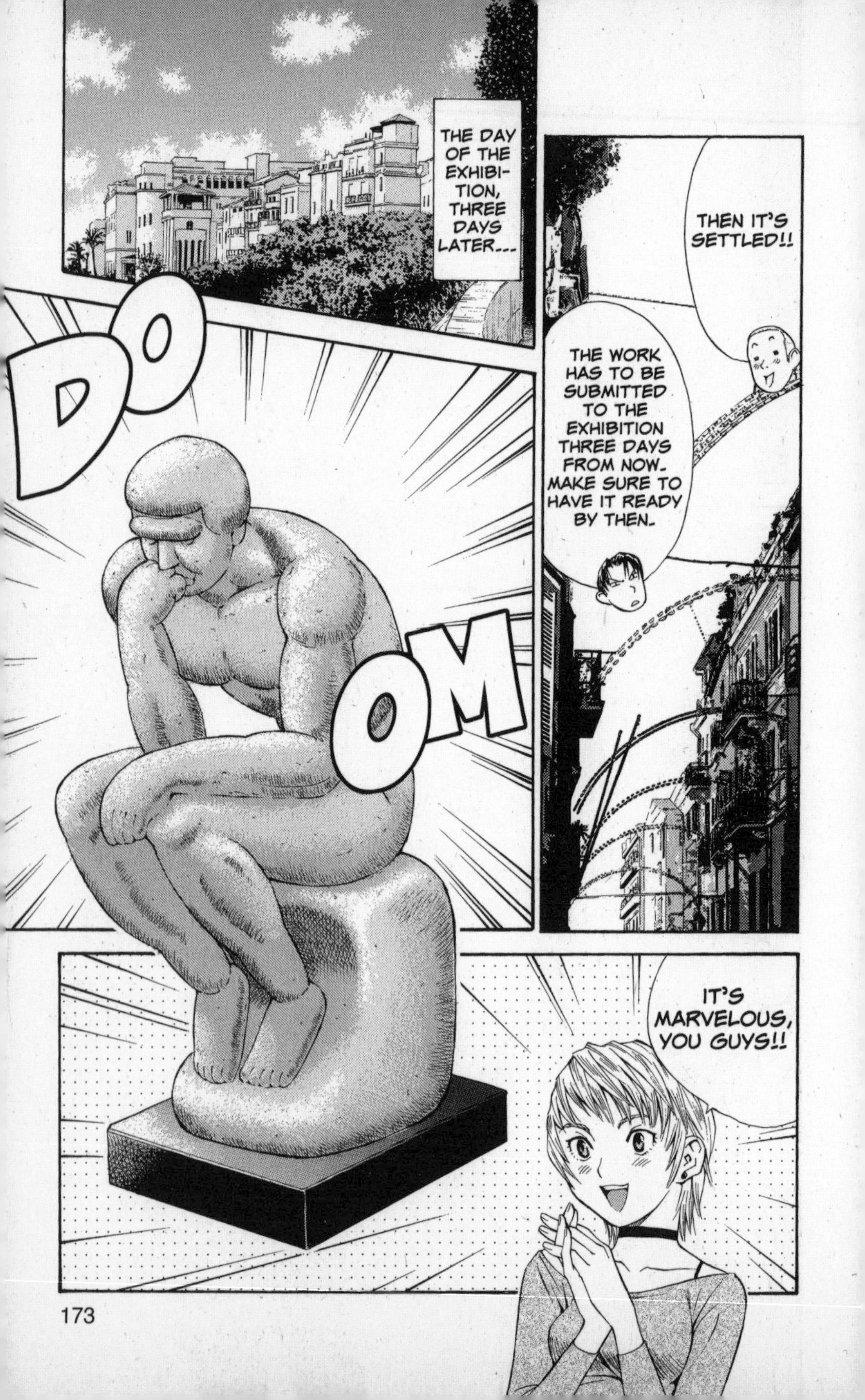
THEN IT'S SETTLED!!
THE WORK HAS TO BE SUBMITTED TO THE EXHIBITION THREE DAYS FROM NOW. MAKE SURE TO HAVE IT READY BY THEN.
THE DAY OF THE EXHIBITION, THREE DAYS LATER...
DOOM
IT'S MARVELOUS, YOU GUYS!!

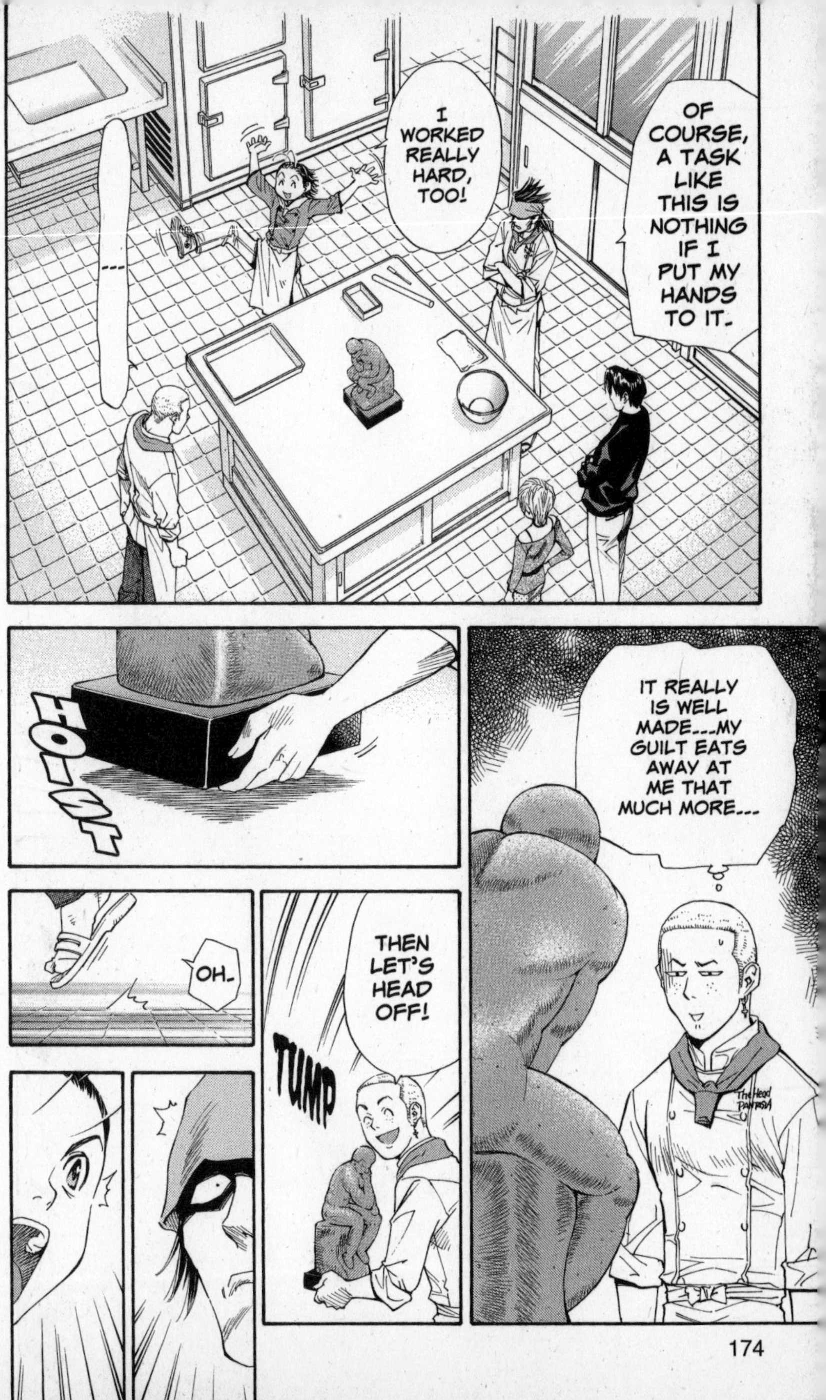
OF COURSE, A TASK LIKE THIS IS NOTHING IF I PUT MY HANDS TO IT.
I WORKED REALLY HARD, TOO!
...
IT REALLY IS WELL MADE...MY GUILT EATS AWAY AT ME THAT MUCH MORE...
HOIST
THEN LET'S HEAD OFF!
TUMP
OH.

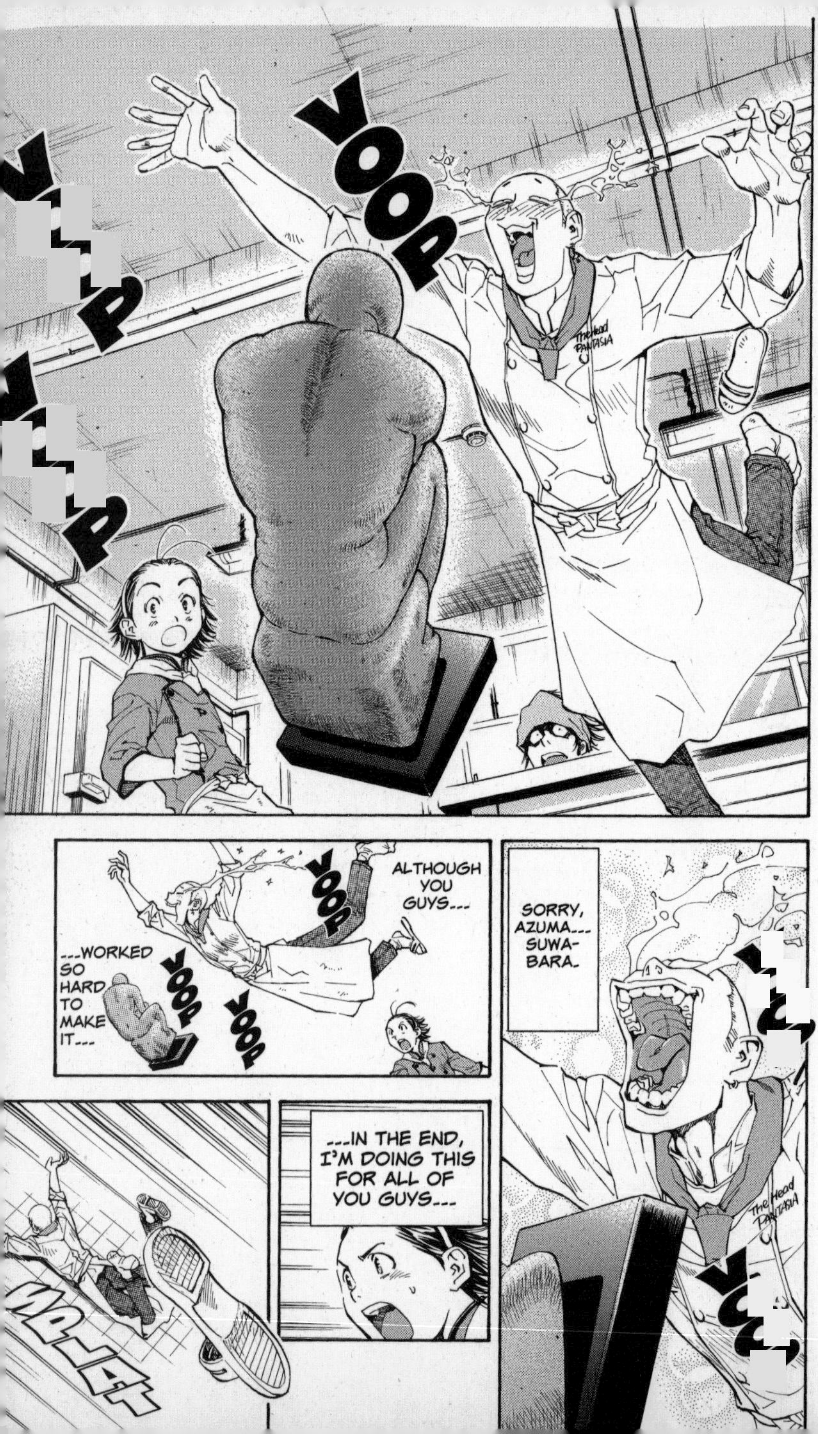
VOOP
The Head PANTASIA
SORRY, AZUMA... SUWABARA.
The Head PANTASIA
ALTHOUGH YOU GUYS...
VOOP
...WORKED SO HARD TO MAKE IT...
VOOP
VOOP
...IN THE END, I'M DOING THIS FOR ALL OF YOU GUYS...

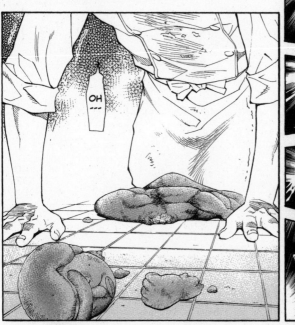

OH

HEY!

AH, HA, HA, HA....
WHAT A KLUTZ....
I TRIPPED AND FELL.
DURR, WHOOPS?

AH

HOW....HOW COULD I HAVE DONE SUCH A THING?!

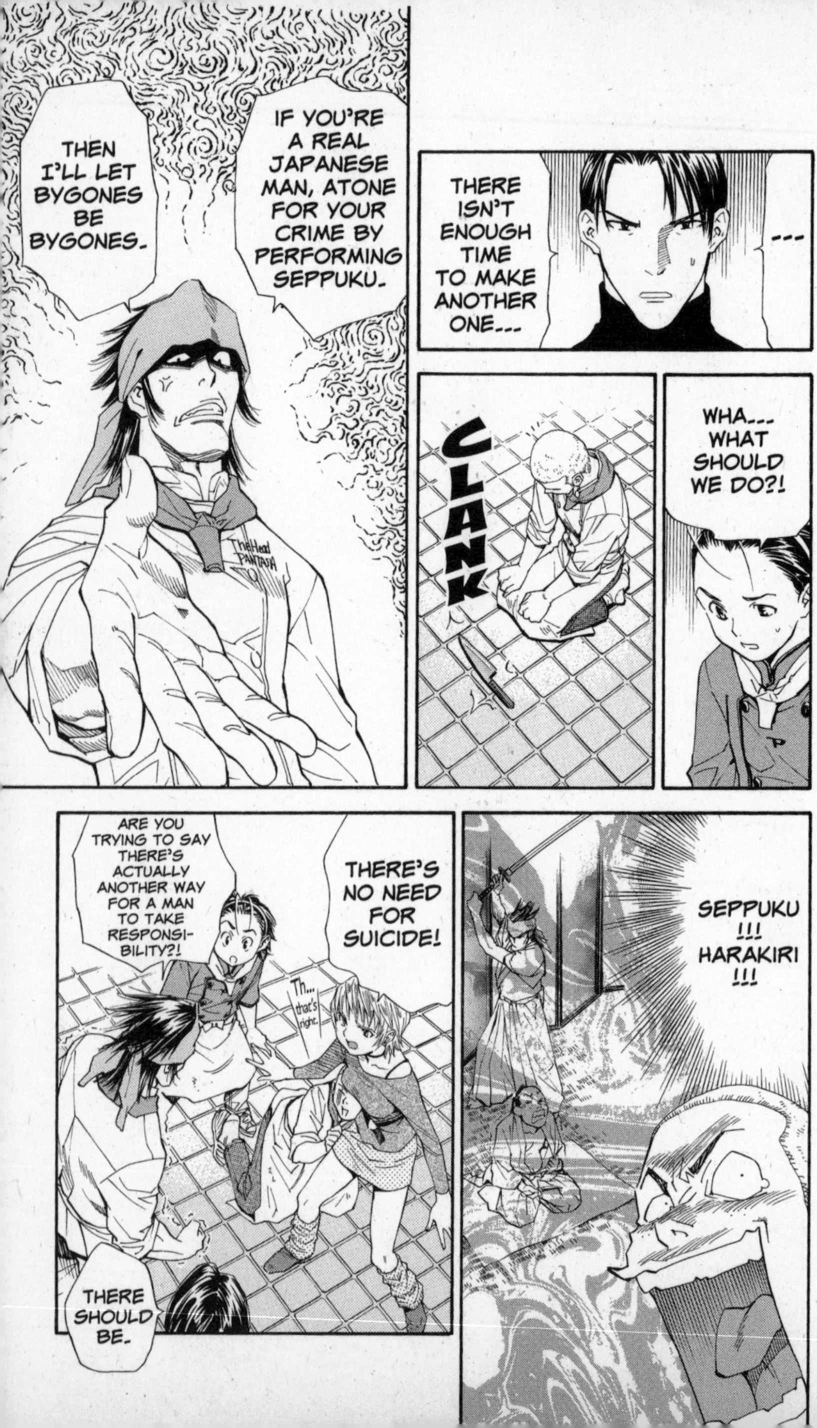
...
THERE ISN'T ENOUGH TIME TO MAKE ANOTHER ONE...
WHA... WHAT SHOULD WE DO?!
CLANK
IF YOU'RE A REAL JAPANESE MAN, ATONE FOR YOUR CRIME BY PERFORMING SEPPUKU.
THEN I'LL LET BYGONES BE BYGONES.
The Head PANTASIA
SEPPUKU!!! HARAKIRI!!!
THERE'S NO NEED FOR SUICIDE!
ARE YOU TRYING TO SAY THERE'S ACTUALLY ANOTHER WAY FOR A MAN TO TAKE RESPONSI-BILITY?!
Th... that's right.
THERE SHOULD BE.

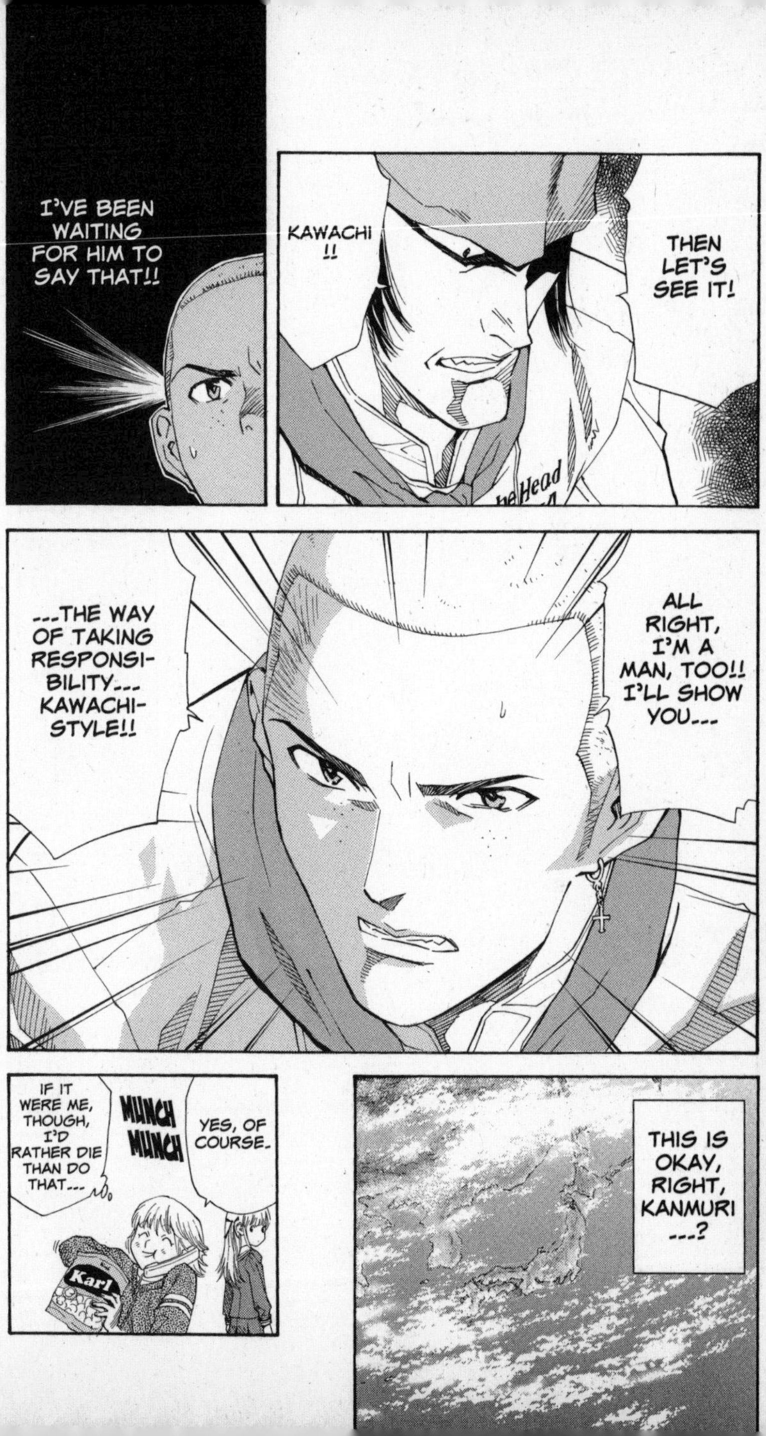
THEN LET'S SEE IT!
KAWACHI !!
I'VE BEEN WAITING FOR HIM TO SAY THAT!!
ALL RIGHT, I'M A MAN, TOO!! I'LL SHOW YOU...
...THE WAY OF TAKING RESPONSI-BILITY... KAWACHI-STYLE!!
THIS IS OKAY, RIGHT, KANMURI ...?
YES, OF COURSE.
MUNCH MUNCH
IF IT WERE ME, THOUGH, I'D RATHER DIE THAN DO THAT...
Karl

TO BE CONTINUED!

Bonus ♥

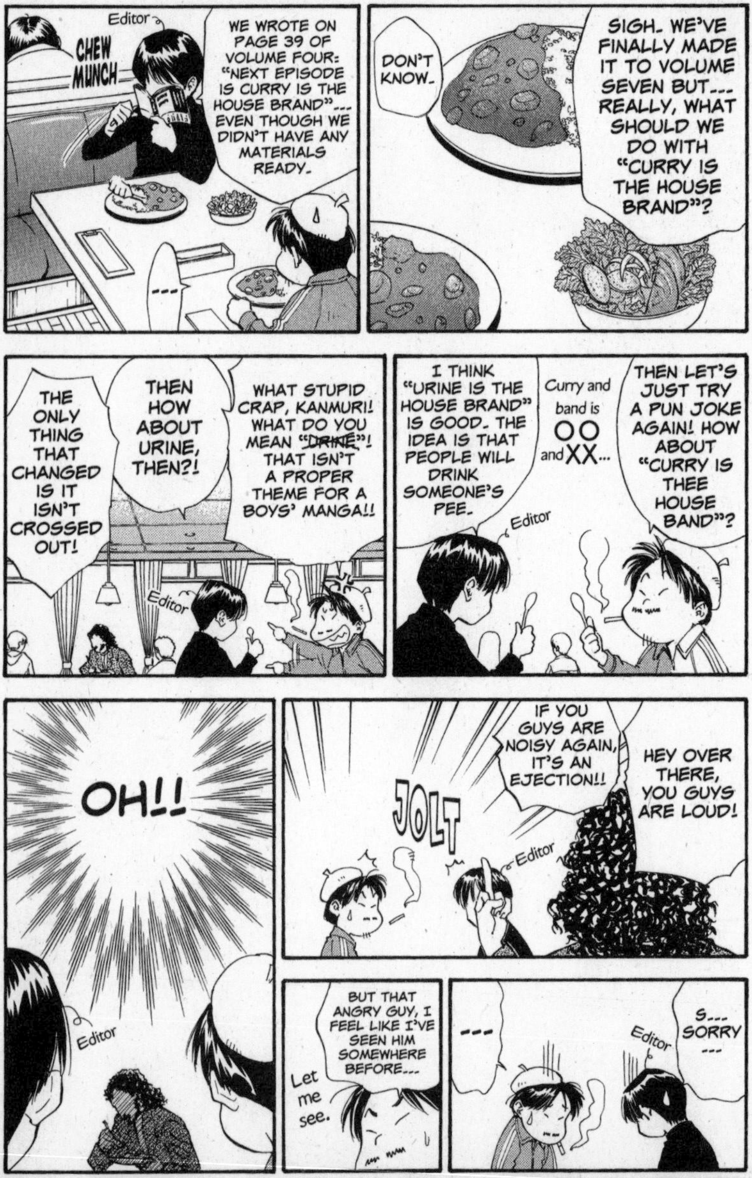

SIGH. WE'VE FINALLY MADE IT TO VOLUME SEVEN BUT... REALLY, WHAT SHOULD WE DO WITH "CURRY IS THE HOUSE BRAND"?
DON'T KNOW.
Editor
CHEW MUNCH
WE WROTE ON PAGE 39 OF VOLUME FOUR: "NEXT EPISODE IS CURRY IS THE HOUSE BRAND"... EVEN THOUGH WE DIDN'T HAVE ANY MATERIALS READY.
...
THEN LET'S JUST TRY A PUN JOKE AGAIN! HOW ABOUT "CURRY IS THEE HOUSE BAND"?
Curry and band is OO and XX...
I THINK "URINE IS THE HOUSE BRAND" IS GOOD. THE IDEA IS THAT PEOPLE WILL DRINK SOMEONE'S PEE.
Editor
WHAT STUPID CRAP, KANMURI! WHAT DO YOU MEAN "~~DRINE~~"! THAT ISN'T A PROPER THEME FOR A BOYS' MANGA!!
THEN HOW ABOUT URINE, THEN?!
THE ONLY THING THAT CHANGED IS IT ISN'T CROSSED OUT!
Editor
HEY OVER THERE, YOU GUYS ARE LOUD!
IF YOU GUYS ARE NOISY AGAIN, IT'S AN EJECTION!!
JOLT
Editor
S... SORRY...
Editor
...
BUT THAT ANGRY GUY, I FEEL LIKE I'VE SEEN HIM SOMEWHERE BEFORE...
Let me see.
OH!!
Editor

Curry is the House Brand

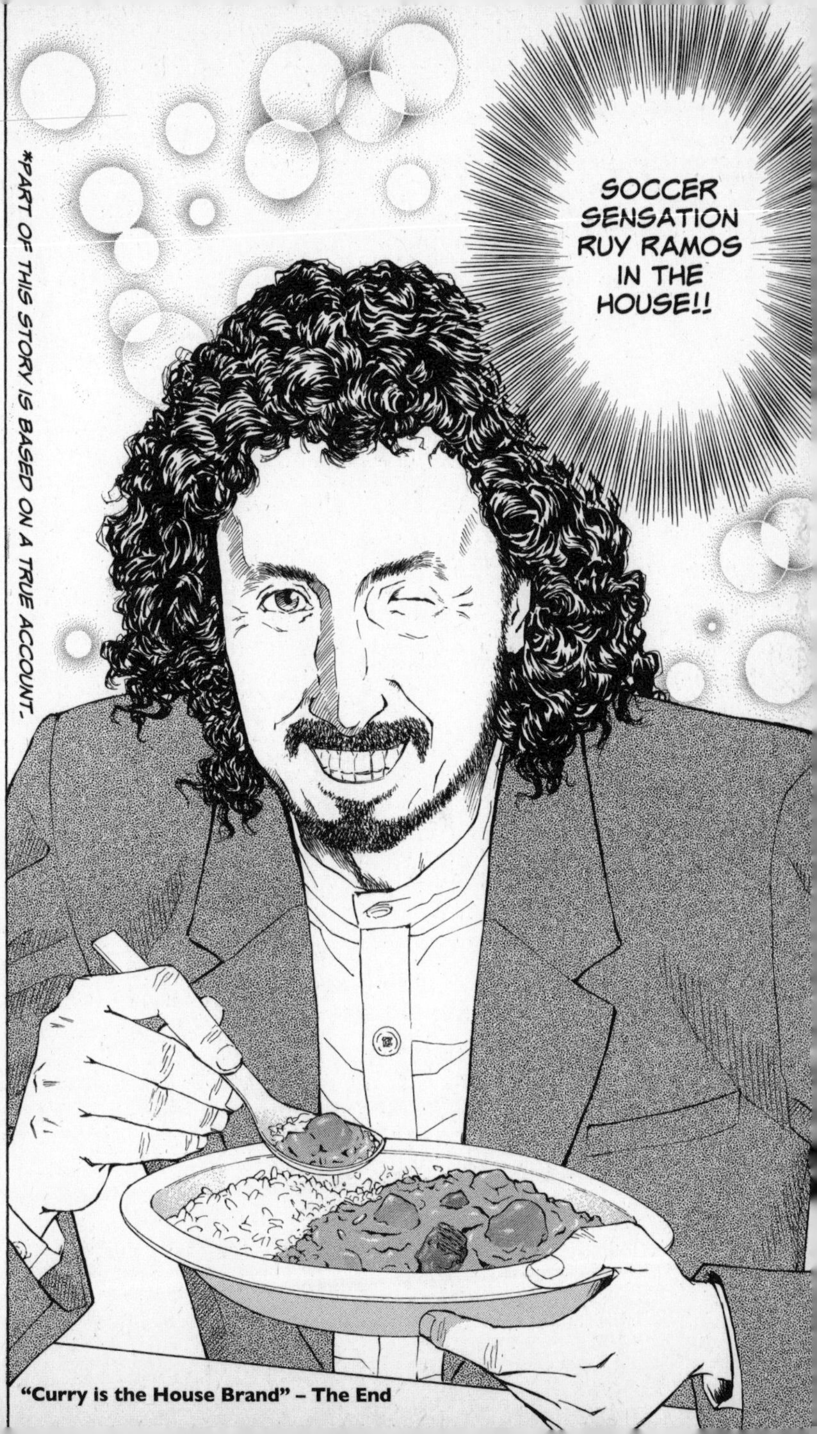
SOCCER SENSATION RUY RAMOS IN THE HOUSE!!
*PART OF THIS STORY IS BASED ON A TRUE ACCOUNT.

“Curry is the House Brand” – The End

Freshly Made!!
Miss Yukino

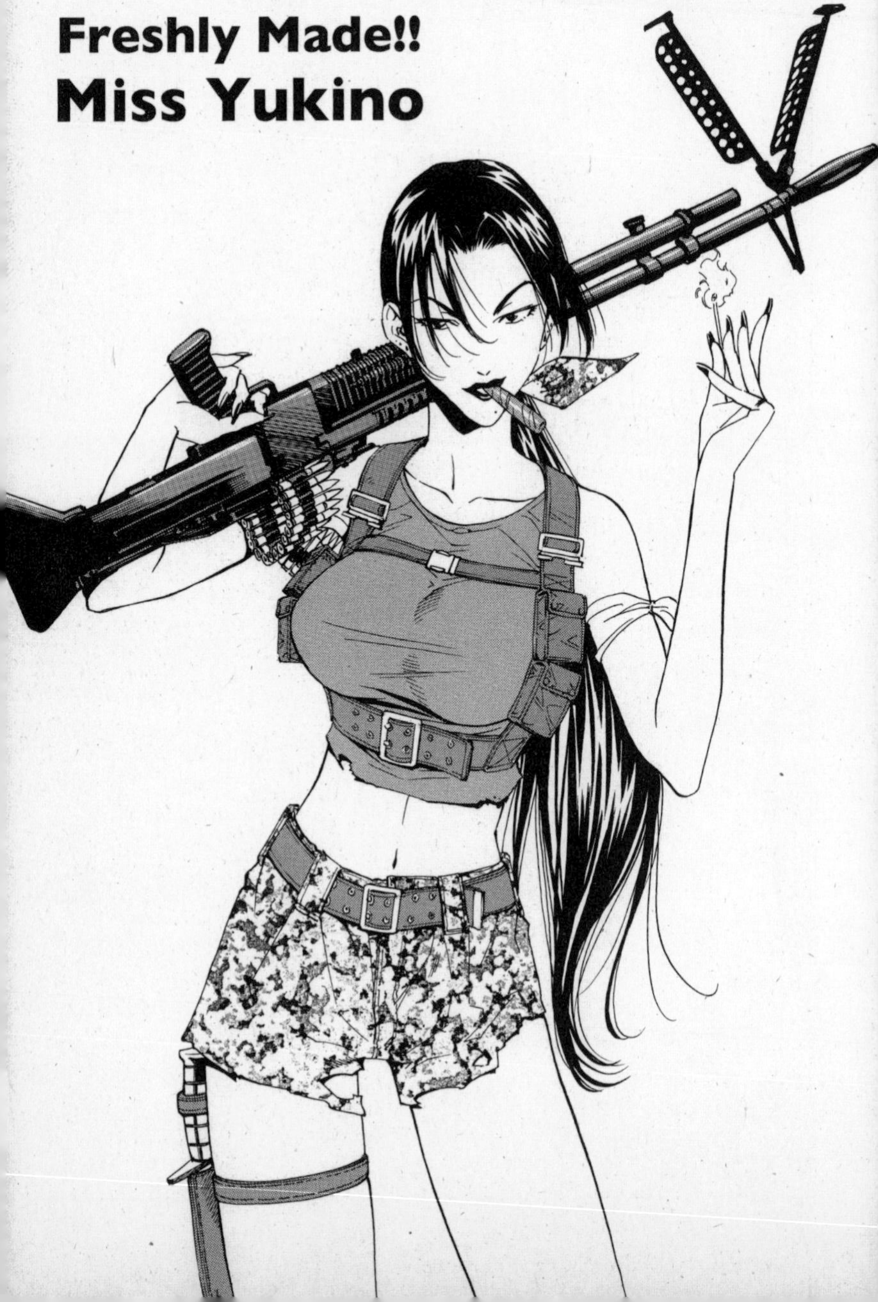

Miss Yukino Is Clean

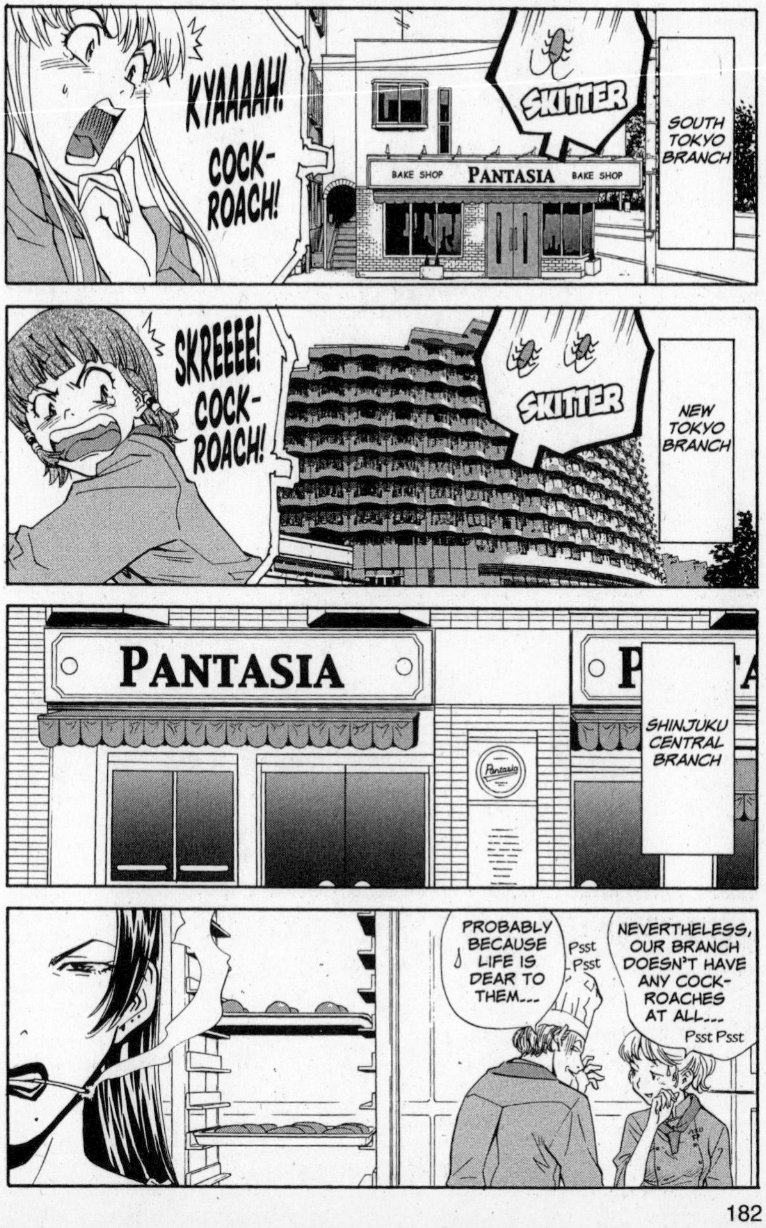
SOUTH TOKYO BRANCH
SKITTER
KYAAAAH! COCK-ROACH!
BAKE SHOP PANTASIA BAKE SHOP
NEW TOKYO BRANCH
SKITTER
SKREEEE! COCK-ROACH!
SHINJUKU CENTRAL BRANCH
PANTASIA
NEVERTHELESS, OUR BRANCH DOESN'T HAVE ANY COCK-ROACHES AT ALL...
Psst Psst
PROBABLY BECAUSE LIFE IS DEAR TO THEM...
Psst Psst

Miss Yukino, Who Is No. 1 in the Universe

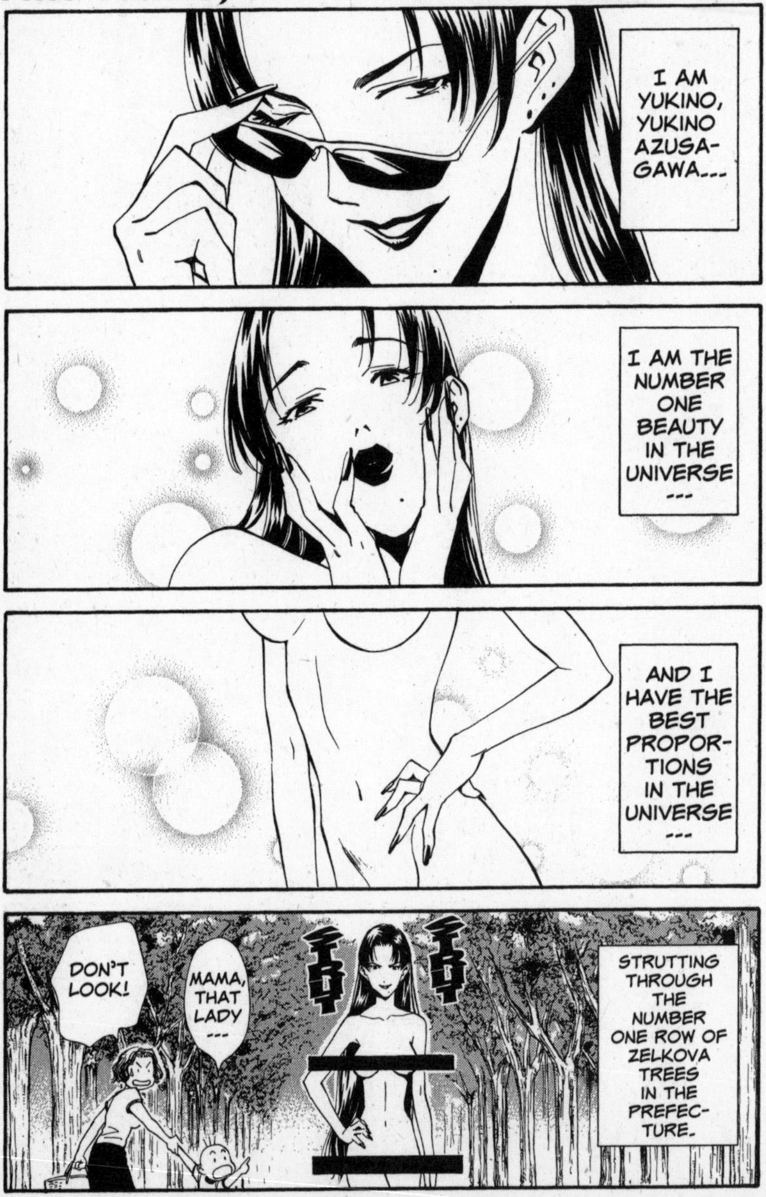
I AM YUKINO, YUKINO AZUSAGAWA...
I AM THE NUMBER ONE BEAUTY IN THE UNIVERSE---
AND I HAVE THE BEST PROPORTIONS IN THE UNIVERSE---
STRUTTING THROUGH THE NUMBER ONE ROW OF ZELKOVA TREES IN THE PREFECTURE.
MAMA, THAT LADY---
DON'T LOOK!

Miss Yukino Is an Inch Ahead

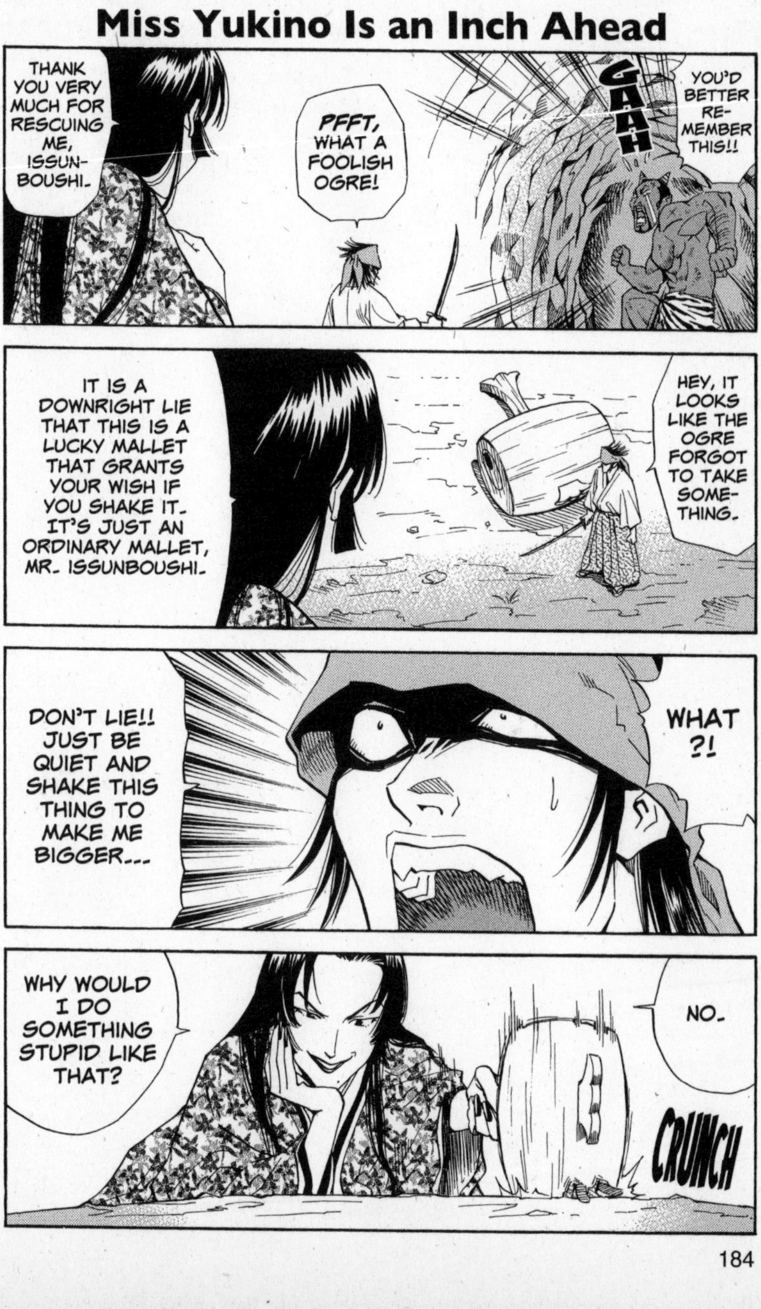
YOU'D BETTER RE-MEMBER THIS!!
GAAH
PFFT, WHAT A FOOLISH OGRE!
THANK YOU VERY MUCH FOR RESCUING ME, ISSUN-BOUSHI.
HEY, IT LOOKS LIKE THE OGRE FORGOT TO TAKE SOME-THING.
IT IS A DOWNRIGHT LIE THAT THIS IS A LUCKY MALLET THAT GRANTS YOUR WISH IF YOU SHAKE IT. IT'S JUST AN ORDINARY MALLET, MR. ISSUNBOUSHI.
WHAT?!
DON'T LIE!! JUST BE QUIET AND SHAKE THIS THING TO MAKE ME BIGGER...
NO.
WHY WOULD I DO SOMETHING STUPID LIKE THAT?
CRUNCH

Freshly Baked!! Mini Information

French Revolution

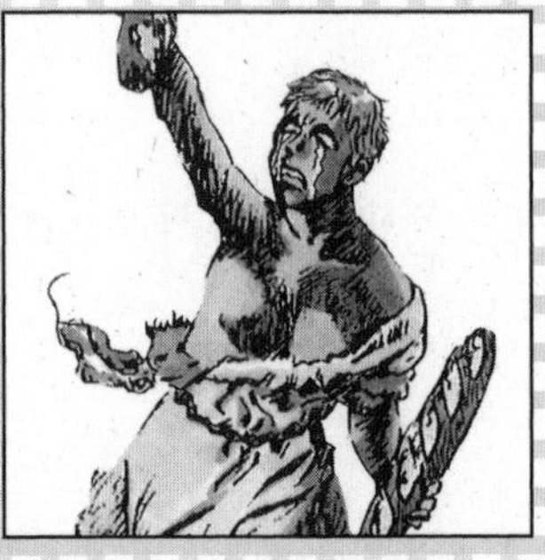

It's said that the French Revolution had a major influence on how French cuisine developed into what it is today.

Court cooks who could no longer work at the court because of the revolution went to the city and started to operate restaurants. It became possible for common people to eat splendid cooking that up until then had only been tasted by royalty.

At this time, how did the common people react? Were there people who staged flamboyant reactions like Kuroyanagi?

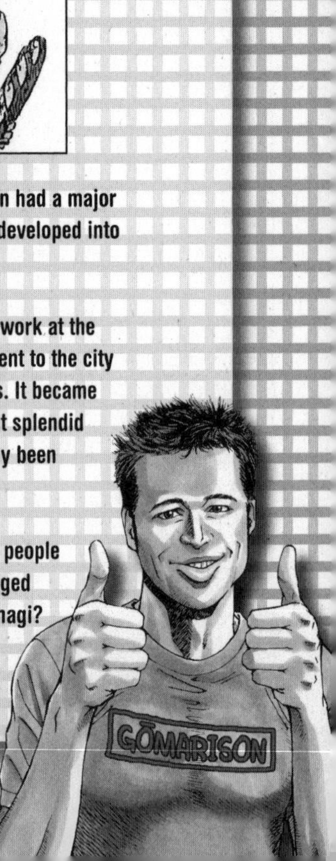
GŌMARISON

YAKITATE!! JAPAN
VOL. 7

STORY AND ART BY
TAKASHI HASHIGUCHI

English Adaptation/Drew Williams
Translation/Noritaka Minami
Touch-up Art & Lettering/Steve Dutro
Cover Design/Yukiko Whitley
Editor/Kit Fox

Editor in Chief, Books/Alvin Lu
Editor in Chief, Magazines/Marc Weidenbaum
VP of Publishing Licensing/Rika Inouye
VP of Sales/Gonzalo Ferreyra
Sr. VP of Marketing/Liza Coppola
Publisher/Hyoe Narita

Printed in the U.S.A.

Published by VIZ Media, LLC
P.O. Box 77010
San Francisco, CA 94107

10 9 8 7 6 5 4 3 2 1
First printing, September 2007

www.viz.com   store.viz.com

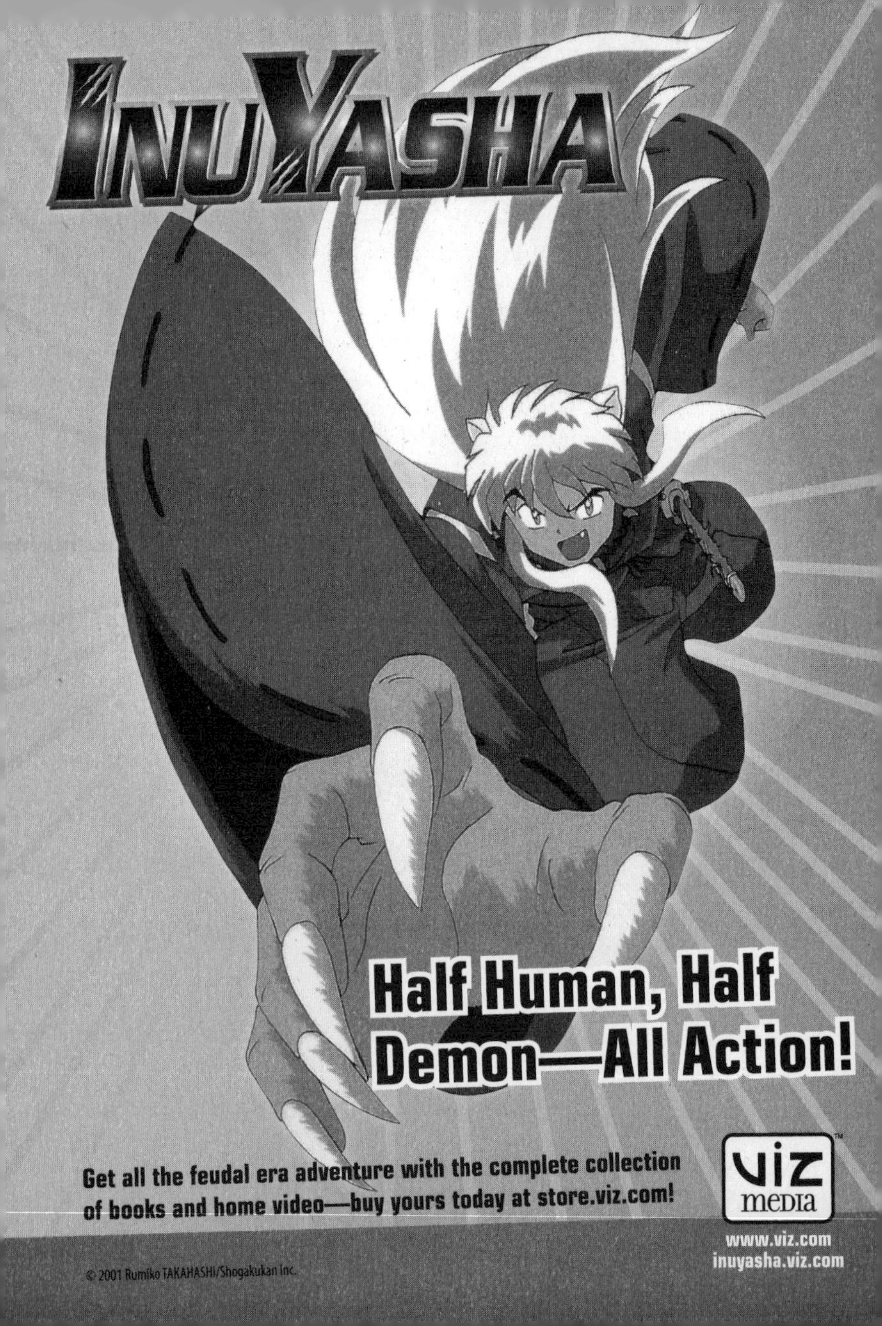
InuYasha
Half Human, Half Demon—All Action!
Get all the feudal era adventure with the complete collection of books and home video—buy yours today at store.viz.com!
viz media
www.viz.com
inuyasha.viz.com
© 2001 Rumiko TAKAHASHI/Shogakukan Inc.

INUYASHA

Read the action from the start with the original manga series

Full color adaptation of the popular TV series

Art book with cel art, paintings, character profiles and more

TV SERIES & MOVIES ON DVD!

See more of the action in *Inuyasha* full-length movies

www.viz.com
inuyasha.viz.com

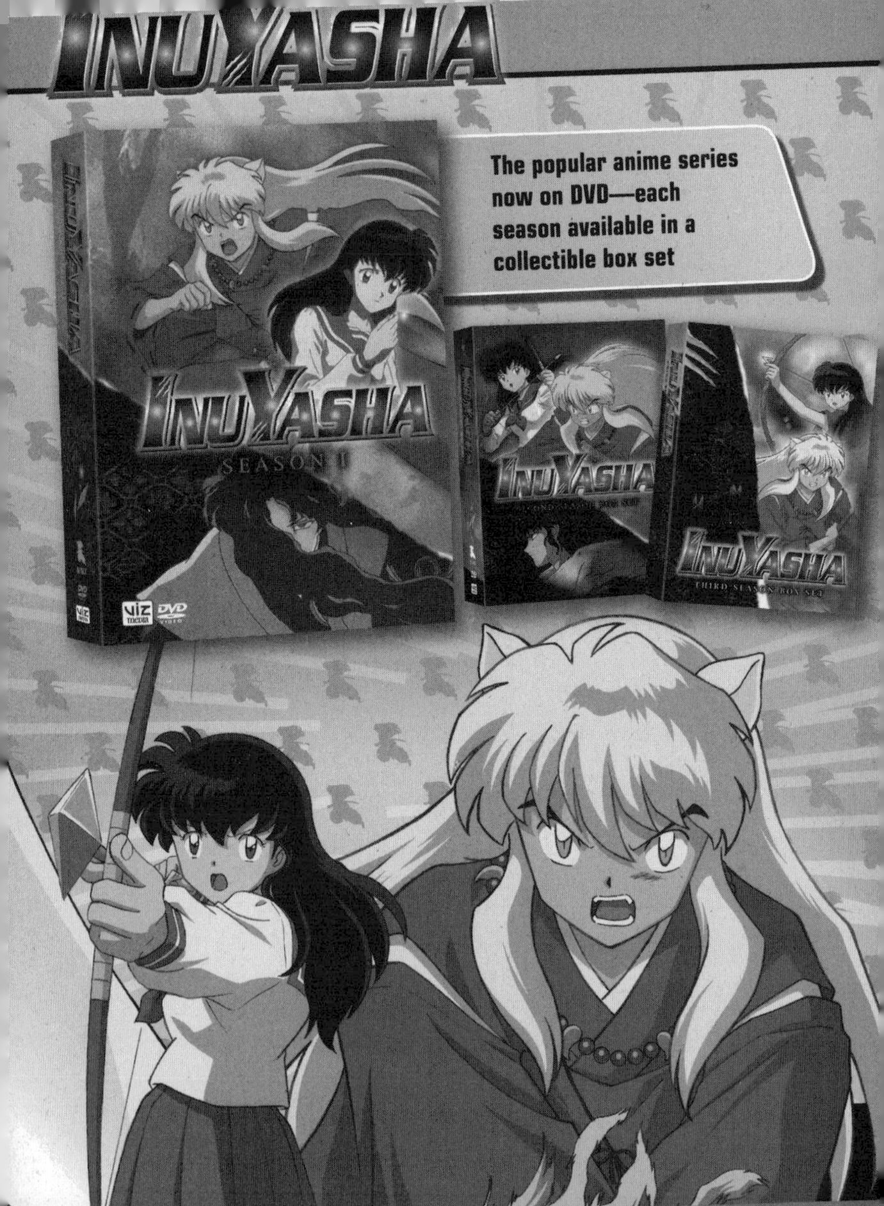
INUYASHA
The popular anime series now on DVD—each season available in a collectible box set
INUYASHA
SEASON 1
INUYASHA
INUYASHA
THIRD SEASON BOX SET

LOVE MANGA?
LET US KNOW WHAT YOU THINK!

HELP US MAKE THE MANGA
YOU LOVE BETTER!

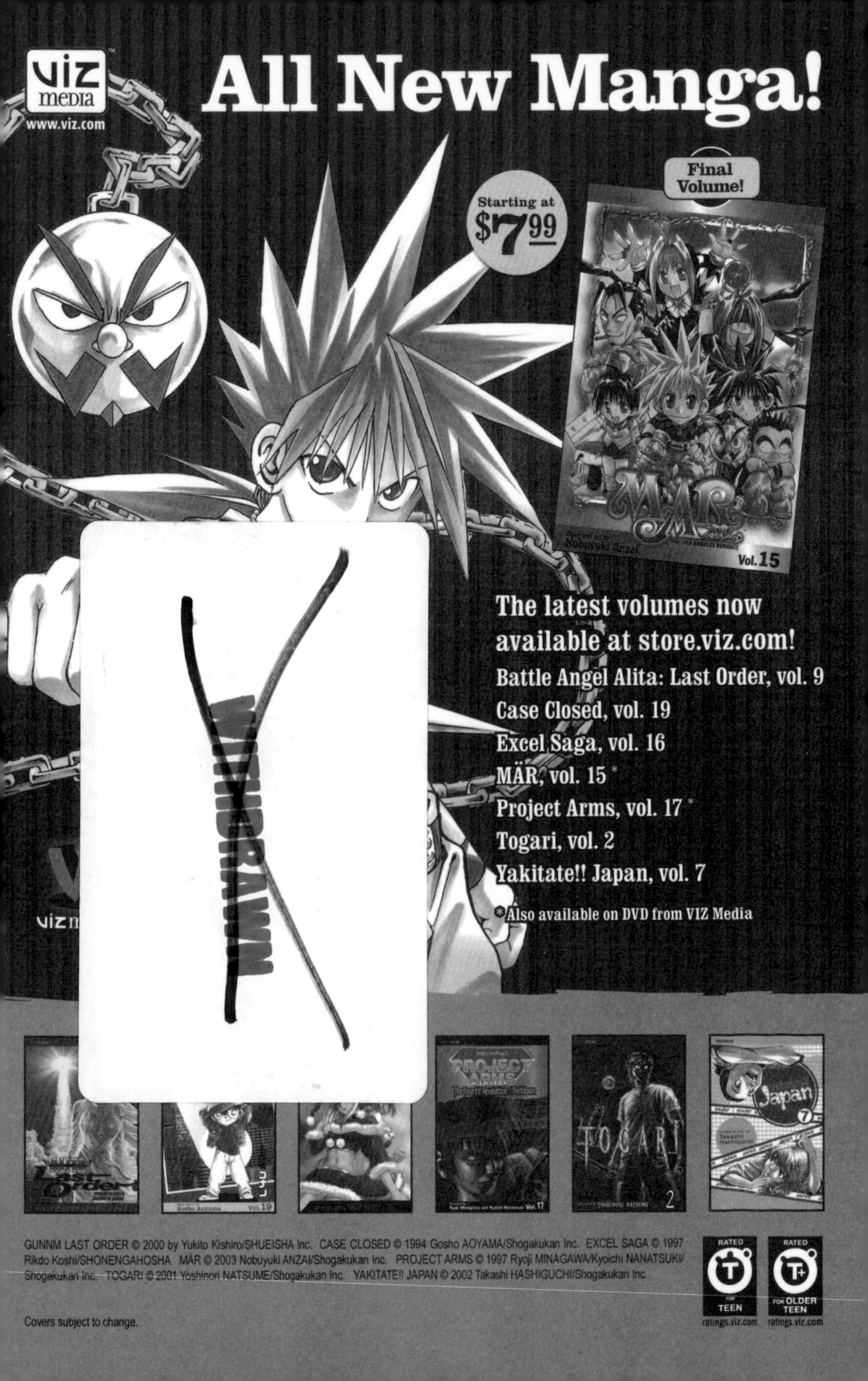
viz media
www.viz.com
All New Manga!
Starting at $7.99
Final Volume!
MÄR
Nobuyuki Anzai
Vol. 15
The latest volumes now available at store.viz.com!
Battle Angel Alita: Last Order, vol. 9
Case Closed, vol. 19
Excel Saga, vol. 16
MÄR, vol. 15 *
Project Arms, vol. 17 *
Togari, vol. 2
Yakitate!! Japan, vol. 7
* Also available on DVD from VIZ Media
Last Order
Gosho Aoyama Vol. 19
PROJECT ARMS
Vol. 17
TOGARI
YOSHINORI NATSUME 2
Japan 7
Takashi Hashiguchi
GUNNM LAST ORDER © 2000 by Yukito Kishiro/SHUEISHA Inc. CASE CLOSED © 1994 Gosho AOYAMA/Shogakukan Inc. EXCEL SAGA © 1997 Rikdo Koshi/SHONENGAHOSHA MÄR © 2003 Nobuyuki ANZAI/Shogakukan Inc. PROJECT ARMS © 1997 Ryoji MINAGAWA/Kyoichi NANATSUKI/Shogakukan Inc. TOGARI © 2001 Yoshinori NATSUME/Shogakukan Inc. YAKITATE!! JAPAN © 2002 Takashi HASHIGUCHI/Shogakukan Inc.
RATED T FOR TEEN ratings.viz.com
RATED T+ FOR OLDER TEEN ratings.viz.com
Covers subject to change.

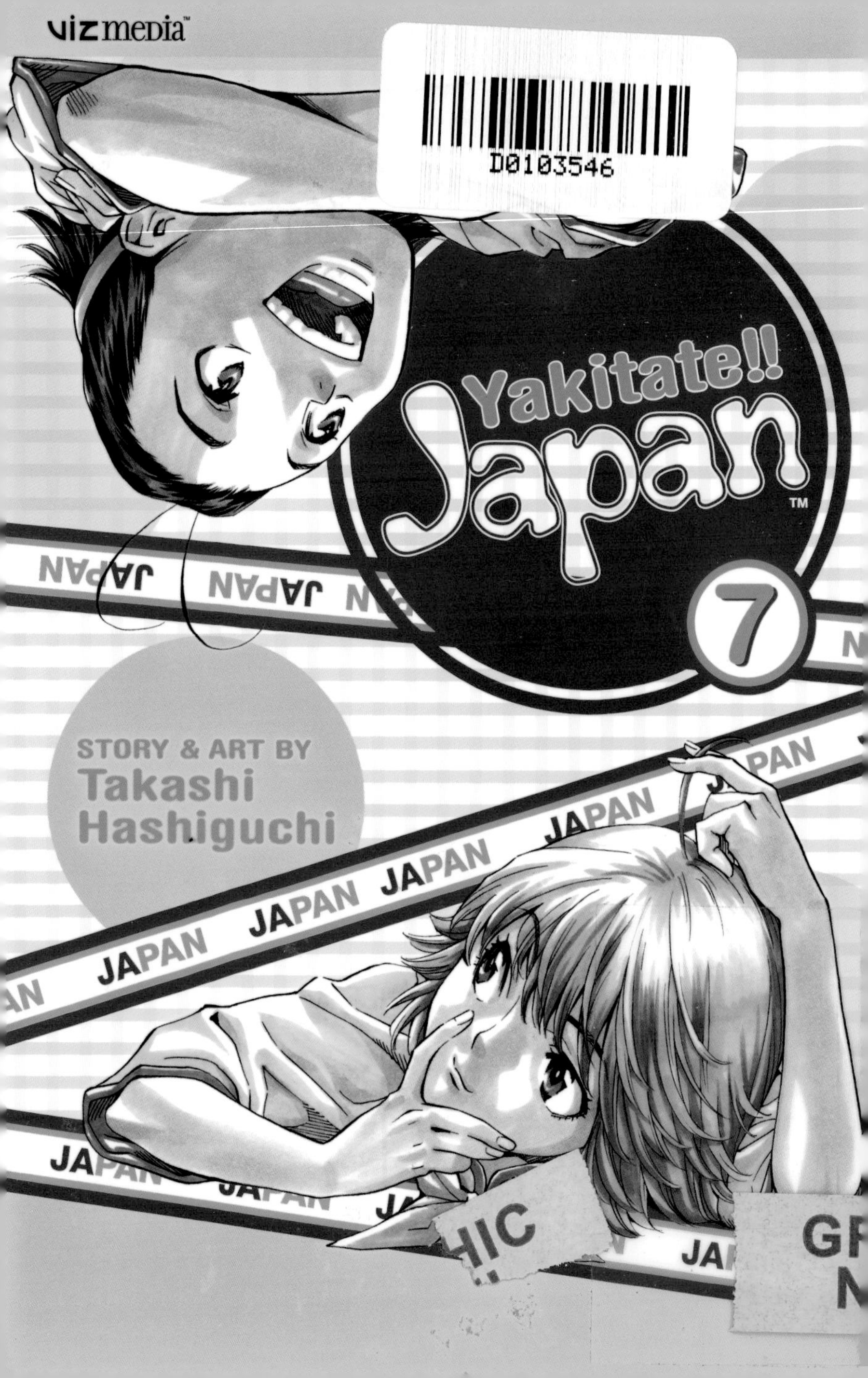
viz media™
D0103546
Yakitate!! Japan™
7
STORY & ART BY
Takashi Hashiguchi
JAPAN